ARISTOTLE'S *NICOMACHEAN ETHICS* BOOK X

Accompanied by a new translation of Aristotle's *Nicomachean Ethics* X, this volume presents a hybrid between a traditional commentary and a scholarly monograph. Aristotle's text is divided into one hundred lemmata which not only explore comprehensively the content and strength of each of these units of thought, but also emphasise their continuity, showing how the smaller units feed into the larger structure. The Commentary illuminates *what* Aristotle thinks in each lemma (and why), and also shows *how* he thinks. In order to bring Aristotle alive as a thinker, it often explores several possible ways of reading the text to enable readers to make up their own minds about the best interpretation of a given passage. The relevant background in Plato's dialogues is discussed, and a substantial Introduction sets out the philosophical framework necessary for understanding Book X, the final and most arresting section of the *Ethics*.

JOACHIM AUFDERHEIDE is Senior Lecturer in Philosophy at King's College London. His research focuses on ancient Greek ethics, an area in which he has published widely.

ARISTOTLE'S
NICOMACHEAN ETHICS
BOOK X

Translation and Commentary

JOACHIM AUFDERHEIDE

King's College London

CAMBRIDGE
UNIVERSITY PRESS

CAMBRIDGE
UNIVERSITY PRESS

University Printing House, Cambridge CB2 8BS, United Kingdom

One Liberty Plaza, 20th Floor, New York, NY 10006, USA

477 Williamstown Road, Port Melbourne, VIC 3207, Australia

314–321, 3rd Floor, Plot 3, Splendor Forum, Jasola District Centre, New Delhi – 110025, India

79 Anson Road, #06–04/06, Singapore 079906

Cambridge University Press is part of the University of Cambridge.

It furthers the University's mission by disseminating knowledge in the pursuit of education, learning, and research at the highest international levels of excellence.

www.cambridge.org
Information on this title: www.cambridge.org/9781107104402
DOI: 10.1017/9781316221594

© Joachim Aufderheide 2020

This publication is in copyright. Subject to statutory exception and to the provisions of relevant collective licensing agreements, no reproduction of any part may take place without the written permission of Cambridge University Press.

First published 2020

Printed in the United Kingdom by TJ International Ltd. Padstow Cornwall

A catalogue record for this publication is available from the British Library.

Library of Congress Cataloging-in-Publication Data
NAMES: Aufderheide, Joachim, author. | Aristotle. Nicomachean ethics. English. 2020.
TITLE: Aristotle's Nicomachean ethics book X / Joachim Aufderheide.
DESCRIPTION: New York : Cambridge University Press, 2020. | Includes bibliographical references and index.
IDENTIFIERS: LCCN 2019039767 | ISBN 9781107104402 (hardback)
SUBJECTS: LCSH: Aristotle. Nicomachean ethics – Commentaries. | Ethics, Ancient.
CLASSIFICATION: LCC B430 .A937 2020 | DDC 171/.3–dc23
LC record available at https://lccn.loc.gov/2019039767

ISBN 978-1-107-10440-2 Hardback

Cambridge University Press has no responsibility for the persistence or accuracy of URLs for external or third-party internet websites referred to in this publication and does not guarantee that any content on such websites is, or will remain, accurate or appropriate.

Contents

Preface	XI
Introduction	1
Translation	32

Commentary: Aristotle's *Nicomachean* Ethics Book X

I Pleasure (X.1–5)	53
X.1 Introduction to the Topic of Pleasure	53
How Pleasure Relates to Life (1172a19–26)	53
Controversy about the Value of Pleasure (1172a26–33)	57
Truth Should Be the Goal of Our Enquiry (1172b3–8)	59
X.2–3 Examining What Has Been Said about Pleasure	61
Pleasure Is the Good: Eudoxus' Hedonism	
The Argument from Universal Pursuit (1172b9–15)	61
Eudoxus' Character Supports His Views (1172b15–18)	64
The Argument from Opposites (1172b18–23)	65
The Argument from Addition Tells against Hedonism (1172b23–35)	68
Pleasure Is Not Good: Academic Arguments against Pleasure	
The Argument from Universal Pursuit Revisited (1172b35–1173a5)	71
The Argument from Opposites Revisited (1173a5–13)	73
Refuting the Argument That Goods Must Be Qualities (1173a13–15)	75
Refuting the Argument That Goods Must Be Determinate (1173a15–28)	77
Refuting the Argument That Pleasure As Movement Is Incomplete and Therefore Not a Good (1173a28–31)	80
Quick/Slow Applies to Movements, But Not to Pleasure (1173a31–b4)	83

v

What Is the Subject of Pleasure and Pain? (1173b4–13)	84
The Pleasures of Eating Are the Wrong Paradigm (1173b13–20)	88

Not All Pleasure Is Good: General Arguments against Pleasure

Deflecting the Argument from Bad Pleasures (1173b20–31)	89
The Pleasures of Flattery Are Not Good (1173b31–1174a1)	95
Some Pleasures Are Not Choice-Worthy (1174a1–4)	96
Some Things Are More Important Than Pleasure (1174a4–8)	98
Upshot: Some Pleasures Are Good, and Some Are Not (1174a8–12)	99

X.4–5 Aristotle's Account of Pleasure	100

Pleasure Is Something Complete and Whole

Pleasure Is Like Seeing (1174a14–19)	102
Pleasure Is Not a Movement (1174a19–b9)	103
There Is Not Even a Coming to Be of Pleasure (1174b9–14)	111

Pleasure Completes/Perfects the Activity

The Most Complete/Perfect Activity of the Senses Is Most Pleasant (1174b14–31)	113
Pleasure As the Bloom on Those in Their Prime (1174b31–3)	118
The Conditions under Which Pleasure Arises (1174b33–1175a3)	120

Corollaries

Reasonable Questions about Pleasure Answered

Why Do We Not Take Pleasure Continuously? (1175a3–10)	122
Why Does Everyone Desire Pleasure? (1175a10–21)	124

There Are Different Kinds of Pleasure

Pleasures Differ in Kind Because They Complete/Perfect Activities Different in Kind (1175a21–8)	127
A Kind of Pleasure Increases the Kind of Activity to Which It Belongs Properly (1175a29–1175b1)	130
A Kind of Pleasure Impedes Any Kind of Activity to Which It Does Not Belong Properly (1175b1–13)	132
The Pleasure Proper to One Activity Acts on Another Activity to Which It Does Not Belong Like the Pain Proper to That Activity (1175b13–24)	135

Pleasures Differ in Value

Pleasure Mirrors the Value of the Activity to Which It Belongs (1175b24–36)	138
Pleasures Differ in Purity (1175b36–1176a3)	140

Different Kinds of Pleasure Belong Properly to
Different Kinds of Animal
   Non-Human Kinds of Animal Show Uniformity in the
   Pleasures Pursued (1176a3–12)   142
   Despite the Variety among Human Pleasures, There Is
   a Pleasure That Is Characteristic of Human Beings
   (1176a12–29)   144

II Happy Lives (X.6–8)   150

X.6 The Life of Pleasure Revisited   150
  Pleasure as a Candidate for Happiness
    The Hallmarks of Happiness (1176a33–b6)   152
    Pleasure Is Chosen for Its Own Sake (1176b6–16)   153
  Against the Life of Pleasant Amusements
    Those Who Live the Life of Pleasure Do Not Know
    about Happiness (1176b16–27)   155
    Pleasure Is Subordinate to Serious Pursuits
    (1176b27–1177a1)   157
    Pleasant Amusements Do Not Require Our Best
    Elements (1177a1–6)   160
    Anyone, Even a Slave, Could Live Happily (1177a6–11)   162
X.7–8 The Theoretical and the Practical Life   164
  Complete/Perfect/Final Happiness Stems from the
  Excellent Activity of Our Best Element (1177a12–17)   164
    Complete/Perfect/Final Happiness Is Theoretical
    Reflection Because It Is:
      Our Best Activity (1177a17–21)   167
      Most Continuous (1177a21–3)   169
      Most Pleasant (1177a23–7)   171
      Most Self-Sufficient (1177a27–b1)   173
      Loved for Its Own Sake (1177b1–4)   176
      Found in Leisure (Unlike the Activities of Practical Virtue)
      (1177b4–15)   178
    Summary of the Preceding Arguments in Favour of
    Reflection (1177b16–26)   181
  The Happy Life Must Be Humanly Achievable
    Our Divine Element Enables Us to Lead the
    Theoretical Life (1177b26–31)   184
    One Should Live in Accordance with the Divine
    Element Because Each Person Most of All Is This
    Element (1177b31–1178a8)   186

The Life in Accordance with the Practical Virtues Is Human and Affords Human Happiness (1178a9–23)	192
The Practical vs the Theoretical Life	
Theoretical Reflection Needs Fewer Resources than Virtuous Practical Action (1178a23–b7)	199
The Gods' Happiness Does Not Stem from Virtuous Practical Action, but from Theoretical Reflection (1178b7–23)	205
A Sign: We Attribute Happiness As Far As Reflection Extends (1178b24–32)	210
Living Happily Does Not Require Many Resources	
Doing What One Should Can Be Done with Moderate Resources (1178b33–1179a9)	213
The Views of the Wise (Solon and Anaxagoras) Confirm This (1179a9–17)	215
Lives and Deeds Must Agree (1179a17–22)	220
The Theoretically Wise Person Is Dearest to the Gods (1179a22–32)	224

III Becoming Good (X.9) — 228

X.9 The End of the EN — 228

The Goal of the EN Is Practical, Not Merely Theoretical: We Become Good by Using Virtue (1179a33–b4)	228
How Do We Become Good?	
Presuppositions	
Words Alone Do Not Make People Good (1179b4–20)	231
Good Character Must Exist Beforehand (1179b20–31)	233
In Favour of Law-Based Education	
Law Helps Educate the Young towards Virtue (1179b31–1180a1)	236
Laws Should Also Govern the Behaviour of Grown-Ups (1180a1–14)	239
Summary: Reasons for a Law-Based Education (1180a14–24)	243
Private Individuals Must Become Proficient in Law-Giving Because Most Cities Do Not Provide for It (1180a24–b7)	246
The Benefits of Individualised, Law-Based Education (1180b7–13)	251
How to Become Proficient in Law-Giving (1180b13–23)	253

Conclusion: An Educator Should Become Proficient
in Law-Giving (1180b23–8) 256
    Politicians Cannot Teach It (1180b28–1181a9) 259
    Sophists Cannot Teach It (1181a9–23) 261
    Learning from Texts Is Not Ideal (1181a23–b12) 264
    Studying a Collection of Laws and Political Theory in
    General Is the Best Feasible Option (1181b12–24) 267

Epilogue 271
List of References 273
Index 280

Preface

On Sources and Translation

Greek Text

I translate the Greek printed in the Oxford Classical Text (OCT) edited by Bywater 1892. Occasionally I prefer Susemihl 1880. Notes on the translation indicate where it deviates from Bywater's text (or from both) in favour of single manuscript readings (those of K^b and L^b) or the most common reading of the manuscripts.

The ancient division of the EN into ten 'books' allows us to single out and refer to larger arguments (on dividing texts into books, see §6). Later editors further subdivided the books into 'chapters', which helped in locating important passages more precisely. However, because referring to chapters is often still too imprecise, scholars have since established the convention of referring to the so-called 'Bekker page' (after the edition of Immanuel Bekker, who produced the first complete critical modern edition of Aristotle's works between 1831 and 1837). While the Bekker page, the column, and the line number suffice to refer precisely and uniquely to a passage, scholars often add the book and chapter numbers to place the passage in context. For example, X.1.1172a19 refers to Book X, Chapter 1, line 1172a19. The Bekker page and line numbers given in the translation approximate those given in Bywater's text as closely as possible.

Translations, Commentaries, and Other Scholarship

There are numerous excellent English translations of the *Nicomachean Ethics*. The translations I found most helpful are Ross 1954, Irwin 1985, and especially Rowe's in Broadie and Rowe 2002. I have learnt much from all of them. Translations from the EN and Aristotle's other works tend to be my own, except for the *Politics*, where I quote Reeve's excellent translation (Reeve 1998). Unlike, e.g., parts of the *Physics* or *Metaphysics*, EN X is beautifully written. It also carries a certain pathos that most translations, including mine, fail to render. To my knowledge, the closest to convey it adequately is the German translation of Dirlmeier 1983.

In my translation I have primarily aimed at accuracy. In particular, where possible, I have tried to render the ambiguities in the Greek text neutrally. There are two exceptions. First, although I have largely refrained from inserting additions that make the text more readable, some additions seem unavoidable. I have put into angled brackets (<...>) uncontroversial additions that the Greek clearly implies. In other places I have added referents that the English obscures ([sc. ...]). But in a few places the text requires more controversial additions to make it intelligible. Those are placed in square brackets ([...]). Here I have opted for legibility over neutrality. The commentary on the relevant lemma usually explains the addition and considers further options.

Second, the Greek text Aristotle wrote did not contain any systematic punctuation or paragraphing. By adding punctuation marks, paragraphs, and chapters, editors take a stance on what they take to be the unit of thought conveyed by a sentence, paragraph, or chapter. These divisions are of course not arbitrary, but take their lead from Aristotle's use of particles (which I have translated where feasible). On the strength of Aristotle's use of the particles, but also taking into account Aristotle's reasoning, I have subdivided the text into units of thought, indicated through my paragraphing. All careful readers will no doubt have their own preferred way of carving up the text. But by dividing the text into relatively small chunks – I ended up with 100 – I hope to put the reader in a position further to subdivide or to cluster together larger units of thought.

Among the numerous excellent commentaries on the EN, I have relied most on the judicious, sometimes judgemental, French commentary by Gauthier and Jolif 1958, the German commentary by Dirlmeier 1983, which excels on the philological aspects, and especially the English commentary by Broadie in Broadie and Rowe 2002. I do, however, only occasionally refer to other commentaries in the lemmata, lest my commentary morphs into a meta-commentary. Similarly, I do not wish the discussion of scholarly literature to detract from engaging with the text itself. So, although my discussion stands on the shoulders of a wealth of excellent secondary literature, the main text of the lemmata does not usually engage directly with that literature. For similar reasons, I keep the work done in the footnotes to a minimum. Two works of scholarship from which I would have liked to benefit came too late: Walker

2018 and Dorothea Frede's commentary on the whole of the *Nicomachean Ethics* (Frede 2020, replacing Dirlmeier 1983), which is only about to be published.

Facts about the Ancient World

While the commentary focuses on the philosophical aspects of Book X, at times some historical background knowledge helps to understand those aspects better. Where possible, I have supplied such trivia as dates and careers from *The Oxford Classical Dictionary* (see Hornblower, Spawforth, and Eidinow 2012).

Acknowledgements

I started writing this book because I thought it needed to be written, and that I was ideally placed to write it. Working on the book made me more convinced of the need for a commentary on *Nicomachean Ethics X*, but less certain about my suitability as the ideal author. I could not have submitted the manuscript to the Press without the help of many others. Without M. M. McCabe's encouragement and enthusiasm for the project, I would probably not have started. I thank the Center for Hellenic Studies (CHS) in Washington, DC for electing me to a fellowship, and Bill Brewer for enabling me to take it up. Much of the book came together under the ideal conditions the CHS provided. I was fortunate enough to present some of the material to discerning audiences at Assos, Columbia University, Cornell University, the CHS, the King's staff seminar, the King's Greek Reading Group, the Yale–UCL workshop, and the Lyceum Society's work-in-progress seminar. I have learned much from all these occasions. I must single out Inés De Asis, Dorothea Frede, Anthony Price, Bryan Reece, and Raphael Woolf, all of whom were kind enough to read and comment on bulky and unwieldy swathes of text. Also, the readers for the Press helped me improve presentation and content at key passages. But I owe my deepest intellectual debt to Sarah Broadie. In addition to overseeing my paideia over the years, she read the first draft of my translation and saved me from more than one solecism. She also helped me with some particularly recalcitrant passages, and especially the ending of the book. Despite all the help I received, I am certain that many readers will not agree with everything I say. This is as it should be. Where they disagree because I made a mistake, that mistake should be attributed to me alone.

Introduction

0. The Commentary

That a reader benefits from a commentary on Aristotle's dense writing should be obvious to anyone who has tried to read Aristotle. Precisely because there exist excellent commentaries on the *Nicomachean Ethics* already (on which, see the Preface), why have a commentary on Book X? First, many readers rightly regard Book X as the pinnacle of the *Nicomachean Ethics*. It is here that he puts the coping-stone on the edifice so artfully constructed in EN I–IX. Other readers, by contrast, find Book X incongruent with the rest of the EN because it seems to propagate an amoral ideal, that of a thinker who flies high above the common run of people and is not subject to their human concerns. So Book X is controversial and will, for this reason, benefit from a fresh discussion.[1]

Second, none of the commentaries I have consulted are comprehensive in the sense that they aspire to comment on the whole of the text of Book X. Usually, they leave out the bits that seem too clear, too boring, or too obscure. While I also do not comment on every single word or line, I nevertheless try to be comprehensive, insofar as I divide the whole text into units of thought, and then go through every unit in the corresponding entry of the commentary. I call the entries by their traditional name, *lemma* (plural *lemmata*, from the Greek *lêmma*: assumption, premise, or argument). Dividing the text comprehensively into lemmata, however, yields more than mere comprehensiveness. It also allows the commentary to trace the flow of Aristotle's thought, to emphasise the continuity of his arguments, and to show how the smaller units feed into the larger structure. So, the commentary tries not only to illuminate *what* Aristotle thinks in each lemma, but also *how* he thinks.

---

[1] I use the traditional acronym 'EN' (which stems from the Latin *Ethica Nicomachea*) instead of the now common 'NE'.

But how do we find out what he thinks? What would help us to understand the point of each unit of thought? One influential line, adopted by many of the ancient commentators, is to explain 'Aristotle through Aristotle'. That is, we adduce other passages from the same author to illuminate the passage over which we puzzle. However, whether, and to what extent, a commentary should rely on this time-tried hermeneutical principle depends on how we understand it. I have eschewed the version employed by many of the ancient commentators, because it seems to rest on shaky ground. In particular, I reject inferences of the type 'Aristotle must mean … in this passage in the EN, because he says XYZ in the *Physics*.' This approach seems to presuppose a more or less rigid system of thought in which one can simply use the building-blocks from one work to patch up apparent holes in another. But his thinking seems more flexible and interesting, as the many signs of reworking the material show (cf. §4). A more promising approach takes into account some flexibility in Aristotle's thought, but nevertheless assumes that the foundations of Aristotelian philosophy remain intact throughout his works. This approach, too, suggests that he expected his readers to know his non-ethical treatises well enough to understand the points made in the EN – even if the transferred building-blocks may need to be cut to size to make them fit. If his ethical philosophy is built in part on non-ethical foundations, it would be the task of the commentary to guide the reader to the relevant passages in the non-ethical works. But there is also an alternative that rejects the common assumption of the first two approaches, namely that the EN rests on principles that are justified in works other than those concerning ethics. This more circumspect approach derives some support from the methodological claim in EN I.3 that an ethical enquiry has its own kind of precision, differing from mathematics and, though not stated here, from first philosophy (what we would call 'metaphysics') and natural science. Indeed, in the same chapter, Aristotle makes demands on the character and age of a suitable audience, but he does not seem to require previous knowledge of Aristotelian logic, natural philosophy, or metaphysics. This might indicate that he takes the latter qualification to be irrelevant to the successful study of ethics.[2]

The goal of this commentary is to bring Aristotle alive as a thinker. To this end, each lemma raises and discusses what seem to me philosophically the most pertinent questions. Usually this requires having an eye on what went

---

[2] Scholars differ over the three hermeneutical approaches. For the latest examples of approaches one and two, see the introduction in Henry and Nielsen 2015. For a trenchant critique, and a staunch defence of the separability of ethics, see Polansky 2017.

on before, both in the immediate context, but also in the larger argument of the EN. So, I whole-heartedly endorse 'Aristotle through Aristotle' as long as the scope is confined to the EN. Of course, where relevant (and perhaps necessary), I also refer the reader to Aristotle's other works – but primarily by way of background illustration. While most lemmata are self-contained, in the sense that they do not rely on other texts to be intelligible, a number of lemmata come properly to life only when read in the light of the Platonic subtext. But does Plato really play this important role, given that the EN contains less than a handful of direct references to Plato? And if he did play that kind of role, why does Aristotle not say that his students must know Plato's philosophical writings? One way of answering the question is to assume that Plato's dialogues are aimed at a wider audience, and that one might expect that a student wanting to study with Aristotle should be sufficiently interested in philosophy to know at least the most important dialogues of Plato.[3] But perhaps one can modify the answer to dispense with the questionable assumption that dialogues such as the *Philebus* and the *Laws* were widely known, and do so in two ways. Very few of the lemmata are self-contained in the sense that they could be understood by just anyone. So, i), some training in, or experience with, philosophical thinking is clearly required. This training may suffice to 'get' the argument on the page. But Aristotle may also expect a specific type of philosophical training, ii), training that partly consists of familiarity with Plato's dialogues. Probably, like Plato, Aristotle wrote the EN for a 'mixed audience', one having some background in i) or ii). Those who discern the Platonic subtext will philosophically get more out of the text, but those who do not may still reach the goal of the EN (on which §3.3). So, to make reading EN X as rewarding as possible, the commentary provides the Platonic background where it is especially fruitful for understanding the philosophical point at issue.

Upshot. The commentary focuses on the philosophical issues that arise in the course of working through the text. Leaving aside philological niceties, the commentary will often explore several possible ways of reading the text to enable the reader to make up her own mind about the best interpretation of a given passage. It concentrates on conceptual questions, individual arguments, and clusters thereof, and their contribution to the overall arch of the argument in EN X. But the enquiry does not take place

---

[3] Robb 1994, 233 suggests that 'some of Plato's dialogues were read aloud with success to sophisticated groups of Athenians'. Cf. Harris 1989, 86 who notes that the works of Protagoras, Anaxagoras, and Isocrates were published in Athens, at least partially, by being read out loud. So, one could pick up some philosophy outside the specialised schools.

in a vacuum, conceptual or historical. To bring out the best in Aristotle's arguments, the commentary places Aristotle's thought in a wider framework. The philosophical framework of the EN on which the commentary relies is sketched in the introduction. The relevant background in Plato's philosophy is given in the commentary.

1. The Guiding Principle of the *Nicomachean Ethics*

The Nicomachean Ethics (EN) is a well-organised work on ethics. It begins, in Book I, with the fairly indeterminate notion of 'the highest good', which it subsequently spells out as happiness. How the highest good structures the whole treatise becomes clear from a postcard-sketch of the EN's content.

In an effort to spell out the highest good as happiness, Aristotle identifies living in accordance with excellence or virtue (*aretê*) as the key to a happy life. The concept of virtue dominates the subsequent discussion. Book II provides a general, almost abstract, treatment of virtue, while Books III and VII contain perceptive treatises on the conditions for acting virtuously. The individual virtues are discussed in Books III–VI; Books VIII–IX deal with the social aspect of virtue.

Book X returns more explicitly to happiness as the highest good. A) The discussion of pleasure (X.1–5) is geared towards connecting pleasure with the happy life, i.e. a life in accordance with virtue. B) The study of three prominent kinds of lives in X.6–8 seeks to determine, finally, the virtue in accordance with which we should live in order to live a completely or perfectly happy life. C) The end of the EN (X.9) examines how we ourselves and others may acquire virtue.

Since happiness as the highest good structures not only the whole EN, but also Book X in particular, I shall discuss both the highest good and happiness in some detail (§§1.1–5) before turning to a briefer sketch of virtue (§§2.1–2) and an outline of EN X (§§3.1–3).

1.1 The Highest Good

The *Nicomachean Ethics* centres on the notion of the highest good. More specifically, it deals with the highest practicable good, the highest human good, or simply *the* human good. Goodness, Aristotle maintains, plays a crucial role in all directed human endeavours, as the beginning of the EN illustrates: 'every craft and every enquiry, and similarly every action and planned undertaking seems to aim at some good' (1094a1–2).

The Guiding Principle of the Nicomachean Ethics

Of course, the goods attained through the various undertakings and even the notion of goodness at play in different domains will differ. Nevertheless, all pursuits and their goods are organised into hierarchies. To take Aristotle's example, bridle-making and other crafts that produce gear for horsemanship do so for the sake of horsemanship. In turn, horsemanship and other pursuits belonging to war are subordinate to generalship. Although both bridle-making and horsemanship are subordinate to generalship, they relate to it in different ways. We can see this by considering how they relate to the goal of generalship, i.e. winning the battle. While bridle-making is purely instrumental in attaining the goal, excellent horsemanship can be more than an instrument. The latter can be part of winning the battle in the sense that excellent horsemanship can constitute (wholly or partially) winning the battle (I.1.1094a9–14). Although the cavalry is employed for the sake of winning the battle, they will not be mere instruments.

The example seeks to illustrate the general relationship between subordinate and superordinate pursuits: 'in all pursuits, the ends of all the ruling pursuits are more choice-worthy than the ends under them, because it is for the sake of the former that the latter too are pursued' (1094a14–16). The superordinate pursuit rules or controls the subordinate in either of two ways.[4] It can a) prescribe the norms internal to the pursuit. For instance, the practice of riding will determine what counts as a good bridle – which would seem appropriate, given the bridle's role as an instrument that facilitates riding. Alternatively, b), the superordinate pursuit can externally regulate the subordinate pursuit. A general need not tell the cavalry how to ride well. That is, the general does not pronounce on the norms internal to horsemanship. Rather, the general decides on how many riders comprise a unit, where to employ them, and when to send them into battle. In this case, the externally regulated pursuit has its own notion of excellence, whereas the internally regulated one does not. As the former has a goal worth pursuing for its own sake (from this pursuit's perspective), it occupies a higher place in the hierarchy of ends.

Introducing planned pursuits as nested hierarchies raises the question of what makes for a complete hierarchy of goals and pursuits. Aristotle argues that there must be end-points that complete the hierarchical structure. In the absence of suitable end-points, we would have to admit to unending hierarchies:

---

[4] Lear 2004, 17–19 distinguishes the two ways of subordination well. See Meyer 2011 for further illuminating discussion.

> If, then, there is some end in our practical pursuits for which we wish for its own sake, and we wish for the others because of it, and we do not choose everything for the sake of something else (for in this way, it will go on to infinity, making our desire empty and vain), it is clear that this is the good, i.e. the best good. (1094a18–22)

The goal that ends the regress is *the* good because the good subordinates all other goals. Aristotle takes care to posit a *single* good that subsumes all other goods. While 'the good' may plausibly refer to the good of a certain domain, the best good towers over and controls *all* other goods.

The proposal has wide-ranging consequences for Aristotle's thinking about goods. Of course, it does not follow from the observation that all planned pursuits aim at some good (1094a1–2) that every good is (to be) aimed at by some pursuit. There may be goods that cannot be attained through action. But, as the beginning of the EN makes clear, Aristotle focuses entirely on practicable goods. And here it is plausible to maintain that any practical good is the good of a practical domain that can be mastered by some kind of practical knowledge. So, corresponding to the hierarchies of goals, Aristotle posits a hierarchy of (kinds of) practical knowledge that govern the practical spheres. If so, the highest good will be the goal of the highest and most controlling kind of practical knowledge. He plausibly identifies the most controlling with the most authoritative practical knowledge. He uses examples to cast political expertise (*politikê*) in this role. Political expertise governs directly or indirectly all aspects of life in a city-state (*polis*): which crafts are needed, how many craftsmen for each, when to wage war; it also legislates what one should and should not do. So, the best practical good will be the goal of political expertise (1094a29–b6).

To identify the most controlling knowledge with political expertise raises the question of the EN's audience. Does Aristotle merely address aspiring politicians? Or does he cast his net more widely? The answer, as so often, is a qualified 'both'. The EN addresses those who seem to lack knowledge of the highest good. Since this knowledge belongs to political expertise, and since the *Nicomachean Ethics* seeks the highest good, it will itself in a way be political (*politikê tis*, 1094b11). However, Aristotle does not seem to address only would-be statesmen.[5] Achieving and preserving the highest good for the city-state is greater, more complete, finer, and more divine than doing the same for an individual. However, the latter

---

[5] *Pace* Bodéüs 1993.

should also be welcomed, because the goal is the same in both cases: the human good (1094b7–11). While he ranks the political expertise successfully exercised by the politician higher than the equivalent on the private level, Aristotle nevertheless seems to acknowledge the private equivalent of political expertise – without seeing the need to find a new name for it. Indeed, he spells out much later in the EN the sameness between political expertise and the expertise required to run a private life well (VI.8). For now, however, the important point is that *we* as private individuals can acquire a kind of knowledge, discussed in the *Nicomachean Ethics*, which aims at the highest good. This knowledge will have a great impact on our lives because, just as every pursuit in the city is subordinate to the highest good, so is every pursuit for a private individual.

1.2 Happiness

Having identified political expertise as the knowledge of the highest practical good, Aristotle seeks to identify its goal more precisely: 'in name, it is agreed pretty much by the majority, for both the many and the distinguished call it "happiness" (*eudaimonia*), and they take living well and doing well to be the same as being happy' (I.4.1095a17–20).

The passage raises two important issues, one about happiness, the other about method. First, 'happiness' does not translate the Greek term *eudaimonia* perfectly. But it is preferable to 'flourishing' or 'well-being', or to leaving it untranslated. All of the translations fail to convey the connection to the divine, clearly present in *eudaimonia*. The word is after all the abstract composite of two words, *eu* and *daimôn*. The former is the adverb for 'good'; the latter means 'god' or 'deity', or, more barbarically, 'higher-than-human-being'. Aristotle cites the tragic playwright Euripides (ca 485–407/6 BC) to connect the two: a person is happy 'when the god gives well' (*hotan ho daimôn eu didô(i)*, IX.9.1169b7–8). While Aristotle and his contemporaries did not necessarily take the god to mete out happiness – this would have to be investigated (cf. I.9.1099b11–13) – the quote from Euripides indicates two points: a) a connection between the divine and human happiness, however ossified, and b) the absence of determinate content of happiness conceived abstractly.

Our concept of happiness, I think, captures the second aspect better than does 'flourishing' or 'well-being'. Like its Greek counterpart, 'happiness' does not have a fixed referent, nor a fixed range of applications. Ordinary people, Aristotle reports, equate *eudaimonia* with pleasure, wealth, or honour. Some do not even settle for a single goal, but adopt a different goal depending on their circumstances. For instance, to those who are ill, health might seem to be happiness. By contrast, philosophers such as Plato distinguish between these ordinary goods and the highest good existing by itself, making the latter the cause of the former (1095a20–8). While we rarely speak about happiness abstractly outside of academic contexts, we do speak a lot about being or feeling happy. Although 'being happy' does not *mean* 'being in an elated mood' or 'feeling pleasure', this common usage fits the conception of happiness employed by the many. For them, being pleased *amounts to* being happy, because they take happiness to be pleasure. However, *eudaimonia* can also be understood as pointing to a more stable or enduring condition (than fleeting happiness). And while being happy may be conceived of as momentary, living well and doing well appear to be more enduring conditions – as if being *eudaimôn* is something more stable than an elated feeling. 'Flourishing' in particular seems more apt for catering for this aspect of the concept of *eudaimonia*, because doing well and living well can plausibly be understood in terms of prosperity – which we can readily capture as flourishing.[6] But 'happiness' and its cognates can also indicate a stable state. Think of the formulaic endings of fairy-tales. 'They lived happily ever after', usually because they have surmounted some obstacle, have found each other, have been rewarded with, say, half a kingdom, and are generally happy. 'Living happily' conveys the stability that being *eudaimôn* can connote, but it stresses the psychological dimension more than 'flourishing' does, for the Prince and the Princess naturally also *feel* happy when they prosper. So, our concept of happiness mirrors the versatility of the concept of *eudaimonia* with which Aristotle begins his enquiry.

Why should we not choose our translation of *eudaimonia* merely for its capacity to capture *Aristotle's* conception of it?[7] We can answer the question by attending to the second point that the passage from I.4 (quoted above) raises. It begins by noting how the word *eudaimonia* is used, and what people think about it. The case of happiness illustrates how Aristotle often operates in the EN. He raises a difficult question, notes either what people of repute and the many say about it (where relevant), and then examines more thoroughly where the existing opinions go right and wrong. He is not usually content with pointing out the mistakes of previous thinkers. In addition, he tries to diagnose what was (or is) attractive about the view,

---

[6] Indeed, this was a widespread use of the term: see Herodotus, *Histories*, V.28; cf. VII.220.
[7] Most scholars focus on Aristotle's own conception of *eudaimonia* and assess its affinity to our conceptions. See especially Kraut 1979.

and often he acknowledges that the other thinkers got *something* right. It would otherwise be a mystery why he would engage with his predecessors at all. So, by dwelling on the views of others, and distilling what truth they contain, he can develop his own view while keeping an eye on the desiderata the examination of others has revealed. This technique seems sensible for anyone who tries to answer difficult philosophical questions – and philosophers still employ it today. But many scholars see an 'endoxic method' in Aristotle's approach, articulated at EN VII.1.1145b2–7, which serves to justify ethical propositions.[8] However, the passage in Book VII seems tailored to its specific context and should not be generalised.[9] And examining how he in fact proceeds in the EN outside of the Book VII passage casts further doubt on the assumption that a set endoxic method is used throughout the EN.[10] In any case, it is clear that Aristotle sees himself in a tradition of theorising about *eudaimonia*. Even when he corrects the mistakes of others and advances his own substantial account, he nevertheless takes himself to be talking about the same thing, *eudaimonia*. Therefore, the translation should be sufficiently wide to accommodate the various accounts, even if only Aristotle's is the correct one.

He begins to think properly about the highest good as happiness by discussing, briefly, three prominent contenders for happy lives in EN I.5: i) the life of consumption (*apolaustikos*), ii) the political life (*politikos*), and iii) the reflective life (*theôrêtikos*). He does so because one's conception of happiness (articulated or not) does influence how one lives – after all, it *is* the overarching goal of all one's pursuits. The first two lives are plausible candidates because of their wide support. The life of pleasure is compelling because living happily requires pleasure and thus goes hand in hand with living a pleasant life (VII.11.1152b6–7). The political life becomes a serious contender if we do not understand it merely as living the life of a citizen in a Greek city-state, but as a more elevated kind of life. Indeed, Aristotle posits honour as the highest good pursued by people living this kind of life (*timê*, 1095b22–3). This goal suggests that the political activity in question should go beyond the ordinary political participation in the assembly or in the jury. Since so many citizens engage in an ordinary way in politics, no one will be especially honoured or deemed especially happy for doing only that. Citizens merit honour only in high office, and it is no accident that offices which involve ruling others (*archai*, e.g. like

---

[8] For a clear statement and defence of this view, see Kraut 2006.
[9] Cooper 2009.
[10] See Frede 2012 for a nice corrective to this assumption.

those of military leaders) were also called 'honours' (*timai*, e.g. *Politics*, II.8.1268a21; III.5.1278a20; III.10.1281a31). The happy political life envisaged in I.5 will, therefore, be a life of political distinction, not merely one of political participation.[11] Both lives home in on important values, but they assign to them a role too important. By judging the life of pleasure as fit only for cattle, Aristotle intimates that pleasure is not a suitable goal for political expertise, the knowledge that enables us to strive at the *human* good (I.5.1095b19–20). By contrast, honour seems all too human, because it requires other people to honour us (I.5.1095b23–6). It is really what people are honoured for, their virtue, that people want. So, neither of the accounts posits a good suitable as the object of a branch of *knowledge*,[12] nor does either one capture the elevated status of the highest good as something divine. Both pleasure and honour should be concomitants of happiness, but fail to capture its essential character.

As it turns out, the discussion of lives only provides a preliminary assessment – evident not least by the choice not to discuss the philosophical life in Book I. Book X fittingly contains the final discussion of potentially happy lives. Having re-examined the life of frivolous pleasure in X.6, Aristotle assesses the happiness of the life in accordance with theoretical wisdom vis-à-vis a thoroughly practical life. Although these lives do not come with the labels 'political' and 'philosophical', they seem to correspond to the lives sketched in I.5, as a close reading of the relevant text (provided in the commentary) suggests.

1.3 Happiness as the Highest Good

Having discussed what people say about happiness in I.4–6, Aristotle turns in I.7 to establishing happiness as the highest human good on less dialectical grounds. In particular, he stresses two criteria for the highest good.

i) The highest good must be *teleios*. The Greek word forms the adjective of the more familiar *telos*, which we can render as 'goal' or 'end'. The adjective conveys 'endyness' (or, better, 'finality'), but also 'perfection' and 'completeness'. We can use *teleios* to rank goods in a hierarchy. A higher good will be more *teleios* (complete/perfect/final) than a subordinate good. The highest good, naturally, will be most so, or, as Aristotle puts it, it will be *teleios* 'without qualification', because it is not subordinate to anything

---

[11] Happiness based on political engagement stems from a sustained and successful effort to shape the city-state's fortunes. Although the offices often lasted only for a year at a time, those who excelled nevertheless managed to be re-elected and to shape the state through their political activity.

[12] Establishing this conclusion is an important task of Plato's *Gorgias*.

(I.7.1097a30–4). Now, happiness fits this role because we do in fact choose all other goods for the sake of happiness, but we do not pursue happiness for the sake of anything else. Even goals we seem to pursue only for their own sake, such as pleasure, turn out to be not unqualifiedly complete/perfect/final. Their character as goods sought in their own right indeed makes them especially suitable: because they are goals or ends, we suppose to attain *the* end through them (cf. I.3.1095b14–16). We can say 'I pursue pleasure in order to be happy', but not 'I pursue happiness in order to have pleasure.' The second sentence is jarring because we grasp, however dimly, that happiness somehow stands above the other goods. (One way to spell this out would be to conceive of happiness as something indeterminate, of which, e.g., pleasure can be a determinant.) So, happiness is the highest good because it is most complete or most final (*teleiotaton*, I.7.1097a30).

ii) The next criterion, self-sufficiency (*autarkeia* I.7.1097b7), also supports the identification of the highest good with happiness. Self-sufficiency is 'what on its own makes the life choice-worthy and lacking in nothing'. Since 'we think that happiness is such [sc. self-sufficient]' (b14–16), this criterion helps confirm happiness as the highest good. But rendering a life choice-worthy and lacking in nothing *just is* rendering it happy. The point becomes evident against the background of Plato's dialogue *Philebus*. Aristotle not only takes the criteria of completeness and self-sufficiency from the *Philebus* (20b–23b), but also the role of the good sought, which, in the *Philebus*, is explicated as 'that state or disposition of the soul which provides a happy life for all human beings' (11d4–6).[13] Both Plato and Aristotle use the criteria to test whether a given candidate for the highest good can fulfil *that* role. Thus, both philosophers share the assumption that the highest good is that which is *responsible* for a happy life – and Aristotle calls this happiness.[14]

The formal remarks on happiness as the highest good leave much room for interpretation. In particular, scholars disagree over a basic question, whether happiness consists of one item (monism) or of several (pluralism). The extreme version of pluralism, 'inclusivism', can readily account for criteria i) and ii), for one sense in which the goods we pursue for their own sake may nevertheless be subordinate to happiness

---

[13] For two excellent studies discussing the relationship between Plato's and Aristotle's use of the criteria, see Lear 2004, 47–71 and Cooper 2004.

[14] For a similar view, distinguishing between the happy life and what makes it happy, see Broadie 1991, 26–7 and nn. 14 and 15, and Cooper 2004, 289–90 with reference to the *Philebus*. See also Charles 2014, 94–8.

would be by constituting happiness. Happiness is *teleios* especially in the sense of 'complete': it comprises a complete array of goods. When I pursue pleasure, virtue, and friendship in order to be happy, I do not use them as instruments for yet something else. Rather, attaining all of them *just is* happiness, because there is no higher goal for the sake of which the collection of goods is pursued, and it makes life lacking in nothing because it comprises *all* such goods required for living well (less-than-fully inclusivist versions of pluralism can also account for the second point).[15]

The monist interpretation, by contrast, takes Aristotle to single out the highest non-composite good. This single good structures the pursuit of all the other goods. Goods such as pleasure, virtue, and friendship will have to be present in a happy life, but individually or even collectively they do not 'make' a life happy. Happiness is a good over and above the other goods, because *it* makes life happy. What underlies the highest good on the monist conception is the metaphysical claim that the highest good serves as 'principle and cause' of other goods (1102a2–4; cf. also I.4.1095a26–8; cf. EE I.6.1213b3–8). An analogy may serve to illustrate the basic point. People suffering from depression may have goods in their lives: friends, good character, wealth, political influence, and more. However, these goods are, in a sense, not goods for the person. When suffering acutely from depression, the person may recognise them as goods, but nevertheless ask, 'What are these goods to me?' If a sane person had the choice to get more of the goods listed at the cost of incurring depression (this need not be a fairy-tale: think of being overworked), she probably would refuse the offer. Similarly, on the monist interpretation of happiness, a private person who leads a happy life would not want to give it up in exchange for immense political power or another good that undermines the goods as good *to her*. For example, if happiness were identical with virtue, selling out one's integrity to acquire a lot of money or political power would not make the person better off in any way. Without happiness, the other goods do not 'count' for the person; they only make a life genuinely better under the influence of happiness.[16]

This rough sketch of the monist and pluralist interpretations of happiness in Book I suffices for the purpose of setting up two different readings of the EN. If the highest good is the guiding principle of the EN, and happiness as the highest good can be understood in a pluralist or a monist

---

[15] See the seminal article by Ackrill 1997, and two recent adaptions, Meyer 2011 and Irwin 2012.
[16] For a foundational discussion of the issue, see Broadie 2007b. Cf. Broadie 2007a and 2007d.

way, then, too, our understanding of the EN as a whole will differ according to our interpretation of Book I. Our understanding of happiness affects in particular how we read Book X, which returns to the topic of happiness. To assess the plausibility of these interpretations, one would have to a) muster and review the textual support for each, and b) spell out in more detail what happiness is in order to see whether it can play the role each interpretation assigns to it.[17] Since this introduction does not aim at settling such controversial issues, but rather at providing an overview of pertinent interpretive questions and answers, I leave aside a), say more about b) in the next section, and return to the different ways of reading the EN in §3.2, which discusses happiness in Book X.

1.4 What Is Happiness?

Having determined the highest good as happiness, Aristotle wishes to say more clearly what it is (I.7.1097b22–4). He does so in the famous 'function argument'. The argument rests on the hypothesis, [H], that if something has an *ergon* or action, then the good, in the sense of excellent achievement, is found in the *ergon* (1097b26–7). The word *ergon* is related to, and can mean, 'work'. Translating *ergon* as 'work' has the advantage over rendering it as 'function' in that 'my work' can refer to both an activity and the product that may result from it – which fits better with the examples Aristotle adduces.[18] The excellence of a sculptor, a carpenter, or a shoemaker seems to reside in their work understood as (detachable) products (b25–9), whereas the excellence of an eye, a hand, or a foot resides in working well (b30–2).

Both sets of examples help motivate the premise of the argument, [P]: human beings have an *ergon*. For, if human beings in a certain role can have an *ergon*, and if the organs that partly constitute a human being also have an *ergon*, it seems at least not implausible to attribute an *ergon* also to human beings (1097b28–33).[19] On the basis of H and P, Aristotle sets out to identify the human *ergon* and the human good. He seeks to locate the human *ergon* by mustering the life-functions for which the soul of each animal is responsible: taking in nutrition, growing, decaying, perceiving,

---

[17] Irwin 2012 does an excellent job for a), and clearly lays out the connection between Books I and X.
[18] Baker 2015 stresses the product–activity ambiguity of the word *ergon*. Unfortunately, we associate 'work' almost exclusively with services rendered for payment. The word therefore smacks of instrumentality, which is not present in Aristotle's use of it.
[19] Barney 2008 reconstructs how Aristotle can argue for P.

desiring, and thinking. The first functions are shared with other animals; only the last activity is characteristic (*idion*) of the *human* way of being alive (1097b34–1098a4). But what does it mean to be capable of thinking, and to use it as one's characteristic activity? Aristotle makes a further relevant distinction: human beings can possess reason either in the sense that they obey reason (and so act in accordance with it) or in the sense that they have reason and use it for thinking.[20] Since the latter expresses the human way of being alive more properly, we arrive at the conclusion, [C]: the human *ergon* turns out to be the soul's activity of reason (or not without reason) (1098a7–8).

However, C does not rule out desire and emotion as functions of the soul that can be characteristically human and thus form part of the human *ergon*. In general, appetites and some other desires belong to the non-rational part of the soul, as non-rational desires come together with the perceptual system (*De Anima* II.2.413b21–4). But human desire seems special 'insofar as it is capable of listening to and obeying reason' (I.13.1102b31). Because human desire *can* listen to reason, it belongs in some way to the reasoning part of the soul. Thus, by extending the domain of reason to include the part of the soul that can listen to reason, Aristotle's account of human nature and the human *ergon* seems to cover all bases of characteristically human behaviour. The final book of the EN, thus, contains a discussion of pleasure, considering how it fits into good human life.

Having established the human *ergon*, we can now build on H to arrive at the human good. Aristotle spells out what the good being found in the *ergon* means by using the example of a cithara player. A cithara player characteristically plays the cithara. Playing the cithara well would be the excellent achievement found in the *ergon* – and the *ergon* does not change in kind merely because it is good. Playing and playing well are the same activity, except that the latter has an additional quality of excellence (I.7.1098a8–12). If the examples illustrate the general point contained in H, then it follows that [C*]: the human *ergon* turns out to be reasoning well.

However, C* leaves out an important aspect of the good, for the example of the citharist illustrates another important dimension of the good. When we qualify the *ergon* with 'good' (or 'bad') as a way of doing things, we usually also add the same qualification to the practitioner. For instance, a good performance is characteristic of a good citharist. The point does

---

[20] While most interpreters take this to be Aristotle's distinction, some reject this claim as a later addition (cf. Susemihl 1880).

not only apply to practitioners of craft, but also to the other set of examples mentioned earlier in the function argument: eyes, feet, and other organs. In general, then, a good *ergon* achieved by X is characteristic of a good or excellent X.

But what is an excellent X? As before, X and an excellent X are of the same kind, the latter differing only in excellence (*aretê*).[21] Aristotle will later spell out the correlation between X's excellence and attaining the good in X's *ergon* in causal terms. An eye's excellence *makes* both the eye and its *ergon* good. *Because of* its excellence, the eye sees well, and counts as a good eye (II.6.1106a15–19). For our present purposes, however, the correlative claim that achieving X's *ergon* well is characteristic of an excellent X suffices (though see 1098a15), for it entails that achieving the human *ergon* well is characteristic of an excellent human being, that is, a human being who possesses excellence and acts in accordance with it [HG]: 'the human good turns out to be an activity of the soul in accordance with excellence' (1098a16–17).[22]

1.5 What Have We Learned about Happiness?

Interpreters seek to discern cues for interpreting HG in the qualifications it receives as [HG*]: 'the human good turns out to be an activity of the soul in accordance with excellence, (i) and if there are several excellences, then in accordance with the best and most *teleiotaton* (this is the superlative of *teleios*: complete, perfect, or final) one. (ii) Moreover, it will be this in a *teleios* life' (1098a16–18). The first qualification may seem puzzling, because so far a certain thing seemed to have only one excellence – which makes sense if we individuate an excellence through the *ergon*. A heavy book may be an excellent doorstop, but not *qua* book. Similarly, a carpenter may be beautiful, a good friend, and generally a good person, but he does not attain these *erga* through being a good carpenter. So Aristotle might hint at the possibility that human beings *qua human* have more than one *ergon* and hence may have several excellences whose exercise

---

[21] Very often 'virtue' seems a more suitable translation for *aretê*, especially when Aristotle treats of the good states of character. But in a general context such as this, where it applies to organs and craftsmen, 'excellence' seems more appropriate.

[22] The phrase 'in accordance with excellence' translates the Greek *kata tên aretên* minimally. A more committal translation would be 'is brought about by excellence' (cf. Pakaluk 2005, 81, n. 18). Although Aristotle clearly stresses that human excellence is the state through which a human being turns out to be good and from which one achieves one's *ergon* well (II.6.1106a22–4), he is less explicit here in Book I.

attains the individual *erga* well. Building on the preceding argument, we can spell out this suggestion as follows. The human *ergon* consists in the activity of reason, but reason can be understood in two ways, as the obedient part that listens to reason, or as the part that itself has and uses reason. Therefore, there are two ways of attaining the human *ergon*, and accordingly two ways of attaining the *ergon* well. And indeed, Aristotle does go on to identify the excellence of the listening part of the soul as the virtues of character, whereas the part that has reason properly hosts several intellectual virtues (I.13.1103a3–7). So he might here envisage a hierarchy between the two ways in which a human being can live a characteristically human life, claiming that the human good is to be attained by the best and most complete/final/perfect excellence.

Importantly, claim i) leaves open whether the highest excellence comprises (all) other virtues or not. We could take Aristotle to mean either a) that the exercise of the complete set of human virtue makes for the highest good (taking *teleios* as 'complete'), or b) that we should regard the exercise of the single *best* virtue as the human good (taking *teleios* as final or perfect). In other words, we have here another important passage that bears on the monist vs pluralist reading of the highest good. Many interpreters think the second qualification of HG* settles the question in favour of inclusivism. They argue that a) the word *teleios* in HG* should have the same meaning in both occurrences, and b) it means 'complete' in its second occurrence, because Aristotle goes on to speak about the length of time, as if a certain quantity was required for completeness (1098a18–20). Therefore c) the complete set of human virtue forms the basis of the human good. However, one may also construe ii) differently, for b) may simply allude to certain constraints on counting a life as a suitable goal. Surely, we would not wish for a life cut short! The point would highlight that the activity of virtue in this short life would not suffice to make it desirable or happy. This does not show that the activity of virtue fails to function as the highest good, but only that we need to specify the life in which it can perform this function: the life has to be goal-like (*teleios*). If that is what Aristotle means in ii), then by the logic of the a-b-c argument, i) would point to the most goal-like or most final activity of virtue.[23]

The professed purpose of the 'function argument' is to elucidate the nature of happiness (I.7.1097b22–4). What, then, does the argument tell us? Many readers take Aristotle to provide a substantial account of the human

---

[23] Similarly, and with further discussion, see Pakaluk 2005, 81–3.

good. In particular, they read HG (or HG*) as if 'excellence' had a fixed referent in human virtues, such as courage, justice, or practical wisdom. However, the argument does nothing to warrant such a conclusion. We should resist the temptation to read the excellences Aristotle later identifies back into the 'function argument', and for two reasons. First, even if we agree on justice and courage as important virtues, this hardly says anything. For instance, Callicles in Plato's *Gorgias* would place justice at the heart of a happy life, but, for him, justice is the capacity to get what one wants (488b–491b). So the function argument does not justify a moralistic account of the excellences or virtues it identifies. Second, regardless of its name, the capacity to attain what one wants seems to be a rational capacity, as it requires deliberation, judgement, etc. Using this capacity well would therefore qualify as a candidate activity for happiness because it has some claim to being the most final one: it can satisfy *all* of one's desires. This 'virtue' has the advantage of bridging the gap between virtue as something that makes its possessor a good human being, and something that is good for its possessor. A good human being would be one who is good at getting what he or she wants – which in turn secures the things that are good for that person to have. Lastly, this 'virtue' can also explain the close link to happiness, for it is plausible to think that being able to get what one wants *does* make one happy. All of this requires further argument. But it should be clear that the 'function argument' provides no more than a formal framework within which we can further enquire. The argument succeeds in narrowing down plausible candidates for happiness, showing that happiness is found in activity, that the activity must be rational, and that virtue or excellence is crucial for attaining happiness – but no more than that. The final account of happiness and of *the* virtue through which we achieve our *ergon* is only achieved through the examination of the three lives in the final book of the EN, in chapters X.6–8.[24]

2. The Body of the *Nichomachean Ethics*: Virtue

Happiness is the central topic that structures the *Nicomachean Ethics*. But how we construe the connection between happiness and the other topics that depend on it through the notion of virtue is influenced by our understanding of the structure of happiness itself, in particular whether we read

---

[24] For a strong defence of the formal reading of the function argument, and an extended discussion of what the function argument *does* accomplish, see Lawrence 2001 and 2006. The latter connects this reading helpfully with X.6–8.

Aristotle as a pluralist or a monist, for he may either go through the goods that are part of happiness or else expand on the conditions that need to be in place for the highest good to make a life happy. The transition to the study of virtue or excellence can be read in line with either the monist or the pluralist approach to the EN: 'since happiness is a certain activity of the soul in accordance with complete/perfect/final excellence, we should examine the topic of excellence, for in this way, we might presumably see the topic of happiness better' (I.13.1102a5–7). We might see happiness better either by seeing what it comprises, or else by seeing what a life that can be made happy by the highest good requires. In any case, by examining the central notion of excellence, we begin to see what hides behind the formula 'activity in accordance with excellence' that stands at the heart of happiness. So, the topic of excellence is subordinate to the topic of happiness, but nevertheless is central to it, insofar as it may illuminate the notion of happiness.

2.1 Virtue of Character

The topic of human excellence, or virtue, runs from I.13.1102a5 to the end of Book VI (1145a11). The discussion falls broadly into two parts, following the crucial distinctions introduced in I.13. In a well-developed soul 'the part of the soul having reason will divide into two parts, the one will have it properly speaking, and in itself, the other has it as something that listens to it as if to a father' (I.13.1103a2–3; cf. I.7.1098a4–5). But since human excellence is found in the activity of reason, Aristotle divides human excellence in accordance with the division in reason. The virtues of character belong to the excellence of the listening part of the soul, whereas the excellences of thought comprise theoretical wisdom, comprehension, and practical wisdom (1103a3–7).

Before discussing the virtues in detail, Aristotle builds the relevant theoretical foundation. By providing insight into what a virtue is, he enables us to discern which states of character should count as virtues and which we should dismiss. Beginning with the acquisition of the virtues of character, he develops the so-called 'doctrine of the mean', according to which an excellent state of character lies (theoretically) between two bad states of excess and of deficiency (II.6). What we choose to do, and how we do it, depends centrally on our emotional response to the situation. Many of our actions are influenced by various forms of pleasant or distressing emotions, such as fear, boldness, desire, anger, and pity (cf. II.5.1105b21–3). As all of these emotions can be excessive, deficient, or in the mean, the associated actions will likewise be excessive, deficient, or in the mean (II.6.1106b18–24).[25] This is why virtue is defined as 'a character state in the mean relative to us issuing in decision, the mean being determined by reason, namely reason by which the wise person (*phronimos*) would determine it' (1106b36–1107a2).

Having established the theoretical background for discussing the virtues, Aristotle now returns to the task set at the end of I.13: 'Resuming our discussion, let us say about each [sc. of the virtues of character] what they are, what sort of things they relate to, and how they do so' (III.5.1115a4–5). He goes on to discuss the following virtues, showing that each of them is in a mean (and hence a genuine virtue): courage (III.6–9); moderation (III.10–12); open-handedness (IV.1); munificence (IV.2); greatness of soul (IV.3); a nameless virtue concerned with smaller honours (IV.4); mildness (IV.5); and the social virtues of friendliness (IV.6), truthful self-presentation (IV.7), and wit (IV.8). A sense of shame falls short of being a virtue, because it is about wrong-doing, and hence not characteristic of an excellent character (IV.9). The whole of Book V deals with justice. It completes the discussion of the character virtues.

2.2 Excellences of Intellect

Aristotle motivates the discussion of the excellences of intellect in two ways. a) He notes that the discussion of the virtues of character rests on the notion of the mean. The notion of correctness contained in the mean needs further elucidation. However, he does not directly discuss the correct prescription that determines the mean (*orthos logos*, VI.1.1138b20; b25; b29; b34). Instead, he turns to the excellences of intellect (1139a1–3), and to the faculty or state that determines the mean in action, practical wisdom (*phronêsis*), an excellence that is implicitly presupposed by the definition of virtue (§2.1).

Aristotle begins defining practical wisdom as an *intellectual* virtue by recalling the distinction from Book I: the rational part of the soul comprises a part that has reason in itself, and a part that listens to reason (I.13.1103a2–3; cf. I.7.1098a4–5). Now, the part that has reason properly, i.e. the intellectual part of the soul, is subdivided into a calculative part (*logistikon*), which reflects on things that can be otherwise, and a scientific part (*epistêmonikon*), which reflects on things that cannot be otherwise

---

[25] For two illuminating studies on the mean in virtue, see Hursthouse 2006 and L. Brown 2013.

(1139a6–12). The best state of the calculative part turns out to be *phronêsis*, or practical wisdom, partly because the calculative part of the soul is closely tied to deliberation. Acting well (in the broad sense) requires good deliberation, and a person who has practical wisdom will be able to deliberate well. However, the remit of *phronêsis* is both broader, insofar as it comprises one's whole life, and narrower, insofar as it deliberates only about a certain range of goods: 'it is thought to be characteristic of the practically wise person to be able to deliberate well about things good and beneficial for himself … [about] what sorts of things conduce to living well in general' (VI.4.1140a26–9).

But merely grasping, intellectually, what is good does not make a person *practically* wise. Practical wisdom aims not merely at grasping what is the good thing to do in this situation. Its true goal can only be achieved when the person's desire agrees with the outcome of good deliberation. In this case, when deciding on a good course of action, both true (practical) reason and correct desire aim at the same thing: acting well (1139b3–4; as opposed to producing something, 1140b7). Now, since the correct desire as motivating force belongs to the virtues of character, Aristotle can argue that the virtues of character and practical wisdom presuppose one another (VI.2.1139a33–4; VI.5.1140b11–20; VI.12–13). Acting well (in the fullest sense) is not possible without both components.

Achieving the goal of theoretical wisdom (*sophia*) does not presuppose the virtues of character in the same way as practical wisdom. Theoretical wisdom aims at truth. Its goal consists merely in understanding the truth, not in doing anything besides understanding. The truth aimed at is fundamental, in the sense that, unlike other branches of scientific knowledge (which also aim at truth), theoretical wisdom also includes a grasp of the starting points or principles (*archai*, VI.6.1141a7–8) of the more specialised kinds of knowledge. So, theoretical wisdom takes a special place among theoretical (or demonstrative) knowledge, because it is the most precise theoretical knowledge, and of the most estimable objects (VI.7.1141a16–20). 'Precision' (*akribeia*) here indicates systematicity and fundamentality: a more precise science relies less on assumptions or starting points taken over from other sciences. In this way, a theoretically wise person will grasp the systematic connections between different branches of science, connections that experts in those particular sciences may well miss.

How are the excellences of the calculative and the scientific part of the soul related? While Aristotle argues that the virtues of character and practical wisdom presuppose one another, he provides no comparable argument for theoretical and practical wisdom. In principle, one person could acquire practical wisdom without an inkling of theoretical wisdom, or vice versa. So, the philosopher and the good person need not be the same (as they are in Plato's *Republic*). But who is better? Which way of life should we prefer? Both intellectual virtues aim at truth, though truth in different domains (changeable vs unchangeable). Practical wisdom enquires about human affairs. But the objects of theoretical enquiry surpass human beings; they are 'much more divine in nature ..., e.g. the constituent parts of the universe' (VI.7.1141a34–b2). May we infer the superiority of theoretical wisdom over practical wisdom because of the affinity of the state and its objects (VI.1.1139a11–12)? The question is important for two reasons. a) Insofar as theoretical wisdom is *a* human good, we must know its true value if we are to take it into account properly in practical situations. b) Insofar as happiness is the activity in accordance with the most complete/perfect/final virtue, we want to to know which one takes pride of place, practical or theoretical excellence. (The latter is especially acute on the monist construal of happiness.)

Unfortunately, b) takes only the back seat in chapters 12–13, a coda to Book VI, which mainly answers the question why we should need practical wisdom in addition to the virtues of character. Aristotle notes that 'it would be strange if <practical wisdom>, although inferior to theoretical wisdom, will be more authoritative, for what produces [X], rules [over X] and prescribes each [thing that X does]' (VI.12.1143b33–5). The puzzle relies on two assumptions, i) that practical wisdom in some sense produces theoretical wisdom, and ii) that Y's practical activities, such as producing X and prescribing a course of action to X, automatically make Y more authoritative than X. Point ii) seems especially plausible in a political context – political expertise epitomises practical wisdom (VI.8) – because a politician oversees all the pursuits in the city-state (I.2.1094a26–b7).

The solution, sketched over only six lines (VI.13.1145a6–11), accepts i), but rejects ii). Practical wisdom does not prescribe anything *to* theoretical wisdom, but *for the sake of* it, which may imply the superiority of theoretical over practical wisdom. But instead of complaining about this excessively brief sketch, we should turn to Book X – which takes up both a) and b).

3. The Telos of the *Nicomachean Ethics*: EN X

Book X comprises three related, but distinct, topics: pleasure, happiness, and some meta-reflection on how the *Nicomachean Ethics* attains its goal as a practical enterprise. I shall give a brief overview of the three discussions in this Introduction rather than at the beginning of each section in the Commentary.

As part of an introduction, the overview in §§ 3.1–3 provides a sense of how the individual discussions a) fit into the plan of the EN as a whole and b) follow one another within Book X. Finally, c), by looking at the topics synoptically, we can discern how they contribute to unified argument in EN X (§3.4).

3.1 Pleasure: X.1–5

The first topic in Book X is pleasure, announced as follows: 'After this topic, presumably, the next to go through is pleasure' (1172a19). Aristotle justifies the need to study pleasure in the introductory chapter (X.1), adducing two important reasons. a) Pleasure is most intimately connected to human nature (X.1.1172a19–20). Just like living with other people, human beings cannot live without it. And as an ineradicable part of human life, pleasure requires philosophical attention in a study such as the EN. b) Because it is a part of human life, pleasure will also be a part of the good human life: 'with regard to virtue of character, enjoying what one should and hating what one should is also thought to be of greatest importance' (1172a21–3). So, the study of pleasure serves not only to understand human nature and the methods of education better (1172a20–1), but also to illuminate the nature of virtue itself, especially insofar as the virtues of character belong, in a way, to the desiderative part of the soul (cf. 2.1–2).

Before Aristotle turns to the elusive connection between virtue and pleasure, he engages with a standing controversy over the value of pleasure: is pleasure the good, or is it plain bad (1172a26–7)? Assessing the argument of hedonists and their opponents alike in X.2–3, he comes out in the middle: some pleasures are good, some are bad (X.3.1174a8–11). But this result raises important questions about the nature of pleasure. Both hedonists and anti-hedonists seem to suppose that there is something in the nature of pleasure that determines its value: pleasure is good (or bad) *because* it is a pleasure. Rejecting the extreme views, one must explain how pleasure has any value at all (and how the value can differ).

Chapters 4 and 5 of Book X develop an intricate, albeit elusive, account of pleasure that sheds light on i) the connection between pleasure and excellence and ii) the value of pleasure. Part of the difficulty of pinning down Aristotle's view stems from the central place allocated to the notion of completion/perfection/finality. Very roughly, he conceives of paradigmatic pleasures as completing/perfecting/finalising (*teleioun*) activities that are themselves complete/perfect/final (*teleios*, X.4.1174b20–33). However we are to understand this exactly (for discussion, see the Commentary), he tries to wrap paradigmatic pleasure into the excellence of excellent activities: insofar as they are most complete/perfect/final, they will be most pleasurable (X.4.1174b19–20).

By attending to less than excellent, or outright bad, activities, we can grasp Aristotle's approach to the value of pleasure, for bad activities, too, can be completed/perfected/finalised by pleasure. Importantly, in both the good and the bad case, we have standards independent from pleasure for assessing the value of the activity. Good activities are made better by pleasure, whereas bad activities will become worse. If we take the kinds of activity to be essentially good or bad, then our taking pleasure in them makes the activities more what they are – and in this sense completes or perfects them. Aristotle takes this picture to illustrate the difference between pleasures. Different kinds of pleasure complete/perfect/finalise different kinds of activity: good kinds of pleasure attend good kinds of activity, whereas bad kinds of pleasure attend bad kinds of activity (X.5.1175b24–33). Underlying this account of the value of pleasure, we have a substantial deviation from the views with which we began. Pleasure no longer is a 'thing' that can be good or bad, but something that exists only by piggy-backing on activities. Pleasure, accordingly, does not have a positive value on its own, but takes on the value of the activity to which it belongs.

Aristotle uses this conceptual framework to approach the overarching topic of the EN, happiness. He argues that the pleasures that properly belong to the happy life, a life in accordance with virtue, enter it through completing/perfecting/finalising excellent rational activities. Through engaging in her characteristic activities, the good person will naturally enjoy the pleasures that stem from virtue. These pleasures are key to a good human life. Those who fail to live in accordance with virtue will miss out on enjoying those primary or key (*kuriôs*) pleasures because pleasure is so tightly bound to the activity that gives rise to it. Instead, they will have pleasures only 'in a secondary way or in ways many times removed, just like the activities' (X.5.1176a27–9). This distinction between pleasures would allow Aristotle to maintain that pleasure in the primary or key sense will be good. That is, the pleasures characteristic of a good human life will themselves be good.

A word on the translation of *hêdonê* and *lupê*. While we might find it odd to say that pleasure and pain accompany every action and affection (as Aristotle does, II.3.1104b13–16), much of the oddness comes merely from translating the Greek as 'pleasure' and 'pain'. I opt for the traditional translation, but the reader should keep in mind that the Greek words cover a significantly wider range of affections than our 'pleasure' and 'pain'. For instance, Aristotle subsumes fear under pain – which we would presumably prefer to call 'distress'. More generally, he thinks it a defining mark of affections such as appetite, anger, fear, confidence, ill-will, joy, love, hatred, longing, envy, and pity that they are accompanied by pleasure and pain (II.5. 1105b21–3). While we might balk at the suggestion that pity or appetite *are* pains, or even that they are accompanied by *pain*, we do nevertheless acknowledge their influence on our hedono-algesic equilibrium. In common usage of the ancient Greek words, this suffices to classify such affections as pleasure or pain.

3.2 Happiness and Happy Lives: X.6–8

Aristotle introduces happiness, the topic of X.6–8, as follows: 'as the subjects of the virtues, friendship, and pleasure have been discussed, it remains for us to treat of happiness in outline' (1176a30–1). Unlike the other topics, happiness does not need any further justification: he discusses it because 'we posit it as <the> goal (*telos*) of human affairs' (a31–2) – which is why the EN practically begins with happiness. So, why come back to happiness? Because only Book X contains the final account of happiness, or rather, an account of final/complete/perfect happiness (*teleia eudaimonia*, X.7.1177a17).

While ending the EN with a discussion of *teleia eudaimonia* seems apposite – given that happiness is the end (*telos*) – there are two main ways to relate X.6–8 to the rest of the EN, pluralist and monist. Both interpretations should start by taking Aristotle's initial summary seriously, including its order. Of all the topics discussed so far in the EN, he singles out virtue, friendship, and pleasure presumably because they are important and desirable goods. Both interpretations agree that virtue, pleasure, and friendship will belong to a happy life. They disagree on how to spell out their place in relation to the highest good. To see how the two interpretations differ, I shall draw on the rough sketch provided in §1.3, and then refine the crucial points that do make a difference.

According to the extreme version of pluralism, inclusivism, all highly general kinds of intrinsic goods are parts of happiness. Since the virtues, friendship, and pleasure satisfy this criterion, happiness would consist in a combination of them. But presumably the goods making up happiness will need to be ordered in a certain way.[26] Aristotle would therefore have reason to return to the topic of happiness in X.6–8 in order to provide

---

[26] In his seminal contribution to the topic, Hardie 1965 very clearly makes order a part of an inclusivist approach. However, many subsequent discussions appear to disregard this important point.

an ordering principle for the goods that constitute a person's happiness. Monism differs from pluralism insofar as it posits happiness to consist of only one good. But monists do not overlook the importance of goods other than the highest. A plausible version of monism would make intrinsic goods such as virtue, friendship, and pleasure parts of the best life, since that life is a life lived in accordance with excellence. However, monists maintain, it does not follow that these goods should therefore form part of happiness, understood as that which makes life happy.[27] So, Aristotle would need to return to happiness in X.6–8 to identify the activity of excellence that makes a life happy, i.e. to identify happiness.

Either interpretation can make sense of what X.6–8 in fact contains. Aristotle begins by re-examining pleasure as a candidate for happiness, thus going back to the life of frivolous pleasure so quickly dismissed in I.5 (cf. §1.2). He rejects it on the grounds that we do not choose pleasure solely for its own sake, despite the appearance to the contrary (X.6). The other two lives mentioned in I.5, the political and the philosophical life, await re-examination in X.7–8. He sets up the discussion at the beginning of X.7 by reminding us that 'if happiness is an activity in accordance with virtue, it is reasonable that it is in accordance with the most outstanding one; and this will be [the virtue] of the most excellent element' (1177a12–13). In a series of arguments (X.7.1177a18–b26) he confirms the claim placed at the beginning, that perfect/complete/final happiness consists in excellent theoretical reflection (1177a16–17). By laying the foundation for establishing the superiority of the philosophical over the practical life (a topic further pursued in X.8), Aristotle in a way resumes the discussion of the relationship between practical wisdom (the guiding virtue of the practical life) and theoretical wisdom (cf. §2.2).

According to the pluralist reading, Aristotle focuses on theoretical wisdom and its activity in order to complete the account of happiness. To take into account the comparative (or competitive) nature of the discussion in X.7, a plausible version of pluralism will assign to excellent theoretical thinking not merely the role of *a* component of happiness, but will cast it as the *key* component – which justifies calling it 'complete/perfect/final happiness'. It could play *that* role if the other goods were ordered in some

---

[27] Scholars used not to distinguish between happiness as that which makes a life happy and the happy life. If pluralism is defined as the thesis that the happy life qua happy contains more than the exercise of theoretical wisdom, then the monist reading sketched here would count as pluralist. However, such a narrow conception of monism makes nonsense of the rest of the EN and should therefore be rejected.

way by reference to theoretical reflection. Theoretical wisdom will not do the ordering – that role belongs to practical wisdom – but it will be that around which the other components of happiness will be arranged. The monist reading agrees significantly with this account, given that the two best lives according to either interpretation will contain the same goods. These goods will also be ordered in a similar way. But the monist account applies different labels. If all the goods that a pluralist includes in happiness are ordered *with a view to* the highest good among them, thus making theoretical reflection central, then, according to the monist reading of the criteria for happiness in I.7, we should regard only this highest good as happiness.

So, how do pluralism and monism differ? For the difference between the pluralist and the monist reading may begin to seem merely verbal. The suspicion may draw support from the fact that Aristotle does not have a clear stance on the issue. Perhaps he would not have regarded the point as important. Since the shape of the philosophical life remains the same regardless of a pluralist or monist interpretation, the difference seems to lack any practical import – and is therefore not germane to the study of ethics. Unfortunately, we cannot dismiss the controversy so quickly, for an important difference emerges when we focus on the second-best life in EN X, the practical life. Theoretical wisdom and reflection appear not to belong to that life. But if happiness *is* theoretical reflection – how can a life that lacks this activity be happy?

The pluralist has a simple answer: the life will be happy because it contains all the parts of happiness except the activity of theoretical wisdom. Although Aristotle stresses the differences between the practical and the theoretical lives, the pluralist *could* maintain, in an effort to explain how the former can be happy, that the parts of happiness are ordered with reference to theoretical wisdom (even if the person living this life does not possess theoretical wisdom). In any case, the life would be less happy than a life that contains *all* kinds of intrinsic goods, but it would nevertheless be recognisably happy, because it contains most of the components that make up happiness.

The monist has a harder time explaining how a purely practical life can be happy. She appears to face the task of elucidating how a life can be happy without *any* happiness in it (assuming that happiness just is the activity of theoretical reflection). She might bite the bullet and write off the purely practical life as a life that is not really happy. Alternatively, and preferably, she must employ considerable scholarly ingenuity to explain how the practical life contains something like the activity of happiness after all. For instance, if theoretical reflection makes us happy because it grasps the truth (*alêtheia*), then excellent practical thinking may make us happy insofar as it yields practical truth (*alêtheia praktikê*, VI.2.1139a26–7).[28] It should be clear that adjudicating between pluralist and monist approaches to the EN goes beyond the question of labels. It concerns our understanding of how the goods in a happy life are related to each other, and consequently makes a practical difference to our pursuit of these goods. So while the take-home message from X.6–8 is simple – the life of theoretical wisdom is better than a purely practical life, and both are vastly better than the life of frivolous pleasure – the details of the ranking, and the reasons for it, remain controversial.

3.3 Becoming Good: X.9

After the discussion of the goal or end of human life (*telos*, X.6.1176a31), Aristotle asks 'if both the present topic [sc. happiness] and the topic of the virtues, and again friendship and pleasure, have been sufficiently discussed in outlines, should one think our plan has reached its end (*telos*)?' (X.9.1179a33–5). In one way, it has, because we have finished the task set out at the beginning of the EN – to identify the goal of human life, and thereby to discuss the most important knowledge for human life (I.2). In another way, the EN remains unfinished, because knowledge of the highest good belongs to political expertise, a branch of practical knowledge. Aristotle now stresses the need to implement the knowledge we have gained through the study of the EN if we are to bring the project to completion.

Many students and scholars tend to see in X.9 a semi-perfunctory transition to Aristotle's treatise *Politics*, because he indeed claims towards the end of EN X.9 that the philosophical study of human affairs is brought to completion (*teleiôthê(i)*) as far as possible through an examination of law-making and a study of political theory – which can be found (arguably) in the *Politics*. This reading certainly chimes well with the EN's approach to studying the highest good as part of *political* expertise (I.2.1094b11). And in the course of the argument, Aristotle seems to address the politician in particular at several junctions. He does so most explicitly, and importantly, when he foreshadows in I.13 the topic to which X.9 returns:

---

[28] In a series of papers, Charles has developed this approach: Charles 1999, 2014, and 2015. Other influential and important monist approaches are defended by Broadie in Broadie and Rowe 2002, 77–8 (cf. Broadie 2016), and Lear 2004.

the true politician 'wants to make citizens good and obedient to the laws' (1102a8–10; cf. I.9.1099b29–32) and hence needs to know about virtue and the basic psychology underlying the account of virtue (1102a18). It seems not unreasonable, therefore, to conclude that X.9 addresses the politician in particular.[29]

However, Aristotle need not have lost view of the private individual. A good person should *also* look to the highest good when educating his children and interacting with his friends and fellow citizens. For, in order to perform both tasks successfully, the good person will need extensive knowledge of the circumstance in which the interaction takes place: the city-state. But in order to understand the city-state in such a way that this understanding can inform our teaching, even the private individual would need to study political theory in general and law-making in particular. X.9 argues that expertise in law-making (whether in a transferred sense or not) lies at the heart of successfully making other people good. But since there is no established route to acquiring the political expertise to which law-making belongs, Aristotle invites the reader to study his *Politics* (or a part of the precursor of the *Politics* as we have them), which does seem to fit the bill.[30] So, the end of the EN does not settle the question of its audience – except that it calls for someone who intends to put the philosophical study of the human good and its related topics into action.

3.4 The Unity of EN X

Contrary to the widely shared opinion that Book X is not a unified whole, looking at EN X from a bird's-eye point of view allows us to see how the three apparently independent topics coalesce into a unity.[31] The concept that unifies Book X is *telos,* together with its cognate *teleios,* and the verb *teleioô.* The concept comprises the notions of an end and finality, and spans completeness, but also connotes perfection. Aristotle may want to

---

[29] Bodéüs 1993 argues that a) the EN should not be regarded as a self-standing treatise, but must be read in conjunction with the *Politics*, and b) aims 'essentially to instruct the politician and above all the politician par excellence, that is, the lawgiver' (39).

[30] Schütrumpf 1991, 80–102, who vehemently opposes both Bodéüs' a) and b), stresses the incongruence between the outline given at the end of the EN and the programme of the *Politics* as we have them.

[31] Natali 2005 provides a clear and recent statement of the common view: 'Book X is not a unitary whole. Rather, it is composed of three different and independent parts', namely pleasure (X.1–5), complete happiness (X.6–8), and 'the necessary conditions for putting the previously established theories into practice' (X.9).

reserve the topics most closely related to the *telos* in ethics for the final book of the EN in order to underline the finality and completeness of the account of happiness and the happy life given in the EN.

We have seen what belongs to a good life in EN III–IX: activities in accordance with virtue and the goods that are required for, or otherwise come with an orientation towards, virtue. Now, in Book X (chapters 1–5) Aristotle argues that pleasure completes or perfects or finalises (*teleioô*) such virtuous activities. It is as if he tries to show that the best life also comes with the best pleasures (much like Plato before him, in *Republic* Book IX). The pleasures attending the best activities, however, are not merely additional goods (such as the best kinds of friendship that also belong to the best life): they make a virtuous life markedly more *teleios* (complete, perfect, or final), for experiencing the right kinds of pleasure adds an important psychological component to the happy life. To call a life happy, it is not enough for us to identify it as happy from the outside, as it were (on the basis of the life's focus and success). The person must also *feel* happy; she must feel that the life is worth living for its own sake. Pleasure or, better, the right kind of pleasure attending virtuous activities provides part of the sought-for finality or completeness of the happy life.

Next, returning in EN X.6–8 to the content of happiness, Aristotle tries to identify the activity responsible for complete/perfect/final happiness (*teleia eudaimonia*). In other words, he seeks to home in on the activity that makes the life, and the person living it, happy. Again, considerations of completeness/perfection/finality play an important role in this discussion, both in the argument against frivolous pleasures (in X.6) and in the arguments for theoretical contemplation (see esp. X.7).

But if we think identifying complete/perfect/final happiness completes what we need to know about ethics, we are mistaken. Aristotle artfully adds another layer of completeness/perfection/finality in X.9. Merely *knowing* what makes the best life happy falls short of completing the EN because the EN is a practical enquiry whose goal (*telos*) ultimately lies in action (1179a35–b4). In order to actualise the knowledge gained, and to bring it to a higher level of completion, we must consider how to implement it. X.9 examines what we would need to study, and how we might acquire the relevant expertise for becoming good and making other people good. Thus, Aristotle outlines a further programme of study that would bring the philosophical study concerning things human to completion (*teleiôthê(i)*, 1181b12–15). So, the notion of completion/perfection/finality ties the three topics of Book X together into a unified whole.

4. The *Nichomachean Ethics* and Other Ethical Works

The *Nicomachean Ethics* is not the only ethical treatise Aristotle wrote. Two further short ethical works have come down to us under his name, the inauthentic *Virtues and Vices* and a work called *Magna Moralia* whose authenticity is disputed. He also authored the *Protrepticus* (an exhortation to philosophy), which survives only in fragments, and another major treatise, known as the *Eudemian Ethics* (EE). The *Nicomachean* and the *Eudemian Ethics* share about one-third of their content: the treatises on justice (EN V = EE IV), the excellences of intellect (EN VI = EE V), and on self-control and pleasure (EN VII = EE VI).

At least since the second-century AD commentator Aspasius, readers of the Aristotelian *Ethics* tended to assign these common books to the *Nicomachean Ethics*. However, Kenny 1978 has challenged the orthodox view by arguing for two theses: i) the books in common initially belonged to the *Eudemian Ethics*, and ii) the EE is the more mature and definitive expression of Aristotle's ethical thinking. While many scholars now accept i) (though not necessarily for Kenny's reasons), few buy into ii). In any case, we can tell two stories about the relationship between the EE and the EN. Either a) Aristotle initially wrote a seven-book ethics (the EN without the books in common), which he then revised and enlarged to the eight-book EE (accepting i) and ii)). Or, b), he wrote the eight-book EE first and then reworked the material into the EN (accepting ii) but not i)).[32] One important reason for revising his course on ethics is a change in framework: the political dimension of the EN is mostly absent from the EE. The prominence of theoretical reflection in EN X marks another important difference from the EE material.

Now, both stories can explain the presence of the books common to the EN and the EE respectively as the result of some editorial intervention. At some point, an editor decided that the EE's treatises on justice, the intellectual virtues, and self-control would complete the EN (either adding them to a seven-book *Ethics* or replacing similar material that was already there) – and so the relevant scrolls were added to the EN.[33] Since a treatise on pleasure was contained in the same scroll as the treatise on self-control (EE VI), the EN came to have two treatments of pleasure. But who did it?

---

[32] a) and b) do not, of course, exhaust all possibilities. They are chosen in order to bring out which assumptions the commentary must make, not in order to engage in textual criticism.

[33] The addition need not have been physical: a change in the catalogue that coordinates the scrolls containing the different treatises would have done the trick.
Andronicus of Rhodes played a key role in 'creating' the Aristotelian Corpus by sorting through the scrolls, ordering them, and cataloguing which belonged together. See Hatzimichali 2016 for an in-depth treatment of Andronicus' editorial activity.

The double-treatment of pleasure seems to suggest that *Aristotle* did not authorise adding the material to the EN, for neither of the two treatises on pleasure acknowledges the other. Worse, on the face of it, they seem to contradict each other. Book VII defines pleasure as the unimpeded activity of a natural state, whereas Book X eschews identifying pleasure with activity, but has pleasure attend the sort of activities that count as pleasures in Book VII. Since *Aristotle* would surely not have contradicted himself in the one work, many scholars blame some later editor for the blunder. But in this case, we would have to be extremely careful in drawing on the books in common for the interpretation of EN X: we should treat them on a par with any other book of the EE that is not shared with the EN.

However tempting the story of the later editorial intervention is, it is not the only good explanation of the double-treatment of pleasure. First, there are good reasons to go back to the orthodox view, maintaining that Aristotle wrote the EN as a ten-book treatise that did not borrow the books in common from the EE.[34] Second, even story b) does not rule out his involvement in adding the books in common to the EN, for EN VI and VII show signs of being revised by Aristotle – whether they are 'mere' revisions (as in the orthodox view) or revisions to adapt the material from the books in common to the EN (as in b)). But revising his thoughts on a topic does not necessarily mean that Aristotle took the superseded version out of the text.[35] He may have rewritten the treatise on pleasure (now EN X.1–5) without deleting the obsolete version in EN VII, presumably because he did not quite finish the process of revising all of the EN to the same polished level.

The commentary operates on the assumption that Aristotle is responsible for the presence of the books in common in the EN. This means in particular that it draws freely on EN VI to work out the relationship between the theoretical and the practical life in EN X. This assumption, however, puts a bracket around the account of pleasure in EN VII.11–14. Just because he says that pleasure is an activity in the Book VII version does not mean that he must hold the same view also in Book X. Although the commentary on EN X.1–5 occasionally mentions the superseded discussion of pleasure, it does so mainly for illustrative purposes. The account of pleasure in EN X must be studied on its own.

---

[34] Frede 2019 persuasively argues for a return to the orthodox view. She notes correctly that whichever of the works originally lacked the books in common had instead something else covering much of the same material (i.e. a) and b) are simplifications). Primavesi 2007 supports the orthodox view especially by taking into account the historical facts of how Aristotle's works were catalogued.

[35] Lorenz 2009 argues that Aristotle's account of the lack of self-control in EN VII.4 contains two versions, and that the revised version, but not the initial one, is distinctive of the EN.

Translation

(X.1)

1172a19 After this topic, presumably, the next to go through is pleasure.

For pleasure is thought to be most intimately connected to our kind, which is why people educate the young through steering them by pleasure and pain.

And with regard to virtue of character, enjoying what one should and hating what one should is also thought to be of greatest importance. For they extend through every aspect of life, having a powerful influence with a25 regard to virtue and the happy life: for people decide on pleasant things and avoid painful things.

And least of all will it seem that a topic such as this should be passed over, especially since it provokes much dispute. For some say pleasure is the good, while others, on the contrary, say it is plain bad, some presumably because they are persuaded that it is so, others because they think it is a30 better for our lives to proclaim pleasure as a bad thing, even if it is not. For, they think, the many incline towards it and are slaves to their pleasures, which is why one must direct them in the opposite direction: this way they may reach the middle.

a35 But this is surely not right. For words about affections and actions carry less conviction than deeds. Whenever the words disagree with things one b1 can see, they earn contempt and destroy the truth besides: for if the person censuring pleasure is ever seen to seek it, he is thought to deviate towards it, as if every pleasure were like that; for making distinctions is not characteristic of the many.

True words, then, seem most useful not only with regard to knowing, b5 but also with regard to life: for, being in tune with the deeds, they carry conviction, which is why they turn those who understand them towards living in accordance with them.

Enough now of such things; let us go on to what people have said about pleasure.

(X.2)

Now Eudoxus thought that pleasure is the good because he saw all things seeking it, both rational and irrational, and that in all cases the object of choice is what is fitting, and that which is most so is best; and[36] the fact that all things move towards the same indicates that this is best for all, since each thing finds what is good for itself, just as with food, and he thought that what is good for all, and what everything seeks, is the good.

His words carried conviction more because of his virtue of character than because of themselves: for he was reputed to be exceptionally moderate; hence, he was not thought to say these things as a lover of pleasure, but rather that things are truly as he said.

It was no less evident, he thought, from the opposite: for pain in itself is to be avoided by everything, so that, correspondingly, its opposite is to be chosen. And most of all to be chosen, he thought, is what we do not choose because of or for the sake of something else; and pleasure, he thought, is by general agreement that sort of thing, for no one asks to what end he is enjoying himself, as if pleasure in itself is to be chosen.

Moreover, he thought that pleasure, when added to any one of the goods, makes it more choice-worthy, such as doing what is just or moderate, and that the good is increased by itself. Now, *this* argument seems to present pleasure as one good among others, and no more so than any other. For every good is more choice-worthy together with another good than on its own. Indeed, with such an argument Plato, too, refutes the claim that pleasure is the good. For the pleasant life is more choice-worthy together with wisdom than without, and if the mixture is better, pleasure is not the good: for the good cannot become more choice-worthy through the addition of anything to it. And it is clear that no other thing will be the good either, if it becomes more choice-worthy together with one of the things good in themselves. What, then, is of this nature, which we too share in? For we are looking for something of this sort.

And those who object that what everything seeks is not good talk nonsense. For what appears to all, this, we say, is so. And the person who objects to this conviction will hardly say anything more convincing. For

---

[36] Following most MSS, reading *de* ('and') instead of K^b's *dê* ('hence', adopted by the OCT).

if unintelligent creatures desire these things, there would be something in what was said, but if intelligent ones do so as well, how could there be anything in what he says? And perhaps even in inferior animals there is some natural element of goodness better than themselves which seeks their own proper good.

And the point about the opposite does not seem right either. For they deny that if pain is bad, then pleasure is good: for bad is also opposed to bad, and both to what is neutral – which they say well enough, but at least in the present case they miss the truth. For if both were bad,[37] both would have to be avoided, and if they were neutral, neither would have to be avoided, or both equally. But as things are, they evidently avoid the one as bad, and choose the other as good: thus in this way they are also opposed.

(X.3)

Again, neither does it follow that if pleasure is not a quality, it is not a good either: for the activities of virtue are not qualities, nor is happiness.

But they say that what is good is determinate, whereas pleasure is indeterminate because it admits of the more and less.[38] Now, if they base their judgement on being pleased, it will be the same with justice and the other virtues, in respect of which they manifestly say that people of a certain character are so more or less, and act more or less in accordance with the virtues, for people may be more just or courageous, and it is also possible to act justly or moderately more or less. But if they judge by the pleasures, surely they do not state the cause, if some pleasures are unmixed, while others are mixed.

And what prevents [us from saying] that just as health admits of the more and less although it is determinate, so too does pleasure? For the same due proportion is not found in everyone, nor is there always some single proportion in one and the same person, but even when it is loosened it remains up to a point, and so differs in the more and less. Thus it is possible that the case of pleasure is of this sort.

Next, supposing that what is good is complete, whereas movements and comings to be are incomplete, they try to show pleasure to be a movement and coming to be.

---

[37] Reading *ontôn kakôn* at 1173a10 with K[b].
[38] Like L[b], I omit the second *to*. Similarly, Plato's *Philebus* has *to mallon te kai hêtton* at 24a9.

But they do not seem to be right even in saying that it is a movement. For quickness and slowness are thought to be proper to every movement, and if not in itself, as for instance the movement of the cosmos, then in relation to something else; but neither of these applies to pleasure. For while it is possible to get pleased quickly, just like getting angry, it is not possible to take pleasure quickly, not even in relation to something else, whereas this is possible for walking and growing and the like. It is possible, then, to fall into pleasure quickly and slowly, but it is not possible to be actively engaged in it (I mean taking pleasure) quickly.

Next, how could <pleasure> be a coming to be? For it does not seem to be the case that anything comes to be from just anything, but rather that what a thing comes to be from is that into which it is dissolved; and pain is the destruction of that of which pleasure is the coming to be. And they say pain is the lack of what is in accordance with nature, whereas pleasure is its replenishment; and these affections are bodily. So, if pleasure is replenishment of what is in accordance with nature, that in which the replenishment takes place would also take the pleasure, namely the body. But the body is not thought to <take the pleasure>; therefore the replenishment is not pleasure either, but when a replenishment occurs, a person takes pleasure, and when he is being cut,[39] he is in pain.

And this view is thought to have originated from the pleasures and pains connected with food: for when people have developed a lack and feel pain beforehand, they are pleased by the replenishment. But this does not happen with all pleasures, for there are no pains involved in pleasures of learning, and in the case of the pleasures associated with perception, those arising through smell; and many sounds and sights and memories and hopes <are painless>. Of what, then, will these be comings to be? For there has occurred no lack of anything of which a replenishment could occur.

And to those who bring forward the disgraceful pleasures, one could reply that these things are not pleasant: for if they are pleasant to those in a bad condition, one must not think they also *are* pleasant, except to such people – just as one must not think either that things healthy or sweet or bitter to sick people also *are* so, nor again that things appearing white to people with an eye-disease also *are* so.

Or one could respond in this way: that the pleasures are choice-worthy, but surely not from these sources, just as being rich is choice-worthy, but

---

[39] Reading *temnomenos* with the MSS (marked as corrupt by Bywater).

not for someone who would have to betray others, and being healthy, but not for someone who would have to eat anything whatever.

Or pleasures differ in kind, for those stemming from fine sources differ from those stemming from shameful sources, and one cannot enjoy the just person's pleasure without being just, nor the musical person's pleasure without being musical, and similarly in the other cases.

And the distinction between a friend and a flatterer is also thought to highlight that pleasure is not good or else <that pleasures> differ in kind; for the former is thought to offer his company with a view to what is good; the latter with a view to pleasure, but the latter is reproached, whereas they praise the former because he offers his company with a view to different things.

Next, no one would choose to have a child's intellect throughout life, even if he would enjoy the things children <enjoy> as much as possible, nor <would anyone choose> to delight in doing something of the most shameful sort, even if he would never suffer any pain coming from it.

Next, many things would be important to us even if they brought no pleasure, such as seeing, remembering, knowing, having the virtues; and if pleasures necessarily accompany them, it makes no difference, for we would choose them even if no pleasure arose from them.

Now, it seems to be clear that pleasure is not the good and that not all pleasure is to be chosen, and that some pleasures are choice-worthy in themselves, differing from others either in kind or source. So let us take it that the things people say about pleasure and pain have been adequately stated.

(X.4)

And what it is, or what sort of thing, becomes much clearer if we start again from the beginning.

Seeing is thought to be complete through any interval of time; for it is not lacking anything whose coming to be at a later time will complete its form; and pleasure too seems to be a thing of this sort. For it is something whole, i.e. there is no interval of time such that, when someone takes pleasure, the form of pleasure will be completed because it lasts longer.

That is why it is not a movement either. For every movement involves time and relates to some end, such as housebuilding, and it is complete whenever it produces what it aims at, either in the whole of the time, or at that moment.

And all movements are incomplete insofar as they consist of parts which also take time, and they are different in form both from the whole and from each other. For fitting together the stones is different from fluting the column, and both of these <are different from> from making the temple. And while the making of the temple is complete (for it lacks nothing towards the proposed project), the making of the foundation or of the triglyph is incomplete, for each is the making of a part. Hence, they differ in form and it is not possible to detect a movement complete in form at any time, except in the whole time [of the movement]. a25

And similarly in the case of walking and the rest. For even if locomotion is a movement from one place to another, it too has different forms: a30 flying, walking, leaping, and so on. And not only that, but there are different forms even within walking itself, for the from-where and to-where are not the same for the racecourse and for part of it, nor for one part and for another, nor is traversing this line the same as traversing that, for the line is not only crossed, but is also in a place, and this line is in a different 1174b1 place from that.

Now, a precise discussion of movement has been given elsewhere, but movement seems not to be complete at every moment of time, but rather its many movements are incomplete and differ in form, since the from-where and to-where determine the form. But the form of pleasure is complete at any time. It is clear, therefore, that they are different from each other: pleasure is something whole and complete. b5

And this would seem to be the case also from the fact that it is not possible to move, while it is possible to enjoy, without taking time. For what occurs in the now is something whole.

And from these points it is also clear that those who say that there is a movement or coming to be of pleasure[40] are wrong. For these cannot be ascribed to everything, but only to things that have parts and are not wholes. b10 For there is no coming to be of seeing, nor of a point, nor of a unit, nor is there any movement or coming to be of these things at all; of pleasure too, then, <is there neither of these> for it is a sort of whole.

And since every sense is active in relation to its sense-object, and is completely/perfectly active when being in good condition and in relation b15 to the finest of its objects (for complete/perfect activity is thought to be of this sort most of all; and let it make no difference whether we say *it* is active or what it is in), in each case[41] the activity of what is in the most

---

[40] Reading *tês hêdonês* with Susemihl (following Ramsauer).
[41] Reading *kath' hekaston* with most MSS.

excellent condition in relation to the most outstanding of its objects is best; and this activity will be most complete/perfect and most pleasant.

For every sense affords pleasure, and so too do thought and reflection, and the most complete/perfect activity is the most pleasant, and most complete/perfect is the activity whose subject is in a good condition in relation to the most excellent of its objects. And[42] pleasure completes the activity. But pleasure does not complete/perfect it in the same way as do the sense-object and the sense when they are excellent, just as health and the physician are not in the same way the cause of being healthy either.

And that pleasure arises with each sense is clear, for we say that objects of sight and sound are pleasant. And it is also clear that it does so most of all when the sense is in the most outstanding condition and is active in relation to an object in the same condition; and when both the sense and the sense-object are like that, there will always be pleasure, at least as long as both what produces [the sense-perception] and what receives <it> are present.

And the pleasure completes/perfects the activity not as the state does, by being present in something, but as some superadded end, like the bloom on those in their prime.

So long, then, as the object of thought or perception is as it should be, and so is what discriminates or reflects, there will be pleasure in the activity; for when the receptor and the producer are similar and in the same relation to each other, the same [sc. effect] naturally arises.

How, then, is it that no one takes pleasure continuously? Is it because one gets tired? For continuous activity is impossible for everything human. So, pleasure does not occur continuously either, for it accompanies the relevant activity. And some things delight when they are new, but later on not so much, because of the same reason. For at first, thought is called forth and is intensely active about them, just as people are with respect to their sight when they look hard at something, and later the activity is not like this but relaxed: that is why the pleasure too becomes dim.

And one might think that everyone desires pleasure because everyone seeks to be alive, too. But life is a kind of activity, and each is active in relation to those things, and with those states, which he also loves most of all. For instance, the musician is active with hearing in relation to melodies, and the lover of learning with thought in relation to objects of reflection, and so on for each of the others. And the pleasure completes the activities, and hence the life that they desire. Therefore, it makes sense that they

---

[42] Following Susemihl's punctuation.

seek pleasure too, since for each person it completes/perfects the activity of living – which is choice-worthy.

But whether we choose to be alive on account of pleasure, or pleasure on account of being alive – this is something we should put to one side for now. For they seem intimately connected and not to allow for separation, for without activity pleasure does not arise, and pleasure completes/perfects every activity.

(X.5)

That is why they seem also to differ in kind. For we think that things different in kind are completed by different things (for it seems to be so both with natural objects and objects produced by craft, such as living things, trees, a drawing, a statue, a house, and an implement); and similarly <we think> that activities that differ in kind are completed by things different in kind. But the activities of thought differ from those involving the senses, and they <differ> from each other according to kind; so, too, do the pleasures completing them.

And this will be obvious also from the fact that each pleasure is thoroughly akin to the activity it completes. For the pleasure proper to an activity increases it. For those who are active with pleasure are more discerning and precise in a given pursuit, for instance those who enjoy doing geometry become proficient in geometry, and understand each aspect of it better, and similarly the lover of music, the lover of housebuilding, and so on improve in the work proper to them when they enjoy it. And the pleasures increase <the activities>, but what increases <something> is proper to it; and where things are different in kind, what is proper to them also differs in kind.

And this will be even more obvious from the fact that the pleasures from other sources impede the activities. For lovers of pipe music are incapable of attending to discussions whenever they hear someone playing the pipes, because they enjoy pipe playing more than their present activity. The pipe-related pleasure, therefore, destroys the activity of discussion. And something similar happens in the other cases, whenever one is engaged in two activities simultaneously. For the more pleasant one pushes the other out of the way, and the more so when they differ much in terms of pleasure, to the point where the other activity stops. That is why when we very much enjoy whatever it may be, we do not do much else, and we do other things when we are pleased only mildly; for instance those who eat snacks in the theatre do so most when the actors are bad.

And since the pleasure proper to the activity makes it more precise, longer lasting, and better, whereas pleasures from other activities spoil it, it is clear that they are distinct by a wide margin. For the pleasures from other activities do almost what pains proper to the activities do, for pains proper to the activity destroy it, for instance when writing or doing calculations is unpleasant, even painful, for someone: the former does not write and the latter does not calculate because the activity is painful. Hence the opposite happens in the case of the activities[43] under the influence of their proper pleasures and pains; and the ones that properly belong being the ones that stem from the activity in virtue of the activity itself. And it has been said that the pleasures belonging to other activities do much the same as pain, for they destroy them, except not in the same way.

Since the activities differ in terms of decency and baseness, however, and some are choice-worthy, others to be avoided, others again neither, pleasures too are like that: for each activity has a pleasure proper to it. Now, the pleasure proper to a worthwhile activity is decent, while the one proper to a base one is depraved; for the desires too for fine things are to be praised, while the ones for shameful things are to be censured. But the pleasures in these activities are more properly tied to them than the desires. For the latter are separate both in time and in nature, whereas the former are so close to the activities, even inseparable, that it is disputed whether the activity is the same as the pleasure. But pleasure does not *seem* to be thought or perception, for that would be odd, but because it cannot be separated, they appear to be the same to some. Just as the activities differ, then, so do the pleasures.

And sight differs from touch in purity, as do hearing and smelling from taste; so the pleasures, too, differ in a similar way, and the pleasures of thought differ from these <perceptual pleasures>, and both <kinds> differ within themselves.

And for each animal there is thought to be a pleasure proper to it (just as it has its <proper> work, too): the pleasure corresponding to its activity. And this will be obvious to anyone who reflects on each case: for a horse's pleasure, a dog's, and a human being's are different, just as Heraclitus says: 'donkeys would rather have sweepings than gold'; for food is more pleasant to donkeys than gold. Now, while the pleasures of different kinds of animal differ in kind, it would be reasonable that the pleasures of animals belonging to the same kind do not differ. But they do differ in no small measure, at least in the case of human beings. For the same things delight

---

[43] Reading *tas energeias* with most MSS (except K^b, followed by Bywater).

some, while causing pain to others, and <the same things> are painful and hateful to some, while being pleasant and lovable to others.

And in the case of sweet things, this happens too: for the same things do not seem sweet to someone having a fever and to someone healthy, nor seem the same things warm to someone sickly and to someone in a good condition. And something similar happens in other cases too. But it is thought that in all such cases what appears to the sound person *is* so. And if this is right, as it seems to be, and it is virtue and the good person (insofar as he is such) that is the measure in each case, then pleasures will be those that appear <to be pleasures> to *him*, and those things will be pleasant that *he* enjoys. And if things odious to him appear pleasant to someone else, that is nothing surprising, for many kinds of corruption and damage befall human beings; and such things are not pleasant except to those who *are* in that sort of state.

While it is clear, then, that the pleasures by common consent shameful should be said not to be pleasures, except to corrupted people – what sort <of pleasure> or which one of those which appear to be decent should we say is characteristic of the human being? Or is this clear from the activities? For the pleasures accompany them. Whether, then, the activities of the completely blessed man are one or several, the pleasures completing/perfecting them will be said to be characteristically human in the primary way; the others will be so in a secondary way or in ways many times removed, just like the activities.

(X.6)

As the subjects of the virtues, friendship, and pleasure have been discussed, it remains for us to treat of happiness in outline, since we posit it as <the> goal of human affairs. So, if we resume what has been said before, the discussion will be shorter.

Now, we said that it is not a state; for [in this case] even someone sleeping through his whole life, living like a plant, could have it, and someone suffering the greatest misfortunes. So, if these [implications] do not satisfy, but one should rather class happiness as some kind of activity, as was said earlier, and some activities are necessary and to be chosen on account of something else, while others are to be chosen for themselves, it is clear that one must class happiness as one of those to be chosen for themselves, and not as one of those to be chosen on account of something else, for happiness does not lack in anything, but is self-sufficient.

The ones to be chosen for themselves, however, are those from which nothing is sought besides the activity. And the actions in accordance with virtue are thought to be of this sort, for doing what is fine and worthwhile is one of the things to be chosen for themselves. But pleasant amusements are also <thought to be like this>. For they are not chosen on account of anything else; for people get harm from them rather than benefit in that they neglect their bodies and possessions. Most of those, however, who are regarded as happy take refuge in such pastimes – which is why those well-versed in such pastimes are highly valued by tyrants, for they make themselves pleasant over the very things the tyrants desire, and the tyrants need people of this sort.

Now, while these things are thought to be characteristic of happiness because those in power devote their free time to them, people of this sort are presumably no evidence at all. For neither virtue nor intelligence, from which worthwhile activities stem, depend on having power. And if they take refuge in bodily pleasures because they have not tasted the unsullied pleasures of a free man, one should not therefore think that the former are more choice-worthy: for children, too, take what is esteemed among themselves to be best. It is reasonable, then, that just as different things appear estimable to children and grown-up men, so too to the bad people and the decent. So, as has been said frequently, both estimable and pleasant things are those that are such for the good person; and for each the activity in accordance with his proper state is most choice-worthy, and for the good person it is the activity in accordance with virtue.

Therefore, happiness does not consist in amusement, for it would be strange if the goal were to be amusement and if being busy and suffering hardship throughout one's life were for the sake of amusing ourselves. For we choose pretty much everything for the sake of something else, except happiness: for it is a goal. But applying oneself seriously and toiling for the sake of amusement seems idle and exceedingly childish. And 'to amuse oneself so that one may apply oneself seriously' (after Anacharsis) is thought to have it the right way round, for amusement resembles taking a break, and people need to take a break because they are incapable of toiling continuously. Taking a break, then, is not a goal: for it occurs for the sake of activity.

And the happy life is thought to be in accordance with virtue, and this life involves seriousness, but does not consist in amusement: again, we say that serious things are better than things that are funny things and involve amusement, and that the activity of what is always better, whether it is a part, or the person, is more serious; and the activity of what is better is more outstanding and thereby is more characteristic of happiness.

Again, just anyone, a slave no less than the best person, might enjoy bodily pleasures; and no one assigns a share in happiness to a slave, unless <one assigns to him a share in> a life also. For happiness does not consist in pastimes of this sort, but in activities in accordance with virtue, as was said earlier too.

(X.7)

And if happiness is an activity in accordance with virtue, it is reasonable that it is in accordance with the most outstanding one; and this will be [the virtue] of the most excellent element. Whether this, then, is intelligence or some other thing which is thought to be naturally such as to rule, lead, and entertain thoughts about fine and divine things, being either divine also itself or the most divine of things in us – the activity of this in accordance with its proper virtue will be complete/perfect happiness.

And that it is reflective activity has been said. And this would seem to agree with both what has been said before and the truth. For this activity is the most outstanding one, for intelligence is the most outstanding of the things in us and [the activity] is of the most outstanding objects of knowledge, the objects intelligence is about.

And further, it is most continuous, for we really can reflect more continuously than do anything else.[44]

Next, we think that pleasure must be mixed into happiness, and the most pleasant of the activities in accordance with virtue is agreed to be the one in accordance with theoretical wisdom. Philosophy at any rate is thought to provide pleasures wondrous in purity and stability, and it is reasonable that this way of life is more pleasant for those who have attained knowledge than for those who seek it.

Next, the talked-of self-sufficiency will be connected most of all to the reflective way of life: for the theoretically wise person and the just person and everyone else need things necessary for living, but when <they are> sufficiently supplied with these things, the just person needs others unto whom and with whom he will perform just actions; and similarly for the moderate person, the courageous, and each of the others, but the theoretically wise person is capable of reflecting even when on his own, and the

---

[44] Reading *theôrein te gar* with most MSS.

wiser he is, the more so; and while he presumably does it better when he has co-workers, he is nevertheless the most self-sufficient.

b1 Next, <reflection> seems to be loved only on its own account; for nothing stems from it apart from reflecting, but from the practical activities we create for ourselves something larger or smaller that remains besides the action.

b5 Next, happiness is thought to be found in leisure: for we busy ourselves in order to have leisure, and we wage war in order to be at peace. Now, the activity of the practical virtues lies in politics or war, and actions in these contexts have a reputation for being unleisurely: a) actions related to war are so completely, for no one chooses to wage war, nor does anyone contrive war b10 for the sake of waging war (for a person will seem completely murderous if he turns his friends into enemies in order to create battles and killings); b) the activity of the politician too is unleisured, and besides doing politics itself it creates for himself positions of power and honours, or at any rate, happiness for himself and his fellow citizens, this [sc. happiness] being different from b15 the activity of politics, and something we clearly seek supposing it to be different.

If, then, of the actions in accordance with virtue those in politics and war stand out in fineness and greatness, but these are unleisured and aim at some other goal, i.e. are not choice-worthy [only] on their own account, while the activity of intelligence, when reflective, is thought to excel in b20 seriousness and to aim at no other goal besides itself and to comprise its own proper pleasure (and this increases the activity), and especially if the elements of the self-sufficient, leisure, and unweariness, so far as possible for human beings, and whatever else is attributed to the blessed person, are evidently characteristics of the activity in accordance with it, then this activity will be the complete/perfect happiness of a human being when it b25 takes a complete span of life, for nothing incomplete is characteristic of things belonging to happiness.

But such a life will be more outstanding than one in accordance with the human element, for one will not live like this insofar as one is human, but insofar as there is some divine element in the person: to the degree that this excels over the compound, to that degree its activity too will excel over <the activity> in accordance with the rest of virtue. If, then, intelb30 ligence is something divine compared with the human kind, so, too, will the life in accordance with this be divine compared with a human life.

But one should not follow those who offer advice, 'think human thoughts because you are human', or 'think mortal thoughts, because you are mortal', instead <one should> put off the mortal as far as possible and do everything to live a life in accordance with the most outstanding thing in us; for even if it is small in bulk, it exceeds everything else in power and esteem by far.

And each person would seem even to be this, given that each is his authoritative and better element. It would therefore be strange if one chose not one's own life but that of some other being.

Again, what was said before will fit also now: for what is proper to each by nature is the most outstanding element and most pleasant for each; and so the life in accordance with intelligence is proper for a human being, if indeed a human being is most of all this. Hence, this life will also be superlatively happy.

(X.8)

And secondarily <so> is the life in accordance with the rest of virtue: for the activities in accordance with it are characteristically human. For we do just things, courageous things, and the rest in accordance with the virtues in relation to each other, observing closely what befits each in contracts, services, and various kinds of action and in affective states; and they all appear to be characteristically human.

Some <of them> are indeed thought to stem from the body, and in many ways virtue of character is thoroughly akin to the affective states. And practical wisdom is also yoked to the virtue of character, and it to practical wisdom, since the starting points of practical wisdom are in accordance with the virtues of character, and the rightness of the virtues of character is in accordance with practical wisdom.

And connected as these <virtues> are with the affective states too, they will be concerned with the compound; and the virtues of the compound are characteristically human; so too is therefore the life in accordance with these, and the happiness. By contrast, the one [sc. virtue] of intelligence is separable. Let only so much be said about it, for going into greater detail is a task too great for the present project.

And it will also seem to need only very few external resources or fewer than <that> of character. For let the need of both for necessary resources be equal, even if the politician is more concerned with bodily toil and things of this sort, for he will differ only by a little, but he will differ much in relation to the activities. For the generous person will need money to do generous things, and the just person, too, for returning benefits (for wishes are invisible, and even those who are not just pretend to wish to do what is just), and the courageous person will need power if indeed he is to achieve something in accordance with his virtue, and the moderate person will need opportunities; for how else will it be clear that he, or any of the other types, is the way he is? Again, it is disputed whether the decision or the actions are more key to virtue, because it involves both. As regards the complete/perfect case, it is clear that it will involve both; and much is needed for the actions, and the greater and finer they are, the more will be needed.

But the person engaged in reflection has no need for such things, at least not for the activity, instead one might almost say they are even impediments, at any rate to his reflecting. And insofar as he is a human being and lives together with many others, he chooses to do what is in accordance with virtue; therefore he will need things of this sort for living a human life.

And that complete/perfect happiness is a kind of reflective activity is also apparent from the following: we hold the assumption that the gods most of all are blessed and happy. But which sorts of actions should one attribute to them? Just ones? Or would they appear ridiculous, making contracts and returning deposits and so on? How about [actions] characteristic of a courageous person, withstanding what is fearful and facing danger because it is fine?[45] Or generous actions? But to whom will they give? And it is absurd if they also have a currency or anything like that. And if[46] they are moderate, in what way would they be <moderate>? Or would it not be low praise, that they have no bad appetites? And to those who go through all the cases, everything pertaining to actions will appear petty and unworthy of gods.

Nonetheless, everyone assumes that they are alive, at least, and therefore active; for surely they do not sleep like Endymion. So, for someone alive, when performing actions is taken away, and producing something even more so, what is left except reflection? Therefore, the activity of the god, superior as it is in blessedness, will be reflective: and therefore of the human activities the one most nearly akin to it will most bear the characteristic of happiness.

And a sign <for this> is also that other animals do not have a share of happiness, because they are completely deprived of activity of this sort. Now, for the gods, the whole life is blessed, whereas for human beings, life is blessed only insofar as a certain similarity with this sort of activity exists: and none of the other animals is happy since they share in no way in reflection. As far, then, as reflection extends, so does happiness, and

---

[45] Lines 1178b12–13 are corrupt. I read *andreiou hupomenontos ta phobera kai kinduneuontos*, as proposed by Bywater 1892, 69.

[46] Reading *ei* with most manuscripts.

to those to whom reflection belongs more, being happy will also belong more, not incidentally, but in virtue of reflection: for it is estimable on its own account. Therefore, happiness will be reflection of some sort.

And happiness for a human being will need external prosperity, for our nature is not self-sufficient for reflection, but also needs the body to be healthy, and the provision of food and other sorts of care. Now, one must really not think that the person who is happy will need a great many of them, even if it is not possible to be blessed without external goods: for what is self-sufficient does not depend on excess, nor does action, and even without ruling land and sea one can do what is fine. For one can act in accordance with virtue also from moderate means (and one can see this clearly, for private citizens seem to do what is decent no less than those in positions of power, but even more), and it suffices to have resources to this extent. For the life of the person active in accordance with virtue will be happy.

And Solon, too, presumably represented happy people well, when he said that they had been moderately provided with external resources, but had done the finest things (in his view), and had lived moderately: for it is possible for those who possess only moderate means to do what one should.

And even Anaxagoras looks to have assumed the happy person to be neither rich nor in a position of power, saying that he would not be astonished if the happy person appeared a strange type to the many, for they judge by the external resources, as they see only them. So it looks as though the views of the wise agree with our arguments.

Now, considerations of this sort carry a certain conviction, but what is true in matters of action is judged from the deeds done and the life lived, for this is key in such questions. One should, therefore, examine what was said before by referring to the deeds and the life, and when it harmonises with the deeds one should accept it, but when it differs assume it to be mere words.

And the person active in accordance with intelligence, and devoting himself to this, seems to be in the most excellent condition and most dear to the gods. For if any attention is paid to human affairs by the gods, as it is thought, it would also be reasonable if they both delight in what is most excellent and closest in kind to them (and that would be intelligence) and benefit in return those who love this most of all and honour it, because they pay attention to what is dear to the gods, and for acting correctly and finely. But that all this is true of the theoretically wise person most of all is quite clear; therefore he is most dear to the gods. And it is likely that the very same person is also superlatively happy; so that, in this way too, the theoretically wise person would be happy most of all.

(X.9)

Well, then, if both the present topic and the topic of the virtues, and again friendship and pleasure have been sufficiently discussed in outlines, should one think our plan has reached its end? Or, as is said, is reflecting on and understanding each topic not the goal in practical matters, but rather applying them?[47] Knowing about virtue, then, is not enough either, but we must try to have and use it, or become good in some other way.

Well now, if words were sufficient to make people decent, 'they would be earning many a handsome fee' (after Theognis), and rightly so, and these [sc. words] would be what needs to be provided. But as things are, they appear to have the strength to turn and exhort the free among the young and to make a character that is well-born and truly loves the fine capable of being possessed by virtue, but to lack the power of turning the many towards refined virtue. For they are not naturally guided by a sense of shame, but by fear, and they do not keep their distance from bad things on account of the disgracefulness but on account of the punishments. Living by passion, they pursue their proper pleasures and what gives rise to them, and they avoid the opposing pains, while they do not even have a conception of what is fine and truly pleasant, as they have had no taste of that. What talk, then, could reform people of this sort? For it is not possible or not easy to remove with talk what has long been absorbed by the traits of character. Presumably, though, we should be content if we acquire a share in virtue when all the factors are in place through which we are thought to become decent.

And people become good, some think, by nature, others think by habit, and again others by teaching. Now, it is clear that the presence of the natural element does not depend on us, but that it is present in those truly fortunate on account of some divine causes; and talk and teaching do not prevail over everyone, but one must have prepared the soul of the listener beforehand with habits for enjoying and hating in the right way, just like soil if it is to nourish the seed. For a person living by passion would not listen to talk that turns him around, nor again would he understand it. And how can one persuade a person in that state to change? Again, in

---

[47] Following Susemihl's punctuation, reading a question mark in b2 and a full stop in b4.

general passion is not thought to yield to talk, but to force. Therefore, the character must exist beforehand in a way akin to virtue, yearning for what is fine and being disgusted by what is disgraceful.

It is difficult to meet from childhood with the right education towards virtue unless one is brought up under laws of the appropriate sort; for living moderately and with self-restraint is not pleasant to most, especially when young. Therefore the upbringing and the practices should be prescribed by laws, for these [sc. practices] will not be painful once they have become habitual.

And presumably it is not sufficient if people receive the right upbringing and supervision when they are young, but even when they are fully grown they should continue to practise these things and be habituated to them, and we would need laws governing these things and in general the whole of life, for the many obey compulsion more than talk, and <they obey> penalties more than the fine.

That is why some think that the lawgivers should i) encourage people towards virtue and exhort them [to act] for the sake of the fine (on the assumption that those whose habits have been decently developed will listen), and ii) that they should exact both chastisement and punishment on those who do not listen and are less suitable by nature, and iii) that they should altogether banish those who are incurable. For <they think> the decent person, living with a view to the fine, will pay heed to talk, whereas the bad person, having an appetite for pleasure, is kept in check by pain, just like a yoked animal. That is why they say that the relevant pains should be opposed most of all to their beloved pleasures.

Well, as has been said, if the person to become good should be brought up and habituated properly and then live in decent ways, i.e. neither willingly nor unwillingly doing what is bad, this should happen if people live in accordance with some sort of intelligent system of right order, provided it has force. Now, a father's prescription does not have the relevant element of force or compulsion, nor, in general, does that of any one man, unless he is a king or something like that, but the law does have the power to compel, being a form of words that stems from practical wisdom of some kind and from intelligence. And while people hate any human beings who oppose their impulses, even if they do that correctly, the law causes no offence in prescribing what is decent.

But only in the city-state of the Lacedaemonians, together with a few others, is the lawgiver reputed to have established the supervision of both upbringing and practices; in most cities the lawgiver does not care about such things, and each man lives as he wants, like a cyclops 'wielding law over children and spouse'. Now, it is best if the care is communal and correct, but when they <sc. practices and upbringing> are neglected on a communal level, it would seem to befit each person to further the virtue of his own children and friends, and for him to be capable of doing it, or, at any rate, of deciding on it.[48]

But from what has been said he would seem to be more capable of this, if he [first] became proficient in making law. For it is clear that communal types of supervision depend on laws, and decent ones on good laws, and whether they are written or unwritten seems to make no difference, nor whether one or many are to be educated through them, any more than it does as in the case of music or gymnastics and in any of the other practices. For just as the legal provisions and customs in a city-state have force, so too do the words and habits of a father in a household, and even more so because of the kinship and the acts of kindness; for they [sc. the children] are naturally predisposed to love and obey him.

And further, individualised regimes of education even surpass common ones, just as in medicine: for while in general rest and fasting help a feverish patient, perhaps they do not help this particular patient, and no doubt the boxing trainer does not prescribe the same fighting style for all. The particular case, then, would seem to be treated with more exactness once there is private supervision, for each more readily attains what is suitable for him.

But a doctor, a gymnastics trainer, and everyone else will provide individualised supervision best when they have general knowledge, knowing what applies to all or to people of such-and-such a type, for the branches of knowledge are said to be, and actually are, of what is common. Still, there is presumably nothing that prevents someone, even though he lacks knowledge, from taking care of an individual person properly, if he has observed accurately through experience what happens in each individual case, just as some people are thought to be their own best doctors, while totally incapable of helping anyone else. Nonetheless, it seems, presumably, that *if* a person wishes to become an expert in a craft and reflective about it, he must ascend to the general, and grasp it as much as possible, for it has been said that the branches of knowledge are about that.

Maybe, then, someone who wishes to improve people, be it many or few, through his supervision, should also try to become proficient in giving law, if it is through laws that we can become good. For it is not possible

---

[48] Adopting Bywater's transposition.

for just anyone to instil a good disposition in whoever is presented to him, but if anyone <can do it>, it is a person with knowledge, just as in the case of medicine and the other cases that involve some kind of supervision and practical wisdom.

So should we examine next from what source or in what way one might become proficient in law-giving? Or, as in the other cases, is it from the politicians? For it was thought to be a part of political knowledge. Or is it evidently not the same for political knowledge and the other branches of knowledge and capacities? For in the other cases, it is the same people who evidently pass on the capacities and exercise them themselves, such as doctors or painters, but as regards political things it is the sophists who profess to teach them, but none of them practises politics, instead this is done by political operators who seem to do this thanks to some kind of capacity and experience rather than by understanding: for evidently they do not write or speak about such matters (though presumably this would have been finer than [making] speeches for the law court or the assembly), nor again have they made their own sons or others dear to them into politicians. But <doing so> would have been reasonable, if they could have, since they could have left no better legacy for their cities, and for themselves they could not have chosen any better possession than this capacity either, nor, therefore, for those dearest to them.

Still, experience does seem to make no small contribution; for <otherwise> people could not have become politicians through familiarity with politics: that is why those who desire to have political knowledge seem to need experience in addition. And those sophists who profess <to have this knowledge> appear to be exceedingly far from teaching it. For they do not have knowledge at all even of what kind of thing it is, or what sort of things it concerns. For [if they did have it] they would not have placed it at the same level as rhetoric or even below, nor would they have thought making laws is easy for anyone who has collected reputable laws; for <they think> one selects the best ones – as if the selection were not a matter of comprehension, and discerning correctly not a big thing either, as it is in music. For those experienced in each case discern the relevant works correctly, and they comprehend through which means or how they are attained, i.e. which sorts of things are in tune with each other; but the inexperienced must be content with not missing whether a work has been produced well or badly, as in the case of painting.

But the laws are like works of political knowledge: how, then, would one become proficient in law-giving, or discern the best ones, from *them*? For people do not appear to become doctors, either, from written texts.

Surely they *try* to describe not only the treatments, but also how to cure and how one should treat each <type of patient>, distinguishing different conditions. But while these <texts> are thought to be beneficial to the experienced, they seem useless to those who lack knowledge. Perhaps, then, collections of laws and constitutions would be especially useful to those who are capable of reflecting on and discerning what goes well or the opposite and which kinds of things harmonise with each other; but those who peruse these things without being in the right condition cannot discriminate well, except as if spontaneously, and they might perhaps then come to comprehend these things better.

Since, then, the topic of law-making is unexamined, left aside by those before us, it is presumably better, rather, if we ourselves examine it, and the topic of a political system in general, so that, as far as possible, the philosophical study concerning things human is brought to completion. First, then, if there is anything on some part of the topic that has been said correctly by our predecessors, we should attempt to go through it, then, on the basis of the collected constitutions, <attempt> to reflect on what sorts of things preserve or destroy cities and what sorts of things preserve and destroy each constitution, and through which causes some cities are governed well and others the opposite. For, having reflected on these matters, we will probably be in a better position to see comprehensively even which constitution is best, and how each is ordered, and which laws and customs it will have. So, let us discuss this from the beginning.

COMMENTARY

I Pleasure (X.1–5)

X.1

1172a19 After this topic ... pleasure.

Aristotle begins Book X by announcing the topic, pleasure. The discussion of pleasure is presented as if naturally continuing the *Nicomachean Ethics*' (EN) main argument. Since the preceding discussion of friendship brims with expressions related to pleasure, a thorough examination of pleasure seems apposite. For instance, a) the famous proof in IX.9 that a happy person needs friends pivots on the relationship between pleasure, virtuous conduct, and life – a connection further illuminated in X.4–5. b) Some friendships form with a view to pleasure, the so-called 'pleasure-friendships'. Could such a relation bring the friends more pleasure than does the friendship between virtuous people? Again, Aristotle answers the question in X.4–5, and expands on it in X.6.

However, there are reasons to doubt that pleasure is neatly integrated in the plan of the EN. A glance at the previous main topics casts some doubt on the place of the present discussion of pleasure. The main topics are virtue (1102a6, from I.13 to VI.13), self-control and the lack of it (VII.1–10), pleasure (VII.11–14), and friendship (Bks. VIII–IX). Now, Book X starts by announcing the topic in the same way as all the other topics – as if pleasure still awaits examination, not re-examination. Since neither discussion of pleasure refers to or acknowledges the other, scholars have surmised some clumsy editorial intervention.

Aristotle composed another long ethical treatise, the *Eudemian Ethics* (EE), following a plan similar to the *Nicomachean Ethics*. Many scholars think he started revising the EE, resulting in 'our' EN I–IV and VIII–X. What about EN V–VII? Currently, most interpreters take the EE to have comprised eight scrolls, including what is now EN V–VII. As the revised *Ethics* left important topics uncovered, such as justice, the virtues of intellect, and the nature of self-control and the lack of it, the relevant treatises were

53

simply added from the EE scrolls – whether by Aristotle or some later editor. Since the scroll containing the topic of self-control also contained the treatise on pleasure, the EN came to comprise two treatments of pleasure. Alternatively, and less 'en vogue', one might find the original home of EN V–VII in the EN as we know it. In this case 1) the scrolls containing the shared material were added to the EE because *it* lacked the relevant discussions or because the EN material was better and could simply replace the EE material, and 2) Aristotle must have been in the process of revising the EN and simply did not have time to remove the treatise on pleasure which was superseded by EN X.1–5.[1]

Endorsing the view that EN V–VII originates in the EE, some scholars find traces of glue even in the topic announcements themselves. For instance, friendship is announced twice: first at the end of VII.14 and then again at the beginning of VIII – as if this helped to stick them together. Since the text also announces our examination of pleasure twice – at end of IX.12 and at the beginning of X.1 – should we suspect its place in the plan of the EN?[2] No, because i) the Book X discussion of pleasure tackles questions arising from friendship (see a) and b) above) more straightforwardly than its counterpart – which might sufficiently justify the connection Aristotle forges between the discussions of friendship and pleasure. ii) The double topic announcements need not smell of glue. Saying 'next, we should discuss pleasure' both at the end of Book IX and at the beginning of Book X makes sense if the text is based on lectures scheduled for different occasions, and/or the reader must take a different scroll (as is the case here). So, on a plausible view of the EN's composition, the treatment of pleasure in Book X comes after the topics Aristotle enumerates at the beginning of X.1. (For further discussion and references, see the Introduction, §4.)

1172a19–21 For pleasure is thought … pleasure and pain.

Aristotle offers three reasons to justify the topic of pleasure (this lemma and the next two). First, he highlights the close connection between being human and pleasure. Although the Greek word *dokei*, translated as 'it is

---

[1] For a trenchant argument against the commonly agreed view, see Frede 2019.
[2] In an effort to establish Aristotle's text, some editors excise the offending duplication. Susemihl's 1880 edition follows the sixteenth-century scholar Denis Lambin (who, in turn, follows unnamed *viri docti*) in taking the end of Book IX (on friendship) to be the beginning of Book X. He excises the first announcement of the topic of pleasure (1172a15–16).

thought' ('it seems' would be an alternative), hides the logical subject who has the appearance or thought, Aristotle presumably expresses a common and uncontroversial view. People in general unthinkingly utilise the close connection between pleasure and human nature in education, or else they educate via pleasure because they grasp its importance for human life.

In what way is 'pleasure most intimately connected (*malista sunô(i)keiôsthai*) to our kind'? According to a more pessimistic reading, pleasure would be something we cannot help but have. Every living organism furnished with perceptual faculties necessarily experiences pleasure and pain, due to appetite (*De Anima* II.2.413b23–4; cf. 414b4–6). As human beings rely on perception, our kind is closely connected with pleasure and pain. While other animals seem to live their lives successfully by appetite, Aristotle attributes living by appetite regularly to the young (e.g. EN I.3.1095a2–11; cf. VIII.3.1156a31–4), recommending we grow out of that way of life. So, even if pleasure forms an ineradicable part of our lives, we need not therefore welcome pleasure.

Alternatively, we could construe the phrase not as 'is an ineradicable part of being human', but as 'most proper or most congenial to our kind'. This reading would evoke a much more optimistic view of pleasure and its relation to education. If pleasure is most congenial to our kind, we will not need to leave pleasure behind in the process of growing up. Pleasure will play a key role in our lives, and contributes to making it fully human. Understood sufficiently widely, pleasure or pain (sometimes both) accompany every affection and action (II.3.1104b13–16). If, as he will argue in X.5, the pleasures and pains *belong* to the relevant actions, the pair will belong to characteristically human behaviour: both action and affection proper are exclusive to human beings.

Tying pleasure and pain to action and affection helps illuminate the point about education. The stick-and-carrot method will usually suffice for animals incapable of other pleasures and pains. These paradigmatic pleasures and pains, however, will not suffice for a characteristically *human* education, as *human* pleasures and pains do not reduce to bodily ones, but tend to have a cognitive component (cf. 'pleasures of the soul', at III.10.1117b28–1118a1). Indeed, if pleasure and pain accompany and belong to actions and affections, we cannot use the former pair merely as a *means* to educate (the function highlighted here), but must instil the proper pleasures and pains as an educative goal in its own right (next lemma). Aristotle will return to and expand on the topic in the first half of X.9, after having discussed which behaviour is most characteristically human (X.5.1176a10–29 and X.7–8, esp. 1177b26–1178a8).

1172a21–26 And with regard to virtue of character ... avoid painful things.

The next reason for discussing pleasure justifies the topic by spelling out why we cannot do without pleasure and pain, and by tying it to the apex of human development: virtue and happiness. Like all other animals, human beings tend to choose what is pleasant and avoid what is painful. If we let ourselves be steered by those basic pleasures and pains shared with other animals, we will hardly live a fully human life, let alone a happy human life. We could either train ourselves to act against inclination (many people read Kant this way), or else train ourselves to enjoy what one should and hate or be distressed by what one should.

Aristotle firmly endorses the latter approach, proposed by Plato (reported at II.3.1104b11–13). He does so because he thinks pleasure and pain influence both individual actions and our character. a) Speaking of human beings in general, 'we do bad things because of pleasure and refrain from fine actions because of pain' (II.3.1104b9–11). For example, imagine I finish all the chocolate truffles I was supposed to share with my family, simply because they taste so good. Having tasted one, I loathed the thought of sharing them: I wanted them all to myself. My pleasure 'makes' me behave like a glutton. b) Individual choices form character: if I continually succumb to the pleasures of gorging on food, I will become a glutton, i.e. a person who habitually enjoys gorging on food (and hates sharing). So, what we enjoy is a sign of our character states (II.3.1104b3–8).

Both a) and b) highlight the importance of taking pleasure correctly for virtue and happiness – and hence the need to educate the young accordingly, for happiness consists in acting well, or doing what one should. But doing what one should against inclination would not be characteristic of what makes a person happy (Kant agrees). For Aristotle (but not for Kant), the happy life must be pleasant because of its central activity (I.8.1099a7). Virtuous action, Aristotle's candidate, satisfies that condition. He doubts that you are acting justly or moderately if you do not enjoy your actions (1099a17–20), for your actions would not seem to stem from virtuous states – pleasure is a sign of character – and properly virtuous actions stem from virtue (II.4.1105a26–b9). So, learning to take pleasure correctly goes hand in hand with acquiring virtue, and should therefore take prime place in education, just as Plato suggested.

But how does one get children to enjoy what they should? And how does one determine what they should enjoy or dislike in the first place? Here, too, Aristotle leans on Plato: the answer must be sought in the context of governing a city-state (*polis*). He expands on the political dimension of education in X.9.

X.1

1172a26–33 And least of all ... reach the middle.

The previous two lemmata justify the discussion of pleasure by tying pleasure to other important topics: human nature, virtue, education, and happiness. Now Aristotle focuses on pleasure itself. Although he writes as if the existence of a dispute about pleasure were a sufficient reason to discuss it, the basis of the dispute, its content, drives the interest: the value of pleasure.

Aristotle mentions only the two extreme positions: normative hedonism (pleasure is the good) and anti-hedonism (all pleasure is bad). Why does he not introduce more nuanced positions? Consider a) all pleasure is good, but not the good; b) some pleasures are good, some bad; c) pleasure itself has no value, but some pleasures have good consequences, whereas others have bad ones. He concentrates on hedonism and anti-hedonism presumably because these positions dominated the debate (see especially Plato's *Philebus*). In any case, the extreme positions set up the subsequent discussion of Eudoxus' hedonism and its detractors (X.2–3).

Aristotle trains the spotlight on the anti-hedonists to make a point about methodology. One can justify one's view on pleasure in different ways. While group A pronounces what they think about pleasure, group B's (official) position seems to be driven by concerns other than the truth of the subject matter. They do not really believe all pleasure is bad. But they do believe that people make many bad choices because of pleasure. They justify representing all pleasure as bad by the expected benefit. If people were to heed their official position, everyone would be wary of pleasure and better able to guard against it – which would be better for all. Since pragmatic concerns (broadly understood) determine group B's official position, we could call them 'pragmatists'.[3]

Does the view of pleasure align with groups A and B? Yes, if we translate the text at 1172a27–30 differently: 'For some [= group A] say pleasure is the good, while others [= group B], on the contrary, say it is plain bad, the former presumably because they are persuaded that it is so, the latter because they think it is better for our lives to proclaim pleasure a bad thing, even if it is not.' On this interpretation Aristotle would insinuate that no one really believes all pleasure to be bad, presumably because no one *can* think that. However, most translators would regard this rendering as an over-translation. If we adopt my translation (or a similar one), we

---

[3] Aristotle portrays the 'pragmatists' as endorsing the distinction between truth in the subject matter, and pragmatic considerations. Pragmatists belonging to the tradition of the philosophical movement popular in the US between the 1870s and 1920s (spearheaded by Peirce, James, and Dewey) would eschew such a distinction.

have three groups: the hedonists, the A-anti-hedonists, and the B-anti-hedonists. Either way, Aristotle focuses on the methodological aspect of propounding a certain view of pleasure.

Interestingly, he appears to share some of the 'pragmatist' concerns: just as the anti-hedonists here warn against pleasure, so Aristotle warns against pleasure, in much the same words (at the end of his general discussion of virtue, II.9). Noting the difficulty of hitting the middle in action, i.e. acting as one should, he observes that we do not judge pleasure impartially – hence we must guard against it (1109b7–9). Indeed, if we 'send pleasure packing', we will get things less wrong and will be in the best position to hit the middle (1109b11–13). So, he shares group B's view that people are prone, often too prone, to pleasure and that one must guard against this tendency – without, however, endorsing their solution, as he makes clear in the next two lemmata.

1172a33–b3 But this is surely ... the many.

Aristotle criticises the 'pragmatist' approach to the value of pleasure, primarily because it fails to deliver what it promises. The 'pragmatists' discredit pleasure in order that people act better. However, because pleasure belongs intimately to human nature, no one can avoid it wholesale (1172a19–20). Even an avowed anti-hedonist must pursue some pleasures. The anti-hedonists' words will therefore, sometimes, conflict with their deeds.

But when the many see a proponent of that view *nolens volens* seeking pleasures, they will be dismayed by the mismatch between words and deeds. They will perceive the anti-hedonist as insincere. The many take the anti-hedonist's condemnation of all pleasure to entail the practical attitude to avoid all pleasure. Now, if the anti-hedonists do not avoid all pleasure, they do not really believe their 'official' view that pleasure is plain bad – which is insincere.

The perceived insincerity undermines the pragmatist goal. For, if a person does not really believe what she preaches, why should we believe her? We tend to believe what someone says (P), because we assume she has (defeasible) reasons to think P true or correct. But when the person's actions betray that she does not take P to be true or correct, why would she say it? In this case, the many may rightly suspect the anti-hedonist to condemn pleasure in order to make them (the many) believe it. But of course, that is no reason for the many to adopt the view!

Aristotle further elaborates on the danger of the pragmatist view. For, if the many were to follow the example of the anti-hedonists, not much would be lost. They would shun many pleasures, and seek only the necessary ones. However, the mismatch between the anti-hedonists' words and deeds makes things worse. The many, Aristotle diagnoses, have difficulties making distinctions (1172b3). They seem to identify only two views: either (all) pleasure is good, or (all) pleasure is bad. So, when the many see an avowed anti-hedonist pursuing pleasure, they take her actions to betray the extreme view that all pleasure is to be pursued. The many readily adopt *that* view, because they infer from her behaviour that the anti-hedonist takes the view to be true or correct. That is, they surmise the 'anti-hedonist' has reasons for the view's truth, even if they may not know them.

Could not a clever 'pragmatist' use the insight into the psyche of the many to reverse-engineer an approach to better their lives? Unfortunately, an inverse strategy yields no better results. If someone were to advocate that all pleasure is good and is then seen to shun pleasure (as perhaps Eudoxus did, X.2.1172b18), should the many not adopt an anti-hedonist outlook? No, because a) the many would hardly become suspicious of pleasure, due to our inherent inclination towards pleasure, noted by the pragmatists (previous lemma), and b) just like an avowed anti-hedonist, the advocate of pleasure would also be seen to pursue pleasure, at least the necessary ones – which undermines the strategy. (For a more extended discussion of the connection between words and deeds, see the commentary on X.8.1179a17–22.)

1172b3–7 True words ... in accordance with them.

The 'pragmatist' criticism of pleasure conceals the truth, misinforming people about the true value of pleasure. However, since the approach aims not at knowledge, but at practical benefit, this does not count as failure (for them). However, the goal cannot justify the means, because the goal of making people's lives better will not be attained by condemning pleasure roundly as bad (previous lemma). In contrast to the pragmatist approach, Aristotle thinks discovering the truth about pleasure will not only yield knowledge, but also improve the lives of those who understand it.

He places two conditions on successfully discussing pleasure in an ethical context. First, the audience must understand the truth about pleasure. 'Understanding' here exceeds understanding the truth-conditions or the ability to make or follow the relevant distinctions. Merely philosophising may yield knowledge about pleasure, but does not automatically improve life (cf. II.4.1105b9–18). One must already be motivated to act in accordance with that knowledge. Hence Aristotle mainly addresses those brought up well, those who are already inclined to act correctly (I.5.1095b4–6).

Second, his view about pleasure carries conviction only if it agrees with the deeds. But whose deeds? Imagine Aristotle were to campaign against slavery. His words could disagree with the deeds and therefore fail to carry conviction either if a) he himself practises slavery, or b) his audience practises slavery. Scenario a) would highlight the insincerity of the person making the proposal: if *Aristotle* does not do as he says, then his words are empty, because he does not believe what he says (cf. previous lemma). So, convincing others in matters of action and life requires harmony between the speaker's words and deeds.

Scenario b) should be familiar to all. If we try to convince a group of slave-owners of the wrongness of slavery, our talk will not usually turn them around. As history has shown, it takes a long and difficult route to change people's minds about slavery. For a successful talk, then, the audience must be 'ready' to receive the words. One must find something the audience already believes and practises with which one's words could harmonise. In this case, words carry conviction and can improve the lives of his audience. The conflict would no longer rest between Aristotle's words and his audience's deeds, but between the audience's beliefs and their deeds. For instance, his audience may see the divine in every human being – which one could show to be incompatible with treating them like chattels.

Returning to pleasure, does either scenario obtain? Although we know too little about Aristotle's audience, the demand on his audience's character rules out a hedonistic attitude. Scenario a) would, in any case, pose the greater threat. Does Aristotle have a coherent attitude about pleasure? In particular, how does his criticism of the anti-hedonists square with his advice that we should guard against pleasure and send her packing (II.9.1109b7–13)? Unlike the 'pragmatists', Aristotle takes himself to be speaking the truth. We must constantly guard against pleasure in the sense that we must not let pleasure make decisions for us – but that does not mean that pleasure is bad, nor does he say so. If his warning implies anything, then it is only that not just any pleasure is to be sought in just any circumstance. (This, presumably, is the sort of complication the many find difficult to understand, 1172b3.)

1172b7–8 Enough now ... about pleasure.

Aristotle now concludes the proem (X.1). He concentrates on what people say about pleasure, especially about its value. He apparently trusts that turning to the things said will help reveal the truth about pleasure – a truth that should manifest itself also in the deeds (see previous lemma).

But why? If we want to find out about pleasure, should we not study pleasure, rather than what people say about pleasure? But how could one examine pleasure anyway? In order to determine the status and nature of pleasure, some, including Eudoxus (discussed in X.2), seek to derive the truth from a universally shared attitude towards pleasure. They base their view of pleasure on observation and subsequent reflection. Aristotle's approach, by contrast, rests more firmly on philosophical reflection. He starts here and elsewhere with reviewing *ta eirêmena*, i.e. things said about a controversial and philosophically interesting topic. However, he does not simply consider the things just anyone has said on the topic. Instead, he musters only views supported by argument, to examine both the views and their support.[4]

But if Aristotle only considers and criticises the views of others, how can he find the truth – unless one of the views happens to be correct? And supposing he wants to make the truth about pleasure his own – how do we find out *Aristotle's* view? Determining *his* view presents perhaps the biggest difficulty for the reader in a dialectically opaque context. If he outlines philosopher A's position and then cites philosopher B's argument against it – does that mean Aristotle subscribes to B's view or even B's reasons against A's view? Not necessarily. Sometimes Aristotle comments on the arguments and signals his colours; sometimes not. Although he completes the discussion of pleasure with his own account (X.4–5), he nevertheless seems to arrive at a preliminary view about the value of pleasure through the dialectical discussion (X.3.1174a8–11). But how he reaches his conclusion becomes apparent only by going through the arguments with Aristotle.

X.2

1172b9–15 Now Eudoxus thought ... what everything seeks, is the good.

Eudoxus of Cnidus (ca 390–340 BC) was a genius known for his accomplishments in mathematics, geography, medicine, law-making, astronomy, and philosophy. His version of hedonism, the thesis that pleasure is the good, merits detailed discussion – unlike sybaritic hedonism, which takes

---

[4] The question of 'Aristotle's Method' is too big to broach here. He starts by going through things said because this is good philosophical practice, not because he has an established method, the so-called 'endoxic method' which he applies here (as pretty much everywhere). For an illuminating discussion of the limits of the 'endoxic method', see Frede 2012.

the life of pleasure to consist in licentiously pursuing bodily pleasures (cf. I.4.1095b14–22, though see X.6 with commentary).

Eudoxus' argument pivots on the observation, O1, that all animals, rational and irrational, pursue pleasure. Together with two further assumptions, a) animals pursue what is good for them, and b) what all animals pursue is the good, Eudoxus can support hedonism, even if his argument falls short of cogently establishing the conclusion, C, that pleasure is the good. Unfortunately, the details of Eudoxus' argument for hedonism have eluded interpreters since antiquity. I shall not try to reconstruct *Eudoxus'* original argument, due to the lack of the textual evidence. Instead, let us think about two ancient versions for which we do have some evidence. Alexander of Aphrodisias (fl. AD 200), the most important commentator of the Peripatetic school, attributes the further observation to Eudoxus, O2, that no other good is pursued by all animals (*In Top*. 226.17, commenting on Aristotle's *Topics* III.1, 116a14–22). With Alexander's added premise, we can construct *a* valid argument:

O1) All animals, rational and irrational, pursue pleasure;
O2) no other good is pursued by all animals;
b) what is exclusively pursued by all animals is the good;
hence C) pleasure is the good.

Few will find the argument of Alexander's Eudoxus cogent, because all the premises seem to lack support. First, premises O1 and O2 do not seem to be observable. Leaving aside worries about induction, how would we observe that animals seek *pleasure*? If we understand pleasure as a feeling, or at any rate something 'internal', we could not straightforwardly observe an animal's pleasure. But even if we move beyond mere observation, and rely on signs that indicate the animal's pleasure, why would we then say the animal pursues pleasure rather than the things that happen to give rise to pleasure? Second, what licenses the move in b) from the descriptive thesis (all animals pursue X) to the normative one (X is the good)?

Aristotle's Eudoxus supports the inference from the descriptive to the normative with the following thought (not based on observation): '[1] in all cases the object of choice (*haireton*) is what is fitting (*epieikes*), and [2] that which is most so is best' (1172b10–11).[5] Invoking 'what is fitting'

---

[5] Other translators take *epieikes* to mean 'decent' (Reeve, Irwin), or 'good' (Crisp, Rowe). While Aristotle often uses the word in this way, his present word-choice may reflect Eudoxus' usage. Warren 2009, 257–9 argues persuasively for the translation adopted here. He discusses many of the points raised here in more detail.

helps to bridge the apparent gap between the descriptive and the normative because it points to an animal's nature: an animal's nature determines what is fitting for it (and in which circumstances, and for how long, etc.). The point bears on the argument in two ways. First, it acknowledges the implicit diversity among animals: because different kinds of animal have different natures, different things will befit them. An elephant and a snake will require different kinds of food, different amounts, and may consume them at different times. Second, many ancient thinkers, including Aristotle and Eudoxus, do not see 'nature' (*phusis*) as a normatively neutral, merely descriptive term (*Physics* II, especially chapter 8). On the contrary, if one finds out what is in the nature of a given species of an animal, one knows what counts as good for this kind of animal, or, in other words, one knows what they *should* choose. So, point [1] supports Eudoxus' assumption a), that animals pursue what is good for them – which combines an observable with a normative claim. An animal's choices reveal some of the norms governing its pursuits.

Point [2] returns to the problem of observability, as it performs the same function as O2, progressing from *a* good to *the* good. All animals pursue what is good *for them*. Aristotle's Eudoxus suggests that all animals' choices converge on one, and only one, good. Given the diversity of animals and their pursuits, Eudoxus' move increases the level of generality dramatically. Even trying to subsume all the choices of an individual animal under one general heading leaves only a few plausible options: pleasure (including desire-satisfaction and avoiding pain), what is natural, and what is good (taking good to be primitive). Now, can Eudoxus really observe the difference between 'all animals pursue what is natural or fitting to them' and 'all animals pursue what is pleasant to them'? Of course not! For 'what is fitting to an animal' and 'what is pleasant to an animal' are co-extensional and observationally equivalent. To support hedonism (rather than nature-ism or what-is-fitting-ism), Eudoxus could invoke the psychological aspect of the good. From this perspective, pleasure has a more important psychological function than what is natural, for while animals by and large do pursue what is fitting for them by engaging, appropriately, in their characteristic activities (eating, mating, building a home), they do not pursue it under this description (if under any). It is much more plausible to claim that animals do what is fitting because it is pleasant to them (cf. 1173a12 and *History of Animals* VIII.1.589a4–589a10). While psychological hedonism, the thesis that all animals pursue pleasure, is logically distinct from normative hedonism, the former implies the latter, for it makes no sense to demand that animals *should* seek something other than pleasure as the good if in fact they are not capable of seeking anything but pleasure. (This also explains why the converse thesis that normative hedonism implies psychological hedonism is not true.)

1172b15–18 His words ... as he said.

Aristotle here interrupts the examination of things said about pleasure to return to the connection between words and deeds (see 1172a33–b7, with commentaries). Given the difficulty of attributing a cogent argument to Eudoxus (previous lemma), we might take Aristotle to remark snidely on the force of Eudoxus' arguments. People would not have found them convincing, or their conclusion, had Eudoxus not lived a moderate life. Earlier, Aristotle described how people become upset when they realise the truth has been hidden from them for ulterior motives (1172a35–b1). Eudoxus passes *this* test, as he does not set up pleasure as the highest good merely in order to justify a pleasure-oriented lifestyle. Pleasure does not addle his mind, nor does pursuing pleasure corrupt his life. He does not extol pleasure *as* a lover of pleasure (*hôs philos tês hêdonês*, 1172b17) whose thinking has been clouded by pleasure. Eudoxus does not state what he *wishes* pleasure to be, but appears to have reasoned soberly, aiming at the truth – as his lifestyle testifies. So, even if his arguments themselves lack power, Eudoxus appears to be sincere, and therefore provides others with some reason to believe in his conclusion that pleasure is the good.

On second thoughts, does this interpretation face a challenge? Remember, a) deeds carry more conviction than words (1172a34–5), and b) only words that agree with the speaker's deeds can sway the audience (1172b5–6). But c) Eudoxus proclaims pleasure as the highest good, while d) he lives moderately. Does c) not clash with d)? Given a), the clash would discredit his words; his deeds would advocate a moderate lifestyle instead of a pleasant one.

The challenge rests on a misunderstanding of Eudoxus' hedonism. He did not distinguish between the goal of rational and irrational animals (1172b10). Human lives, including his own, should gravitate towards pleasure in the same way as other animals' lives (on which, see commentary on previous lemma). Animals tend to choose what is natural and fitting when, and only when, it is good for them. In order to enjoy eating or drinking, an animal must be hungry or thirsty, and similarly with other characteristic pleasures. Animals, in other words, do not usually indulge in excesses, because the excessive activity would not be pleasant to them: it would be unnatural.[6] By pursuing pleasure, animals pursue what is beneficial for them (at that time). Human beings *qua* animals should therefore also aim to pursue only those pleasures that are beneficial.[7] So, by living his philosophy, Eudoxus would indeed appear moderate because he would not eat or drink excessively or indulge in any other bodily pleasures beyond what is appropriate (in Aristotle's view, moderation extends to bodily pleasures only, III.10). So, like any credible advisor, Eudoxus practises what he preaches. His deeds *do* agree with his words, but not everyone understands his words correctly.

Once it is established that Eudoxus did live by what he said, his predilection for intellectual pursuits provides a glimpse of his view of *human* nature. Eudoxus excelled in several fields: mathematics, geography, medicine, law-making, astronomy, and philosophy. If he lived by what he said, he found these pursuits pleasant. Since we tend to enjoy what is natural to us, intellectual pursuits would be natural to human beings. Thus, Eudoxus' ethics overlaps significantly with Aristotle's. Both advise avoiding excess (and deficiency) in favour of what is appropriate (Aristotle's famous doctrine of the mean, cf. Introduction §2.1), both take appropriate action to be pleasant, and both regard human beings as rational animals. Although both build their ethical theory on the notion of human nature, they differ in that Eudoxus promotes pleasure as the highest good, whereas Aristotle thinks pleasure (merely) a concomitant of the activity central to the highest good.

1172b18–23 It was no less ... pleasure in itself is to be chosen.

Aristotle attributes a second argument for hedonism to Eudoxus, which falls into two parts. The first part (up to 'its opposite is to be chosen') supports the key premise of the first argument (1172b9–15): everything pursues pleasure. The second part further expands on why pleasure is 'most of all to be chosen' (*malista haireton*, b20; cf. b11 in the first argument) and therefore plays the role of the highest good. We do not know whether Eudoxus (or Aristotle's Eudoxus) proffers this argument as an independent defence of hedonism, or whether it supports the first argument (see commentary on 1172b9–15).

---

[6] Neither Aristotle nor Eudoxus question why pleasure *should* be lined up with what is good for the animal, but take the connection for granted. However, at 1173a4–5 Aristotle postulates a divine element (possibly on Eudoxus' behalf) that seems responsible for matching pleasure with what is good for the animal.

[7] A further complication: what would Eudoxus make of harmful pleasures? For further discussion, also of the points raised here, see Broadie 1991, 353–5.

Eudoxus establishes or confirms the universal pursuit of pleasure by appealing to the universal attitude towards pain:

i) 'pain in itself is (to be) avoided (*pheukton*) by everything';
ii) the opposite of what is (to be) avoided is (to be) pursued *(haireton)*;
iii) pleasure and pain are opposites; therefore
iv) pleasure in itself is (to be) pursued by everything.

The bracketing of 'to be' indicates an ambiguity in the Greek verbal adjectives *pheukton* and *haireton*. The verbal adjectives can either express a factive attitude (pain in itself is avoided) or a normative attitude (pain in itself should be avoided). If we take the present argument together with the previous one, the difference between these two readings vanishes, for animals tend to do what they should do: they pursue what benefits them, and avoid what harms them.

The first premise would be implausible if 'pain' were not qualified as 'pain in itself', for many animals, including human beings, readily endure pain (exercise; territorial fights; giving birth; bringing up children). So, do they pursue what is painful? Yes and no. 'Yes', insofar as their pursuit has a painful component, but 'no' insofar as they would not choose the painful component if they could avoid it. In Eudoxus' words, they do not choose pain in itself, but endure pain for the sake something else. No animal would endure pain just for the sake of having the pain.

What justifies premise i)? It should be clear that we cannot simply observe it, as we need some theoretical background to explain away the occasions on which animals do seem to pursue pain. Premise ii) helps, if read normatively rather than descriptively, and understood in the framework of his first argument. The first argument established that animals should pursue pleasure, because pleasure goes hand in hand with what is good for the animal. Given premise iii), animals *should* avoid pain, because pain tends to go hand in hand with damage to their nature. When animals experience pain, they tend to suffer something that is bad for them. The prospect of attaining a (greater) good may justify suffering pain, but animals should not, and generally do not, suffer harm just for its own sake. (Note, Aristotle further discusses and defends premise ii) against a criticism in 1173a5–13.)

What does this argument add, if it relies on the first argument? First, it changes perspective. Some may have doctrinal reasons for denying that animals pursue pleasure, for instance because they take pleasure to be plain bad (X.1.1172a28). However, few, if any, have reasons for denying that animals avoid pain. Second, adding 'in itself' to the objects of pursuit and avoidance helps with difficult cases. When pain seems to be chosen, the animal does not choose pain in itself (but rather a greater pleasure), and when pleasure seems avoided, the animal still aims at (greater) pleasure itself.

Aristotle prefaces the argument by 'it was no less evident', which seems to refer to the thesis that pleasure is the good. Going beyond iv), Aristotle's Eudoxus seeks to establish pleasure as the good by focusing on goods as ends in the second part of the argument. (Note, Aristotle's Eudoxus does not state vii) to ix): I have supplied them to reconstruct an argument that Aristotle represents only in a curtailed form.)

v) 'Most of all to be chosen … is what we do not choose because of or for the sake of something else';
vi) 'pleasure … is by general agreement that sort of thing', i.e. not chosen because of or for the sake of something else; therefore
vii) pleasure is most of all to be chosen.
viii) What is most of all to be chosen is the good; therefore
ix) pleasure is the good.

Premises v) and viii) reflect the connection between goods and ends. Suppose goods G, E, and F are all choice-worthy. But if we choose G only because of, or for the sake of E, then E is a higher end than G, and more choice-worthy. But if we choose E in turn for the sake of F, and F not for the sake of anything else, then F would be the most choice-worthy good of the three, or *the* good if G, E, and F exhaust the set of goods.

Does the argument establish ix)? The general agreement with which Eudoxus supports premise vi) does the job: people treat pleasure as if it were (to be) chosen in itself, an attitude that surfaces when you ask them what they enjoy themselves for (1172b22–3). However, this only places pleasure among the goods chosen for themselves.[8] There could be other goods which we *also* choose for themselves. But Eudoxus' argument requires pleasure to be *the* thing most of all to be chosen. His full supporting argument might run as follows. If we were to ask people why they do what they do, they would eventually cite pleasure as their ultimate reason. They will justify everything else by reference to pleasure, even apparently self-standing goods such as friendship (on the relationship between goods and the highest good, see the commentary on the next lemma). If so, Eudoxus could confirm not only the descriptive claim that people (and animals) seek pleasure, but also the assumption made in the first argument that objects

---

[8] Contrary to Eudoxus, Aristotle argues later that at least some pleasures are for the sake of something else, even if we surmise those pleasures to be final ends (X.6.1176b27–1177a1).

of choice are chosen insofar as they appear pleasant to the one making the choice.

If indeed people would respond in the way envisaged by Eudoxus, he could establish pleasure as the highest good. But a) people may be confused about what they ultimately pursue, and b) similar versions of the argument predict a different answer. Plato, for instance, writes as if everyone will choose what appears fine and good to them in order to be happy (*eudaimôn*, *Symposium* 204d–205a). Eudoxus, in fact, could agree, but insists that pleasure is what makes a life happy. Plato considers whether pleasure could play the role envisaged by Eudoxus in his dialogue *Philebus*.

1172b23–35 Moreover, he thought ... we are looking for something of this sort.

The interpretation of Eudoxus' next argument, and Aristotle's response, proves especially difficult, despite its deceptively simple form. He reports Eudoxus as maintaining that a) adding pleasure to any good G makes the resulting good more choice-worthy than G by itself, and b) the good is increased by itself. Why would a) and b) support hedonism?

Aristotle points to a gap in the argument, for a) seems to derive its strength from an underlying principle, something like a*) whatever good makes any G better through its addition is the good. But, he objects, a*) and a) will not do, because it does not rule out alternatives to pleasure. Besides pleasure, there may be other goods whose addition also makes any G better. Indeed, Aristotle seems to embrace a dubious value-theoretic principle, both here and elsewhere (I.7.1097b16–20), namely (V): for all goods X and Y, X + Y is more choice-worthy than X or Y alone. We should understand the goods over which the variables quantify as intrinsic goods, or goods in themselves, to render (V) plausible. Aristotle presents a few lists of such goods in the EN: 'having a sound mind, seeing, some pleasures and honours' (I.6.1096b16–19), 'honour, pleasure, intelligence and every virtue' (I.7.1097b2–3), and perhaps 'seeing, remembering, knowing, having the virtues' (X.3.1175a5–6). While he grants Eudoxus' point that we would prefer to have honour together with pleasure, Aristotle adds that we would also prefer to have honour together with virtue.[9] If virtue also makes every good better, then, given a*), there

---

[9] For our present purposes, we must leave aside the intricate difficulties that arise when we think about the structure of the compound good. Eudoxus does not suggest that honour is improved by the pleasure we derive from a chocolate truffle. Instead, he seems to suppose we take pleasure in our honour or what caused us to receive the honour. Similarly, Aristotle does not suppose honour and virtue to stand next to each other, but that we merit honour on account of our virtue.

would be two referents of the unique identifier '*the* good' – which is absurd. To avoid absurdity, he suggests weakening a*). Taking a cue from (V), we should maintain a**) whatever good makes any G better through its addition is good in itself.

Now, Aristotle seeks to corroborate his criticism by referring to Plato, who explicitly used this kind of argument. The dialogue *Philebus* deals with establishing the right relation between knowledge and pleasure in the good life. In an effort to displace both pleasure and intelligence (*phronêsis*) as the good (cf. 20b6–9), Socrates asks his interlocutor to consider whether either intelligence devoid of any pleasure or pleasure devoid of any intelligence could play the role of the good. Neither option is choice-worthy. Aristotle reads the argument as if pleasure on its own failed to be the good, because i) the addition of another good would make pleasure more choice-worthy, but ii) *the* good does not become more choice-worthy through the addition of another good. Note that Plato's argument in the *Philebus* does not explicitly rely on i) or ii). The original argument only concludes that a life of only pleasure, but no cognition, memory, or awareness, fails to be choice-worthy because pleasure alone falls short of being sufficient. Hence, pleasure cannot be the good because it misses one of the hallmarks of the good (21a–d with 20d4–6). So, *Plato's* argument need not be designed to show that either intelligence or pleasure is an intrinsic good. It may merely show that an unmixed life may be humanly unattainable and therefore not choice-worthy.[10]

Scholars debate the extent to which Aristotle endorses Plato. They are especially interested in the status of the assertions 'that no other thing will be the good either, if it becomes more choice-worthy together with one of the things good in themselves' (1172b31–4) and that we are looking for a good of this nature (b34–5). Scholars attend to this passage to support their respective approach to the vexed question of whether Aristotle's highest good consists of one, several, or all intrinsic goods, which arises in Book I (chapter 7, 1097b16–20, see Introduction §1.3). If he endorses ii) in b31–4, and reasoning inspired by Plato more generally, Aristotle seems to suggest that we cannot improve the good because it already comprises all goods (inclusivism). But does he endorse ii)? We might think he cannot do so, because ii) conflicts with (V), a principle to which he evidently subscribes. There are two ways in which we can plausibly ease the clash between ii) and (V). First, we may take Aristotle merely to report Plato's view until the end of the lemma – in which case he would use ii) merely as a borrowed tool to point to

---

[10] See Evans 2007 for pertinent discussion.

a difficulty in Eudoxus' thought. Second, and more interestingly, we might take Aristotle to endorse ii), but to limit its scope. Without a restriction in scope, Plato's reasoning would make the good practically impossible (b31–4), because, with (V), we can always improve any candidate for the highest good. Hence, we have to look for a candidate that cannot be improved and thus stands outside the scope of (V). Without trying to decide these interpretive difficulties, we should note that Aristotle allocates a special role to the highest good that sets it apart from the other intrinsic goods, for the highest good tops a hierarchical structure that subsumes all other goods (I.1–2; I.7), and it is the 'principle and cause' of the other goods (I.12.1102a2–4). So, (V) might plausibly apply only to intrinsic goods other than *the* good.[11]

Now, if we opt for the second interpretation on which Aristotle excludes his highest good from the scope of (V), how does his argument against Eudoxus fare? The question arises because (on this reading) his conception of the highest good seems to share a formal feature with Eudoxus': no other good added can make the highest good better. Indeed, when explaining his conception of the highest good, Aristotle approvingly cites Eudoxus to illustrate the structure of the highest good (I.12.1101b27–34). But if *Aristotle's* highest good does not fall within the scope of (V), why should (V) apply to *Eudoxus'*? We need either a good reason for the difference, or else take the tension between (V) and ii) as evidence that Aristotle does not endorse ii). That is, we might fall back on the option that he simply uses Plato's argument without subscribing to its premises, unless Eudoxus' conception of the highest good saliently differs from Aristotle's, despite the structural similarity of both. A salient difference between Aristotle's and Eudoxus' conceptions emerges when we turn our attention away from a) towards b). Aristotle may restrict the scope of (V) to the plurality of goods which he acknowledges as independent goods (see lists cited above). But he may exclude his highest good from the scope of (V) by making it different in standing or kind from the lower-level goods. This reasoning is not available to Eudoxus. Eudoxus' good is enhanceable insofar as the good is increased *only* by itself (=b). The combination of a*) and b) points towards a pervasive monism about goods, counting pleasure as the only good. So, if two lower-level goods become better when combined, then necessarily also the highest good must become better when a lower-level good is added to it: more pleasure is better than less pleasure, regardless of the relevant goods' place in the hierarchy of goods.

---

[11] For a philosophically rewarding exploration of the questions raised in this paragraph, see Lawrence 1997.

But Eudoxus' hedonism seems more defensible than Aristotle's criticism lets on, for Eudoxus need not deny that his highest good falls within the scope of (V) – but only on condition that there be no genuine plurality of goods. According to Eudoxus, there is only one good, the highest good, in virtue of which every other good is good. All things good in themselves have in common that their goodness stems from the highest good inherent in them. This monism bears on the argument from addition. If A) pleasure improves acting justly, B) acting justly is good in itself, and C) what is good (another translation for *to agathon* at 1172b25) is improved through itself, then D) acting justly must be good in virtue of its pleasure. So, E) the addition of pleasure would not conjoin two different goods, but merely add more of the same to the good already present. That is, the *Philebus* argument, and Aristotle's adaption (i and ii above), does not threaten Eudoxus' theory, because there are no goods besides pleasure that could make any good better. So, claim b) provides the means for filling the gap that Aristotle detects in Eudoxus' argument. It supports the uniqueness of pleasure as an 'improver' of goods, required for a*), and thereby allows Eudoxus to block Aristotle's argument which relies on the principle (V) and a genuine plurality of goods.

1172b35–1173a5 And those who object ... their own proper good.

Aristotle now turns to rebutting objections to Eudoxus' arguments for hedonism (this lemma and the next), before addressing attacks on the goodness of pleasure more generally. Eudoxus' 'argument from universal pursuit' relies heavily on the thesis (T) that what all animals pursue is the good (see 1172b9–15 with commentary):

1) All animals, rational and irrational, pursue pleasure;
2) no other good is pursued by all animals;
T) what all animals pursue is the good; hence
C) pleasure is the good.

The (unstated) objection that dominates the present lemma denies (T): there might be some goal G that all animals pursue, but nevertheless G would not be the good.

Now, Aristotle does not state any reasons for rejecting (T).[12] Instead, he deems doing so 'nonsense', because what appears to all is so

---

[12] For a different approach to the difficulties with (T) from the one pursued here, see commentary on 1172b9–15.

(1172b36–73a2).¹³ Presumably, he means that in all cases what appears F to all is F, where F does not only range over value-properties (or else it would be too close the restating T). Aristotle does not in general take a thing *a* to be F because we all believe *a* to be F. Instead, there are some independent facts on which animals may pick up. If they *all* take *a* to be F, this would for Aristotle constitute indefeasible evidence for *a*'s being F. One would need a very powerful error theory to explain away universal agreement on *a*'s being F, one that explains the systematic error of both rational and irrational animals. To motivate the error theory, one cannot use the apparent diversity of goals pursued as evidence that *the* good does not exist. This move would attack premise 1), not (T).¹⁴ But if the unnamed objector does not demote 'good' and 'the good' to specious properties, the objector seems to be saddled with an etiolated theory of the good that seems unable to explain the attraction of the good. Unless the objector adds a theory of the good supporting the alleged phenomena, Aristotle insinuates, she will not have anything convincing to say.

He explores the resources of the objection more thoroughly. If Eudoxus' argument had relied entirely on the testimony of irrational animals, then the objector would be in a stronger position, for she might think that the good attracts only those who grasp it intellectually – in which case we could indeed discount the behaviour of irrational animals as evidence. *Their* common pursuit of X would fall short of establishing X as *to be* pursued by all. So, the objector seems have a point if we disregard *universal* pursuit: the evidence of irrational animals does not seem to tell us much, if anything, about the good for rational animals (*qua* rational), at least not without further assumptions. However, Aristotle strengthens the evidence for Eudoxus' theory by making explicit a further underlying assumption that renders even the behaviour of irrational animals relevant for what is to be pursued by all. Even irrational and therefore inferior animals presumably¹⁵ possess some natural element that moves them towards their proper

---

[13] Some translators render the Greek neuter plural as plural in English. E.g Reeve translates 'things that seem to be so to everyone, these, we say, are'. Both translations are possible; the sense is the same in both.

[14] Mackie 1977, 36–7 uses the Argument from Relativity to support his error theory about morality.

[15] Aristotle's 'presumably' or 'perhaps' (*isôs*), here as elsewhere, does not necessarily express hesitation or even doubt. Just as 'I guess' in the American vernacular often does not express the utterer's uncertainty, so Aristotle often uses *isôs* merely as a polite phrase to blunt his opposition. Or, as Bonitz has it, he asserts 'cum modestia quadam' (Bonitz 1870, 347b32–43, with examples).

good (1173a4–5).[16] Animals tend to find what enables their well-functioning, i.e. they tend to pursue what befits their nature, and thereby attain their own good (Aristotle agrees with Eudoxus on this). Animal behaviour, then, seems goal-oriented, not willy-nilly. And precisely because they lack the cognitive resources to deliberate about what is good for them, there should be some other element that steers them reliably towards their goals. So, animal behaviour can at least show what is good *for them*.

Aristotle rests his argument there, but we could develop it further. Animals have an element guiding them reliably to their good. The element, therefore, is good-oriented insofar as it responds to what is good for the animal. Now, if we have a theory of the good that automatically subsumes all goods under *the* good, then the element would also be oriented towards the good – not merely towards what is good for this (kind of) animal. The objector, of course, need not take this step, but both Eudoxus and Aristotle do, though in different ways (see commentary on previous lemma). For Eudoxus, anything that is good in itself (such as an animal's well-functioning) is good because of the pleasure inherent in it. So when an animal seeks anything that benefits it, it pursues pleasure, i.e. the good.

Aristotle, note, does not mention pleasure at all, but defends (T) on independent grounds, compatible with his own theorising about the good (on which, see the previous lemma). Thus, he does not defend Eudoxus' hedonism – he may object to premises 1 and 2 – but rather the methodological assumption that universal pursuit points towards the good. And indeed, the *Nicomachean Ethics* begins with a related, but more restricted, inference: all rational pursuits aim at some good; hence, all rational pursuits aim at the good. So Aristotle adopts (T), insofar as he endorses the inference from the universal pursuit of a good (in a certain domain) to postulating *the* good as the goal (in this domain). The objector has not put forward an argument that would undermine this point.

1173a5–13 And the point about ... they are also opposed.

Aristotle parries another stab at Eudoxus' hedonism. Roughly, Eudoxus argues i) pain is to be avoided; ii) the opposite of what is to be avoided is to be pursued; iii) pleasure and pain are opposites; therefore iv) pleasure is to be pursued (see 1172b18–23, with commentary for analysis and discussion).

---

[16] The context rules out the alternative translation 'bad people' (taken thus by Aquinas) instead of 'inferior animals'.

Unnamed opponents ('they') try to derail Eudoxus' train of thought by finding a fault in its logic. Premise ii) presupposes only one contrary of a bad state, namely the relevant good state. But, so the objectors, 'bad is also opposed to bad, and both to what is neutral' – where the second clause could mean either a) both bad and good are opposed to what is neutral, or b) both bad states are opposed to what is neutral.[17] Either way, if bad does not necessarily oppose good, and the properties of *haireton* (to be pursued) and *pheukton* (to be avoided) are anchored in goodness and badness, then premise ii) turns out to be false, and Eudoxus' argument loses its soundness.

Aristotle agrees in principle with the logic of the objection. Eudoxus' conclusion follows only if all contraries of bad are to be pursued. But not all contraries of all bad things are to be pursued. For example, I should not pursue the excess of food merely because the deficiency is to be avoided (*Categories* 13b36–14a6). In the present case, however, the alternatives sketched by Eudoxus' opponents fail to convince. If pleasure were opposed to pain as bad, both would have to be avoided; if pleasure were opposed to pain as something neutral, pleasure would have to be neither sought nor avoided. But people very clearly (*phainontai*, 1173a11) differentiate between pleasure and pain through their behaviour. They pursue the former and avoid the latter. (The remark may in fact be even more pointed: if 'they' in a11–12 refers back to the same people who put forward the objection, then they themselves pursue pleasure and avoid pain – which brings them into the camp of those whose words do not agree with their deeds, cf. 1172a33–b3.) So, while the objectors discover logical space in which ii) fails, Aristotle saves the truth of the premise in the present context.

The defence highlights why he takes the trouble of defending Eudoxus' argument. Aristotle does not want to rescue hedonism, but the principle on which Eudoxus rests his case: the argument from universal pursuit (on which see the previous lemma). More specifically, Aristotle seems to defend the assumption underlying the argument from universal pursuit by defending *ta phainomena* (what one can see; what is obvious) against mere logical possibility: the former will always be more plausible. Indeed, he does not seem to care very much about Eudoxus' argument, for he seems to begin from the observation that people avoid pain and pursue pleasure to conclude the further point (indicated by *kai*, 'also') that they are

---

[17] Reading a) mentions all options of opposing the bad, whereas b) only has the new ones not yet considered by Eudoxus. Reading b) runs perhaps more smoothly, as a) must supply 'good' as part of the subject from before the 'for'-clause.

opposites, whereas Eudoxus seeks to derive the goodness of pleasure from the badness of pain.

Interestingly, the *Nicomachean Ethics* contains a parallel dialectic in the other discussion of pleasure in Book VII. At EN VII.13.1153b1–7 Aristotle puts forward his own version of the argument from opposites to argue that pleasure is good, but not *the* good – which is probably why he does not mention the hedonist Eudoxus as his inspiration. He also defends it against an objection similar to the one just discussed. Aristotle attributes the Book VII objection to Speusippus (407–339 BC), Plato's nephew and first head of the Academy after Plato's death in 427 BC. Some interpreters take the two passages to be slightly differing accounts of the same dialectical bout and hence seek to illuminate the present passage by infusing it with Speusippus' views on pleasure (most notably Gauthier and Jolif 1958, 823–4). But we should be careful, because a) the Book VII argument establishes a different conclusion (pleasure is a good vs pleasure is the good), and b) Warren 2009 rightly stresses the dialectical character not only of Aristotle's discussions, but also of Speusippus' objection. So, bringing the two arguments together requires us to take account of the context in which they are presented.[18]

X.3

1173a13–15 Again, it does not follow ... nor is happiness.

In his preface to the examination of pleasure in X.1, Aristotle outlines only the extreme positions in the battle over pleasure: 'some say pleasure is the good, while others, on the contrary, say it is plain bad' (1172a27–8). Subsequently, he examines one of them in X.2, Eudoxus' hedonism. Now we would expect him to assess the merit of anti-hedonism, the claim that pleasure is plain bad. But he does not do so. Instead, he addresses arguments designed to show pleasure is not good (arguments which, when successful, would refute hedonism). One influential editorial tradition of subdividing books into chapters, followed in anglophone translations and commentaries, marks a new chapter here (X.3), to emphasise Aristotle's shift in topic, however slight. Another tradition, prevalent on the European continent, takes its cue from the last line of X.1 – 'let us go on to what people have

---

[18] For a careful study of the type of argument, and its application to pleasure in the context of Plato's Academy, see Cheng, in press.

said about pleasure' – a project that continues until 1174a12 (the end of X.3 in my translation).

In any case, Aristotle continues to present the arguments against pleasure in a very curtailed way. He apparently expects his audience to be familiar with the reasoning for and against pleasure. Nevertheless, the bare bones of the thought presented in this lemma shine through well enough: i) if X is a good, then X is a quality; ii) pleasure is not a quality; therefore iii) pleasure is not a good. He refutes the argument by attacking premise i). While virtue is a good and belongs in the category of quality (I.6.1096a25), the exercise of virtue surpasses the mere having of it in goodness (I.4.1095b30–1096a2; cf. I.8.1098a30–3) – but the exercise is not a quality. According to Aristotle, happiness, the highest good, also does not belong to the category of quality, since happiness is most of all an activity (*energeia*, I.7.1098a16).[19]

Whether his counter would convince those who put forward the argument originally does not seem to be central to Aristotle. He seems to object to i) for two reasons. First, he maintains that 'good' is said in as many ways as 'being'. So, just as the account of X's being depends on the category of being to which it belongs (substance, quality, quantity, etc.), so also X's goodness depends on the category to which X belongs. The virtues, for example, exemplify goodness in the category of quality, whereas the right measure does so in the category of quantity (I.6.1096a23–7).[20] So, premise i) would seem to be plainly wrong. Second, and more pertinent to our context, the i)–ii)–iii) argument supports neutralism, the thesis that pleasure has no value at all. But Aristotle seems committed to rejecting neutralism, because he regards the pleasures added to other goods as genuine goods in themselves (see commentary on 1172b23–35). At first sight, the argument's conclusion – pleasure is not a good – appears compatible with pleasure's being neutral or bad. However, if X's being a good requires X to be a quality, then, presumably, X's being bad *also* requires X to be a quality. But if pleasure does not belong to the category of quality, as ii) stipulates, pleasure could not have any value, positive or negative. Thus, by undermining premise i), which implies that only qualities have value, Aristotle averts the danger of neutralism.

---

[19] I leave aside the complication whether several goods constitute happiness, or only one (on which, see Introduction §§1.3 and 3.2). All sides agree that the central component of happiness is an activity.

[20] See *Topics* I.9.103b20–104a3 for a list of the ten categories and the homonymy of being.

1173a15–23 But they say that what is good ... while others are mixed.

Another anonymous and curtailed argument, this time focusing on the alleged nature of what is good. The Greek *to agathon* is usually rendered as 'the good', but because of the argument's origin – discussed below – 'what is good' seems more apposite. We can reconstruct the reasoning as follows:

i)   what is good is determinate;
ii) what admits of the more and less is not determinate;
iii) pleasure admits of the more and less; therefore
iv) pleasure is not good.

Where does the argument originate, and why should we, or anyone, believe its premises? In the analysis of virtue in II.6 Aristotle cites approvingly the Pythagorean belief that bad belongs to the unlimited and good to the limited (*peperasmenou*, 1106b29–30). He does so to support his view, a corollary from his account of virtue, that there is often only one way of 'getting it right', whereas there are infinitely many ways of getting it wrong. Thus, the good and correct action and feeling would be limited, whereas bad responses are unlimited. While falling short of defending i), the thought nevertheless provides some support for it. We can find a fuller defence (though a less plausible one) if we turn to Plato's reworking of the Pythagorean material in the *Philebus*. With a view to examining the goodness of pleasure, the dialogue establishes a fourfold ontology of all things, consisting of limit (*peras*) and unlimited (*apeiron*), as well as the entities resulting from imposing limit on what is unlimited, and the cause of such mixtures (23c–27c). Next, all genuine mixtures are good. This thesis gains plausibility when we consider that good mixtures consist of unlimited material that has been limited by the *right* limit, such as music, the seasons, health, beauty, strength, and good states in the soul: having the right measure or right proportion makes something a proper entity (26a–b). Now, if we regard the right limit as equivalent to, or at least entailing, determinateness, then the *Philebus* supports i*) what is determinate is good – the converse of i) (of which Aristotle approves at IX.9.1170a20–1). Although i*) does not yield i), we can nevertheless appreciate the close connection between the determinate and goodness at which i) points. Moreover, if not having a limit entails not being determinate, the dialogue supports ii), as admitting of the more and less puts an entity in the class of unlimited things (24a–b). Finally, the interlocutors place pleasure in the class of unlimited things because it admits the more and less (27–28a). Thus, we can find premises i) to iii), or relevantly similar theses, supported in the *Philebus*.

Aristotle leaves the reasons given in the *Philebus* to one side and considers on his own whether the more and less applies to pleasure. He distinguishes two ways the argument for iii) could go: pleasure admits of the more and less because a) one thing can be enjoyed more or less (a17–22), or because b) some pleasures are better or more pleasurable than others (a22–3) – in which case pleasure itself has no firm limit or determination. (In the next lemma, he also objects to premise ii.)

We may represent the first interpretation of premise iii) as a supplementary argument for iii):

iii–a) a person can have more or less pleasure, and
iii–b) if a person can have more or less pleasure, then pleasure admits of the more and less.

The underlying thought seems very plausible. Just as I can read for a longer or shorter time, so I can enjoy the book more or less. Neither my reading nor my enjoyment of reading seem to have an inherent limit: they do not come with the 'right amount'. But if enjoying anything whatever does not have a limit, then pleasure itself does not seem to have a limit. Despite its intuitive appeal, the interpretation leads to absurd consequences. Barring special pleading, iii–b) seems to rest on a more general principle, iii–b*) if a person can have more or less X, then X admits of the more and less. But, Aristotle objects, iii–b*) cannot be correct, for a person can have more or less justice, i.e. she can be and/or act more or less justly. If iii–b*) were correct, justice would admit of the more and less. Together with premises i) and ii), we would have to conclude that justice is not good – an absurd consequence which strongly tells against iii–b*). But could we not hold on to iii–b*), and hence to iii–b), in the following way? The assailant of pleasure could admit to their *speaking* about having more or less virtue (*enargôs phasi*, 1173a19), while restricting virtue and virtuous actions to certain perfections that do not admit of the more and less. Even if an action does not quite measure up to perfection, they, together with everyone else, may *call* it virtuous. (Aristotle notes the difficulties of measuring a person and their actions, II.9.1109b16–20.) This move, however, creates an opening for the defendants of pleasure. They could follow suit by stipulating that only perfect enjoyment counts as pleasure; all similar affections that fall short of the perfection we only *call* 'pleasure'. So, in this case, perfect pleasure would be something determinate and good – just like perfect justice or virtue.

The second interpretation of premise iii) proves difficult, because Aristotle does not expand on the original argument. What does 'if they judge by the pleasures' mean (1173a23)? The plural (*hêdonais*) does not seem to highlight the several instances of pleasure (mine, yours…), but to point to a criterion by which we can differentiate between pleasures. Pertinent to the present context, one might reconstruct the thought as follows:

iii–c)   some pleasures are pleasures more than other pleasures;
iii–d)   if some pleasures are pleasures more than other pleasures, then pleasure admits of the more and less.

But why should we believe iii–c)? Aristotle may allude again to Plato's *Philebus* and *Republic*, which distinguish between pure and impure pleasures. Impure pleasures are necessarily mixed with pain, whereas pure pleasures always remain unmixed. Both dialogues consider the pure pleasure superior and more of a pleasure, and perhaps rightly so: if a certain type of pleasure necessarily includes its opposite, pain, then this type of pleasure may seem further from instantiating the essence of pleasure than pure pleasures.[21] So, different types of pleasure would be pleasure more or less – which might justify applying 'more and less' to pleasure. However, Aristotle complains, iii–c) appears convincing only if presented without the supporting background, i.e. only if the objectors suppress their own reasons for differentiating between pleasures, since the pure pleasures (many pleasures of seeing, hearing, smelling, or learning) turn out to have measure, i.e. they belong to the class of measured and good things (*Philebus* 52c1–d2). Only impure pleasures belong to the unlimited, not least because of their intensity (*sphodrais hêdonais*, 52c–3), intensity being itself a marker of the more and less (24c1). Now, if the opponents of pleasure had stated the reason for claiming pleasure to be more or less, they could not have made their argument: first, because the unlimited pleasures are not unlimited insofar as they are pleasures, but insofar as they are mixed with their opposite, pain; and second, because their approach also posits pure and unmixed pleasures, pleasures that are good – contrary to iv).

1173a23–28 And what prevents … pleasure is of this sort.

In this lemma, Aristotle presents his concluding thoughts on the following argument against pleasure:

i)   what is good is determinate;
ii)   what admits of the more and less is not determinate;

---

[21] In the *Republic* 586b7–8, Plato calls mixed pleasure 'images and shadow-paintings of true pleasure', whereas the *Philebus* classifies them as real, but false pleasures (45a–47a).

iii) pleasure admits of the more and less; therefore
iv) pleasure is not good.

Aristotle sympathises with premise i), but objects to iii), partly on dialectical grounds (see commentary on previous lemma). Now he takes issue with the premise ii). Rejecting ii) enables him to maintain that goods are determinate (= i) while allowing for varying degrees of those goods. For example, people are just or moderate more or less, and they act justly or moderately more or less (1173a17–22), and are, consequently, more or less happy (III.9.1117b9–11). The same with pleasure: while it does admit of the more and less, it need not, for this reason, lose its goodness. So, Aristotle sets out to show that some goods that people have or instantiate may admit of the more and less – without, thereby, becoming indeterminate.

To deny the link, prominent in the *Philebus*, between indeterminateness and the more and less, Aristotle cites health as a counter-example: health 'consists in a blending of hot and cold elements in due proportion, in relation either to one another within the body or to the surrounding' (*Physics* VII.3.246b4–6; cf. *De Anima* I.4; cf. Plato's *Philebus* 25e7–8). But despite the notion of 'due proportion' in its definition, health allows for variation between people, and even within one and the same person. For some people, a temperature of 37 degrees Celsius indicates a slight fever, whereas for others that temperature is normal. And vigorous exercise may raise an athlete's temperature without making her ill. So, although hot and cold elements stand in due proportion to each other, the measure defined by their proportion admits of the more and less. Thus, the instances of health, a determinate good, will come with slight variations and will therefore admit of the more and less – without jeopardising its status as goods. But if the example of health renders premise ii) false, then Aristotle can retain the connection between determinateness and goodness, even if the more and less applies to instantiations of those goods, such as happiness, virtue, and pleasure.

> *1173a28–31 Next, supposing that ... pleasure to be a movement and coming to be.*

Now we come to the most prominent argument against pleasure, the so-called kinesis or genesis argument (in contrast to the previous lemmata, Aristotle here states the *argument*, but leaves the conclusion to be supplied). We can gage the argument's importance by the sheer space allocated to it. Following its exposition, Aristotle spends almost a whole Bekker page developing his own responses to it (up to 1173b20). He returns to the connection between pleasure and movement or coming to be at the beginning of X.4 for another one-and-a-half Bekker pages. The parallel discussion of the argument in Book VII also spans a whole Bekker page. His interest in the argument, and its prominence, stems from Plato: several of his dialogues contain versions of it, most notably the *Philebus* and the *Republic*.

The argument runs as follows:

i) what is good is complete/perfect/final (*teleios*);
ii) movements and comings to be are not complete/perfect/final;
iii) pleasure is a movement or coming to be; therefore
iv) pleasure is not good.[22]

The argument starts from a plausible assumption about the nature of what is good. In the first chapters of the *Nicomachean Ethics*, motivating the enquiry into the highest good, Aristotle regards a good and an end (*telos*) almost as equivalent: every genuine end is good, and goods are ends (encompassing higher and lower ends). So, the property of being an end (*teleios*) will attach to the property of being good.

What does 'good' mean here? We can elucidate the first premise (as well as the second and third) by turning to its source, Plato's *Philebus*:

> Socrates: But that for the sake of which what comes to be for the sake of something comes to be in each case, ought to be put into the class of the things good in themselves (*en tê(i) tou agathou moira(i)*), while that which comes to be for the sake of something else belongs in another class, my friend.
> (*Philebus* 54c9–11, tr. Frede)

So, the dialogue asks about the status of pleasure as a good in itself.[23] This works well with the explanation given, that the hallmark of being a good in itself is not being for the sake of something else. Despite using a different term, Aristotle's first premise corresponds to Plato's point, because Aristotle, too, thinks being *teleios* points to being a good in itself (I.7.1097a24–34).

---

[22] An alternative interpretation translates 'supposing that *the* good is complete …'. I render the Greek *to agathon* as 'what is good' (as in 1173a16) because of the dialectical interchange with Plato (see below).

[23] Albeit difficult to interpret, most scholars agree that the argument does not merely show that pleasure is not *the* good (*pace* Delcomminette 2006, 493–4), but that pleasure is not intrinsically good (Carone 2005, 108), or unqualifiedly good (Frede 1993, lv), or a perfect end (Evans 2008, 134–42). Evans points out that the same phrase, *moira tou agathou*, appears also in 20d1–10, where it, being complete and sufficient, contains all and only things that are worth pursuing as ends in themselves – and these things would be good in themselves.

Premises ii) and iii) use two different words to describe the nature of pleasure: movement (*kinêsis*) and coming to be (*genesis*). However, the focus (here) lies on pleasure as *genesis*. Aristotle, as his objections to Plato's argument will show (in the next three lemmata), understands *genesis* literally as bringing something into existence. Plato's use of the same term encompasses a much wider range. Bringing things into existence, such as shipbuilding, is but one special case of a *genesis* (54a5–b5). Creating something has all the characteristics of a process, such as taking time, etc., and would, therefore, count as a *genesis* or *kinêsis* for Aristotle. For Plato, however, the key feature of a *genesis* is its subordination to some other, and better, good. In Plato's words, a *genesis* is for the sake of something else, a relation that must be understood broadly so as to include the pair 'manly lovers' and the objects of their love, 'fine and good youths' (53d9–10). Perhaps Aristotle passes over the niceties of the original argument because the pleasures Plato cites in the coda to his argument *do* fall under the special case of coming to be:

> Socrates: But this same person [sc. the persons who indicated that there is always only generation of pleasure] will also laugh at those who find their fulfilment in processes of generation (*genesis*).
> Protarchus: How so, and what sort of people are you alluding to?
> Socrates: I am talking of those who cure their hunger and thirst or anything else that is cured by processes of generation (*genesis*). They take delight in generation (*genesis*) as a pleasure and proclaim that they would not want to live if they were not subject to hunger and thirst and if they could not experience all the other things one might want to mention in connection with such conditions.
> Protarchus: That is very like them.
>
> (*Philebus* 54e1–55a1, tr. Frede)

The quotation brings home the intuitive appeal of Plato's argument. If pleasure is a process whose main goal consists in remedying some defect, then we will have to welcome the defect in order to have pleasure as remedy. But, so Plato, it would seem much better not to suffer the defect in the first place: if we value the good state as something good in itself, then pleasure derives its value from some other good. Therefore, we should not put these two goods in the same class: pleasure is inferior to goods in themselves.

Plato's cases also illustrate the rationale for regarding pleasure as a process of coming to be, i.e. a movement. The obvious cases of eating and drinking, both processes, suggest as much. Interestingly, Aristotle himself proposes to define pleasure as 'a kind of movement of the soul a settling back into one's proper nature, both massive and perceived' in the *Rhetoric* (1369b33–5). Here, however, over the next few lemmata, he firmly opposes Plato's conception of pleasure.[24] He refutes premise iii) by marshalling three arguments against pleasure as coming to be, and one against pleasure as movement. He reserves the bulk of the discussion of premise ii) and the explanation why movements are incomplete and why pleasure is not a movement for X.4.

1173a31–b4 But they do not … mean taking pleasure), quickly.

Plato defines pleasure as *genesis* (coming to be) in his dialogues *Philebus* and *Republic*. He proffers arguments to show why pleasure falls short of being a good in itself, due to its nature as *genesis* (see previous lemma). However, Plato also regards 'the coming to be of either the pleasant or the painful in the soul as a sort of motion (*kinêsis tis*)' (*Republic* 583e9–10, tr. Grube/Reeve), thus associating pleasure with motion or movement (*kinêsis*). Aristotle reconstructs Plato's argument with both terms. In this lemma he focuses on pleasure as movement, before turning to pleasure as coming to be in the next lemmata.

Aristotle's riposte relies on the connection between movement and time. He undermines Plato's understanding of pleasure by arguing that a) if X is a movement, then X can happen quickly or slowly, but b) pleasure does not happen quickly or slowly. He does not argue for the first point, but simply takes it for granted. In his theoretical works, Aristotle applies the word *kinêsis* to all processes of change except coming to be and passing-away, i.e. to changes in quantity, quality, location, positing locomotion as the most basic change underlying all the other kinds of change (*Physics* VIII.7). He defines movement (*kinêsis*) as 'the fulfilment of what is potentially, insofar as it is potential, – e.g. the fulfilment of what is alterable, insofar as it is alterable, is alteration' (*Physics* III.1.201a10–11). But fulfilling the potential to change takes time and can happen slower or faster (cf. *Physics* VI.2.233b20–1). Not all movements, however, can happen faster or slower compared with themselves, insofar as they can speed up or slow down. Most prominently, the speed of the sphere of the stars, its circular motion, is fixed. We can, nevertheless, compare their speed with other movements – in relation to which the movement of the stars can be quick or slow.

---

[24] See Dow 2011 for a helpful discussion of the question whether Aristotle's view in the *Rhetoric* clashes with his views in the *Ethics*.

To establish the key premise, b), Aristotle understands 'pleasure' (*hêdonê*) as 'enjoying' or 'being pleased' (*hêdesthai*), likening it to being angry. We distinguish between getting angry and being angry: being angry implies, usually, having got angry, but getting angry does not entail, nor does it always lead to, being angry. So, we can regard getting angry as a movement – without, thereby, regarding anger (understood as being angry) as a movement: anger and becoming angry are two different things. The same move, Aristotle implies, applies to pleasure. Allowing that we can become pleased quickly does not entail that 'quickly' applies to pleasure (understood as being pleased or taking pleasure),[25] either in itself or in relation to something else. From here he concludes that we cannot characterise pleasure as quick or slow – which entails that pleasure is not a movement.

The reasoning has some intuitive appeal, but fails to argue, positively, that 'quick' and 'slow' do not apply to pleasure. But why would the pair not apply to pleasure or anger? Consider 'her anger passed quickly'; or 'his joy faded more quickly than dawn broke'. Both snippets seem well-formed and do not seem odd or stilted, and both seem to attribute 'quick' to anger and pleasure – despite Aristotle's opposition. However, he could explain the examples away by insisting that both describe the process of an emotion's fading. Just like getting angry, so ceasing to be angry is a process – which does not imply that anger (being angry) is a process.

1173b4–13 Next, how could <pleasure> be ... he is in pain.

Aristotle now examines the key premise of Plato's chief argument against the goodness of pleasure in its most prevalent formulation. If pleasure is a process of coming to be (*genesis*), Plato maintains, then pleasure is not good in itself (see 1173a28–31, with commentary for details). While Aristotle clearly objects to Plato's argument, the extent of his criticism is less clear, for the opening sentence can be rendered a) 'Next, how could <pleasure> be a coming to be?', or b) 'In what way is <pleasure> a coming to be?' The first reading would set up a wholesale rejection of Plato's view of pleasure, whereas the second would instead point to problems and ask for clarification. Unfortunately, the text does not tell one way or the other;

---

[25] Note, however, that Aristotle does not usually take the aorist of being angry (*orgisthênai*) or being pleased (*hêsthênai*, both at II.6.1106b18–20) to imply a process rather than the result of that process, as he does here at 1173a34 and b1.

getting *any* argument out of the text already proves a formidable task. The following representation should, therefore, be used cautiously:

i) Pleasure is a process of coming to be. (Plato's thesis)
ii) Coming to be is a process of X's coming to be from Y, and
iii) if X comes to be from Y, then X dissolves into Y. ('For it does not seem to be the case that anything comes to be from just anything, but rather that what a thing comes to be from is that into which it is dissolved.' 1173b5–6)
iv) If pleasure is a process of coming to be of X, then pain is the destruction of X. ('Pain is the destruction of that of which pleasure is the coming to be.' 1173b6–7)
v) In regard to pleasure and pain, the reference point, X, is the natural state. ('Pain is the lack of what is in accordance with nature, whereas pleasure is its replenishment.' 1173b7–8)
vi) The natural state is a state of the body. (Unstated premise.)
vii) Hence, pleasure and pain are bodily, i.e. they take place in the body. ('These affections are bodily.' 1173b8–9) (From i to vi.)
viii) If pleasure takes place in B, then B takes the pleasure, i.e. B enjoys. ('If, then, pleasure is a replenishment of what is in accordance with nature, that in which the replenishment takes place would also take the pleasure.')
ix) Hence, the body takes pleasure ('namely the body.' 1173b9–11)
x) 'The body is not thought to <take the pleasure>.' (1173b11)
xi) 'Therefore the replenishment is not pleasure.' (1173b11)

While the conclusion looks as if it favours reading a) – providing a reductio of i) – it does not preclude reading b). Aristotle may question how to understand the 'is' in premise i). If Plato *identifies* pleasure with a process of coming to be, then, as Aristotle's train of thought shows, we run into difficulties. If, however, it describes looser connection, then Plato may have a point, for Aristotle agrees 'when a replenishment occurs, a person takes pleasure' (1173b12) – in which case the replenishment may cause the pleasure, but is not identical to it. In any case, the argument dislodges a certain identity-view of pleasure and a process of coming to be, as characterised by i), v), and vii).

Aristotle does not argue for premises ii) and iii), but seems to rely on his theoretical works (and expects his audience to do likewise). In *Physics* I.7 he posits three principles to account for change: subject, form, and privation. The change's start and end-point oppose each other as contraries. A change, then, is the process that takes place to bring the subject from not having a certain form (roughly: quality) to having it. For example, I start out as an unmusical person (i.e. the privation of being musical applies to me) and become proficient in music through practising an instrument. But – and this is important for the present argument – if I forget my music lessons, I will lose my proficiency in music again. By losing the newly gained quality, the subject will revert to its previous condition. Premises ii) and iii) thus introduce a framework for understanding processes.

The theoretical background readily applies to pleasure and pain on Plato's assumption that pleasure is a process. The proponents of the *genesis* theory of pleasure identify pain with the depletion of some natural state, and pleasure with its replenishment, thus opposing pleasure and pain as the coming to be and destruction *of* the same X, the natural state. Again, Aristotle seems to sum up views found in Plato's dialogues. The *Republic*, points to the natural state because 'being filled with what is by nature appropriate is pleasant' (585d11). More explicitly, the *Philebus* provisionally maintains '[w]hen the natural combination of limit and unlimitedness that forms a live organism [i.e. its good order] … is destroyed, this destruction is pain, while the return towards its own nature, this general restoration, is pleasure.' (32a8–b4, tr. Frede). Both texts suggest that pain is the destruction of the natural and harmonious state, as iv) claims.[26]

The dénouement centres on the subject of pleasure – which the *genesis* theorists allegedly get wrong. Aristotle tacitly takes the natural state that helps define pleasure and pain to be a state of the body. While the passages quoted from Plato do not need to be read this way, at least the examples with which the *Philebus* motivates its view of pleasure and pain support Aristotle's reading. Socrates speaks of thirst as 'a destruction and pain, while the process that fills what is dried out with liquid is pleasure', and adds that the 'unnatural separation and dissolution, the affection caused by heat, is pain, while the natural restoration of cooling down is pleasure' and that 'the unnatural coagulation of the fluids in an animal through freezing is pain, while the natural process of their dissolution or redistribution is pleasure' (31e10–32a8, tr. Frede). All the examples seem to concern bodily phenomena, because the relevant states belong to the body. But if pleasure *is* the restoration of a bodily state, then pleasure would also be a bodily affection (premises vi and vii).

[26] We should not read the text at 1173b12–13 ('when he is being cut') as a reference to a surgical procedure, as this albeit initially painful process would aim at restoring the natural state. The cutting here seems to be simply an example of bodily harm. Cf. *Timaeus* 65b2–3.

Now, premise viii) might seem to express an uncharitable take on Plato's account of pleasure, for it would be wrong to suppose that *a*'s φ-ing in B entails that B φs. For example, Socrates' death takes place in prison, but it does not follow that the prison dies. A defender of the genesis theory might emphasise the distinction between pleasure (*hêdonê*) and enjoyment (*hêdesthai*). Identifying the restoration of a bodily state with pleasure does not entail that enjoyment itself is a bodily process. The former may give rise to the latter – without being identical to it. So, if *enjoyment* is the phenomenon that we wish to explain, then Aristotle's criticism does not seem to apply. But the rejoinder threatens to undermine the genesis theory, in two ways. First, a process of coming to be requires only three principles: the subject, the form, and the privation. But now the *genesis* theorist introduces a further essential entity: someone who takes pleasure. How does the person fit into the scheme? Second, the examples in the *Philebus* illustrate pleasure as a restorative process. If we distinguish between pleasure and enjoyment, they do nothing to support the claim that *enjoyment* is a process of replenishment. So, unless the *genesis* theorists expand on their theory, Aristotle seems justified in assuming that the restoration theory of pleasure purports to explain the whole phenomenon of pleasure – not just a part of it – which justifies premise viii). But in this case, pleasure would not only take place *in* the body, but also be *of* the body. The body would be the subject of pleasure, i.e. the entity that has the pleasure – which strikes us as wrong (ix and x).

The conclusion 'the replenishment is not pleasure' affords a weaker reading and a stronger reading. According to the latter, Aristotle would, via *modus tollens*, reject premise i). This reading, however, requires the other premises to be true – a strong assumption. The weaker reading would merely find some fault with the genesis view. It would leave open whether to reject (or refine) premises vi) to viii), or to reject the strong identity statement between pleasure and a process of coming to be, perhaps by distinguishing between enjoyment and pleasure (as suggested at 1173b12–13). Either way, it might strike us as odd that Aristotle writes as if the *genesis* theorists were unaware of this point. First, Plato explicitly contrasts bodily pleasures with restorations of the soul at *Republic* 585b–e. Second, Plato requires even bodily pleasures to involve some motion or agitation of the soul (*Republic* 583e9–10, quoted in previous lemma; cf. 584c4–7). He goes to great lengths in the *Philebus* to make a similar point. Mere bodily changes will not necessarily result in pleasure and pain; only changes of sufficient size produce (*apergazontai*) pleasure and pain (*Philebus* 43b7–9). The causal language – bodily restorative processes produce (*poiousi*,

43c4–6) pleasure – speaks against strictly identifying pleasure with bodily restorations. So, if Plato as the main exponent of the *genesis* theory agrees with Aristotle, what does the criticism amount to? Regardless of reading a) or b) above, Aristotle makes clear that we cannot uphold the strict identity thesis between bodily restorations and pleasure. The argument points towards a distinction between enjoyment and pleasure, where the former is a function of the soul. But in order to cash in on the distinction, the *genesis* theorist needs to explain how enjoyment can be a restorative process in the soul – a task that Plato hardly tackles explicitly in his dialogues.

1173b13–20 And this view ... a replenishment could occur.

Aristotle has put forward a strong reason against the *genesis* theory of pleasure. Taken at face value, the theory seems to imply that pleasure (and pain) belong to the body, but we do not regard the body as the subject of pleasure (see previous lemma for details). In this lemma, he diagnoses the source of trouble for the genesis theory. Charitably interpreted, the theory works well for such bodily pleasures as eating and drinking: being hungry or thirsty usually *is* painful, and eating or drinking tend to be pleasant only if preceded by some kind of lack, signalled by hunger or thirst. While Aristotle objects to identifying pleasure and pain with the restoration and dissolution of a natural state, he nevertheless grants a looser connection: whenever we experience the dissolution of a natural state, we experience pain, and whenever we experience its restoration, we experience pleasure (cf. 1173b11–13). So, for the prime examples of the so-called bodily pleasures, associating pleasure with restoration seems plausible (1173b14–15).

The *genesis* model, however, does not extend beyond the special cases from which it was developed. Aristotle now points towards a set of counter-examples. The pleasures of learning, smelling, of many sounds and sights, and memories and hopes come without pain, i.e. no pain precedes them. These pleasures, he argues, do not fall under the genesis theory, for a) the theory posits a strict connection between a lack and pain (the former either constitutes or causes the pain). So, b) the absence of pain would entail the absence of a lack. But c) without lack, there can be no restorative process (*genesis*), and hence no pleasure. Therefore, the genesis model does not apply to the set of pleasures mentioned. The genesis model applies only to a subset of pleasures, but should not be taken for a general account of pleasure.

The defendant of the genesis theory can push back – not by denying the examples, but by rejecting a) and b). In the *Republic,* Plato introduces painless pleasures: the pleasures of smell neither require an antecedent pain (an equivalent of hunger of thirst) nor leave any pain behind when they stop (585b5–8). In the *Philebus*, Plato takes a further step against a) and b). He postulates an unperceived lack that precedes the painless pleasures. These painless or pure pleasures are '[t]hose related to colours we call beautiful (*kala*), for instance, or to shapes, most pleasures of smell, and those of hearing, and generally anywhere the deprivation is imperceptible and without pain and which supply perceptible replenishments which are pleasant' (*Philebus* 51b3–7, tr. Gosling, slightly altered). Since all these pleasures restore an unperceived lack, they will not involve any pain or desire. So, 'there is no inevitable pain mixed with them' (speaking of the pleasures of smelling, 51e2), nor is there any pain 'that could be called inherent by nature' (speaking of the pleasures of learning, 51a8). So, Aristotle's examples do not seem to undermine the genesis theory, but merely provoke clarification.

In light of Plato's resources, does Aristotle attack a straw man? Not necessarily – for two reasons. First, he may criticise the hypothetical nature of Plato's account. Roughly, Plato reasons i) pleasure is unified, i.e. the same definition applies to all pleasures; ii) food-related pleasures are or are caused by replenishments of a lack; therefore iii) painless pleasures, too, are caused by replenishments of a lack. Hence, iv) Plato must postulate an unperceived lack. Now, Aristotle can see what sort of lack food-related pleasures presuppose: the lack of nutriments or moisture. But what lack do the pure pleasures of smell or sight presuppose? Which natural state is being restored when one enjoys certain smells? It is surprisingly hard to avoid an ad hoc answer and to develop a reasonable account.[27] Second, the simple genesis theory has morphed into the theory that *perceived* processes of destruction and restoration are or cause pain and pleasure. If I am to experience pleasure, I must be aware of the restorative process. But this blurs the difference between [G], pleasure is the perceived restoration of a natural state, and [P], pleasure is the perception of the restoration of a natural state. While [G] keeps the fundamentals of the genesis theory, [P] counts, instead, as a perceptual theory of pleasure. Plato seems to offer no reason for preferring [G] to [P] other than the simple cases of eating and drinking in which perception does not figure prominently.

> *1173b20–25 And to those who bring ... the eye-diseased also are so.*

Discussing what people have said about pleasure – the project begins at 1172a19 – Aristotle has so far considered theories, or theoretically informed views, about pleasure. They tend to assign a value to pleasure based on

---

[27] As Taylor 2008b shows.

theoretical assumptions (and arguments) about the nature of pleasure and goodness. Changing tack in the final stretch of discussing the *endoxa* (i.e. well-reputed positions or arguments), Aristotle leaves behind the 'philosophical' opinions about pleasure and turns to a different kind of opinion that pronounces directly on the value of pleasure – without theoretical underpinning.

The first of these 'arguments' focuses on pleasures that bring reproach. We can garner the point by recalling a passage from Plato's *Gorgias* to which Aristotle probably alludes. Callicles posits pleasure as the good. Living pleasantly, for him, means living well. Socrates then infers that a) a life spent in pleasantly scratching one's itches would be happy, and, similarly b) the life of a catamite[28] would count as happy as long as it is pleasant. Callicles concedes a), but balks at b), thereby giving up the identity between the pleasant and the good (494c–495a). Some pleasures, e.g. the catamite's, are not good. So, the existence of disgraceful pleasures undermines both hedonism (pleasure is the good) and the weaker thesis that all pleasures are good. As before, Aristotle continues to devise strategies of dealing with the objection to pleasure – without, however, committing to any of them. Of the three strategies – marked off by an 'or', *ê* in Greek, at b25 and b28 – the first two allow pleasure to remain good (this lemma and the next), whereas the third gives up that view.

As a first response to the argument from bad pleasures one could deny that the things enjoyed are pleasant (*hêdea*). How does this bear on the existence of bad pleasures (*hêdonai*)? Socrates' argument in the *Gorgias* draws its strength from extending pleasure beyond a mere feeling that all pleasures may share. Feeling in a certain way does not on its own give rise to praise or blame: there would be no difference between good and bad pleasures. Instead, as examples a) and b) show, pleasure encompasses also that which gives rises to them: scratching an itch, or sex. But if pleasure comprises both an 'internal' and an 'external' element (the feeling and its cause), Aristotle has an opening for a rejoinder. Taking the internal element for granted, he questions whether the external element of pleasure is really pleasant. If scratching an itch does not count as pleasant, this casts doubt on the status of the resulting experience which encompasses both the scratching and the enjoyment.

To substantiate his move, Aristotle compares the experience of pleasure with the experience of sweetness – which likewise comprises an internal and an external element. Just as we cannot automatically infer

---

[28] A 'boy-toy', usually the young and passive partner in homosexual relationships between men.

from 'x tastes sweet to subject S' that x is in fact sweet, so we cannot infer from 'x is pleasant to S' that x is in fact pleasant, for if S perceives the sweetness under conditions that deviate sufficiently from the norm, then her judgement 'x is sweet' must be relativised to those in a similar condition, for only then will their senses reliably produce a similar experience. Later, Aristotle suggests the norm governing the use of the predicate 'sweet' is the healthy and fully developed person. Only when x tastes sweet to this sort of person can we truly say, without qualification, that x is sweet (cf. 1176a10–15). Analogously, he posits an ethical equivalent of the healthy person who functions as the norm for pleasure (more at 1176a15–29). If 'pleasures' that bring reproach will not be pleasant to that sort of person, we can deny their status as pleasures, just as we would discount certain 'sweets' if they taste sweet only to patients who suffer from a certain illness. But as long as we can differentiate between 'normal' and 'sick' pleasures, Aristotle's strategy may provide Callicles with reasons to push back against Socrates. Thus, Callicles could explain why we call certain pleasures 'bad' without admitting that pleasure itself is bad.[29]

1173b25–28 Or one could ... eat anything whatever.

The existence of bad pleasures undermines both hedonism and the claim that all pleasures are good. But why do some pleasures count as bad? Unless we reject the feeling itself of pleasure as bad, we need to consider other factors also, such as the occasion, the motive, the source (or what gives rise to pleasure). Doing so allows for a finer-grained approach that will make some pains good and some pleasures bad, such as rightful anger at an underserved provocation, or the pleasure of having succeeded in seducing a friend's spouse.

The previous response sought a) to integrate what gives rise to pleasure into the experience called 'pleasure', and b) to dismiss bad pleasures as based on, and incorporating, what is not really pleasant. The present proposal takes a different route. Instead of integrating pleasure and its source, it separates them. Properly speaking, pleasure, so the thought goes, consists only in the feeling of enjoyment. So, all the other factors are, strictly speaking, irrelevant to assessing the value of the pleasure: they do not have

---

[29] There is, of course, a question as to what extent this move is compatible with Callicles' hedonism. Aristotle need not worry about the difficulties, because he lays out how one can defend the thesis that all pleasure is good, not that pleasure is *the* good.

the power to 'make' any pleasure itself bad. To support the move, we can cite other goods that behave similarly, such as wealth and health. The examples indicate the separability of the good in question from its source. Just as the ways of acquiring or maintaining health or wealth are external to and separable from health or wealth, so too is the source of pleasure separable. Just as the money collected from urine taxes does not stink, so the pleasure from shameful sources is not itself shameful.

But distinguishing between pleasure itself and its source forms only half the answer. The other half consists in explaining why the so-called bad pleasures are *called* 'bad' – without admitting pleasure itself to be bad. Aristotle might suggest an interesting two-tier strategy. First, since one cannot get any of the goods in question without its source, the source, though not part of the relevant good, must be chosen as well. How, and by what means, I acquire a good belongs to the 'package' of my choice. If I can attain pleasure in a particular situation only from a bad source, the package ceases to be good without qualification, and may even be called 'bad'. But since I would be choosing the package only because of the pleasure, people call the pleasure 'bad', even if it itself remains good.

But does this account not contain the seed of its own destruction? Consider an objection sometimes levelled at hedonists. If all pleasure is good, then the pleasure a sadist enjoys from torturing his unconsenting victim is good. But surely there is nothing good in this situation! Hence not all pleasure is good. Moving on to the second level, Aristotle hints at a response: 'being rich is choice-worthy, but not for someone who would have to betray others, and being healthy, but not for someone who would have to eat anything whatever' (1173b27–8).[30] If we distinguish between 'good' and 'good for' we can explain why the sadist does not get any good from torturing, despite his enjoyment. While wealth and health are choice-worthy, they are not choice-worthy *for* those who perform certain actions to attain the relevant good. Thus, the focus may shift from the source to the sort of people who would choose bad sources to attain a good. For *them* the relevant goods are not choice-worthy, because what is good for a certain person depends on their constitution or circumstances more generally: medicine benefits only the ill; instruction benefits only the

---

[30] Most translators take the datives in Greek (*prodonti*, b9; *phagonti*, a10) to be broadly instrumental 'but not if you have to betray someone' and 'but not if it requires you to eat anything and everything' (Irwin). Taking the dative as the dative of benefit (as translated here) encourages the second-line response explored in the text.

ignorant; and food benefits only the hungry. In the ethical case, too, what is good for a person, i.e. what makes a person's life go well, may depend on her state of character. And for a person who willingly embraces a bad source in order to attain some end for herself, attaining the end may not in fact be good, as the end will not contribute to the life's going well (one cannot live well with a character like *that*).

Does Aristotle's suggestion undermine the status of the goods in question? Plato's Socrates might think so. In the dialogue *Euthydemus,* he argues that we should count 'goods' that do not always benefit their possessor as neutral, i.e. neither good nor bad (280c–281e). If so, pleasure would count as neutral rather than good. However, the answer ultimately depends on one's account of the good and goodness more generally. Some goods may be intrinsically good, even if they are only conditionally good.[31] So, it is possible that Aristotle considers pleasure an intrinsic good conditional on character. However, from this lemma, we cannot determine his position, as he merely sketches possible options.

1173b28–31 Or pleasures differ ... in the other cases.

Finally, Aristotle sketches an apparently different response to the problem of bad pleasures. The first two solutions devise strategies to account for so-called 'bad pleasures', explaining why these pleasures may not be bad properly speaking (1173b20–5) or in themselves (b25–8). Both aim at keeping the tenet (T): all pleasure is good. Now, he seems to drop (T) in order to pursue the solution proposed in response perhaps to the original argument from shameful pleasures (on which, see commentary on 1173b20–25). In Plato's *Gorgias*, Socrates diagnoses the oversight of distinguishing between pleasures as the source of Callicles' predicament. By differentiating between kinds of pleasure, Callicles could avoid conceding that even shameful pleasure makes a life happy. But, he notices, he must give up (T) in return (494e–495a). But should a hedonist have conceded the point to Socrates?

To answer that question, we must first examine the evidence for the distinction. The previous proposal emphasised the uniformity of the good in

---

[31] A prominent example would be happiness in Kant's moral philosophy. For further elucidation on Kant's account of conditional intrinsic goods, see Bader 2015 – his paper in The Highest Good in Aristotle and Kant (Aufderheide and Bader 2015). Engstrom's and Barney's contributions to the same volume illuminatingly compare ancient conceptions of conditional goodness with Kant's (see Engstrom 2015 and Barney 2015).

question. No one would postulate different kinds of money or health. Even if we can differentiate between them according to their sources (birthday money, blood money, salary...), money and health remain uniform. Now Aristotle points to a difference. While I can have the same money as a millionaire (just not as much), or the same health as an exercise enthusiast, I cannot have the just or musical person's pleasure – unless I am just or musical (1173b29–31). The argument seeks to tease out the intuition that I miss out on a certain sort of enjoyment if I cannot play an instrument. I can have the pleasure of playing the harmonica from nothing but playing the harmonica. Thus, in contrast to the previous argument, the present proposal does not take pleasure to be a uniform feeling, but rather an experience that differs according to its source.

But where to locate the source of a pleasure? We might be tempted to regard the activity as the source. If I get pleasure from a shameful activity, then my pleasure will also be shameful. However, *Aristotle* offers a different, and more interesting thought. He does not say that I cannot have the just person's pleasure without *doing* what is just. Rather, I cannot have the just person's pleasure without *being* just (1173b29–30). Now, suppose that on occasion I can do, and enjoy doing what is just, even though I am not a just person.[32] Why would I not have the same pleasure as the just person? Pleasures divide into kinds, the proposal suggests, not insofar as they stem from different activities, but insofar as the activities stem from differently developed states. Thus the source (Greek: *apo* with genitive) extends beyond activities and must include the states of the soul responsible for the activity. Alternatively, we may question whether the just person and I really perform the same activity. The identity of the activity may already depend on the state from which it stems. Either way, with the activity and states of character Aristotle has suggested two plausible factors for determining the value of pleasure. He develops a version of the present proposal in X.5, when he differentiates pleasures into kinds (1175a21–b16). He assigns the same value to the kind of pleasure as to the kind of activity that they accompany (1175b24–36).

Where does the proposal leave (T)? On its own, it cannot save (T). But combined with the other two attempts, the hedonist could pursue the following responses: either a) the bad kinds of pleasure are not really pleasures, or b) it is not the pleasure that makes bad pleasures bad, but rather the bad character of the people who indulge in them.

---

[32] The assumption seems plausible in light of Aristotle's account of habituation in EN II.4.

1173b31–1174a1 And the distinction ... a view to different things.

Aristotle now reports a further consideration against pleasure that may support either of two conclusions: 'the distinction between a friend and a flatterer is also thought to highlight that [a] pleasure is not good or else [b] <that pleasures> differ in kind' (1173b31–3). The considerable difference between [a] and [b] stems presumably from differing conceptions of friendship presupposed by the argument.

A simplistic argument for [a] could run as follows. A flatterer seeks to provide pleasure, whereas a friend's concerns gravitate around more serious issues, such as virtue, family, politics, etc. The friend seeks to help her friend's life go well (cf. VIII.5.1157b25–1158a1), whereas the flatterer only seeks to make it pleasant (if that). And since people praise friends but reproach flatterers, their respective aims, central to what they are, seem likewise praiseworthy and worthy of reproach. Hence, [a].

The argument has several defects, and [a] seems to overstate what it can establish, for in order to conclude [a], we must add further premises. Why does reproaching flatterers say anything about pleasure? Because flatterers aim at providing pleasure. Unfortunately, this answer creates a dilemma. Aristotle distinguishes between pleasure-based, honour-based, and virtue-based friendships in VIII.3–4. While virtue-friendships take centre-place, he regards the other kinds of friendship nevertheless as genuine. But pleasure-friendships form with a view to pleasure. So, either we have to discount pleasure-friendships as real friendships, counting pleasure-friends merely as flatterers, or else we also have to reproach pleasure-friends for providing pleasure. But Aristotle suggests neither of these two options. Pleasure-friends are genuine friends and, as such, not to be censured. Now, if the present lemma still addresses the question of bad pleasures, i.e. if we understand [a] to imply that pleasure is bad, then the answer that flatterers are bad because they provide pleasure faces an even greater difficulty, for we would have to censure all friends, because every kind of friendship also provides pleasure (EN VIII.3 and *Rhetoric* I.11.1371a17–24), and doing so would be objectionable, given [a]. Either way, the fact that flatterers provide pleasure does not seem to be a sufficient reason to censure them.

How, then, do flatterers bear on the question of pleasure? The flatterer, not being a friend, deliberately acts to appear as a friend. By providing pleasure to his 'friend', he seeks to influence the flattered person for his own self-benefit or other ulterior purposes. We censure the flatterer because he dissembles his true motives (cf. IV.7). But we also censure the deceived person, because she lets herself be misled by pleasure (cf. VI.7.1121a7). So, we may indeed regard the pleasure involved in flattery as something bad. But the reasons for doing so cannot be generalised, because the flatterer tends to provide pleasure for a specific purpose, and not all pleasures lend themselves to flattery. For example, the pleasure of a shared walk in beautiful surroundings may be part of a pleasure friendship, but hardly something a flatterer could use for his purposes. So, the argument points to a difference in kind between the pleasures of friendship and that of flattery, as [b] would have it.

Curiously, Aristotle does not in any way respond to the thought. Does his silence indicate agreement? Not necessarily, for he has already outlined at least two ways that would allow him to discount the pleasures involved in flattery as genuine (see 1173b20–25 and b25–28 with commentaries). He leaves it open as to whether the argument successfully undermines the thesis that all pleasure is good.

1174a1–4 Next, no one would choose ... pain coming from it.

Aristotle adds two further points against pleasure. As in the previous lemma, he does not venture a reply to the objection. Whether we take his silence to express consent, or confidence in our ability to respond for ourselves, depends on what we take the two thoughts to mean.

a) Let us suppose childhood to be the most pleasant stage of life because of the way children enjoy their games, toys, parents, and each other. But one can have these outstanding pleasures only in the right frame of mind – a child's frame of mind. However much we enjoy dreaming about being a child again, faced with the choice, the argument predicts, no one would actually choose to be mentally a child, just for the sake of the supreme pleasures. What follows? We might take the argument to show that pleasure differs from the good, for if pleasure and the good were identical, the life of pleasure would have to be choice-worthy – but it is not (cf. the 'mollusc-argument' in Plato's *Philebus*, 20b–23b). Although this reading works, it does not seem to exhaust the resources of the argument. The argument could more specifically i) point to values about which we care more than about pleasure. Alternatively, and in light of the preceding arguments, ii) we might take the argument to corroborate the differences in kind between pleasures (cf. 1173b28–31).

b) Fear of future pain (in the form of remorse, reproach, or any other form of punishment) provides another reason for passing over a certain occasion for pleasure. Now, if you had a way of making sure your shameful action and pleasure would not be discoverable – would you be swayed by the pleasure? Perhaps not. Astonishingly, the argument predicts *no one* would go for such pleasure! If so, then, just as before, the argument would seem to show that pleasure is not the good, and that either i) we value other things higher than pleasure, such as virtue and integrity, or ii) pleasures differ in kind (shameful kinds being not choice-worthy).

Both a) and b) suffer from several defects. The problem with a) consists in neglecting the normative dimension of pleasure. While doing child-like and even childish things befits children, it does not befit grown-ups, whatever their state of mind. Those influenced by Eudoxus may refuse to choose the childish frame of mind not because of i) or ii), but because they do not expect to enjoy doing child-like things. Child-like pleasures will not be in accordance with their (mature) nature, and hence should not be pleasant to them (cf. 1172b9–15). So, followers of Eudoxus' hedonism may reasonably deny the premise that *they* would enjoy the greatest pleasures, were they to choose a child's life. They think they would have to become a child in order to have those pleasures.

Argument b) falters when we question whether really no one would choose to have the shameful pleasures. Consider Plato's story in the *Republic* (359c–360b). If an unjust person had a ring rendering him invisible, of course he would go into people's houses and have sex with anyone he wished (360b), and perhaps even a fairly decent person could not resist the temptation. So, taking any future pain out of the equation would only leave the imminent pleasure and its disreputable source. It seems naive to suppose that no one would be tempted if the pleasure comes 'for free'. The argument would be much stronger if it concentrated on only the good people: *they* would never choose a shameful pleasure even in these circumstances; and, being good, they must know.[33] But the stronger version of the argument already presupposes that pleasure and the good are different. But perhaps we should restrict the scope of 'no one' to Aristotle's audience. Since they are decent (cf. I.3.1095a10–11), *they* would not succumb to the power of the magic ring. But again, *they* already take pleasure and the good to be different – which leaves it unclear exactly what the argument adds.

Presumably, Aristotle leaves the interpretation of the arguments deliberately open. He mentions them, because they seem to belong to the stock arguments used in the academic discussion of pleasure. He has already given us the means to process them, either strengthening the case against pleasure, or else rebutting their apparent force.

---

[33] Cf. Cicero, *De Officiis*, III.38–9.

98 I Pleasure (X.1–5)

1174a4–8 Next, many things would ... if no pleasure arose from them.

In contrast to the previous lemma, the final argument against pleasure leaves little room for different readings. The present lemma highlights more directly that we care about things other than pleasure, things we would choose even if they brought no pleasure at all. Hence pleasure and pain do not function as the sole criterion for choice. Other things are good and choice-worthy not merely on account of being a pleasure, but in their own right. Pleasure would only be one good among others.

The argument distinguishes between pleasures and their sources. Pleasure is not the same as, e.g., seeing, remembering and so on, but those activities *bring* pleasure (*epipheroi hêdonên*, 1174a5), or pleasure *arises from* them (*ginoit' ap' autôn hêdonê*, a8). So, by conceiving of pleasure as something different from, and additional to,[34] the activity, we can consider these activities apart from their pleasure, even if pleasure necessarily follows them. So, while one could reject the actual separation of pleasure from its source-activities, we can nevertheless separate them in thought and consider how we would choose.

What does Aristotle think about this argument? i) He does not, here, assert that seeing, remembering, and so on are goods. Elsewhere, he counts the following as goods: 'having a sound mind, seeing, some pleasures and honours' (I.6.1096b16–19), and 'honour, pleasure, intelligence and every virtue' (I.7.1097b2–3). So, he seems committed to endorsing the conclusion that there are other goods besides pleasure.

ii) He does not assert in his own voice that pleasure necessarily follows seeing, remembering, knowing, and possessing the excellences, partly because he says nothing about the objects of seeing, remembering, and knowing. Would Aristotle think that we ought to choose seeing and remembering even if we could only see or remember extremely ugly scenes? His remarks at IX.7.1168b13–19 make clear that such memories and perceptions would at any rate not be pleasant – and perhaps not choice-worthy. (In the context of tragedy, however, we do enjoy what would otherwise be painful, *Poetics* 4.1448b7–12.) Further, properly having a certain state entails using it (cf. VII.3.1147a11–14). But now suppose that the state giving rise to 'virtuous action' does not at the same time conduce to our enjoying those actions. Aristotle would doubt whether we could have the virtues without also enjoying virtuous action (I.8.1099a15–23). So, the conceptual tie between pleasure and virtue seems too close for the thought experiment to work in this case.

---

[34] Signified by the *epi* in *epipherein*, a verb that also means 'adding' (LSJ, s.v.).

1174a8–12 Now, it seems to be clear ... have been adequately stated.

Aristotle now sums up the results of discussing what people have said about pleasure and pain: a) 'pleasure is not the good' (1174a4–8), b) 'not all pleasure is to be chosen' (a9), and c) 'some pleasures are choice-worthy in themselves' (a9–10). Together, b) and c) indicate some difference among pleasures which we can explain either by d1) differentiating kinds of pleasure, or d2) classifying pleasures according to their sources.

Some scholars (Ramsauer, Susemihl, Stewart, Festugière) reject these lines as inauthentic, partly because they take them to sum up lines 1174a1–8 only – which do not discuss *the* good explicitly. Some manuscripts read 'good' instead of 'the good' in line 9, referring back to 1173b32–3 ('the distinction between a friend and a flatterer is also thought to highlight that pleasure is not good'). The transmitted text would seem more integrated, and less suspicious. But why restrict the upshot's scope anyway? Why would Aristotle not sum up the whole discussion of 'what people have said about pleasure'? The problem about the good disappears if we take him to sum up all of X.2–3 here. He started out in X.1 with the extreme positions 'pleasure is the good' and 'pleasure is plain bad' (1172a28), positions whose support he subsequently discusses. He seems to endorse the argument Plato puts forward in the *Philebus* that pleasure cannot be the good because pleasure alone is not sufficient for a good life (see 1172b23–35, with commentary; cf. 1174a1–8). So, Aristotle does seem to derive a) from the preceding discussion.

How about b) and c)? By endorsing the *Philebus* argument, Aristotle not only rejects pleasure as the only good, he also thinks it establishes the pleasures added to good things as good in themselves – summed up as c). The difficulty now resurfaces as b), for in X.2–3 he takes great care to defend pleasure against those who argue that, because of its nature, pleasure could not be good in itself (goodness and quality, 1173a13–15; goodness and determinateness, 1173a15–23; pleasure as movement or coming to be, 1173a28–31 and 1173a31–b20). The defence at least leaves it open as to whether all pleasure might be good. Moreover, he agrees with Eudoxus that i) people pursue pleasure as good (1173a11–13), and ii) what all pursue is good (1172b35–1172a2). While he does not share Eudoxus' further point, iii) that people pursue only pleasure, Aristotle's commitments nevertheless bring him close to maintaining that all pleasure is good. So, why would he assert b), 'not all pleasure is to be chosen'? We can read b) in two ways. On the strength of 1174a1–8, he might claim that not all pleasures are to be chosen. If the choice involves choosing something bad in addition, or if it (permanently) precludes having some other, greater good, we should let the pleasure pass. Alternatively, we might take him to use the term 'pleasure' broadly, so as to include pleasures not without qualification (bad pleasures bring pleasure only to certain people…). In this case, he could maintain that all unqualified pleasures are good, while writing off the qualified pleasures as bad. Both d1 and d2 would provide a suitable starting point for developing this interpretation (for details, see commentaries on 1173b25–8 and 1173b28–31).

To conclude, Aristotle nicely sums up the main results from discussing the things said about pleasure. We may want to question the status of the results. While he discusses things said, he surely does not consider *all* things said. And even if he gathers the most important sayings – why would going through things *actually* said give definitive answers? People might simply get things wrong about pleasure. But if the answers are not definitive – why go through the exercise? Aristotle safeguards his conclusions by cementing them into a broader basis than just the things said. He has supported his claim that pleasure is a controversial topic – which precludes him from being able to accommodate every opinion (as demanded at I.8.1098b10–12). But he has also appealed to what we can evidently see – people pursuing pleasure and avoiding pain. The discussion is not merely 'dialectical', but also draws on observation and life. So, by cutting down the extreme positions of hedonism and anti-hedonism, Aristotle arrives at a plausible view of pleasure: some kinds of pleasure are good, while other pleasures (conceived broadly) are bad. His own account of pleasure should therefore try to vindicate his conclusions, as they stem from both a thorough examination of arguments and the role of pleasure in human life more generally.

X.4

1174a13–14 And what it is … from the beginning.

Aristotle makes a fresh start – marked as a new chapter by later editors – by asking two programmatic questions about pleasure. What is pleasure (*ti esti*)? What sort of thing is pleasure (*poion ti*)?

Aristotle tends to use *ti esti* as a formula rather than as a real question. The *ti esti* – literally the what-it-is – of something, X, points towards the thing's essential properties, the properties that make X what it is. Often the *ti esti* serves to identify more generally the kind to which X belongs, in particular the highest genus to which X belongs. Socrates, for example, belongs to the genus 'animal'. But this does not suffice to tell us what Socrates is, because there are many animals that differ in kind from Socrates. We also need the specific differences between other animals and those to which Socrates belongs. Socrates belongs to the genus of human beings, and it is essential for human beings to be able to use reason (cf. *De Anima* III.3.428a16–24; cf. EN I.7.1098a7–8). So, to give an account of what Socrates is, we need both the highest genus and the all specific differences (land-dwelling, biped, rational…).

Aristotle uses this approach in EN II.5 when trying to determine the nature of virtue. He first examines the *ti esti* of virtue to identify its genus (it belongs to states, *hexeis*, 1106a12), and only then considers its *poion ti*. By considering what sort of *hexis* virtue is, he arrives at the differences that mark off virtue from other states. And by putting together its genus and specific differences, Aristotle arrives at the definition of virtue (II.6.1106b36–1107a2).

Coming back now to the present lemma, when Aristotle asks for the *ti esti* and the *poion ti* of pleasure, we might expect an enquiry that results in a definition of pleasure. But nowhere in X.4–5 (or anywhere) does he identify the genus and specific differences of pleasure, nor does he offer a definition. And although he repeatedly likens pleasure to activity, he never identifies pleasure with a certain kind of activity (which would go some way towards saying what pleasure is). So perhaps we should take Aristotle to correct himself when he says 'what it is, or what sort of thing' (1174a13). Where we would expect an attempt to define pleasure, we should content ourselves with finding out what sort of thing pleasure is, i.e. what qualities it has – which might work well through likening pleasure to activity.

Aristotle, however, does more than liken pleasure to activity. By detailing what pleasure, and presumably nothing else, *does*, he highlights pleasure's specific function or work (*ergon*). While a 'functional definition' of pleasure falls short of giving us the genus and specific differences, it nevertheless comes close to indicating what sort of thing pleasure is. For those qualities of a thing that play a crucial role in performing its function would seem to be essential – thus pointing towards the *ti esti*.[35] Now, we might still want to ask why he stops short of giving a proper definition of pleasure, for a functional approach to X does not preclude defining X. For example, he arrives at the specific differences of virtue only through considering its specific function (II.6.1106a15–17). Still, there are two reasons against a definition of pleasure, one economical, one metaphysical.

---

[35] Hadreas 2004 explains and develops the functional definition of pleasure.

First, Aristotle thinks he needs to give a sufficient theoretical background to help the political leader instil virtue in his subjects (I.13.1102a7–26). A definition of virtue surely contributes to that project, not least because it helps political leaders to find their target. Pleasure differs in this respect, because we do not have any trouble identifying instances of pleasure. Unlike virtue, everybody has some! So, he does not need to define pleasure. In fact, doing so would not, strictly speaking, belong to a treatise on ethics, because it serves no practical purpose.

Second, apart from considering the economy of writing an ethical treatise, Aristotle may be unable to give a definition of pleasure. He has already criticised Plato's approach to pleasure (1173a28–b20) and will continue to do so in X.4. Perhaps Aristotle does not merely criticise Plato for giving the wrong definition of pleasure, but for trying to give a definition at all. Pleasure may be too diverse to fall under one definition (we might fare better to classify pleasure by family resemblance). However that may be, Aristotle chooses to gather pleasures by their function.

1174a14–19 Seeing is thought ... because it lasts longer.

In the first lemma of X.4, Aristotle promised a fresh start by examining the nature of pleasure. In the Greek, this lemma reads as if it would give a reason or rationale for doing so. He uses the word *gar* ('for') which usually marks some kind of explanation. He tends to propose a thesis and then uses *gar*-clauses to structure and subordinate reasons: the *gar* looks backward.[36] Here, however, Aristotle *starts* with a *gar*-clause. To make sense of the Greek text, we should not understand the *gar* as looking backward to the previous lemma, but as forward-looking (inceptive or anticipatory),[37] and either translate as 'now', 'so', or similar, or leave it untranslated.

He starts his investigation by considering the metaphysics of pleasure. Because he makes a fresh start, we must expect him to cover some of the same ground as earlier in X.3, where he responded to, and repudiated, other theories of pleasure. Now, however, he does not develop his view as an antithesis to some other view, but prepares his own approach to pleasure in his own terminology. He makes four points:

i) Seeing is complete through any interval of time; [1174a14–a15]
ii) [for] any instance seeing is complete in its form at all times; [a15–16]

---

[36] See Netz 2001 for a painstaking analysis.
[37] Denniston 1934, 68–70.

iii) pleasure too seems to be a thing of this sort; [a16–17]
iv) [for] any instance of taking pleasure is complete in its form at all times. [a17–19]

Thesis iii) finds support from two sides. On the one hand, seeing a) illustrates the kind of quality attributed to pleasure, and b) suggests a similarity to pleasure which suffices to transmit the quality. On the other hand, Aristotle explains in iv) how we should understand 'pleasure' for iii) to be true.

To i) and ii). Sight is complete in form at any time because no length of time makes it more complete. Even if I have to go through a process that is not complete in form at every time before I can see (taking off my eye-mask, opening my eyes, turning on the light), seeing itself is complete in form as soon as it starts. In *De Anima* II.5 Aristotle carefully contrasts the sort of affection one undergoes when 'changing' from not perceiving to perceiving with ordinary changes. I undergo a change when I become musical (a process that takes time), but not really when I put my musical knowledge to use. Seeing, and perceiving in general, resembles not the acquisition of knowledge, but its use. While watching a play can be interrupted and is therefore not complete at every time, the bare act of using one's eyes for seeing cannot be interrupted in the sense that its going on longer would bring the act of seeing to completion.

By juxtaposing pleasure and seeing, Aristotle anticipates the close connection between pleasure and perception that drives the discussion from 1174b14 onwards. But he does not rely on it here. Instead, he gives a reason, in iv), why we should regard pleasure as some kind of whole (*holon ti*). Understood as taking pleasure, or enjoying, pleasure does not take time to have its form completed. No length of time will make someone's taking pleasure more complete. Why? Again, while you can interrupt my temporally extended enjoyment, you do not thereby prevent me from having enjoyed myself. Compare: if you interrupt me baking a cake, we can describe my activity as gathering ingredients and starting on a batter. I was not really baking a cake (yet). But if I enjoy the (interruptible) process of baking the cake, then your interruption half-way does not mean that I was only half-enjoying myself. I was enjoying myself fully – until you interrupted.

Aristotle will go on to cover similar ground in the next few lemmata.

1174a19–21 That is why ... at that moment.

Having determined in the previous lemma what sort of thing pleasure is (*poion ti*), Aristotle now turns to examining what it is (*ti esti*). He does so, in part, by arguing at length what pleasure is not: a movement (*kinêsis*). He uses 'movement' to capture all sorts of change, including qualitative change (*auxêsis*) and quantitative change (*alloiôsis*), as well as locomotion (*phora*). Sometimes Aristotle contrasts *kinêsis* with coming to be (*genesis*) – in which case he tends to use 'change' (*metabolê*) as the most general term capturing both (*Metaphysics* 8.1.1042a32–b5; 11.1.1069b3–14). Sometimes, however, he uses *kinêsis* in the same way as *metabolê* (e.g. *Physics* V.1.225a34ff; V.5.229a31), to subsume all kinds of change, including coming to be and passing-away. He focuses here on *kinêsis* in the narrower sense, in contrast with the X.3 discussion, which focused on pleasure as coming to be (1173b4–b20, though see the 'quick–slow' argument against pleasure as movement at 1173a31–b4).

Aristotle here begins an excursion on the form of movement that he relates to pleasure only from 1174b5 onwards. Everything that comes in-between supports the main premise (M): a movement is not complete. Together with the claim, established in the previous lemma, that the form of pleasure is complete through any interval of time, he can conclude that pleasure is not a movement. How does he support (M) in this lemma? He illustrates the general claim that a movement relates to some end with housebuilding. The example also makes vivid that movements take time to be completed. But if movements can be completed, does this not open the door to analysing pleasure as movement after all? Pleasure as a movement and something complete would occur when the movement reaches its end! In response, Aristotle considers two options. We could locate a complete movement either in the whole of the time the movement takes from beginning to end or else only in the last moment (1174a21).

But if a moment does not take time, nor is in time (*Physics* IV.11.220a18–22), and is therefore not part of the movement that takes time and is in time – is the second option even coherent? One may even suspect the text (as do Gauthier and Jolif 1958, 834). Indeed, one manuscript offers only the first suggestion: 'and it is complete whenever it produces what it aims at in the whole of the time it takes' (*ê en hapanti dê tô(i) chronô(i) toutô(i)*). However, this reading may miss the point, for the second option may make room for the possibility that completions of processes do not, properly speaking, belong to the process. In any case, the movement comes to completion only when it is over – whichever option we adopt. So, pleasure could not be both complete and a movement, because we would have the pleasure as something complete only when the movement no longer occurs. Unlike in X.3, Aristotle does not here encourage us to think that a movement may give rise to pleasure (cf. X.3.1173b11–13). His point is simply the metaphysical claim that pleasure does not itself belong to the class of movements.

1174a21–29 And all movements are incomplete ... the whole time [of the process].

Aristotle further considers the relationship between pleasure and movement – albeit without mentioning pleasure. Having argued that pleasure is complete in form at any moment it occurs, he started to highlight the differences between pleasure and movements in the previous lemma. While movements occur, they are incomplete. Now he considers a further way one might try to account for pleasure as movement.

Complex processes, such as building a temple, consist of many ordered subprocesses. Their individual completion enables and often partly constitutes the completion of the overarching process. While the subprocesses take time, just like any other movement, most of them will be completed before the overarching process. Thus, complex processes may harbour a way of accounting for pleasure-as-movement. The overarching process consists of *complete* parts and would therefore no longer be wholly incomplete at any time, but will have some completeness. So, to the extent that the overarching process is completed, to that extent it can be pleasurable. More precisely, the pleasure of the overarching process could consist in the completed subprocesses.

Two reasons forestall this attempt. Each subprocess, such as setting the foundation or inserting the triglyph (an ornamental element between the column and roof of a Doric temple), is a) different from the overarching process and b) itself incomplete. The first point stresses the difference of enjoying building a temple from enjoying laying the foundation. We cannot simply replace the former with a series of enjoyments derived from completing some subprocesses. i) While we would thus identify some pleasures, we would not account for *the* pleasure of building a temple. Thus, ii) we would not account for the pleasure as a movement, because the pleasures stemming from the subprocesses require the processes to be completed.

The second point, b), undermines any attempt to locate pleasure in completed subprocesses. Although the jobs of setting the foundation and of inserting the triglyphs must be finished before the temple, they need not, thereby, be complete. Insofar as they are parts of a larger project, a project reaching its end with the completion of the temple, they remain incomplete. A triglyph is only a triglyph of a temple when the temple is completed. So, Aristotle here seems to allocate priority of the whole over its parts. The completion of subordinate processes depends on the completion of the whole: no movement is complete unless the whole project finishes.

So, the building of the temple contains no complete movement 'at any time, except in the whole time [of the movement]' (1174a27–9). Hence, if pleasure were a movement, and pleasure had to be complete, there could be no pleasure in, e.g., building a temple while the process occurs.

1174a29–b2 And similarly in … a different place from that.

Aristotle now considers in more depth one of the reasons pleasure cannot be a movement – again without mentioning pleasure. However, the thesis that pleasure is something complete, but movements are not complete, informs the present lemma. In the previous set of examples (temple-building, 1174a21–9), Aristotle first analysed the overarching process into several subprocesses and then focused on the incompleteness of subordinate processes: insofar as they are subordinate, they are not complete until the overarching process reaches its end. Hence, we cannot locate the pleasure of the overarching process in completed subprocesses. Now he concentrates on the difference in form. Even if the subordinate processes can be completed in a way, they differ in form from the overarching process, and hence cannot account for the pleasure of *that* process. The point needs no elaboration for building, as the different stages of building obviously differ. But one may easily overlook the formal differences in moving from place to place (locomotion) – the topic of this lemma.

Aristotle puts forward two distinct arguments. First, he suggests that movement is less unified than it seems, for the different modes of moving from A to B (flying, walking, leaping) result in different forms of movement. So, if pleasure were a movement, we would have to take into account the mode, as well as having traversed the distance to account for the pleasure properly. Now, his point may be that a) those who propose pleasure as movement do not take the mode of conveyance into account. So, if they identify pleasure with locomotion *tout court*, they could not account for the difference in motions. Implausibly, the pleasure of walking from A to B would be the same as the pleasure of leaping from A to B. Alternatively, b), Aristotle may cavil at the alleged generality of their definition. Since motions differ in kind according to the mode of conveyance, there simply is no pleasure that is identical with locomotion *tout court*.

Second, even any single kind of locomotion turns out to be more complex than it appears initially and less conducive to identifying pleasure with movement. Suppose we were to account for the pleasure of walking as having traversed a certain distance. But walking (or running) falls into subprocesses: the racecourse in the stadium divides into smaller subsections or parts, marked (as they were) by lines across the racetrack. Now, if locomotion is a movement from one place to another, then start point and end-point determine the form of the locomotion (cf. 1174b5). But in this case walking (or running) the whole racecourse differs in form from completing just a part. The difference, Aristotle stresses, lies not in the different distance covered. Even if we traverse two equally long parts of the track, our walking differs in form whenever the from-where and to-where differ. What do we gain by highlighting the formal differences in locomotion? Consider the following thought: running the racetrack from start to finish takes time to complete. But once I start running, I have completed part of the racetrack, and since I do the very same thing, running, I have already completed a version of the same process in which I am engaged. Hence I can locate the pleasure of running in something complete. Aristotle can block the move in two ways. Either he could, as in the previous lemma, insist on the incompleteness of the subordinate movements – in which case they could not account for pleasure. Or else he can stress the differences between having completed this or that part of the racecourse, and running all of it. We could not explain why we enjoy running rather than having run, because our present running differs, formally, from the running we have completed.

1174b2–7 Now, a precise discussion ... is something whole and complete.

Aristotle sums up the preceding lines and, returning to the point of departure, explicitly relates the discussion to pleasure. First, he sums up why movement is incomplete (discussed at 1174a19–b1), and then reiterates the point of 1174a14–19, 'pleasure is something whole and complete'. He can thus confirm the preliminary conclusion that pleasure is not a movement (stated at 1174a19).

Aristotle has shown that a movement consists of many incomplete movements, i.e. subprocesses, which differ in form both from one another and the overarching movement. But what does this mean for movement in general? One might wonder what exactly he takes himself to have shown. If we read *oud' en tô(i) hapanti chronô(i)* at 1174b3 (with Susemihl) instead of the OCT's *ouk en hapanti chronô(i)* the text would translate 'but movement seems not even to be complete in the whole of time' – in which case Aristotle would renege on his earlier tentative concession that a process is complete in the whole of time (1174a28–9). However, both text and sense work in favour of the weaker reading: 'movement seems not to be complete at every moment of time'. a) Virtually all manuscripts support the OCT. b) Aristotle sums up movement with a view to comparing it with pleasure. Pleasure's being complete at any time (*hotôoun chronô(i)*, b5–6) suffices to establish the difference between pleasure and movement, as long as movement is not complete at every time. Thus, the weaker reading serves to distinguish between pleasures and movements: pleasure belongs to things whole and complete in form (cf. 1174a17–19), whereas movement does not.

The positive assertion 'but rather…' can be read in two different ways because the key phrase, *hai pollai* [sc. *kinêseis*] can be translated in two ways. Either c) it refers to the many subprocesses of which every movement consists (as adopted in the text, thus also Irwin, Reeve), or else d) to most movements (thus Rowe, Ross). While the latter serves to illustrate the point that pleasure is not complete at every time, it adds little. Reading c) by contrast explains better why movements are not complete at every time: the subprocesses that make up every movement are incomplete (argued at 1174a21–9), and they differ in form because their start and endpoints are different (as argued at 1174a29–b2).

How different are pleasure and movement, metaphysically? Aristotle refers to a 'precise discussion of movement', presumably at *Physics* III.1–3, which defines movement as 'the fulfilment of what is potentially, insofar as it is potential, e.g. the fulfilment of what is alterable, insofar as it is alterable, is alteration' (III.1.201a10–11). In his definition of movement in the *Physics*, he regards movement as an actuality (*entelecheia*) and activity (*energeia*), although he stresses its incompleteness (*energeia men … atelês de*, *Physics* III.2.201b31–2). Since he has focused on the completeness of pleasure and the incompleteness of movement, he only rules out that pleasure is an *incomplete* activity. What he has said so far about the nature of pleasure is compatible with classifying pleasure as a *complete* activity. And indeed, by likening pleasure to seeing, Aristotle may suggest that pleasure *is* a complete activity, because seeing is a complete activity (1174a14–19). In this case, those who define pleasure as movement would not be fundamentally mistaken about the nature of pleasure – they realise that pleasure is something active – but they fail to appreciate that pleasure is something complete. However, Aristotle never says pleasure is a complete activity.[38]

---

[38] In the other treatise on pleasure, EN VII.12.1153a13–15, Aristotle suggests that we should conceive of pleasure as an activity (*energeia*), not as a coming to be (*genesis*). Many scholars take him to imply complete activities there. For references, and the dissenting view that *energeia* encompasses both complete and incomplete activities, see Aufderheide 2013.

1174b7–9 And this would seem to be ... now is something whole.

Aristotle now offers a further, and apparently independent, argument for 'this' (*touto*). 'This' could refer either to A) 'they [sc. pleasure and movement] are different from each other' (1174b6–7), or to B) 'pleasure is something whole and complete' (b7) from the previous lemma. Since either reading also involves the other 'conclusion', the readings differ more in emphasis than substance. According to reading B), Aristotle further justifies taking pleasure to be something whole and complete, thus supplementing the reasoning in 1174a14–19. But since he has argued at length that movements are not complete, he would thereby also support A). If, however, we opt for reading A), then he would offer a more direct argument, perhaps parallel to the previous considerations, for the difference between pleasure and movement. While the extremely terse writing allows for both readings, A) reads more naturally:

i. It is not possible to move without taking time (1174b3);
ii. it is possible to enjoy without taking time (b8–9); therefore
iii. pleasure and movement are different from each other.

If we need more support for premise i) than ordinary experience, we can turn to the *Physics*. He differentiates between time (which is divisible) and the now (which is indivisible). The now is the point that divides, and connects, past and future. Like spatial points, it does not have an extension, or else it would be divisible (*Physics* IV.12). But, as Aristotle has argued in 1174a21–b2, every movement divides into subprocesses that differ in form. So, if movement were to occur in the now, the now would be divisible – which is false (cf. *Physics* VI.3.234a24–31). Hence i). Further, the *gar*-clause 'for what occurs in the now is something whole' would bolster premise ii), provided we find it plausible that pleasure occurs in the now. Presumably, he goes back to the thought at 1174a15–19 that we can enjoy a fully fledged pleasure instantaneously: its lasting longer does not change the form of the pleasure, only the 'amount' (cf. B).

The last move may puzzle us, for two reasons. First, how can pleasure last a time, if it occurs instantaneously? For if pleasure does not take time, how can we enjoy something for a while? Our puzzlement derives from thinking the wrong way round. If we add two things that lack extension, we will arrive at a third thing that also lacks extension. Aristotle, by contrast, conceives of an extensionless point as a cut in a magnitude. He does not suggest that pleasant experiences consist of many successive extensionless instances of enjoyment, like pearls on a string. Instead, he seems to presuppose that pleasant experiences last a while, but that we can 'cut' the experience at any moment, and will find the same (form of) pleasure.

Second, experience takes time. So, how can we experience a pleasure instantaneously? Just as every physical cut in a line has extension, so a 'mental cut' in the experienced pleasure will also have extension. But then, how can our experience support premise ii) in any way? We can develop an answer, admittedly speculative, from some puzzling remarks Aristotle makes about time:

> But neither does time exist without change; for when the state of our minds does not change at all, or we have not noticed its changing, we do not think that time has elapsed, any more than those who are fabled to sleep among the heroes in Sardinia do when they are awakened; for they connect the earlier 'now' with the later and make them one, cutting out the interval because of their failure to notice it. So, just as if the 'now' were not different but one and the same, there would not have been time, so too when its difference escapes our notice the interval does not seem to be time. If, then, the non-realization of the existence of time happens to us when we do not distinguish any change, but the mind seems to stay in one indivisible state, and when we perceive and distinguish <some change> we say time has elapsed, evidently time is not independent of movement and change. It is evident, then, that time is neither movement nor independent of movement.
>
> (*Physics* IV.11.218b21–219a2, tr. Hardie and Gaye in Barnes 1991)

Aristotle concludes from this passage that we assume there is no time without change. Now, assume a) that you enjoy something for a while, i.e. you do not enjoy different kinds of pleasure successively, and b) that the intensity of the pleasure does not change. In this case, if you were to attend purely to your enjoyment, you would not notice time passing. Like those who sleep in the heroes' caves in Sardinia, you would join up the last and the first moment. In-between, as if in an instant, you have your pleasure. So, our experience might after all support the claim that it is possible to take pleasure in the now.[39] If we wish to strengthen this tentative interpretation, we need to explain how we can purely attend to our enjoyment. Is enjoyment something to which we can attend? Aristotle provides material that helps answer these questions, especially in X.5.

---

[39] For the interdependence between mental activities, change, and time, see Coope 2005, esp. 37–41 and 159–72.

X.4

1174b9–14 And from these points ... it is a sort of whole.

Aristotle claims to investigate the nature of pleasure at the beginning of X.4. Having established pleasure as something whole (1174a14–19), he draws out the differences between pleasure and movement (*kinesis*) (until 1174b9). The present lemma concludes this part of the investigation, while the next one begins the positive account of what pleasure is.

How does Aristotle conclude the negative part of his enquiry into the nature of pleasure? There are two interpretations, depending on which text we read. The two texts differ in two letters. In line b10, the OCT prints the text transmitted by the manuscripts, which has 'pleasure' in the accusative (*tên hêdonên*). It translates 'those who say that pleasure is a movement or coming to be are wrong'. The emended text, proposed by Ramsauer, does not have 'pleasure' in the accusative, but in the genitive (*tês hêdonês*). It translates 'those who say that there is a movement or coming to be of pleasure are wrong'. What hangs on the change?

Interpretation A. If Aristotle wrote *tên hêdonên*, he would for the last time be pointing out the mistake of those who count pleasure as a movement. But by adding 'or coming to be', he would correct his own term 'movement', *kinêsis*, replacing it with the opponents' term, *genesis*. This would show how the previous discussion relates to the genesis theory of pleasure that he has already discussed in X.3.1173a29–b20, for he would be following the pattern of the discussion in X.3, albeit with a difference in emphasis. In X.3 he *first* argues against pleasure as *kinêsis* (1173a31–b4), before devoting the bulk to refuting the *genesis* theory. Here, he denies first that pleasure is a *kinêsis* from 1174a19–b9, and then that pleasure is a *genesis* from 1174b9–14. Some interpreters think the structural similarity supports interpretation A.[40]

Interpretation B. If Aristotle wrote *tês hêdonês,* he would be shifting focus. Having established that pleasure is not a *kinêsis* at 1174a19–b9, he would be turning in b9–14 to a related, but different, claim. There is not even a *kinêsis* or *genesis of* pleasure. The claim entails two related and important points. First, there is no process whose completion ends in pleasure. Adding this point as a sort of footnote to the previous discussion seems reasonable, for while he has shown pleasure – something complete – to be different from processes, he has not ruled out a modified

---

[40] Thus Gauthier and Jolif 1958, who follow the paraphrast (sometimes identified with Heliodorus of Prusa). The text, whoever wrote it, is printed in Heylbut 1889.

process-view of pleasure, according to which pleasure is the completion of a process or movement. So, second, Aristotle would be further engaging with the view that pleasure is a movement, for if pleasure were the completion of a movement, the pleasure would belong to the movement. But movement, as he repeats here, consists of temporal parts, different in form (cf. 1174a21–b2). The complete change comes to be through the successive completion of subprocesses. So, if there is no coming to be *of* pleasure, pleasure will neither be a process nor belong to it as completion.

Are both interpretations equally plausible? In favour of A speaks the manuscript authority; B will have to explain the scribe's mistake. But doing so proves easy: the scribe, writing *tên hêdonên* instead of *tês hêdonês*, simply assimilated the grammatical case to those of 'movement' and 'coming to be' – a common enough error. Which interpretation does Aristotle's reasoning at 1174b10–13 support? The text allows for two readings, corresponding to A and B. At b13, after having made the point that there is no coming to be *of* seeing, a point, or a unit, he adds *oude toutôn outhen kinêsis oude genesis*. We can translate either as a) 'nor is any of these a movement or coming to be', or b) 'nor is there any movement or coming to be of these things at all'. The difference consists in taking *outhen* either adverbially ('not at all'), or else as an indefinite pronoun ('any'). The next point, *oude dê hêdonês*, translates most naturally and literally as 'and hence not of pleasure either' – which readily continues b), but not a), and thus favours interpretation B. To make sense of the three words, interpretation A has to go back to the point from line b11 – 'these [sc. movement and coming to be] cannot be ascribed to everything' (*ou ... pantôn tauta legetai*) – and apply it to the present line. This would yield 'hence they are not ascribed to pleasure'. The move may be grammatically possible, but just barely. So, Aristotle's reasoning seems to support B rather than A.

One final point. Interpretation A can easily accommodate the instances at which Aristotle says that pleasure comes to be (*ginetai* at 1174b27 and 1175a21). Does this not rule out interpretation B? For this seems to say what B denies, namely that there is a coming to be of pleasure. No, because 'X *ginetai*' does not have to mean 'X comes to be'. It can also indicate a conclusion that arises from a certain set of premises ('X turns out to be F', cf. I.7.1098a16–17), or more generally that X arises under certain conditions. So, when Aristotle says that pleasure *ginetai* from the senses (1174b27), or not without activity (1175a21), he can mean that pleasure *arises* from the activity of the sense that expresses a kind of dependence – without implying a process of coming to be.

1174b14–20 And since every sense is ... most pleasant.

At the beginning of X.4 Aristotle sheds light on the nature of pleasure by comparing it to seeing. Like seeing, pleasure is formally complete (*teleios*) in the now, i.e. without taking time (1174a14–19). Because movement is incomplete, pleasure differs from movement or coming to be (1174a19–b14). In this lemma, he returns to the example of perception. Going beyond its feature of formal completeness, Aristotle expands on the sense in which perception is *teleios*, for he now speaks of *teleios* in the superlative – which does not easily square with formal completeness.

The *Metaphysics* distinguishes two senses of the word. It applies when a) 'that outside which not even one portion is to be found, as for instance the complete time of each thing is that outside which there is no time to be found which is part of that time' (*Metaphysics* 5.16.1021b12–14, tr. Kirwan), and when b) 'that which in respect of excellence and goodness cannot be surpassed relative to its genus, as for instance a doctor is complete and a flautist is complete when they are without deficiency in respect of the form of their own proper excellence' (*Metaphysics* 5.16.1021b14–17, tr. Kirwan). At first sight it is easy to see how *teleios* as 'perfect' (=b) can admit of a superlative, but not how *teleios* as 'formally complete' (=a) could do so.

How are the two senses of *teleios* related? One proposal capitalises on the two senses of *teleios*, stacking the perfection of pleasure onto its formal completeness, suggesting that only formally complete things can be perfect. For example, we cannot call your racing 'perfect' before you finish the race (or only in a qualified way).[41] According to this proposal, Aristotle would have established pleasure as something complete in the previous discussion, and now, firmly seizing on b), draws out a further characteristic of pleasure. i) A sense is perfectly active (*teleiôs*) only when in good condition and directed at the finest (*kalliston*) object of its range (b14–16). ii) The activity ensuing from the interaction of such an object and sense is perfect (*teleia*, b16). iii) In every case, the activity is best (*beltistê*, b18) when the sense is in the best condition and is active in relation to the most outstanding object (*kratistos*, b19) in its domain. iv) Such an activity (i.e. best) is also most perfect (*teleiotatê*) and most pleasant (b19–20). Thus, Aristotle moves beyond formal completeness as a mark of pleasure, links it to activities of perception, and correlates pleasantness with the activity's perfection.

---

[41] Bostock 1988, 259–60 sponsors the interpretation outlined in this paragraph. Gonzalez 1991 denies a shift in focus.

Can we do without postulating an unannounced shift in the meaning of *teleios*? Yes, if we read Aristotle as elaborating on the formal completeness of pleasure, for formal completeness can also come in degrees. Processes divide into subprocesses whose completion constitutes the completion of the overarching process. The subordinate processes, however, will be complete in a way (e.g. the fluting of the column), but incomplete in another (because the fluting of the column of a temple depends on the temple's being built; see commentary on 1174a21–9). The subordinate goals can be reached fully only on attaining the superordinate goal.

Mentioning 'finest' and 'best' perceptual activities suggests an interpretation that relies on the sub- and superordination. 'Fine' often contrasts with necessary and subordinate activities that, due to their subordination, cannot be fully *teleios* (cf. I.7.1097a22–b6). When animals perceive, their perceptual activity will be formally complete, and often be perfectly executed. Despite their keen senses, animal perception falls short of being fully *teleios* insofar as their perceiving and the pleasures they derive from it are confined to the necessary. Every perceptual pleasure an animal may have takes its root in necessary activities, such as eating (cf. EN III.10.1118a16–22). An animal cannot take non-necessary pleasures, such as enjoying the smell of flowers (EE III.2.1231a10–11). Animal perception thus belongs to essentially subordinate activities. Some characteristically human perception also belongs to essentially subordinate activities, such as crafts. But not all: the finest and best perceptual activities are not essentially subordinate – and hence can be most *teleios*. So, superlative pleasantness will not be a function of a perfectly executed activity, at least not primarily. Rather, the finest object requires a well-functioning sense, whose activity will not be subordinate to anything. It will therefore be maximally complete.[42]

1174b20–6 For every sense affords ... being healthy either.

In this lemma, Aristotle formulates the central claim of EN X.4–5, [CC]: pleasure completes the perfect activity. He introduces it after having extended points i)–iv) from the previous lemma to include thought (*dianoia*) and reflection (*theôria*). So, perception, thought, and reflection will be most complete/ perfect when the best objects activate the best states. Being most complete goes hand in hand with being most pleasant. How should we understand CC, especially in relation to the correlation between completeness and pleasantness?

---

[42] See Aufderheide 2016, 292–7 for further discussion. For the alternative (pleasure arises with perfectly executed sense-perception), see Price 2017, 193–6.

Many interpreters assume an explanatory link between pleasure and perfection. According to them, the best activities are most complete/perfect because pleasure *is* their perfection/completion or, more weakly, because pleasure contributes in some other way to their perfection. Alternatively, we may take Aristotle to offer 'and pleasure completes the activity' (1174b23) not as an explanation for the completeness or perfection of the activity, but as something additional.[43] He has, the thought goes, already specified the conditions under which an activity is complete/perfect, namely when a good state is active in relation to a good object (1174b22–3), and pleasure therefore adds a further completion/perfection.

The text does not favour either of the two readings. Aristotle uses the all-purpose connective particle 'and' (*de*) – not the explanatory *gar* ('for'). A writer can use *de* to introduce an explanation, though rarely in prose (Denniston 1934, s.v. de, 169–70). Nevertheless, reading a colon before 'and pleasure completes the activity' (printed in Bywater's OCT) would help to understand CC as explanation. But since punctuation was only added by later editors, reading a colon as opposed to a full stop already rests on interpretation and should not constrain how we read the text. Susemihl, for example, prints a full stop, marking off CC as a new point.

Whether or not pleasure completes an already perfect activity or an otherwise imperfect activity – how *does* pleasure complete or perfect it? Aristotle starts with a negative point. Pleasure does not perfect the activity in the same way as the sense-object and the sense do. His point is straightforward if we assign two completions/perfections to an excellent activity, one due to sense and sense-object, the other to pleasure. In this case, Aristotle highlights their difference. But his negative point does not decide between the two readings, for we may also construe his thought differently. We can keep pleasure as *the* perfection if a) the interaction between a good sense and sense-object gives rise to pleasure and b) pleasure in turn completes the activity. Since pleasure perfects the activity directly (through giving rise to pleasure), whereas the sense and sense-object do so only indirectly, they would complete pleasure in different ways.

We might find ourselves disappointed at so little in support of CC – Aristotle simply asserts it, and does not seem to elaborate on it. Does he not give us any clues how we should understand CC positively? Many interpreters look to the medical analogy which expands on the different completions/perfections or different ways of completing/perfecting. If pleasure is a *cause* of the activity's perfection and falls under one of the

---

[43] So taken by Owen 1986, Irwin 1985, 306, van Riel 2000, and Broadie and Rowe 2002, 436.

four causes (e.g. *Physics* II.3) – does pleasure cause the perfection as material, efficient, formal, or final cause? Taking the cue from 'health and the physician are not in the same way the cause of being healthy either', we might try to analyse pleasure analogously. If the doctor acts as efficient cause and health as formal cause of this patient's health, then a good sense and sense-object would complete the activity as efficient cause, whereas pleasure would complete it as formal cause.[44]

Two reasons speak against reading off anything positive from the analogy. First, activities such as seeing are formally complete with or without pleasure; hence pleasure cannot be their formal completion (1174a14–19). Second, Aristotle will say that pleasure arises with perception, or depends on it (*ginetai*, 1174b27, cf. 1174a8) – which would not characterise a formal cause.[45] Given the difficulties, we should focus on the negative point only. The medical analogy forestalls the following reasoning: if two things perfect an activity, then they perfect it in the same way; hence pleasure must perfect seeing in the same way as sense and sense-object do, because they both perfect the activity. Instead, Aristotle points out, one can use the same term to indicate different ways in which something operates. Both health and a doctor are causes of health, but they cause health in different ways. Likewise, the sense-object and sense, as well as pleasure, may perfect the activity, but they can do so in different ways. Either by causing (in a wide sense) different kinds of perfection or by causing the same perfection in different ways.

1174b26–31 And that pleasure arises ... and what receives <it> are present.

In the previous lemma Aristotle puts forward the central claim of EN X.4–5, [CC]: pleasure completes the perfect activity. Following CC, he examines how pleasure completes the activity. Since he has so far only outlined how pleasure does not complete activity, we would expect him to continue elaborating on CC in this lemma. But the text as we have it thwarts our expectation. After repeating the connection between an outstanding activity and maximal pleasantness, Aristotle seems to comment on the duration of pleasure: pleasure will be present as long as the good activity. Some

---

[44] So Stewart 1892, 427, Gosling 1973, and Gosling and Taylor 1982, 212–13. Gauthier and Jolif 1958, 839–41 suggest health as a final cause, but Gosling and Taylor 1982, 244–7 effectively refute this suggestion.

[45] By making pleasure the formal *and* efficient cause, Shields 2011, 207–8, seeks to explain how pleasure can be both dependent on the activity and nevertheless perfect it.

scholars have objected to the text. They think the present lemma disrupts the line of thought, because he returns to CC at 1174b31–3, and then says more about the duration of pleasure in 1174b33–1175a3. The paraphrast[46] omits the lines of this lemma in his paraphrase of EN X; Gauthier and Jolif simply transpose the present passage, fitting the lines after b33. However, in the absence of any textual reason for transposing these lines we must keep them at their present location – even if the thoughts would be better organised were the paragraphs switched around.

The exposition seems less disrupted if we do not focus on the duration, but on the conditions under which pleasure arises – *that* topic runs from 1174b14 to 1175a3. In the present passage *aisthêsis* refers to the organ of perception (cf. 1174b14 and b20), not to the act of perceiving. Aristotle claims that pleasure arises with each sense, supported by the observation that we call objects of sight or hearing 'pleasant' (1174b27–9). Presumably, he presents an abbreviated list, as we also call objects of touch, smell, and taste 'pleasant'. In any case, he seems especially interested in the conditions under which pleasure arises most. When the sense and the object are good and the activity perfect (cf. 1174b15–18), pleasure will always arise. So Aristotle seems to postulate a necessary connection between pleasure and perfect activity.

How does this further point affect our understanding of CC? We may understand Aristotle to propose pleasure either as (A) *the* perfection of a perfect activity, or (B) *a* perfection (at least in addition to formal completion). According to A, the necessary connection between pleasure and activity poses no obstacle, and indeed may seem to confirm it, as the activity's perfection just is pleasure, or else cannot be attained without pleasure. B seems a more perilous interpretation, for if we take pleasure to be a further completion/perfection, we face the more difficult task of explaining why pleasure should necessarily follow an otherwise perfect activity.[47] Why should I not be able to engage perfectly in looking at a beautiful object without enjoying it?[48] Note, however, that the dialectal advantage of A over B turns out to be weaker than it appears, for in order to capture Aristotle's project of identifying the conditions under which

---

[46] The elusive paraphrast is sometimes identified with Heliodorus of Prusa (of whom we know hardly anything else). In any case, the paraphrase is edited in Heylbut 1889, and might have been written as late as the fourteenth century AD. See Gauthier and Jolif 1958, 105–7 for details.

[47] See commentary on previous lemma for the two interpretations of CC, as well as more details and names.

[48] Van Riel 2000 pushes this line, arguing that Aristotle has nothing to answer the question with. This paragraph draws on Aufderheide 2016, who develops a solution to the problem.

pleasure arises, A must also find a way of specifying the almost-best activities which, when enjoyed, become best and perfect. But A must do so without reference to pleasure, or else their account would be circular. However, once the activities are identified without reference to pleasure, the connection between the best activities (or almost-best) and enjoyment ceases to be necessary – in which case we must ask, again, what entitles Aristotle to claim that pleasure in the sense of enjoyment always accompanies the best activities.

> *1174 b31–3 And the pleasure completes/perfects the activity ... on those in their prime.*

Aristotle now characterises the workings of pleasure more directly. He begins by contrasting, again, pleasure's perfecting or completing an activity with a different way: 'pleasure completes/perfects the activity not as the state does by being present in something' (1174b31–2). Only then, and only in a simile, does he indicate that pleasure completes or perfects an activity 'as some superadded end, like the bloom on those in their prime'. Aristotle's account of pleasure remains elusive, partly because the image hardly illuminates how pleasure completes an activity as some supervenient end. Almost everything in this sentence sparks controversy, both because of its inherent unclarity and its central position in his account of pleasure.

The negative point may highlight one or both of two points. The relevant state is the good state of the sense, referred to earlier at 1174b15, b18–19 and b22. This state can complete or perfect the activity in either of two ways by being present in the activity. i) For objects that can be perceived through several senses, the sense actually used determines the form of the perception (e.g. seeing as opposed to hearing). ii) As a dull sense does not interact perfectly with a good object, a good sense may be said to complete or rather perfect the activity. Since Aristotle contrasts pleasure with the state, i) would indicate that the kind or form of the activity is not determined by pleasure (in X.5 he argues it is the other way round). More controversially, according to ii), pleasure would either a) not contribute to the activity's quality or else b) would not contribute to it in the same way as the state's goodness, for pleasure and the state present in the activity may perfect it in different ways, or effect the same perfection in different ways (see commentary on 1174b20–6).

The phrase 'as some superadded end' (*hôs epiginomenon ti telos*) characterises positively how pleasure completes or perfects an activity. But what does this mean? First, one may wonder why we should translate *telos* as 'end' if it illustrates how pleasure completes or perfects an activity. Would not 'perfection' or 'completion' be more suitable? No, because Aristotle implicitly continues to disagree with Plato on the nature of pleasure (cf. 1174b14–20). By making pleasure some kind of end, he opposes the Platonic view that pleasure is essentially subordinate and therefore not an end.[49] This reading also suggests that the indefinite *ti* does not put distance between pleasure as a *kind of* superadded end and *proper* ends (such as good activities). Translating 'a certain superadded end' would likewise mislead the reader if it implies that the superadded end is the same for all activities (more on this in X.5). Due to the level of generality – his account should fit all the best pleasures – the *ti* leaves the exact nature of the superadded end open.

Aristotle seeks to explain how pleasure completes or perfects an activity as a supervenient end with the help of a simile. Unfortunately, the Greek allows for several readings, and therefore fails to convey *the* way in which pleasure completes or perfects the activity. In particular, 'bloom' (*hôra*) and 'those in their prime' (*akmaiois*) leave room for interpretation. *Akmaios* has a temporal sense, referring to a certain stage in the life of a person. But the different ways of taking *hôra* ('bloom') suggest very different ways of understanding the simile and hence pleasure. *Hôra* has to do either 1) with timing, and can be translated as 'springtime of life', 'height of youth', or 'time of maturity'; or 2) with physical appearance, and so could be translated as 'beauty'.[50] These two different translations suggest two opposing ways of interpreting the simile, one emphasising the necessary connection between pleasure and perfection, the other making out pleasure as something additional. If *hôra* refers to time, be it to the 'height of youth' or 'time of maturity', then *hôra* and *akmê* refer essentially to the same thing, as both refer to a certain time in a man's life. A man would be in his prime because he is in the springtime of his life. The springtime's setting-in perfects (*teleioi*) his life such that he is now in his prime.[51] The point, then, of the simile would be that pleasure completes or perfects an otherwise imperfect activity: the activity is perfect or complete (*teleios*) be*cause* pleasure completes or perfects it – not as an efficient cause, but as the perfection of the activity. So, pleasure in a perfect activity is not anything

---

[49] Warren 2015 nicely brings out Aristotle's dialectic with Plato: even the simile alludes to the *Philebus* argument where Plato condemns pleasure to the class of things that are not goods because they are subordinate (53c–55c).

[50] LSJ s.v. *hôra*.

[51] Some supporters of this interpretation, such as Bostock 2000, 157, think that Aristotle elucidates the way in which pleasure perfects the activity by reference to health at X.4.1174b25–6. However, this is not an essential feature of this interpretation, cf. Strohl 2011, 275–6.

extra in the sense that it is something over and above the activity, but rather 'it is the further fact that the activity is perfect' (Bostock 2000, 157).

Alternatively, if *hôra* refers to beauty, then the beauty superadded to those in their prime is something different from, and additional to, being in one's prime, as being in one's prime does not entail physical beauty. Here, we can differentiate between two ways of spelling out the age of those in their prime. A) Aristotle's use of the word *hôra* in the discussion of friendship points towards youth. When discussing the different kinds of friendship based on pleasure, he turns to the one based on good looks: 'in the case of the lover (*erastês*) and beloved (*erômenos*) … one of them takes pleasure in seeing the other, while he takes pleasure in being looked after by the lover; and sometimes as soon as the bloom (*hôra*) comes to an end, so too does the friendship' (VIII.4.1157a6–9). Traditionally, Greek society looked favourably upon male homosexual relationships within certain limits, one of which was that the beloved had not yet grown a full beard, i.e. that he was not yet a man.[52] However, that Aristotle wants to associate pleasure with something perfect speaks against A) and in favour of B), i.e. taking 'prime' to refer to maturity. Accordingly, the analogue in the simile should refer to a man in his prime, not to one who is not yet fully developed. Moreover, in his biological works, *akmaios* likewise refers to a mature man.[53] And at *Rhetoric* I.5.1361b11, he explicitly locates the *akmazôn* between young and old; in *Rhetoric* II.14.1390b9–11 he declares the body to be in its prime (*akmazei*) from 30 to 35, whereas the mind peaks at about 49. Whether we opt for A or B, this interpretation stresses that pleasure is something other than the perfect or complete activity, or *the* perfection of that activity. Like beauty, pleasure is something additional to the perfection or completion that the activity already has.[54]

1174b33–1175a3 So long, then, as the object … the same [sc. effect] naturally arises.

So far, from 1174b14 onwards, Aristotle has stressed the connection between pleasure and the best activities. He identifies the most complete/perfect activities with the most pleasant ones (1174b19–20). Before he

---

[52] Plato's *Protagoras* remarks on this contrast at 309a1–5. Warren 2015 contains a full discussion of the allusions to the pair lover–beloved in Plato's and Xenophon's writings.

[53] See especially Hadreas 1997. Cf. van Riel 2000, 57 and Bostock 2000, 156.

[54] Proponents of this interpretation are Owen 1986, Irwin 1985, 306, van Riel 2000, and Broadie and Rowe 2002, 436.

turns to answering questions raised about pleasure, he indicates how to account for pleasure in less-than-perfect activities. Extending the account also tells us about which aspect of pleasure completes the activity.

For Aristotle, pleasure consists of two key components. The objective component hangs on the notion of pleasantness; the subjective component is the pleasure taken. While I can enjoy something that is not really pleasant, my pleasure would not be a pleasure without qualification. Indeed, he suggested writing off bad pleasures as not really pleasant (X.3.1173b20–8). Since he used superlatives (*teleiotatos, hêdistos*) to correlate the quality of the activity and its pleasantness, we might reasonably think activities of middling quality middlingly pleasant, and activities of bad quality not pleasant at all. Although the objective component plays a role, Aristotle instead focuses on the subjective component in X.4, the agent's enjoyment. A parallel passage from Book II.3 proposes 'the pleasure or pain that is superadded to what people do should be treated as a sign of their dispositions (*hexeis*)' (1104b3–5). Here, the superadded pleasure (*epiginomenên hêdonên*, 1104b4) must be understood as the pleasure taken in or occasioned by that activity (*chairein*, b6), i.e. the agent's enjoyment. Since Aristotle uses the same expression, a participle of *epiginesthai*, X.4.1174b31–3, to make a point about the connection between pleasure and the activity, 'pleasure' should mean the same in both cases.

But if he talks about the pleasure taken, rather than what the pleasure is taken in, correlating the best activities with the most pleasure becomes much less plausible. Does Aristotle propose that the degree of the agent's enjoyment stands in proportion to the quality of her activity? Not necessarily, and the present lemma explains why: 'when the receptor and the producer are similar and in the same relation to each other, the same [effect, i.e. pleasure in the activity] naturally arises' (1175a1–3). By dropping the superlatives here, he suggests a more basic condition for enjoyment, the similarity between sense and object. Since the notion of similarity works only in a limited range of cases, we should think of it as 'fit'. Further, the quoted passage does not seem to state a sufficient condition for enjoyment, but rather a necessary one. So, we should formulate Aristotle's insight as [F]: for pleasure to occur, there must be a fit between the underlying state and the object that activates the state.

Earlier, he had already commended Eudoxus for linking pleasure with what is fitting by nature (cf. X.2.1172b11). Now, homing in on the subjective aspect of pleasure, he picks out the fit between the state activated and the activating object as the prime condition for what gives rise to the agent's enjoyment, which allows for the relevant variation. While F does not explicitly take into account degrees of enjoyment, it lends itself towards [F*]: the better the fit between the object and the state, the more the agent will enjoy the activity. So, how much the agent enjoys the activity is not determined by the quality of the activity, but rather by how well the activity befits the agent. In any case, both F and F* confirm a thought explored in X.3.1173b22–5, where Aristotle suggested that what people in a bad condition enjoy is not enjoyable for everyone. The point was not that one *should not* enjoy these things, but rather that people of a good disposition *cannot* enjoy them. According to F (and F*), they cannot do so because of a lack of fit.

Note, however, that F does not suggest pleasure could *perfect* just any activity. While a bad person may enjoy a depraved activity immensely, Aristotle would hesitate to speak of perfection or completion, given that neither the states involved nor the objects activating them are excellent. Since he tries so hard to attribute perfection to the activity before he says that pleasure perfects it (1174b23), we should not assume that pleasure in any real sense perfects substandard activities (though see *Metaphysics* 5.16.1021b17–19).

1175a3–10 How, then, is it that ... pleasure too becomes dim.

Aristotle's theory of pleasure so far consists of two elements – the core claim [CC]: pleasure completes the perfect activity; and the necessary condition [F]: for pleasure to occur, there must be a fit between the underlying state and the object that activates the state. He elaborates on the theory in light of two questions arising from the dialectical part of his discussion (X.2–3). a) Why does no one take pleasure continuously? (This lemma.) b) Why does everyone desire pleasure? (Next lemma.)

The question about the continuity of pleasure arises because Aristotle rejects the *genesis* theory of pleasure, which identifies pleasure with a movement (X.4.1174a19–b14). Movements have an internal cut-off point. If pleasure is a movement, and every movement ceases when it attains its goal, then continuous enjoyment seems impossible. The movement theory of pleasure accurately captures phenomena such as slaking one's thirst. Initially, quenching one's thirst is satisfyingly pleasant, but when the process of rehydration is completed, drinking water ceases to be pleasant. If the theory were to apply also to all the other pleasures we might have, including perceptual and intellectual pleasures, then all of these activities and pleasures would have an internal cut-off point – which would explain why we cannot take pleasure continuously.

How can Aristotle account for the phenomenology without identifying pleasure with a movement? He answers by stressing pleasure's dependence on the activity. For the pleasure taken in movements he has already suggested that pleasure occurs *while* the movement occurs (X.3.1173b12). According to CC, the pleasure will cease when the relevant activity related to the movement ceases.[55] CC helps to extend the correct prediction beyond movement-pleasures. Although seeing and reflecting do not have an internal cut-off point, we cannot experience continuous pleasures, because our human faculties are incapable of being active continuously. So, the pleasure dependent on perception will stand and fall with the activity.

However, Aristotle seems to address also a more disquieting problem, namely, why something like F is not a sufficient condition for pleasure. Sometimes I engage in a formally complete and qualitatively perfect activity without enjoying myself. Or rather, first I do, but then I don't. Aristotle may suggest that the activity loses its edge. However fine the artworks and however good my critical eye – after hours in the gallery, my gaze tends to grow dull. The activity is no longer perfect, and hence pleasure need not complete it. But how does the solution work? For the constitution of the sense activated hardly changes (fatigue does not change the *hexis* at 1174b32),[56] nor do the objects change. But if something like F were sufficient, and the interplay between a good state and a suitable object constituted perfection, then the activity *should* still be supremely pleasurable. The solution falls into place if we take him to add agent-related *ceteris paribus* clauses to his account of pleasure. Pleasure will necessarily accompany the best activity of perception *provided* the agent is not too tired to engage fully in the activity. A further related addition concerns familiarity – which can also kill pleasure. If you've been to the gallery too many times and know every detail of every artwork, you will probably not go to the trouble of discerning all the details and their interplay: you will take a broader look. But, Aristotle seems to suggest, a perfect activity of seeing requires intense attention – which explains why familiarity can take away the pleasure.

He does not attempt to give a full list of *ceteris paribus* clauses, but rather indicates how the agent's condition (as opposed to the *hexis*) can undermine pleasure. But especially the second clause may cause a problem. Excessive

---

[55] For the present problem, it does not matter whether we take the relevant activity to be the perception of the movement (so Bostock 1988) or whether we take it to be the activity that causes the movement (Aufderheide 2013 on EN VII), for both will cease when the movement ceases.

[56] Cf. *eu diakeimenês* 1174b15; *eu echontos* 1174b22.

familiarity explains why we do not always or continuously enjoy activities that we perform perfectly (think about routine). But does this fit with the apex of pleasure, theoretical reflection, or contemplation (1177a23–7)? Contemplation or reflection (*theôria*) do not consist in finding out new things, but in contemplating a certain kind of knowledge that one already possesses, and hence presupposes familiarity. But if familiarity can dampen the enjoyment, then contemplation may fail to be superlatively pleasant. Aristotle may respond that either a) the material to be contemplated far exceeds the human mind, so that we shall never become too familiar with the objects of thought, or b) the objects are inherently so interesting that we shall never become bored with them. Answer a) does not account for Aristotle's god who constantly engages in contemplation, continuously enjoying the same simple pleasure (VII.14.1154b26). While god does not tire, he will be familiar with the objects of contemplation if anyone is. It is therefore important to note that familiarity *can* kill pleasure, but whether it does so on any given occasion depends on further factors, such as the objects that give rise to pleasure.

1175a10–17 And one might think ... which is choice-worthy.

When discussing Eudoxus and his detractors, Aristotle agreed with the former that pain is to be avoided and pleasure, its opposite, to be sought (1172b18–23). If all living things desire what is suitable and good for them, Eudoxus can explain why everyone desires pleasure, since he identifies pleasure with what is good. Aristotle, by contrast, takes pleasure to depend on an activity: it completes a perfect activity like 'some superadded end' (X.4.1174b31–3). Does he regard pleasure as an extra good that people might also desire? If not, why should we desire pleasure, rather than the good activity that gives rise to it? He offers a twofold answer. He questions the presumed implicit contrast between pleasure and activity in the next lemma. But before that, he explains in this lemma why, according to his theory, everyone *should* desire pleasure. He develops his answer in four steps.

a) Aristotle locates the source of desire for pleasure in life, or more specifically in our seeking to be alive (1175a11–12). While he acknowledges a primary sense in which we are alive – actively thinking and perceiving (IX.9.1170a18–19) – he concentrates here on more complex activities and lives.

b) He connects love and the activities central to one's life: 'each is active in relation to those things, and with those states, which he also loves (*agapa(i)*) most of all' (1175a12–13).[57] The beloved activities take a central role in the person's life, sufficient to distinguish between the lives of a lover of learning and a musician – even if both lives contain elements of both. Ideally, a lover of understanding leads a life in which understanding is central, whereas the musical person leads a life in which performing or listening to music is central 'and so on for each of the others' (1175a15).

c) While love explains how a person will most want to live, it also explains what a person enjoys. In Book I, Aristotle has reminded his readers of the well-known connection between a person's being a lover of X, i.e. a trait of her character, and her habitually enjoying X or X-related activities (*chairein* 1099a17–20): 'to each person that thing is pleasant in relation to which he is called "lover of" that sort of thing, as for example a horse is to the horse-lover, a spectacle to the theatre-lover and in the same way what is just is also pleasant to the lover of justice, and generally the things in accordance with excellence to the lover of excellence' (I.8.1099a8–11). For the lover of X, there is an internal connection between engaging in the beloved activity and habitually enjoying it. Even if pleasure and the activity are distinct, for the lover of X they come as a package that she desires as a whole *because* she loves X.

d) Everyone desires pleasure because everyone desires and pursues the beloved activities central to a life. A person's life is shaped by the activities she loves, and those are the activities she most enjoys, as pleasure will complete or perfect them (for her). Hence, Aristotle surmises, it makes sense that they seek pleasure (1175a16–17).[58]

His solution suffers from two problems. First, assuming every life to be shaped by beloved activities seems naive. Many people live lives that centre on difficult and laborious activities – hard physical labour. Eking out a living in these hard conditions affords them very little pleasure, and what pleasure they get does not stem directly from their graft. Here the

---

[57] Instead of rendering *toutois* (1175a13) as 'with those states' (so also Reeve) – literally 'with these things' – one might translate 'in these ways' (Irwin), or more narrowly 'with those faculties' (Rowe; Ross), on the strength that Aristotle goes on to illustrate the claim with hearing (*akoê(i)*, a14) and thought (*dianoia(i)*, a14). Whiles 'states' is wide enough to encompass faculties, it can also refer more narrowly to an ability in mathematics as opposed to creative writing – both of which would belong to 'thought'. Cf. X.5.1175b1–6.

[58] Aristotle does not here distinguish between seeking (*ephiêmi*) and desiring (*oregomai*), as he starts out to explain why everyone desires pleasure, but ends by having shown why everyone seeks pleasure.

connection between being a lover of X and leading an X-related lifestyle seems broken, and hence Aristotle's solution does not seem to apply. One might modify the solution slightly to accommodate these cases, for the solution requires only two points, i) that the person live for something, and ii) that what she lives for be pleasant to her. One might then locate a labourer's source of pleasure in more basic life-activities, such as being with one's family or sharing a hard-earned meal. If the labourer lives for these moments, and desires life, he will also desire pleasure, as long as he enjoys those activities.

But the modification highlights the deeper problem. Does not the solution rest on a fallacy? Consider: I desire to exercise; exercise is painful for me; therefore I desire pain. *That* conclusion does not follow because 'desire' creates an intensional context. Usually when we say 'S desires X' we mean to focus on what S takes herself to desire (*de dicto*), not what her desire is in fact directed at, perhaps unbeknown to her (*de re*). So, Aristotle does not seem entitled to move from 'S desires music' to 'S desires pleasure (of music)'. Or does he? Return to the example. I do not desire the pain of exercising, because I would happily forego the pain exercising brings and merely enjoy its pleasures. While it does not make sense to attribute to me the desire to feel the pain of exercising, it does make sense to attribute the desire to feel the joy of making music to the musician and the joy of learning to the lover of learning. Because of their characteristic love for the relevant activity, *for them* there is no real distinction between their preferred activity and the pleasure of it – which blurs the *de dicto* – *de re* distinction in this case.

1175a18–21 But whether we choose ... completes/perfects every activity.

Everybody desires pleasure. In the previous lemma, Aristotle tries to explain how his theory can accommodate this fact. He does so by pointing to the more specific case that a lover of a certain activity will both choose and enjoy the activity: [LCA] if a lover of activity A desires A, she will also desire the pleasure the activity gives her. But why should the conditional LCA be true? Aristotle now expands on the solution that someone who desires to be alive hardly distinguishes between activity A for which she lives, and the pleasure A brings (see also commentary on previous lemma). If a person S lives for A, then S tends to find attaining A pleasant. Attaining A serves as an end, and enjoying A reinforces the end-like nature (for S) of A. So, S lives for something pleasant. Now, does S choose A on account of the pleasure S brings, or does S choose pleasure on account of A? In other words: which is prior in S's motivational set, pleasure or the activity?

Instead of answering it, Aristotle dismisses the question (and never comes back to it). While we can theoretically distinguish between pleasure and activity A, *for S* the distinction does not arise, as presumably a) S would give A a less central role in her life if S did not enjoy A, and b) S would not be satisfied if the pleasures she tends to get from A were substituted with pleasures from other sources. S regards A and A-related pleasures as an inseparable package: without A, the relevant pleasure does not arise, and pleasure completes or perfects every activity (1175a20–1). ('Every activity' here must mean 'every activity that plays the role of X', where X is an activity for which a person lives, as is clear from Aristotle's way of framing the question at 1175a18–19.) For S, there is no priority: A and the pleasure of A are almost the same.

Although Aristotle has made pleasure metaphysically dependent on the activity, his approach to the question rings true to the phenomenology. Often we do not distinguish whether we engage in a pleasant activity on account of the pleasure, or whether we have pleasure on account of the activity. But does Aristotle not forget about an important distinction? Suppose my life revolves around being a good person. I try to be generous, just, courageous, and all the rest of it. It matters greatly which of these describes my attitudes: a) I donate money to charity and enjoy doing so, vs b) I donate money on account of the enjoyment I get. While a just person will act justly with pleasure (I.8.1099a17–20), she will not perform the action for the sake of pleasure, or on account of pleasure, but rather for the sake of the fine (e.g. III.8.1116b31; IV.2.1123a24–6; IX.8.1168a33–4). If we take the present lemma to be Aristotle's final word on the question, he would suggest that it does not matter to the good person whether pleasure or the good activity is her primary object of desire, because both are so intimately linked. True, she will perform the actions for the sake of the fine (*de re*), but she need not conceptualise the actions in this way.

X.5

1175a21–8 That is why they seem ... the pleasures completing them.

Aristotle now returns to differentiating between pleasures, exploring in detail one of the responses to reproachful pleasures outlined at the end of X.3. He opts for the third response – pleasures differ in kind – which he develops in his own name (translating 1175a21–2 alternatively as 'this is why people think pleasure also differs in kind' gives the wrong impression that people other than Aristotle invoke the function of pleasure to differentiate between kinds of pleasure). While all editors mark here the beginning of a new chapter, Aristotle clearly sees the difference between kinds of pleasure as stemming directly from the main claim of X.4, that pleasure completes activity.

To show that pleasures differ in kind, he argues as follows:

1. If A and B differ in kind, then what completes/perfects A will differ in kind from what completes/perfects B. (1175a22–3)
2. [Therefore?] if activity a and b differ in kind, then what completes/perfects a will differ in kind from what completes/perfects b. (1175a25–6)
3. The activities of thought differ in kind from the activities of perception, and the activities of perception differ in kind from each other according to the sense used. (1175a26–8)
4. Pleasure completes/perfects the activities of thought and perception. (From before, 1174a20–1175a3)
5. Therefore, pleasure differs in kind. (1175a28)

The argument stands and falls with 1, especially if 2 is meant to instantiate the more general claim in 1. And indeed, Aristotle tries to justify only the first premise, taking the others for granted. He supports the first premise with a few examples. They are supposed to show that if we divide substances or form–matter compounds into natural and artificial, any member of either class is completed or perfected by something different.

Unfortunately, the text leaves open whether the examples illustrate a point about formal completion (FC), or rather about qualitative perfection (QP). At first glance, the examples seem to support the former reading. Consider, while young animals possess the form of their kind in some way, they do not fully manifest it; only adult animals have fully actualised their potential and thus manifest the form completely. While animals differ in kind simply by belonging to this or that species – whether mature or immature – their coming to maturity and thus fully displaying the differences in form will also differ. Hence, what completes each kind of animal will differ in kind. Similarly for all living things that undergo a process of maturation.

The alternative reading focuses on qualitative perfection. According to QP, the text does not compare immature with mature animals, but focuses only on mature animals. Each kind of animal will have a characteristic set of behavioural patterns which include procreating their kind. Aristotle calls their characteristic behaviour *ergon* ('function' or 'work', cf. 1176a3–4). Now, some individuals will be better at performing their work, and if they tend to do so reliably, we could attribute excellence (*aretê*) to them, because excellence makes its possessor accomplish the *ergon* well (II.6, esp. 1106a15–24). Thus, those animals that perform their *ergon* well have excellence, whereas the other ones do not. But Aristotle calls excellence a perfection (*Metaphysics* 5.16.1021b14–23, quoted in commentary on 1174b14–20). Therefore, since the characteristic behaviour differs between species, so does the excellence.

Aristotle may see little difference between FC and QP, for if a thing's essence is defined functionally, i.e. via its characteristic work, it may come to be fully what it is only when it performs its work or function well, i.e. when it possesses excellence: 'excellence is some perfection (*teleiôsis tis*), for when anything acquires its proper excellence we call it "perfect" (*teleion*), since it is then really in its natural state: e.g. a circle is perfect when it becomes really a circle and when it is best' (*Physics* VII.3.246a13–16). So, it looks as if a thing only completes its nature when it attains excellence. Here, formal completion seems to presuppose qualitative perfection. By likening pleasure in this regard to excellence, Aristotle would suggest that pleasure not only makes the difference between an ordinary and an excellent activity (as per QP), but also that it makes the activity more what it (really) is (as per FC).

Having spelled out the first premise, we can evaluate Aristotle's argument. As it stands, premise 1 seems to invite counter-examples. a) Two gems may differ in kind, but both are perfected/completed by the same kind of cut and polish. b) Two metals may differ in kind, but both are perfected/completed by the same process of purification. c) A new pair of shoes and a new saddle both need to be broken-in to be perfected. The process is the same in both cases: use it. Now, one might push back against a) and b) by pointing out that the pairs do not really differ in kind, and hence should be perfected by the same process or activity. However, c) is designed to deflect that comeback, as the two items do not belong to the same kind. It will not help to move up to a higher kind that encompasses both, because this move would threaten premise 3. While all senses differ from one another in kind, it would be possible – contrary to the drift of the argument – to classify them simply together as perceptual senses. Thus, we cannot save the argument by insisting on fundamentally different kinds. So, if 2 is supposed to follow from 1, we would need more work to bridge the gap between 1 and 2. But may not 2 stand on its own legs? Perhaps so, but Aristotle does not give any support. But without it, we have no reason to follow his thought. Why would pleasure not perfect different kinds of activity without differing in kind itself? The counter-examples to premise 1 at any rate suggest the possibility that pleasure as a nice feeling could accomplish that task. But perhaps we should regard the present lemma not as a failed attempt at a cogent argument, but rather as a warm-up for the arguments to come (beginning in the next lemma).

1175a29–b1 And this will be obvious ... proper to them also differs in kind.

The present lemma adduces further support for 'this', i.e. the thesis that pleasures differ in kind, by turning to what pleasure does.[59] He tries to tie a specific kind of pleasure to a specific kind of activity by arguing that each kind of activity has its own or its proper (*oikeion*) pleasure which increases it ('enhance' or 'intensify' also translate *sunauxei* well). Put in argument form, we can represent Aristotle's reasoning schematically as follows:

1) The pleasure of activity A increases A.
2) If z increases A, then z is proper to it.
3) If activities A1 and A2 differ in kind, then what is proper to them differs in kind.
4) A1 and A2 differ in kind.
5) A1 is increased by the pleasure of A1 (=P1); whereas A2 is increased by the pleasure of A2 (=P2). (From 1; cf. 1175a30–1)
6) Hence: P1 is proper to A1, and P2 is proper to A2. (From 2 and 5)
7) Hence P1 and P2 differ in kind. (From 3, 4, and 6)

Aristotle seems to support premises 1 to 3 (and indirectly 5 and 6) with some examples: 'those who enjoy doing geometry become proficient in geometry, and understand each aspect of it better ... and so on' (1175a31–5). Unfortunately, the examples do not sufficiently support the case. First, while doing something with pleasure tends to go hand in hand with a better performance, this observation does not necessarily support 1, for it does not show that people are more discerning and exact *because of* their enjoyment. Why should they not enjoy the activity precisely because they engage so intensely in it (cf. X.4.1175a6–10)? If so, person S might become especially expert in the relevant activity because she engages in it so intensely. S's activity will be more perfect than the activities of people less discerning and exact – hence S's activity should be more pleasant given the link between perfection and pleasantness in X.4. In this case, pleasure would be increased by the activity, not the other way round, as stated in 1.

---

[59] He also follows a 'functional approach' in X.4. See the commentary on 1174a13–14.

Premise 3 also suffers from lack of support. Remember, at the end of X.3, in response to the problem of reproachful pleasures, Aristotle sketched various ways of keeping the good pleasures apart from the bad ones. One option was that pleasures do not differ except in their sources (1173b25–8) – just like being healthy and being rich. Nothing said here rules out that option, as we can observe people to be more discriminating and exact when they get paid more for their work. For all the argument says, we could spell out 'the pleasure of' in premise 1 along the lines of 'the payment for'. This would allow Aristotle to make pleasure proper to a certain activity (just like pay). However, pleasure would nevertheless resemble money in its uniform character, even if it is tied to specific activities. So, premise 3 would turn out to be false.[60]

Perhaps the present passage does not play the role of an independent argument, but rather corroborates the case made for pleasure in the previous lemma (though see commentary). The point was that those who enjoy the activity are much better at it than those who do not. Now Aristotle could highlight that this observation goes well with i) the distinction between kinds of pleasure (as per the previous argument) and ii) the claim that pleasure increases the activity. But if we *assume* pleasures to differ in kind and to increase the activity – what would there be left for the argument to show?

Aristotle's examples also raise a question about the nature of pleasure. In the first part of X.4, he likens pleasure to activities, such as seeing and contemplating (even if he eschews calling pleasure an 'activity'). Since none of the criteria for being a movement or a process like housebuilding apply to the activities of perception or thought (X.4.1174a14–b14), they also fail to apply to the pleasures accompanying them.[61] The present lemma mentions the lover of housebuilding and his pleasures. The pleasure would seem to stem from a movement (cf. X.4.1174a20). How can Aristotle account for the pleasures of movements, given that pleasure and movements seem to differ so significantly? In particular, a) pleasure is said to be 'in the now' and something complete in form at every time, whereas building extends over time and is not complete at every moment (1174b2–9, with commentaries). b) Housebuilding falls into many subprocesses that differ in kind from the superordinate process (1174a21–3). Although a builder will enjoy

---

[60] Of course, we may try to find salient differences between pleasure and pay. For instance, if I have enough money, pay may not motivate me to do anything, whereas pleasure, or the prospect of it, more directly affects my motivation.

[61] Heinaman 2011, 9–16, lists twenty characteristics of processes. He discusses the problem I sketch here at greater length.

many different kinds of pleasure while building, pleasure does not follow the process all the way, for processes are infinitely divisible, but the builder will not enjoy infinitely many different kinds of pleasure.

We may develop a solution on behalf of Aristotle that takes its cue from his conception of activity. An activity actualises some potential. In the case of seeing or contemplating, the actualisation is complete at any time. However, actualising the capacity to build *this* house takes time to come to completion. Nevertheless, whether engaged in laying the foundation or in thatching the roof, the builder actualises his capacity for building a house — and here the characteristics fit. As soon as the builder starts building, he makes use of his housebuilding knowledge (in general, craft is 'accompanied by rational prescription', VI.4.1140a6–10). And actualising knowledge is not a process (*De Anima* II.5). Hence enjoying the use of one's housebuilding knowledge would not be a process either. The solution works if housebuilding *just is* the activation of expertise in housebuilding, and similarly for other processes or movements. While the proposal explains the pleasures we obviously take in processes such as building, walking, eating and so on, we must await confirmation before we can attribute the proposed solution to Aristotle (see next lemma).[62]

1175b1–13 And this will be even more obvious ... when the actors are bad.

Aristotle takes himself to make his point even more obvious than in the previous lemma. But which point does he refer to? Probably, he has in mind the immediately preceding claim that a) pleasures proper to activities differ in kind in accordance with the activities (1175a36–b1). Alternatively, we may take him to corroborate only the weaker claim that b) pleasures are proper to their activities. The language suggests a), because 'this will be even more obvious' (1175b1–2) alludes to 'this will be obvious also' (1175a29) from the previous lemma – which was supposed to show that pleasures differ in kind. There are, however, philosophical reasons for thinking that Aristotle establishes only b).

Neutrally described, Aristotle adduces two sets of examples that suggest the pleasure of one activity can diminish or destroy another activity. But we can explain the phenomena only if pleasure belongs to one activity

---

[62] Gosling and Taylor 1982, 313–14, propose a similar interpretation (also discussed by Heinaman 2011, 24–6). Neither, however, conceives of the capacity activated as knowledge. Aufderheide 2013 doubts whether we can account for the pleasures in movement by conjuring up a complete activity; see especially 154–6.

rather than another, i.e. only if pleasure is proper to 'its' activity. For if the pleasure I get from different activities were the same, the pleasure of the one activity could not impede the other activity. And if pleasure were not specific to a certain activity, then the pleasure I get from one activity may well increase any activity, if pleasure is such as to increase activity (1175a30–1). However, pleasures alien to an activity have the tendency to interfere with the competing activity, especially when intense. Therefore, we should regard pleasure as specific to a given activity. Minimally, Aristotle seems to rely on the conditional claim, [C]: if the pleasure of activity A1 impedes A2, then the pleasure of A1 is proper to A1 (and not to A2). This would suffice to try to establish b). In order to aim for a), Aristotle must invoke a further premise, taken from the previous lemma, [P]: pleasures proper to different kinds of activity themselves differ in kind.

The argument for a) suffers from two problems. The first problem, which also infects the reasoning in the previous lemma, is due to P. Problem 1: pleasure could be like money. Suppose pleasure bore no differences in form or quality, but merely in quantity. This view of pleasure would predict exactly the same phenomena as Aristotle's thesis that pleasures do differ in kind. For if I am drawn to pleasure, I would concentrate on the activity that affords more pleasure. Hence, a more pleasant activity would impede a less pleasant one (cf. 1175b4–5, 'because they enjoy pipe-playing more than their present activity'). As in the previous lemma, we can interpret the alternative explanation as an attack on P. For if we spell out 'the pleasure of activity A' analogously to 'the payment for', the pleasures that accompany or complete different activities may count as proper to them. But since pleasure on this theory does not allow for differences in form or kind, P turns out to be false. (Note, this criticism leaves C intact.)

Problem 2: C seems too strong, at least if combined with P. Aristotle seeks to justify the division of pleasure into kinds by suggesting that different kinds of activity come with different pleasures proper to them. If proper pleasures, in turn, correspond to different kinds of pleasure, Aristotle can successfully tie kinds of pleasure to kinds of activity. But this attempt faces a dilemma. For the sake of argument, let us grant the consequence of C and P, that if the pleasure of A1 impedes A2, the pleasures of A1 and A2 differ in kind. Now we can formulate a dilemma:

[D] Either every proper pleasure corresponds to a kind of pleasure, or it does not.
    NO The negative response to D will not do, at least not if we see Aristotle as trying to establish a) rather than b), for this

move requires us to deny that one kind of activity comes with exactly one proper pleasure. So, one kind of activity could host several proper pleasures, or a certain pleasure could be proper to several kinds of activity. But if we do so, the role of proper pleasures in distinguishing pleasures into kinds becomes unclear: proper pleasures would not seem to do any work for that conclusion.

YES The positive response to D, that every proper pleasure corresponds to a kind of pleasure, has at least the advantage of making clear why Aristotle bothers with proper pleasures. However, this path is problematic as well, because it leads to a further dilemma:

[*d*] Either every kind of pleasure corresponds to only one kind of activity, or it does not.

NO Aristotle cannot choose the negative path of *d*, because he has argued that a certain kind of pleasure completes/perfects a certain kind of activity (1175a22–3): pleasure and the activity match in kind.

YES But the positive path does not work either, for it leads to two problems:

First, it goes against the grain of this lemma and the previous one, which suggest we should individuate the activities broadly. The present lemma contains material to support the suggestion that we should individuate the activities broadly, according to the different kinds of knowledge activated. Importantly, Aristotle seems to source all his examples in 1175a30–1175b6 from the same place, Plato's *Philebus*. More specifically, he gathers them from the discussion of kinds of *knowledge* in the *Philebus*: geometry (56e8), music (56a3), building (56b8), and pipe-playing (56a5), and perhaps even 'paying attention to a discussion' (*tois logois prosechein*) corresponds to the activity of dialectic (*dialegesthai*, 57e6–7).[63] But, in contrast to the broad-grained individuation of activities, C seems to encourage a much finer-grained division. The pleasure of listening to pipe-music may distract me from listening to the lyre. And listening to Famous Artist's pipe-music may distract me from listening

---

[63] See Harte 2014, 308.

to Average-Joe's playing the pipes. C explains my behaviour by postulating different pleasures proper to the different performances – which, on the present response to *d*, would entail different kinds of activity.

Second, the fine-grained division of kinds of activity seems simply wrong. Why should listening to Average-Joe's playing the pipes differ in kind from listening to Famous Artist? The latter will be better, and more pleasant, but not different in kind.

Upshot. Reading a), i.e. Aristotle's attempt to establish or support the differentiation of pleasures into kinds through proper pleasures, faces serious difficulties. If he individuates proper pleasures via C, then he creates a dilemma for himself that does not allow for a straightforward solution. Moreover, the examples he adduces do not rule out an alternative explanation that does without kinds of pleasure. The problems would not arise so readily if reading b) is correct. For reading b) does not, on its own, make any claims about kinds of pleasure, and hence does not generate D. So far, then, Aristotle's kinds of pleasure stand on shaky ground.

1175b13–24 And since the pleasure proper ... except not in the same way.

Aristotle musters a further reason that pleasures belonging to different activities differ significantly from one another. An activity affords not only a pleasure proper to it, but also a certain corresponding pain (closely related to disliking the activity). Proper pain and proper pleasure obviously differ from one another, as the former increases the activity, whereas the latter destroys it. Since the pleasure proper to activity A_2 destroys activity A_1, the pleasure of A_2 functions like the proper pain of A_1 (albeit differently: the one through making the person feel good, the other through making her feel bad). But since the proper pain and the pleasure of A_1 differ significantly – they have the opposite effect – the pleasure of A_2 also differs significantly from the pleasure of A_1.

Aristotle says too little about the way in which an alien pleasure destroys an activity. His thesis that alien pleasures destroy an activity faces two problems. First, the argument does not show that the pleasures of A_1 and A_2 differ. Again, we might think of the difference in quantitative rather than in qualitative terms. Suppose I can only perform either A_1 or A_2. I am engaged in A_1, but if A_2 promises more pleasure, I am inclined to stop A_1 and continue with A_2 instead. The pain proper to A_1 and the pleasure of A2 function similarly, in that they threaten to, and often do, destroy A1. Both do so because A1 lacks (sufficient) pleasure for the agent to continue with it. Aristotle, note, says nothing to rule out this alternative explanation.

Second, the assumption that a person cannot enjoy two activities at once invites counter-examples. Doing the dishes is only mildly pleasant. Listening to music is more pleasant than doing the dishes. But listening to music while doing the dishes does not necessarily destroy the latter activity. Indeed, it often makes washing up go more smoothly and faster (depending on the music). Now we can take the objection in two directions. i) Together with the claim from the previous lemma that the pleasure which increases an activity belongs to that activity (1175a30–1), it would seem as if the pleasure belongs to the wrong activity. If listening to music (A2) makes doing the dishes (A1) better, then the pleasure of A2 should belong to A1. But it is false to attach the pleasure of listening to music to doing the dishes. To avert i), one might think that ii) a general level of pleasantness does the job. A2 need not directly increase A1 – it also increases doing other chores. One way of spelling out the suggestion would be by postulating a general level of enjoyment that the pleasure of A2 increases. If a person feels good in this general sense (rather than morose), she will perform whatever task better. However, introducing a general level of enjoyment undermines the correspondence between activities and their proper pleasures.

Despite these problems, the passage throws light on how Aristotle supposes a proper pleasure to increase the activity to which it belongs (*sunauxei*, 1175a30). A proper pleasure makes the activity 'more precise, longer lasting, and better' (1175b13–15). The activity becomes more precise if pleasure causes people to be more discerning and exact in the relevant activity, as said before (1175a31–2). The heightened exactness helps explain why the activity lasts longer. An activity peters out when the objects of thought or perception become old and dull (X.4.1175a7–10). So if pleasure helps keep up an intense engagement with the objects, it will last longer. While these two characteristics could plausibly be explained by a general level of pleasure, the third one may require tying pleasure more closely to activity, depending on how we understand 'better'. Pleasure can make an activity better in two senses. a) Pleasure makes an activity more valuable. If we take the claim that 'the pleasure completes/perfects the activity … as some superadded end' (1174b31–3) to mean that pleasure is an additional good, then pleasure would always add positive value to the activity, even to bad ones. This notion of 'better' can operate with a more general notion of pleasure. However, Aristotle will argue in the next lemma that pleasure increases the positive value only of good activities. Therefore reading b) seems more plausible: pleasure makes the activity better in the sense that it makes the activity more what it is (cf. commentary on 1175a21–8). Bad activities, like adultery, would become worse in terms of value, but better of their kind, when the perpetrator enjoys it. Taking pleasure to be specific and proper to the activity especially encourages this view of pleasure and its value.

Finally, a textual point prompts us to reflect further on the individuation of kinds of pleasure. The OCT prints the genitive singular of 'activity', *tês energeias*, at 1175b20 (with K^b, a very reliable manuscript). The other manuscripts have the accusative plural *tas energeias*. According to the latter, Aristotle speaks about the 'activities under the influence of their proper pleasures and pains' (b20–1), whereas the OCT has him sketch what happens to '*the* activity under the influence of its proper pleasures and pains'. The difference between the two texts is that the OCT attributes several proper pleasures to a single activity, whereas the other manuscripts leave open whether a single activity harbours only one or several proper pleasures. The plural in 'and the ones that properly belong being the ones that stem from the activity in virtue of the activity itself' (b21–2) could take up the plural of the activities (*tas energeias*) and explain that, for each of them, the pleasure that stems from engaging in the activity is proper to it.

What philosophical difference does the textual variation make? The text bears on the question of how to individuate pleasant activities. The OCT suggests a particular way of a fine-grained division of pleasures and activities. According to the OCT, several pleasures belong to one activity as proper pleasures. How is that possible? We can make sense of the claim by means of an example. The activity of housebuilding comprises many subordinate tasks. These tasks properly belong to the overarching activity. In this case, the pleasures of various housebuilding activities (tiling the bathroom, laying the floor) would (also?) belong to housebuilding – in which case housebuilding hosts many different proper pleasures. The text of the other manuscripts (the one translated here) does not suggest this way of dividing pleasures but has a proper pleasure correspond to just one activity. That Aristotle tends to write of the proper pleasure in the singular rather than the plural (1175a30–1; b5–6; b13–14; the plural at 1175a36 refers back to the several examples considered so far) tells against the OCT text. Similarly, he tends to say 'the pleasure completes/perfects the activity' (1174b33; cf. 1175a21) – as if *the* pleasure proper to an activity completes it (as opposed to *one of the* proper pleasures). In this case, the pleasure of painting the bathroom and the pleasure of painting the bedroom will belong to different activities and not be subsumed under the general activity of housebuilding to which they belong. This way of parsing the pleasures chimes with the claim that pleasures that can interfere with each other belong to different activities.

> *1175b24–36 Since the activities differ ... so do the pleasures.*

Leaving behind the attempt to differentiate pleasures into kinds, we return to a squarely ethical question. Do different pleasures differ in value? Aristotle presents his positive answer by relying on the notion of proper pleasure (developed in 1174a29–b24), and by comparing pleasure with desire.

What does desire have to do with pleasure? Elsewhere, Aristotle suggests that desire is for pleasure,[64] that a rational desire always precedes the enjoyment of an action (without desire we would not decide to perform the action),[65] and that enjoying X tends to instil a desire for X in the agent. Here, however, Aristotle seems to operate with a notion of desire independent from pleasure – he mentions none of the connections between the two. Indeed, using an independent notion of desire makes for a much stronger argument. As highlighted in the introduction to the discussion of pleasure, people disagree strongly about the value of pleasure (1172a26–33). But no one seems to dispute about the value of desire as such. Since bare desire does not exist, everyone will grasp the main point of bringing in desire, namely that its value depends on the object of the desire.[66]

Aristotle may liken pleasure to desire because he has argued in X.4 that bare pleasure does not exist either. Pleasure completes or perfects an activity, and thus depends on the activity. Now he brings home the point, implicit in his conception of pleasure, that pleasure *as such* does not have any value, positive or negative. Although he does not explicitly locate the source of desire's value, he points to the objects of desire as an important factor – which would explain why a desire tends to mirror the value of

---

[64] In fact, Aristotle's claim is more restricted. He thinks that appetitive desire (*epithumia*) is for pleasure, even if he sometimes uses the more general term *orexis* to express the point (so at *De Anima* II.3.414b5–6; cf. EN III.12.1119b5–7). For a nuanced discussion, and references, see Pearson 2012, 91–110.

[65] See the discussion of deliberation, wish, and decision in EN III.2–4.

[66] Epictetus comes close to regarding desires *qua* desires as bad (*Encheiridion* 2 and 48) – some three centuries after Aristotle. While Callicles in Plato's *Gorgias* does exhort desire, he emphasises the fulfilment of as many desires as possible, not merely *having* desires (494a–c).

the desired object. Now, we can desire doing a good deed without coming round to performing it. But we cannot enjoy doing a good deed without performing it. So, pleasure belongs much more closely to the enjoyed activity than does desire to the desired activity – almost to the point of indistinguishability (1175b31–3). Pleasure's greater proximity to the activity lets Aristotle conclude, by a fortiori argument, that pleasure also mirrors the value of the activity.

How far does the analogy go? Aristotle argues explicitly *that* pleasure mirrors the value of the activity – and then stops. Presumably, he omits investigating the value of pleasure further because it makes no practical difference. Unlike desire, we cannot enjoy pleasure without engaging in an activity. So, it suffices for practical purposes to know *that* pleasure takes on the value of its activity. However, the philosophically minded reader might wonder *how* pleasure takes on the value of its proper activity. Does Aristotle suggest pleasure's value also depends on its object, as in the case of desire? He would have the resources for doing so, for, just like desire, pleasure tends to be directed at some object, something the pleasure is about: enjoyment needs an object with which I am actively engaged.[67] If so, the object of pleasure factors large in determining pleasure's value, just as it does with desire. A good pleasure would be good largely because it is the pleasure taken in a good object, not merely because it increases a good activity. The other relevant factors for determining the value of pleasure stem from the list of things that explicate the elements that determine whether emotions, including pleasure, are taken as one should: the right time, the right object, in relation to the right people, etc. (II.6.1106b21–3).

Supposing Aristotle endorses the explanation – what are the objects of pleasure? The question is difficult to answer because he seems almost deliberately vague about the object of enjoyment. In X.4, he speaks of pleasure perfecting/completing the activity (*passim*), of pleasure arising from the activity (1174b27; 1175a5; b20–1), and of pleasure accompanying the activity (1175a5–6) – which leaves open which objects we enjoy. Two different sets of objects suggest themselves. a) The agent might enjoy the activity insofar as she enjoys the object with which the activity puts her in touch. At 1174b27–9 Aristotle writes that we enjoy sights and sounds, and presumably all other kinds of perceptual objects. Alternatively, b), he also puts forward the activity as the object of enjoyment (1175a33–4),

---

[67] Distinguishing between 'enjoying' and 'being pleased', Penelhum 1964, 82, notes that 'being pleased that' does not require active engagement with the object, but merely some awareness or cognisance of it.

as well as the work proper to an activity (its *ergon*, a35). His insouciance makes little difference for determining the value of pleasure. All the activities mentioned in X.4–5, activities of perception and thought, necessarily have some object they are *about*. So, even if the activity served as primary object, what the activity is about would serve as secondary object. So, the two options would largely coincide.

1175b36–1176a3 And sight differs from touch ... within themselves.

The present lemma has puzzled many readers and interpreters. Aristotle has distinguished between good and bad pleasures in the previous lemma. But which pleasures are best? Before he expands on the obvious answer — the pleasures associated with the best activities – he puts forward a different proposal in this lemma, introducing the notion of purity. The present lemma may have the character of a) a footnote in which Aristotle simply records, and then drops, another difference between pleasures via the notion of purity, or b) a premise for the larger argument that fills the rest of X.5 (so Gauthier and Jolif 1958), or c) something in-between.

If b) or c) are right, we must explain how purity bears on the present line of thought. Some Platonic background helps illuminate the function of purity in this context. In the *Republic*, Plato regards all pleasures as fillings of some sort. In order to rank pleasures in terms of goodness, Plato introduces two distinctions: i) pure vs impure and ii) intellectual vs bodily pleasures, distinctions that he tends to run together. Pleasures that necessarily presuppose or otherwise involve pain are impure, whereas pain-free pleasures are pure. Plato observes that many so-called 'pleasures', coming through the body, are merely a relief from pain (584b–c) – which sure enough *seems* pleasant. But the appearance is misleading, since only the juxtaposition to pain makes the condition seem pleasant; in itself it is not pleasant. By contrast, the philosopher's pleasures do not require a contrasting pain to appear pleasant: they *are* pleasant (to a lover of knowledge) and hence true to their appearance. Thus, Plato has a means of ranking pleasures in terms of pleasantness, where 'X is more pleasant than Y' does not mean that X gives pleasure more frequently, or that X-pleasures are more intense than Y-pleasures (584b). Rather, iii) the real criterion for pleasantness is whether X-pleasures are purer than Y-pleasures. So, in the *Republic*, Plato tries to discredit bodily pleasures as mixed, less real, and less pleasant than intellectual pleasures (585b–586c). The *Philebus* carefully eschews aligning i) and ii), as certain pleasures of sight, hearing, and even smell turn out to be pure (51b–e, though Plato mentions smell already at *Republic* 584b). Nevertheless, the *Philebus* retains iii) (cf. 52d–53c). So, in both dialogues, Plato uses the notion of purity to rank pleasures in terms of pleasantness. When a pleasure is not mixed with its opposite, then pleasure is more what it is – a pleasure.

Does Aristotle share Plato's conception of pure/impure pleasures? No, he does not define impure pleasures as mixed with pain. In fact, he does not define them at all (or pure pleasures). A closer look at the passage helps to see how he seems to revive Plato's initial suspicion of the body as a source of impurity – but for different reasons. Although Aristotle distinguishes between pleasures of the body and pleasures of the soul (III.10.1117b28–9), pleasure belongs properly to the soul (I.8.1099a8). All the activities mentioned here (smelling, hearing, etc., 1176a1–3) are taken from III.10, most of them verbatim – as if he wanted to draw attention to the distinction between bodily and psychic pleasures. He might now suggest that bodily involvement taints pleasure, making it less what it really is. The less the body is involved, the purer – and the more pleasant – the pleasure.[68] Thus, for Aristotle, the life of pure thought would be the most pleasant life.[69]

Despite the differences in detail, alluding to Plato's criterion of purity nevertheless helps Aristotle make his point. Like Plato, he rejects a quantitative notion of pleasantness in favour of a qualitative one. This helps him to rank pleasures in terms of their pleasantness. According to b), the present lemma continues the argument from the previous one. Aristotle has just distinguished between good and bad pleasures; now he introduces a criterion to single out the best pleasures – as if greater purity automatically yields greater goodness (as in Plato). By contrast, reading c) proceeds more carefully. While purity introduces another relevant factor for assessing the pleasures of the best life (the topic of the remainder of X.5), it keeps purity/pleasantness and goodness apart. My enjoying pleasure A may be purer than your enjoying pleasure B, but still your pleasure may be better, if you enjoy it at the right time, for the right amount of time, in relation to the right person etc., whereas I do not. It is not the purity of an activity that alone determines the pleasure's value, but ethical considerations (broadly understood) also need to be considered.

---

[68] Gonzalez 1991, 151–9, reaches a similar conclusion through linking purity, pleasantness, and completeness.

[69] Plato concedes in the *Philebus* that the life of our thought life would be neither pleasant nor painful (55a), if 'pure thought' designates the calling-up and entertaining of knowledge rather than its acquisition. This is due to the conception of pleasure as a restorative process. Aristotle critically examines this view at X.3.1173a29–b20.

1176a3–12 And for each animal ... lovable to others.

Building on the previously established concepts 'proper pleasure' and 'kinds of pleasure', Aristotle seems to add a third distinction among pleasures. Having separated the good from the bad (1175b25–36), the more pure from the less pure (1175b36–1176a3), he now seeks to differentiate between the pleasures proper to human beings and those that are not proper to us (this lemma and the next two). Roughly, he argues that i) each kind of animal has a pleasure proper to its characteristic activity (its *ergon*); ii) human beings are animals [unstated]; therefore iii) there is a pleasure proper to the characteristically human activity. But why the argument, and why now?

Identifying the pleasure proper to an animal as the pleasure stemming from performing its *ergon* allows Aristotle to capture the spirit of Eudoxus' argument from universal pursuit without espousing his hedonism. According to Eudoxus, each kind of animal pursues what is fitting for them, i.e. what is natural for them (1172b11, with commentary). Unlike Eudoxus, Aristotle distinguishes between what is pleasant and what is good. The notion of proper pleasure helps him to capture what is right about Eudoxus' thesis.[70] If we understand a set of characteristic behavioural patterns, namely pursuing what is fitting, as the animal's *ergon* (function or work), and the pleasure taken in achieving the *ergon* as its own proper pleasures, then proper pleasures will belong to activities that are good for the animal.[71] But since the pleasure takes on the value of the activity to which it is proper (1175b24–36), proper pleasures will be good for each animal. Perhaps Aristotle goes even further by alluding to Heraclitus' observation that donkeys do not find gold pleasant (1176a6–8; DK 22 B9): if animals find pleasant *only* what is good for them, pleasant *to* and good *for* a kind of animal would always go hand in hand.[72] That is, Aristotle does not merely try to identify the proper pleasure for different kinds of animal – including humans – but he does so with a view to value. The pleasures proper to a kind of animal are good for the animal, and are the only ones an animal should pursue seriously.

Aristotle seeks to support and adapt Eudoxus' central insight by focusing on a problem with iii) which he attempts to solve in the next two

---

[70] In *Hist. An.* IX.1.589a8–9 Aristotle follows Eudoxus closely: 'and what is natural is pleasant, and all [animals] pursue their natural pleasure'.

[71] Aristotle, in fact, thinks that we attribute virtue or excellence to animals on the basis of their performing their *ergon* well, II.6, esp. 1106a15–24.

[72] Another Heraclitean fragment on the same topic is cast in terms of pleasure: 'Pigs enjoy muck more than clean water' (DK 22 B13).

lemmata. However, he seems to overlook two problems with i). First, the choice of examples, human vs canine vs equine pleasure, supports i) because of the obvious differences in their respective *ergon*. But consider different kinds of animal whose characteristic behavioural patterns overlap, such as horses and donkeys (both mentioned here). Why should we think *their* proper pleasures differ? Aristotle, who does not consider the question, could pursue different lines of response. He could a) highlight the species-specific differences in the *ergon*. Procreation, for instance, belongs to an animal's *ergon*, and while the activity of mating may not differ much, what is begotten does differ in kind – and so the pleasure stemming from it. Alternatively, he could b) individuate the *ergon*-related activities partly via the animal-specific sense-organ or 'reason'. So, a donkey's tasting hay and a horse's tasting hay would be two similar, but different, activities, insofar as they are the activations of different sense-organs. But if the activities are different, so are the associated pleasures.[73] Second, we can observe a variety of different behavioural patterns among animals belonging to one kind. Rover the dog enjoys chasing after a ball, while Fido prefers to sleep on the sofa. Kitty the cat shuns wet food and only eats biscuits, whereas Puss disregards biscuits and only eats wet food, and so on. Does the observation not undermine i)? No, because all the behaviour displayed befits the animals: it is natural. So, while the *ergon* allows for some variation, as long as the animals do what is good for them, it does not matter whether they enjoy biscuits or wet food. In either case, they perform their *ergon*, and hence enjoy the same proper pleasure.

Human life also displays significant variation in pursuits. Individual human beings can and do enjoy things directly opposed to each other, as Aristotle observes (a10–12). However, iii) requires that all human beings enjoy the same proper pleasure, at least in a sense (cf. 1172b36–a5 on the universal pursuit of the good). Unfortunately, the 'fix' developed in the previous paragraph does not work, because human lives are much more complexly organised, and therefore admit of a much greater variety, than the lives of most animals. An animal's kind (together with its characteristic environment) determines to a large extent how an animal lives. A herbivore's eating meat or a gregarious animal's living in solitude *are* deviations from the norms of their kind: it is not what such a kind of animal does. While some

---

[73] One could spell out this suggestion by appealing to the priority of the whole over the part (cf. EN IX.8.1168b31–3). Here we could say that the identity of a part depends on the whole to which it belongs. Although the sense-organs of horses and donkeys will be very similar, they differ insofar as they are parts of different wholes. A donkey's sense of taste helps sustain a donkey, not a horse.

kinds of animal have complex 'societies', the different roles in that society are few. Human beings, by contrast, differ insofar as different societies satisfy their basic needs in different and opposed ways: some through farming, some through hunting, others by being nomads (for further ways of life, see *Politics* I.8.1256a13–b7). Unlike other animals, many humans have the opportunity to follow and dedicate themselves to pursuits not related to meeting their basic needs.[74] So, within human societies, different individuals can play significantly different roles: some are producers, others magistrates, others artists, and so on. Human lifestyles can and do vary. At 1175a10–17 Aristotle highlights the fact that people's lives differ, depending on their central activity: a music-lover's life will differ from that of a lover of learning — and so will their characteristic pleasures. Therefore, even if all human beings pursue the human good in some sense, the way they pursue it allows for much more significant variation than does that of any kind of animal.

To conclude, Aristotle *does* put his finger on an important difference between human beings and other kinds of animal that threatens iii). A life's central pleasures are determined for all animals by the kind to which they belong – human beings excepted. While the variety among human pleasures need not undercut the inference 'human beings tend to enjoy X if and only if X is good for human beings', it does undercut the inference from 'this normal human being tends to enjoy X' to 'X tends to be good for human beings'. Over the next two lemmata, Aristotle examines which individual pleasures to discredit, and which one to elevate to *the* pleasure proper to the human *ergon*.

1176a12–22 And in the case of sweet things ... in that sort of state.

In the previous lemma, Aristotle has begun to argue for the existence of *the* proper human pleasure. If successful, the argument allows him to privilege this pleasure and to run goodness and (proper) pleasantness together (see commentary on previous lemma). However, he is rightly worried whether we can single out any one pleasure as *the* proper human pleasure, since human lives and the pleasures central to them vary so much. The present lemma reins in the sheer variety of pleasures by identifying a standard with which we can determine whether a given pleasure is central to human life or not.[75]

---

[74] Aristotle distinguishes between naturally shared desires and their pleasures on the one hand, and private or peculiar pleasures (*idioi*) on the other, at III.11.1118b8–27.

[75] In a way, Aristotle sets himself a bigger task than Plato in *Republic* IX, 581c4–583a11, where a competent judge decides between 'merely' three different ways of lives and their associated pleasures.

First, he points to familiar cases of differing perceptions. The same object, O, may seem sweet or warm to a sick person, whereas O appears neither sweet nor warm to a healthy person. We take the healthy person's perception to be authoritative: one *should* perceive O as the healthy person does. Nevertheless, we do not deny that O *seems* sweet or warm to the sick person. The sick person's perception simply deviates from the norm. Second, assuming similar norms for human conduct, Aristotle postulates not the healthy person as authoritative, but the *spoudaios* (good, decent, sound, 1176a16). If the good person perceives or discerns correctly in all cases to do with human conduct, she will also be right about pleasure. What is pleasant without qualification will appear pleasant to her *insofar as she is good*. The proviso importantly restricts the unqualified pleasures, for a good person will enjoy water when thirsty or might enjoy white wine more than red wine. But neither is characteristic of a good person (bad people may enjoy the same pleasures). By contrast, enjoying acts of virtue belongs to the good person *qua* good (cf. I.8.1099a17–21). As before, what is pleasant to someone with distorted taste (either through illness or depravity) is pleasant only in a qualified way, pleasant-to-them. Again, these abnormal people really do enjoy X, but X cannot be recommended for enjoyment to anyone but to those in a similar condition. Hence, X will not be pleasant without qualification (1176a19–22).

How do the argument's two steps relate to each other? The text argues as follows: i) the healthy person judges authoritatively in perpetual cases (1176a13–14); ii) the *spoudaios* judges correctly in all such cases (a15–16); iii) [therefore?] the good person judges correctly about pleasure (a18–19). Now, Aristotle either equivocates between *spoudaios* and the good person in ii) and iii), or he does not. If we assume that he does not equivocate, then he seems to maintain that the *spoudaios* is the norm of every kind of perception, as if *that* was characteristic of a good person insofar as she is good! While implausible, we can see why Aristotle would want to make the *spoudaios* the norm not only of conduct, but also of ordinary perception. For insofar as ordinary perception informs conduct and ethical judgement, the *spoudaios'* perceptual apparatus must be impeccable. For instance, if I mistake the bloodstains on an injured person's shirt for batik, I will not seek the sort of medical help I should seek – and thus fail to do what I should. So, even if the good person does not perceive everything correctly in virtue of his good character, he nevertheless must perceive those things that could make an ethical difference correctly. Alternatively, and more plausibly, Aristotle uses i) to motivate the general claim in ii), that whoever counts as *spoudaios* in a certain domain will judge correctly.

Thus, *spoudaios* does not designate the ethical paragon as it does in most of the EN, but the paragon of any domain. In iii) he then narrows down the domain to that of human conduct, where the good person plays the role of the *spoudaios*.

His reasoning broaches a metaphysical question about the connection between the judgement and what is judged, for an object P might count as pleasant without qualification *because* the good person (*qua* good) judges P to be pleasant, or else the good person might judge P as pleasant *because* P is pleasant without qualification. In other words, is it the good person's response to P that transfers the status to P, or does P have the status as pleasant without qualification independently of the good person's response? The answer might seem obvious to us. 'Aristotle's comparison of pleasant with sweet is useful insofar as perceptible qualities such as sweet are plausibly construed as 'response-dependent', that is, as essentially involving a disposition to produce a specific response in an observer.'[76] So, the suggestion goes, pleasure is also response-dependent. But Aristotle seems to have a different view of pleasure's comparanda. In his scientific works, perceptual qualities such as warm/cold and sweet/bitter are what they are in virtue of their explanatory role, not in virtue of our responses to them. Sweetness, for instance, serves as a nutriment to the body (*De Sensu* 442a2) – whether we perceive our food to be sweet or not makes no difference to its nutritional value, and hence to its sweetness.[77] If 'pleasant' works like 'sweet', 'pleasant' would be response-independent.

While Aristotle need not give the same metaphysical account of 'sweet' and 'pleasant', some passages in the EN work well with a response-independent construal of 'pleasant'. In an argument designed to highlight the pleasantness of the virtuous life, Aristotle maintains that the good person's life is pleasant because 'things pleasant by nature are pleasant to the lover of the fine and virtuous actions are of this kind' (I.8.1099a13–14). To avoid a vicious circle, the reasoning must presuppose a response-independent distinction between things pleasant by nature and not pleasant by nature – independent at least from the good person's judgement.[78] So, the good person will lead an unqualifiedly pleasant life not because what she judges to be pleasant thereby

---

[76] Harte 2014, 315.
[77] For further discussion of this point, see Aufderheide 2017, 213–15.
[78] For what it is worth: in the *Eudemian Ethics* Aristotle identifies what is good without qualification with what is pleasant without qualification (1235b31; 1236b26; 1237a27). So, to the extent that goodness is response-independent, to that extent pleasant *can* be so as well.

becomes pleasant without qualification, but rather because she is perfectly attuned to enjoying what is pleasant by nature or without qualification.[79]

1176a22–29 While it is clear ... just like the activities.

In this lemma, Aristotle completes the task of identifying the proper human pleasure, begun at 1176a3–12. While we can single out the pleasures proper to other kinds of animal through their characteristic activity (*ergon*), human nature (and with it human pleasure) proves too complex for this expedient. Even if we eliminate shameful or otherwise objectionable pleasures, there remain a plethora of human pleasures. Aristotle has introduced, in the previous lemma, the good person as competent judge, i.e. as someone who reliably discerns qualified pleasures from unqualified pleasures (1176a12–22). Now he addresses the question *what sort of* or *which* pleasure the good person singles out.

His argument relies on the central thesis established in X.4, that pleasures depend on and accompany activities (by completing or perfecting them). Together with the claim that pleasures are proper to the activity that gives rise to them (1175a29–b13), Aristotle can turn his attention to identifying the activity proper to human beings. Since he has made the good person the measure of all things concerning human conduct, the good person's actions, insofar as she is good, will reveal the pleasures proper to human beings (cf. 1176a15–18 with commentary). For an accurate judgement, Aristotle does not merely look to the good person, but to the completely happy person (*teleios kai makarios*), because external factors might impede the good person's actions, in which case she would not count among the happy (as happened to Priam, I.10.1099b22–1101a8). So, whatever actions are characteristic of a completely happy person will yield the pleasure(s) proper to human beings.

However, Aristotle shifts from 'pleasure proper to human beings' (implied in 1176a3–12) to speaking about 'the pleasures characteristic of human beings in the primary way (*kuriôs*)' (a27–8), which allows him a more gradual approach to human pleasures, warranted by the complexity of human life. For other animals, an activity is either natural or unnatural. If natural, it will benefit the animal and count as a proper pleasure. But a binary distinction proves too crude to account for human pleasures.

---

[79] Taylor 2008a, 102–3 likewise attributes an objective construal of 'pleasant' to Aristotle (on the basis of I.8). However, he problematises the passage because he takes Aristotle to advocate 'pleasant' as a response-dependent quality in X.5. Cf. 2008b, 252–4.

Discounting the unnatural and perverted pleasures still leaves a wide variety of pleasures that are characteristically human, in the sense that no other animal can perform them. They are much more closely related to *the* proper or primary human pleasure than the activities of other animals; and they differ among themselves by being more or less closely related to the primary human pleasure. So, the primary human pleasure serves as a standard and focal point to rank pleasures in terms of appropriateness for human beings.[80]

Aristotle omits to specify which activities he counts among the primary human ones. The omission does not weigh heavily against Aristotle's account, but stems from the structure of the EN. In I.7, the so-called *ergon* or function argument, he seeks to clarify in virtue of which activity a life is happy. The argument locates the direction in which to find human happiness by thinking about human nature. Reason, he argues, must play a key role in human happiness. Human activities characteristically involve reason, such as sculpting and playing the flute (indeed all crafts, cf. 1097b25–6), but also ethically good action and theoretical thinking. If his claim is so general, then the conclusion of the *ergon* argument that 'the human good turns out to be the activity of the soul in accordance with virtue, and if there are several virtues, in accordance with the best and most complete/perfect/final one (*teleiotatên*)' (1098a16–18) need not refer to any particular virtue. The argument entitles him to claim only that happiness rests on excelling in 'the activity of the soul in accordance with reason, or not without reason' (1098a7–8) – whatever that activity may be.[81] So, Aristotle does not name the best activity which, together with its proper pleasure, will be human in the primary sense because he has not yet identified the best activity.[82]

The reference to the function argument suggests as characteristically human the pleasures that stem from reasoning (broadly understood). It thus reinforces the point made through the criterion of purity: the less a pleasure involves the body, the more it is what it is for something to be a pleasure (1175b36–1176a3 with commentary). For human beings, the best pleasures will not only be *unqualifiedly* pleasant, but also *most* pleasant, because least bodily. So, the end of X.5 raises the question which activity

---

[80] For further reflections on Aristotle's use of *kuriôs*, see Charles 1999 and Scott 1999.
[81] Note that Aristotle, having foreshadowed the twofold division of reason to follow in I.13, posits the active life to be more properly (*kuriôteron*) human – which may privilege the active use of reason over the passive act of 'listening' (I.7.1098a3–7).
[82] For a defence of this reading of the function argument, see Lawrence 2001.

best satisfies both the criterion of purity and makes best use of reason. In X.7–8, Aristotle takes up the task of identifying the best activity by comparing theoretical reflection with virtuous action. Do both the intellectual aspect of virtuous action and purely theoretical thought yield pleasures that can be called with equal right 'primarily human', or does one top the other? The answer requires thinking further on what it is to be human – which Aristotle does at X.7.1177b26–X.8.1178b32. In other words, the question of which pleasures count as primarily human depends on which life counts as primarily human (and the best human life). Thus, Aristotle sees the discussion of pleasure, or at least one important question, as continuous with the discussion of the best life in X.7–8.

II Happy Lives (X.6–8)

X.6

1176a30–33 As the subjects ... will be shorter.

The two sentences with which Aristotle leads on to the next topic raise numerous questions. Why does he write as if he has only discussed three topics? Why does he write as if happiness still remains to be discussed, given that Book I treats of this topic at length? And why should he discuss it only in outline (*tupô(i)*)?

The answers fall in place if we examine the use of the word *tupô(i)* in the EN. Right from the beginning, he stresses that successful practical agency requires us to grasp the highest good in outline – just like archers need to have a goal (I.2.1094a25). But why only an outline? Successful archers do have a precise grasp of their target, so why should we as practical agents not also have a precise target? In response, Aristotle distinguishes between different levels of precision suitable for different kinds of enquiry. While we aim for a single, exact answer in mathematics, practical affairs such as ethics or political science allow more variation, due to their complexity. In contrast to mathematics, we should be content with broad-brush outline statements (*pachulôs kai tupô(i)*) as the appropriate level of precision for ethics (I.3.1094b19–25; cf. II.1.1104a1–2 *tupô(i) kai ouk akribôs*). This sense of *tupô(i)*, a), indicates the absence of unsuitable precision, and would be appropriate in our lemma, as a discussion of happiness is a paradigmatically practical affair for Aristotle.

However, a related use of the word *tupô(i)* also seems to be at play. By discussing a topic 'in outline', Aristotle can b) indicate that he will not go through all the possible cases relevant to answering a problem, but will selectively concentrate on the main ones only (*katholou ... kai tupô(i)*, I.11.1101a27). Both a) and b) have the same purpose: to make the sheer variety of cases in practical affairs manageable. But b) also has a further purpose. Treating a topic in outline may require a more precise account later.

We can find *tupô(i)* used in this way at II.7.1107b14–16, where Aristotle promises to fill the very schematic characterisation of the virtues with content later. Similarly, at III.5.1114b26–1115a6, he summarises the preliminary discussion of virtue (II.2–III.5), and says that he has discussed the different virtues together, in outline. Having summed up what is characteristic of all virtues and virtuous action, he then begins to discuss the specific virtues. The word *analambanein* ('resume' or 'take up again', 1115a4) signals the continuity between the outlined framework and the more specific account. However, due to a), even the more precise account will remain in outline (III.9.1117b20–2). So, the word *tupô(i)* can indicate different levels of enquiry, but whether it indicates a preliminary sketch of the framework or the most specific account suitable for a treatise in practical philosophy depends on the context.

Let's return to happiness. In Book I, Aristotle identifies happiness with activity of the soul in accordance with (the highest) virtue in a complete life (I.7.1098a16–20). Using painting metaphors, he stresses that he has only outlined (*perigegraphthô*, a20) the good because one needs to lay down a well-sketched outline (*hupotupôsai*, a21 with a23) before one can usefully fill in (*anagrapsai*, a22 with a23–4) the details. While the outline of happiness will suffice to guide much of the EN's argument, it needs further filling in. So, Aristotle appears to approach happiness in the same way as virtue. In Book I he gives a general account of happiness that schematically sketches the role, criteria, and logical category of happiness. The account may apply to several species or determinants, candidates that will have to be examined in a more precise account. The present lemma signals the resumption of the topic. In fact, he uses the same word as in the account of virtue, *analambanein* (1176a33), to signal the next stage of his enquiry. We resume the enquiry into happiness, but we do so within the confines of the framework established earlier. So, since we need to consider only those candidates that appear to fit the outline of happiness drawn earlier, the discussion will be shorter than starting from scratch or considering every possible candidate (a33–4). In fact, Aristotle discusses only the life of pleasure (this chapter), the life of politics or virtue, and the life of reflection (the next two chapters). So, only in X.6–8 does he give more definite content to the Book I sketch of happiness.

Aristotle's word choice further confirms this approach. He introduces every topic in Greek by *peri* with genitive, governed by a verb of speaking, discussing, or enquiring. In this way, he highlights virtue, friendship, and pleasure as the main topics of the EN that Book I put on the stage, taking the other topics to be subordinate. He has not, however, introduced happiness as a topic in this way, but does so only now. That is, only now does he consider himself to treat of happiness as a proper topic (rather than setting the stage). Due to a), however, he cannot help but give even a more precise account in outline only. But that restriction applies to every major topic, as he notes at the beginning of X.9: 'the present topic <sc. happiness> as well as the topic of the virtues, and again friendship and pleasure, have been sufficiently discussed in outlines' (*tois tupois*, 1179a33–4).

1176a33–b6 *Now, we said that ... but is self-sufficient.*

In the previous lemma Aristotle announced he was taking up the topic of happiness again, based on the results gained earlier. Book I of the EN begins by establishing the highest good as the goal of all human endeavours. To develop the framework for the other topics treated in the EN, he argues in Book I that i) the highest good is an activity (rather than a state), and ii) we should identify the highest good with happiness. In the present lemma, he reiterates some of the points supporting i) and ii). He does so not with a view to establishing those points again, but in order to examine which activity best satisfies the role of happiness.

He begins by reminding us of the nature of happiness as an activity. In doing so, he alludes to I.5, where he briefly considers three lives based on different conceptions of the highest good. Having quickly brushed aside the life of pleasure, he turns to the life of politics, which posits honour (*timê*) as the highest good and end (1095b22–3). Honour alone, however, will not do. Politicians want to receive honour for being good (and from good people) – which makes virtue a more appropriate goal. Still, virtue falls short of being a sufficient goal (*atelestera*, b32) because we would not call people happy (*eudaimonizein*, 1096a2) if they had virtue but were constantly asleep, or did nothing, or suffered great misfortunes. By alluding here to the latter set of arguments (and he will do so again at 1178b18–23; cf. I.8.1098b30–1099a7 for emphasis on activity), Aristotle calls to mind that happiness is not a thing, but an activity that shapes a life. Note, 'activity' here seems to be understood broadly so as to include pleasure (next lemma). While pleasure may or may not be an activity according to the Book X account (scholars are divided), pleasure as something active clearly contrasts with states.

To narrow down further what sort of activity happiness might be, Aristotle distinguishes between activities choice-worthy in themselves and activities to be chosen on account of something else. In effect, he reminds us that happiness as the highest good must be *teleios*, which can be translated as 'complete', 'perfect', or 'final' (I.7.1097a24–b6). The criterion rules out a vast number of activities (in the broader sense). For example, housebuilding and other processes fail to qualify as candidates for the activity of happiness because they do not satisfy the criterion of being *teleios*. Building a house is not choice-worthy for its own sake, but for the sake of the house. Any candidate for the activity of happiness must, by contrast, be chosen for its own sake. In Book I, Aristotle notes, moreover, that some activities are choice-worthy both in themselves and for the sake of X (1097a34–b1). More specifically, in Book I he identifies the X for the sake of which we may undertake activities choice-worthy in themselves with happiness. Now he examines which of the activities to be chosen in themselves turns out to *be* happiness.

Finally, completeness/perfection/finality closely relates to self-sufficiency (*autarkeia*, 1097b7), a further criterion for happiness. Here Aristotle writes as if self-sufficiency could explain why happiness is complete/perfect/final: 'for happiness does not lack in anything, but is self-sufficient' (1176b5–6). Although the Book I discussion of the criterion rather seems to suggest that being *teleios* entails self-sufficiency (1097b6–8), Aristotle here calls to mind what stands behind the criterion. Any candidate for the highest good must be self-sufficient in the sense that it can 'on its own render the life choice-worthy and lacking in nothing' (1097b14–15). This does not mean that the happy and self-sufficient life is one that could not be improved because it already has all the goods. Rather, he seems interested in the psychological aspect of self-sufficiency: when a person attains happiness, she will not be dissatisfied with her life and wish it contained other goods besides. Happiness stops the lingering desire for more goods whose prospect is dimly perceived to make one happy. Whoever engages in the self-sufficient activity of happiness will have all she needs for living well.

1176b6–16 The ones to be chosen ... people of this sort.

Aristotle's outline-examination of happiness makes progress by considering a necessary condition that any candidate must satisfy: any activity that purports to play the role of happiness must be choice-worthy in itself. He presents two candidates that appear to satisfy the condition: virtuous action and pleasure.

Importantly, the condition does not rule out activities that may be both choice-worthy in themselves and for the good consequences they tend to bring, for virtuous action aims at some good beyond itself that a successful action brings about. However, Aristotle stresses that *doing* fine and worthwhile actions (*ta kala kai spoudaia prattein*, 1176b8) satisfies the finality criterion, even if we also welcome the fine and worthy things brought about by the action. He has supported this view of virtuous action in Book VI by contrasting actions guided by practical wisdom (*phronêsis*) with those guided by productive expertise. We clearly seek something beyond the activity in the latter: they aim at a product to which the action is entirely subordinate. We build houses for the sake of having the houses, not vice versa. The former differ in this respect, Aristotle argues. Virtuous action aims primarily at acting well (*eupraxia*, VI.5.1140b7), a goal internal to the action, not subordinate to the result. We can act well even if the desired result does not follow, but we cannot build well if the house does not ensue. We can, and do, choose virtuous action without necessarily seeking anything besides the activity.

The case for pleasure seems more straightforward. Unlike virtuous action, pleasure does not seem to aim at or tend to bring about some further good. The first reason Aristotle cites on behalf of pleasure's candidacy brings this point home. By choosing pleasure, people do not gain anything for themselves besides pleasure – indeed, they may even spend their fortune and harm their bodies (1176b11). But the point seems true only if we understand the 'pleasant amusements' (*tôn paidiôn ... hai hêdeiai*, 1176b9) in a certain way. For why would I harm myself by pursuing cultured pleasures, such as playing games, making or hearing jokes, listening to music, and perhaps going to the theatre? Which pleasures is Aristotle talking about?

The verbal echoes of the virtue of wittiness (in IV.8 witty people are *eutrapeloi*, here rendered 'well-versed') in the context of amusement (*diagôgês meta paidias*, 1127b34) might suggest a refined pursuit of pleasure which we could call 'culture hedonism'.[83] However, the second reason for pleasure's candidacy further underlines the difficulty with this suggestion. People take tyrants to be especially happy, and tyrants take refuge in such pastimes, i.e. in the sorts of pleasure at issue. But few tyrants were known for their pursuit of culture.[84] Instead, tyrants were known for their pursuit of baser pleasures. So, Aristotle seems to conjure up the caricature of the luxury-loving tyrants he himself perpetuates in the *Politics* (V.10.1313a4–11).

---

[83] So Pakaluk 2005, 320–1 and Kullmann 1995, 255. On culture hedonism, see *Politics* VIII.5.1339b31–41.

[84] Hermias, tyrant of Atarneus, may be one of the few exceptions – Aristotle writes only 'most of those' (although the reports of his character are extremely controversial). In any case, Aristotle and Hermias were friends, and Aristotle composed a hymn to his friend's virtue on the occasion of the latter's death. Natali 2013, 32–42, translates the sources and provides a well-balanced account.

He depicts them invariably as interested in sex, heavy drinking, and effeminate behaviour. They lavish money on 'prostitutes, foreigners, and craftsmen' (1314b3–4), presumably because they are well-versed in providing the tyrants with pleasure. Going to excess in *those* activities indeed leads to declining wealth and health; culture hedonism seems comparatively salubrious.[85]

By examining the suitability of pleasure, Aristotle apparently alludes to the life of pleasure mentioned briefly in Book I. Understood as the life of consumption (*bios apolaustikos*, I.5.1095b17), he quickly dismisses it as worthy only of cattle. However, he notes that something can be said in favour of this sort of life because high-powered people like Sardanapallus devote their lives to pleasure (1095b19–22).[86] So here in Book X Aristotle seems to reconsider the case for pleasure on the strength of its satisfying the criterion of self-sufficiency. The next lemma will examine how strong the case for the life of consumption really is. This lemma only puts pleasure in the race, and indicates *that* he talks about this kind of life, not a more refined version of hedonism.

1176b16–27 Now, while these things ... in accordance with virtue.

In the *Politics*, Aristotle connects the tyrant's excesses with happiness. Some tyrants 'not only begin their debaucheries at dawn and continue them for days on end, but they also wish to be seen doing so by others, in order that they may be admired as happy and blessed' (V.11.1314b29–32, tr. Reeve). Tyrants generally succeeded in this: they were thought to be paradigms of happiness (cf. previous lemma). In this lemma Aristotle first hints at the reason tyrants were thought to be happy, and then musters arguments against taking tyrants as paradigms.

Tyrants play a special role in popular thinking about happiness. Their judgement seems to have special weight, because of the close connection between free time or leisure (*scholê*) and happiness (explored further in X.7.1177b4–15): i) everyone wants happiness most of all and ii) in leisure

---

[85] On a semantic level, the text also speaks against culture hedonism: Aristotle uses the same word 'seek refuge' (*katapheugousi*) at 1176b12 and b21 to describe the tyrants' behaviour. Since the latter concerns bodily pleasures, 'pleasant pastimes' at b12 should do so too.

[86] While Sardanapallus was in fact the last great Assyrian king (or one of the last; he ruled ca 667–647 BC), the Greek imagination took him to exemplify all the traits of pleasure-loving tyrants. We can still find reverberations of this view in Delacroix's monumental painting *The Death of Sardanapallus* (1827), and in Thoreau's *Walden* (1854, in the section 'Economy').

time one can do what one wants most. Now, people might reason as follows: iii) tyrants can do whatever they want, especially in their leisure time[87] (even tyrants need to spend some non-leisure time on organising their bodyguards, crushing uprisings, extorting money etc.). Therefore (tacitly assuming i), iv) what tyrants choose to do in their leisure time will be most characteristic of happiness. v) Tyrants choose excessive bodily pleasures on a large scale. Hence vi) such activities bring happiness. Thus, tyrants are thought to be paradigmatically happy because they make use of their opportunity to lose themselves in pleasure. They can do things ordinary people cannot do, such as hosting and wallowing in prolonged debaucheries. Since such activities set them apart from everyone else, their preferential choice to engage in these activities is taken to be authoritative and thereby picks up on what is characteristic of happiness. So, even if ordinary people try to follow the tyrants' examples in opting for bodily pleasures, they will attain only a shadow of the tyrants' supposed happiness because they do not have the means to live the life of consumption in the same way as tyrants do.

Aristotle criticises people for taking their lead from tyrants in matters of happiness. He offers two reasons. First, having political power (*dunasteuein*) does not by itself improve one's judgement. Having the power to do what they want does not guarantee that tyrants will do what is worthwhile. Rather, since virtue and intelligence engender worthwhile (*spoudaia*) activities, the tyrant *qua* powerful does not shed light on what makes us happy (1176b18–19). The force of the argument depends on the context in which we place it. If the enquiry were open, limited only by the two constraints that the activity of happiness be choice-worthy in itself and be self-sufficient (1176a33–b6), then we would not have any conception of worth to go by – *that* should stem from whatever happiness turns out to be. However, Aristotle explicitly widens the context in which to place the argument. At the beginning of X.6 he notes that he would shorten the discussion by resuming what has been said before (1176a32–3). So, he is entitled to presuppose a conception of worth. In particular, he seems to rely on two related points: a) happiness, the ultimate source of what is worthwhile, must stem from the activity of reason in accordance with virtue (I.7.1098a16–17); b) therefore, the person who has virtue is the measure of worthwhile activities (X.5.1176a17–18; cf. a24–9) – not the tyrant.

---

[87] Polus confronts Socrates in the *Gorgias* (466b–c) with the popular view of tyrants. Socrates tries to undermine this picture both in conversation with Polus and Callicles. For a remarkable corrective of the popular view, see also Plato's *Republic* VIII.565d–579e.

Aristotle's second reason carries on the thought contained in b) and makes it explicit in the end. Having undermined power as a credible source for good judgement, he now suggests that experience would be a much more suitable indicator of authoritative judgement. Proper value-judgements require experience of the things valued – but tyrants lack the relevant experience. Tyrants value (base) bodily pleasures so highly only because they do not know the unsullied pleasures of a free man (1176b19–21). The argument obviously alludes to *Republic* IX.583–7, where Plato attributes much of the tyrant's erroneous behaviour to ignorance of true pleasures, i.e. the pleasures of reason and philosophy. Aristotle, however, does not merely rely on Plato's argument, but offers his own reasons to undermine the tyrant's judgement. What children value, he points out, does not outstrip their experience – which explains why they and grown-up men esteem different things, and so likewise do good and bad people (b21–4).

Finally, and in addition to the rhetorically effective insinuation that tyrants suffer from arrested development, Aristotle provides an argument to clinch the point that the tyrant's judgement falls short. Authority in value-related judgements belongs to the good man (*spoudaios*), a point made first in III.4.1113a25–33 and invoked later at IX.4.1166a12–13, 9.1170a14–16, and most recently in X.5.1176a12–22. What is really good and pleasant is so *to* the good person *qua* good person – and this will be activities in accordance with virtue (1176b24–7). The 'good man argument' performs two functions. First, it serves to undermine the tyrant's judgement. Second, it also pulls the rug out from under the tyrants' pleasures. The tyrant and his admirers think that prolonged orgies provide the most pleasure. However, according to the good man, these are not pleasures in the primary sense (cf. 1176a22–9). So, the tyrant does not get what is really pleasurable, and nor do his 'pleasures' contribute anything to happiness. One can, perhaps, perceive the lack of self-sufficiency of the tyrant's pleasures in the fact they display their lifestyle for others to admire – as if they needed outside confirmation for their happiness (cf. *Politics* V.11.1314b29–32, quoted above). In any case, his preferential choice to engross himself in such pastimes should not be regarded as sound.

1176b27–1177a1 Therefore, happiness does not ... for the sake of activity.

In the previous lemma, Aristotle successfully discredited tyrants as good guides to happiness. Authority in value-judgements belongs to the good man who allocates a central role to the activities of virtue and the pleasures stemming from them, not to pleasant amusements. However, the point that motivated the whole discussion, that pleasant amusements seem to satisfy the finality criterion for happiness, still needs to be addressed.[88] Pleasure seems to be a genuine end because we do not seek anything beyond itself (1176b9–10). In fact, Eudoxus used this observation to identify the good with pleasure (X.2.1172b18–23).

Aristotle tries to dispel the charm of pleasure by arguing that pleasure *could not* play the role of the highest good. He puts forward two related reasons: 'And applying oneself seriously and toiling for the sake of amusement i) seems idle and ii) exceedingly childish' (1176b32–3). The first reason asks what the point is of taking the trouble to exert oneself. We can explain that we take trouble over that which we suppose makes us happy. We busy ourselves and suffer hardship on account of happiness because we subordinate everything else to it. A tyrant may need to take considerable trouble over his pleasures, as his debaucheries require extraordinary resources. But the initial argument relies on some shared experience. Everyone takes pleasant amusements to be ends! Now, if simple pleasures were sufficient for a happy life, then why would we busy ourselves and suffer hardship on account of happiness? The amusements in which everyone shares do not require toil – and yet toil we do. So, our lives do not chime with the thesis that amusements suffice for happiness. We should be idle, but we are not.

Second, toiling for the sake of amusement (*paidia*) would be childish (*paidikon*). As before, at 1176b21–4, Aristotle imputes arrested development to those who identify pleasure with happiness – this time in the form of a wordplay (setting *paidia* as the goal is *paidikon*). The substantial point, however, goes beyond name-calling. We get children to apply themselves seriously by giving them some pleasant reward. First you do your homework and clean up your room, then you can go and play. Children do serious things for the sake of pleasant amusements. So, if grown-ups still reward themselves for their more serious pursuits with pleasant amusements, then their value-structure resembles that of children – and Aristotle's jibe goes much beyond mere rhetoric.

Especially the second aspect of Aristotle's invective highlights a point about value. Anacharsis, a wise Scythian nobleman who travelled Greece in the sixth century BC, brings out clearly that amusing oneself (*paizein*, from the same root as *paidia*) should be subordinate

---

[88] On the finality criterion, see 1176a33–b6, with commentary. Cf. Introduction §1.3.

to serious pursuits, not vice versa. One should 'amuse oneself so that one may apply oneself seriously' (1176b33). Growing up, then, requires reversing the roles of amusement and serious pursuit in order to orient one's outlook towards that which is really valuable. His take on the value of pleasure and serious pursuits also gives Aristotle a nice answer to the question raised by i), namely, why pleasant amusements should be part of the happy life if happiness consists in serious pursuits. We cannot continuously do serious things, and need to take breaks, and an amusement (*paidia*) resembles taking a break (*anapausis*). But what licenses assimilating amusement to taking a break? Could I not take a break from serious activities without thereby pleasantly amusing myself? Of course, but Aristotle merely requires that whenever I do amuse myself, I am not pursuing anything serious – which seems right for the most part. Thus, if amusing myself is taking a break from serious activities, and breaks have a certain place in the hierarchy of ends, then amusements will take up that place. By likening pleasant amusements to taking a break, Aristotle subordinates pleasant amusements to something else and thereby argues, effectively, against those who extol it as the highest good.[89]

But what has happened to our shared experience that pleasure seems to satisfy the finality criterion for happiness? We should not cavil at the mismatch between our experience – pleasant pastimes *do* feel as if they are an end in their own right – and Aristotle's theory. He has argued that pleasure as a value is subordinate to more serious pursuits that are more central to happiness. He has not argued that pleasure is not *also* desirable in itself. For example, socialising with friends can be both useful for the sake of serious activities and good in its own right. Importantly, however, our experience need not reflect accurately how things really are. In the case of pleasant amusements it seems in fact important that our experience does not reflect the value-structure properly. Focusing on the further purpose of pleasant pursuits would undermine their point. If enjoying oneself were felt to be for the sake of serious activity, one would not feel as if one were taking a break, but still under the yoke.

---

[89] When Aristotle recommends amusement as a suitable means for recreation, he of course does not have in mind the tyrant's pastimes, but other, more suitable, amusements. Presumably he would think of getting a massage in the gym (III.10.1118b3–8), and especially socialising with friends. The latter he calls a 'playful amusement' which has its place in taking a break, or relaxation more generally (*anapausis*, IV.8.1127b33).

1177a1–6 And the happy life ... conducive to happiness.

Of the two candidates that seem to satisfy the conditions for happiness (cf. 1176b6–10), Aristotle has eliminated pleasant amusements – which entitles him to allocate centre stage to the other candidate, virtuous activity. Before determining more precisely *which* virtuous activity plays the role of happiness *best* (starting a few lines further down in X.7), he adds to his argument against the life of pleasure two sets of further considerations or afterthoughts (this lemma and the next). These further arguments seem to have the status of being endoxic – in this case, arguments familiar to the audience (more on endoxic arguments in the commentary on 1172b7–8). They corroborate the arguments against pleasure by showing that the arguments agree with what is said about the issue, if what is said seems true (cf. I.8.1098b12).

In this lemma, Aristotle gives two arguments for putting pleasure in its place. The first rehearses the well-established connection between happiness, virtue, and *spoudê*. The Greek word is here translated as 'seriousness', but also connotes the worth that merits serious pursuit. In particular, the cognate adjective *spoudaios* often means 'good' or 'excellent'. Now, going by the adjective, those who rely on what has been said before (1176a32–3) will readily follow Aristotle's point. At two key junctions – the function argument (at I.7.1098a7–18) and his account of virtue (at II.6.1106a17–24) — he invokes the generic connection between being good (*spoudaios*) in a certain domain and having the relevant virtue or excellence. The latter passage suggests that virtue 'makes' its possessor and what he/she/it does good. While Aristotle often refers to the virtuous person as *spoudaios* (most recently at X.6.1176b24–7), he also stresses that the person's actions, too, have the quality of being *spoudaios* (1176b7–9 and 1176b18–19). Since the happy life is the life in accordance with virtue, the happy life will involve *spoudê* (worthwhile seriousness) both through the person and her actions.

The second argument examines further the good and serious activity. Aristotle breaks down activity into its two basic components: a state or capacity, and what activates it. On both counts, he contends, virtuous activity fares better than merely amusing oneself. First, he highlights (again) that serious things surpass those that are not serious. The claim that 'serious things are better than things that are funny things and involve amusement' (1177a3–4) seems unduly restricted. Why not say that serious things are better than anything laughable? As if to answer the question, the text of one of the MSS differs and would translate 'serious things are better than funny things and [better than] things that involve amusement'. In either case, however, the lack of argument for the superiority of the serious over the ridiculous does not affect Aristotle's point as long as we class the funny/ridiculous with the non-serious. For he has argued in the previous lemma that activities lacking in seriousness are subordinate to the serious ones, and that therefore only the latter can stand at the heart of happiness (1176b27–1777a1, with commentary).

The second point focuses on what, ultimately, performs the activity. It does not hark back, but looks forward to the task of adjudicating between the different candidates for the virtue central to happiness, which begins in a few lines. Aristotle takes the soul to be the source of all human action. He distinguishes between the rational and the non-rational part of the soul (I.13.1102a26–32). The non-rational part divides into nutritive (the fourth part of the soul, VI.12.1144a9) and another part which, when trained well, can listen to reason (I.13.1102a13–1103a1). The rational part of the soul divides into the practical or calculative and theoretical (VI.1.1139a8–15, with VI.11.1143b14–17 for the corresponding virtues). Aristotle ranks the rational parts of the soul higher than the non-rational parts, and within the rational part of the soul, the theoretical part of the soul surpasses its practical counterpart (VI.13.1145a6–8).[90] Now, if we locate the pursuit of amusement in the appetitive part of the soul, whereas virtuous action springs from the rational part of the soul (though it requires the subrational part), then virtuous activity will exceed the pursuit of pleasant amusements because it stems from a better part of the soul. The result transfers to a person if we take a person to be guided by one part of the soul. The pleasure-seeker would follow appetite, whereas the virtuous person follows reason.

Finally, Aristotle lines up the two points and returns to happiness. Roughly, we can represent his thought as follows:

1. Serious things are better than non-serious ones. (1177a3–4)
2. The activity of the better part of a person is more serious than the activity of a lesser part. (a4–5)
3. [Therefore?] The activity of a better person is more serious than the activity of a lesser person. (a4–5)
[4. Therefore, engaging in serious things requires either the better part of a person or a better person than what is required for engaging in non-serious activities.]
5. The activity of a better part or person is more outstanding. (a4–5)
6. What is more outstanding is more characteristic of happiness. (a5–6)

---

[90] How could one possibly justify this ranking? In the context of the *Ethics*, Aristotle may simply rank the different functions of the soul in terms of what is more an expression of human excellence – which rules out the nutritive part of the soul (I.13.1102b11–12). Aristotle resumes the question of what human nature essentially is in X.7.1177b26–1178a8.

[7. Therefore, the activity of the better part of the person and of the better person is more characteristic of happiness.]

[8. Therefore, engaging in serious things is more characteristic of happiness.]

Aristotle does not state conclusions 7 and 8, but we can supply them readily from the context. While premise 6 seems contrived – often 'better' (*beltion*) and 'more outstanding' (*kreittôn*) are used interchangeably[91] – it nevertheless succeeds in zooming out from a narrow focus on the activity (as in the previous two lemmata).[92] Both what sort of person you are, and which part of the soul guides your life are relevant for happiness. A better person's life is more characteristic of happiness.

1177a6–11 Again, just anyone ... was said earlier too.

The second set of afterthoughts to the discussion of pleasure picks up on the conclusion of the first (previous lemma) by focusing on the person. It presents a *reductio* argument. i) The life centred on bodily pleasures is the happy life. ii) Anyone can get bodily pleasures: living *that* life does not require any special qualities. So, iii) even a slave could enjoy the same activities as the tyrant, and live as happily, were she offered the opportunity. But iv) 'no one assigns a share in happiness to a slave' (1177a8–9). From the clash between iii) and iv), Aristotle implicitly draws support for his view that i) is false. This would leave the other candidate for the happy life, the life of virtuous activity, as the only contender. Unlike the life of pleasure, not everyone can live the life of virtue. The virtuous life does require special qualities, qualities that slaves lack. According to Aristotle, slaves cannot act virtuously because they lack both practical wisdom and the virtues of character.[93] So, enabling a slave to lead a happy life would require extensive training, which would have to do away with his status as slave (cf. iv).

---

[91] In the *Politics* Aristotle distinguishes the two terms at one point (III.13.1283a41), noting that the majority is both 'stronger' (*kreittôn*) and 'better' (*beltion*) than the minority.

[92] In doing so, Aristotle appears to follow Plato. After proving an argument against pleasure in the *Philebus* at 53c–55c, he adds some further considerations, highlighting how wrong the hedonistic picture is if we take into consideration also the state of the soul (55c–d).

[93] Aristotle distinguishes between natural and non-natural slaves in *Politics* I.5–7. The latter may be ordinary people who have been reduced to slavery in war. Only the former have a nature that predestines them to be slaves. The present lemma seems to envisage natural slaves. In *Politics* I.5 Aristotle asserts that natural slaves lack reason as the ruling element of the soul, which would be required for virtuous actions. See esp. 1254b20–4.

The argument effectively reverses the paradigms for the life of pleasure, in line with Aristotle's initial reaction against it. At the first mention of that life, he castigates those who choose to live it as slavish (I.5.1095b19–20). However, its defenders take powerful tyrants to exemplify the life (1176b13 with commentary). But a) if a feeble slave can engage in the same happy-making activities as the all-powerful tyrant, then the tyrant's personal qualities seem irrelevant. This contrasts with virtuous activity, insofar as worthwhile activities depend on virtue or intelligence but not on having power (1176b18–19). b) Aristotle drives home the point that tyrants have no experience of the pleasures of a free man (b20): tyrants only experience pleasures (of the kind) slaves also can enjoy. But if slaves can partake in happy-making activities, they could lead happy lives – which runs against both common and considered opinion.

Could not the defender of the life of amusement push back? Consider: even if slaves can in principle enjoy the same pleasures as powerful tyrants, in fact they cannot, because they are not given the opportunity – which explains iv). The status of a person, and the power she has, does play a role. For if someone gets promoted from slave to tyrant, he could live happily, but he would no longer be a slave. Although Aristotle agrees that being reduced to a slave will hinder a person from living happily, he does not think the status alone hinders slaves from being happy. More importantly, slaves do not have 'a life'. Two Greek words can render 'life': *zôê* and *bios*. The former tends to denote life or aspects of life in the biological sense, whereas the latter tends to denote a mode of life.[94] Surely, slaves have both: they are alive and live a certain way of life! So what does Aristotle mean by denying them a *bios*? Presumably, and in line with his view on natural slaves, he denies them a life that aims at living well, rather than merely living. Slaves cannot aim at living well because they proverbially lack leisure (*Politics* VII.15.1334a20–1), and leisure is required for living well (cf. 1176b16–27, with commentary). In this sense, slaves may be on a par with those who make a living from retail, the vulgar arts, and other servile occupations – all of which are pursued only out of need (EE I.5.1215a25–32).[95] A slave's life fares worse, however, because he does not lead a life but, rather, is led. His master will make decisions for him, including life-important decisions. So, the slave aims neither at living well nor at living, because all the aiming is done through his master. In this sense, then, the slave does not have a

---

[94] Scholars disagree on what a mode of life entails: is it an aspect of a life (Gauthier and Jolif 1958, 862) or, rather, an all-encompassing way of life (Cooper 1975, 160)? (Further, Keyt 1989.)

[95] Following the MSS rather than Walzer's seclusion of 'for the sake of need'.

human life, and hence has no prospect of human happiness.[96] So, activities in which a slave *can* engage cannot be central to human happiness.

X.7

1177a12–17 And if happiness is … complete/perfect happiness.

The present lemma belongs to the outline examination of happiness, which spans X.6–8. (The beginning and end-points are flagged at X.6.1176a30–1 and X.9.1179a33–4 respectively.) Most modern editions mark a new chapter at the beginning of this lemma. But the division could indicate either of two readings: i) after having dealt with pleasure, Aristotle moves on to the next candidates for the role of happiness; alternatively, ii), the discussion leaves behind happiness as discussed in X.6 and moves on to the next level. The two readings are possible because Aristotle moves within this lemma from speaking about happiness (1177a12) to speaking about complete/perfect happiness (*teleia eudaimonia*, a17).

Corresponding to i) and ii), there are two ways of understanding complete/perfect happiness. I) Although without precedent in the EN, the phrase alludes to the conclusion of the function argument, according to which the human good turns out to be activity in accordance with virtue, 'and if there are several virtues, then in accordance with the best (*aristê*) and most complete/perfect one (*teleiotatê*)' (I.7.1098a16–18). Since Aristotle has not yet identified the highest virtue – even X.6 speaks simply in terms of virtuous activity – he embarks on this task now. So, *teleia eudaimonia* at 1777a17 does not mean something different from 'happiness'. Aristotle adds *teleia* to emphasise the finality or completeness of happiness and its account. This interpretation can easily explain why he drops the qualification *teleios* later, as if to identify happiness *tout court* (1178b31–2). Alternatively, II), Aristotle has already defined happiness sufficiently in I.7. Now, by introducing *teleia eudaimonia* he shifts the topic from 'mere' happiness to perfect/complete happiness. If this reading suggests that we can have ordinary happiness without complete/perfect/final happiness, it immediately raises questions about the status of X.7–8. Is it an add-on? Or is it an essential part of the EN? Why do we need to know about perfect/

---

[96] At *Politics* III.9.1280a32–4, Aristotle claims slaves cannot make decisions – or at least, just like animals, they cannot lead a life in accordance with decisions. So, even if a slave had character, he would not be able to guide his life through his character, but would be knocked about by external influences, such as his master.

complete happiness? So, the two different readings not only differ philosophically, but also shed different lights on the EN as a whole. If we adopt I), we would expect Aristotle's answer to be contained within, or at least compatible with, the rest of the EN, whereas II) may introduce an afterthought that relates to the rest of the EN, but need be neither expected nor fully compatible with it (similar to how some of Plato's myths are taken to stand to their preceding 'arguments').[97]

Whichever of the options we choose – what is the argument? Going back to the distinction between the quality of an activity and the quality of the state giving rise to it (X.6.1177a3–6), Aristotle tries to home in on our best state or element in order to identify the best activity that springs from this element as happiness. But how he fills in the formal point that happiness is the best activity of our best element is a more controversial issue. He argues for the existence of the best part in us: this is intelligence (*nous*) or some other thing. He does not seem to care about names as much as about the characteristics: '[C1] to be naturally such as to rule, lead, and [C2] to entertain thoughts about fine and divine things' (1177b14–15). That to which C1 and C2 apply counts as divine itself, or as the most divine element in us (b15–16). So, Aristotle aligns our best element with its being most divine. But his reasoning may go in either of two directions: a) our best element E has the characteristics C1 and C2 because E is divine; or, b), because E has C1 and C2, it counts as divine. According to b), Aristotle would justify intelligence's status as best element in the sense that it cites the grounds for its elevated status. In particular, one might think that its practical role as natural ruler and leader designates intelligence as the highest element (C2 would do so, too, on the assumptions that i) entertaining thoughts about fine and divine things is the highest achievement, and ii) that no other element does that). But, according to a), E's leadership role may be no more than a sign for the elevated place of intelligence. Rather, because intelligence is divine, or our most divine element, it may be natural for it to rule – in which case the elevated place of intelligence is shown, but is not justified, by its excellence at ruling.

Having singled out the best element, identifying the activity of happiness should be straightforward: we only need to identify the best activity. Unfortunately, Aristotle complicates the argument by introducing 'the

---

[97] Most interpreters follow along the lines of a). Long 2011 argues for b), as do, in a different way, Scott 1999 and Bush 2008. The issue resurfaces at 1177b26–1178a23. Among a), we can distinguish between pluralist and monist approaches. Since their interpretations of this passage can be very similar, I do not discuss them individually. See Introduction §3.2.

proper virtue' of intelligence – as if there might loom a plurality of virtues. And indeed, executing C1 well seems to require a practical virtue, whereas excellence at C2 requires a theoretical virtue. Going back to what was said before (as per X.6.1176a32–3), EN VI introduces a sharp distinction between practical and theoretical intelligence, each of which comes with its own distinct virtue (1.1139a3–17).[98] Now, if both action and theoretical reflection are functions (*erga*) of the best part of the human soul, should there not be *two* proper virtues, both of which make us happy?[99] No, because Aristotle does not consider a thing to have two independent functions. A plurality of functions must, in some way, be ordered – which allows the best function to take centre stage (cf. *Protrepticus* B 63–5 Düring). That is, one of the virtues must take priority over the other. He takes up the task of identifying *the* proper virtue of intelligence because *its* activity yields perfect/complete happiness (1177a16–17).

One may wonder whether the present lemma contains an argument in favour of theoretical activity – and by implication theoretical wisdom as the proper virtue of intelligence. Indeed, most editors and translators take the next line ('And that it is reflective activity has been said') to belong to the present train of thought – as if it constituted the conclusion of an argument contained in this lemma. It would do so if we relied on the assumptions, already mentioned above in relation to C2, that i) entertaining thoughts about fine and divine things is the highest achievement, and ii) that no other element does that. Alternatively, the present passage may simply serve to set up the quest for *the* proper virtue of intelligence and the best activity, rather than decide it. In this case, the proper argument in favour of reflection (introduced with *gar*, a19) begins immediately after stating the position to be justified. In any case, assuming that there is *the* best human activity, Aristotle provides six (further?) reasons in favour of reflection over the next six lemmata. Only then does he address the important question – going back to a point left open at the end of X.5 (1176a22–9) – whether the best activity suits human nature, i.e. whether it is the best activity *for us* (1177b26 to 1178a8). A key task, one to which Aristotle alludes here, will be to determine the relationship between the (merely) human and the divine. Here he

---

[98] This distinction, somewhat confusingly, does not line up with another important distinction, which classifies theoretical wisdom (*sophia*), comprehension, and practical wisdom (*phronêsis*) as intellectual virtues, whereas liberality and moderation count as ethical virtues (1103a5–7). So, not all intellectual virtues belong to the theoretical, as practical wisdom and the ethical virtues mutually depend on one another and can only exist in the sphere of action (VI.13.1144b30–1144a6).

[99] Pluralist accounts of Aristotelian happiness (note 97 above) stress this point.

anticipates that the best activity will stem from our most divine element, but leaves open whether it is only relatively divine or properly divine.

1177a17–21 And that it is reflective ... objects intelligence is about.

In the previous lemma, Aristotle stresses the importance of identifying complete/perfect/final happiness (*teleia eudaimonia*, 1177a17). Now he puts forward thesis [T]: reflective activity (*theôrêtikê*) is the activity at the heart of complete/perfect happiness. But he does not present T as something new, claiming instead that T 'has been said before' (1177a17–18). In this lemma, he supports T with a two-part argument: i) intelligence is the most outstanding element in us, and ii) the (proper?) activity of intelligence deals with the most outstanding objects of knowledge. Over the next lemmata, he will give five more arguments in support of T.

Thesis T may surprise both first-time and seasoned readers of the *Nicomachean Ethics*. Contrary to the assertion that this 'has been said', the EN up to this point does not contain a passage expressly stating T. What can we infer from this? Scholars have been tempted to make bold claims about the composition of the EN: a) the EN once contained a passage that has now fallen out, such as the 'Nicomachean' version of the common book EE V = EN VI (Susemihl);[100] b) others take him to refer to some earlier work, such as the *Protrepticus*. Fragments B58–70 (Düring) contain much of the thought expressed in 1177a13–21 (Gauthier). Alternatively, and less boldly, c) he may be recalling a point that broadly goes in the direction of T. One could point to I.5.1096a4–5 where he mentions the life of reflection, but only to set it aside for later investigation. So, an alert reader with an astonishing attention span will expect Aristotle to come back to the topic! Or one could take the text to allude to the Book VI passage that subordinates practical wisdom (*phronêsis*) to theoretical wisdom (*sophia*, 13.1145a6–11). Finally, d), the text may refer to a thesis well-known to his audience, either through debate in Aristotle's school or through some other philosopher (perhaps Plato's *Phaedo*).

Option d) has greater explanatory power at a lesser cost than a) and b). In particular, it would explain why Aristotle continually comes back to this reputed opinion (*endoxon*) in different ways and in different contexts, such as b) and c). If he had stated the point in the EN, as a) and c) claim, he would not need to go out of his way to say to state that the thesis agrees with what

---

[100] On the EN's relation to the *Eudemian Ethics*, see Introduction §4.

has been said before – everybody presupposes that it does. But the answer raises a further question. Does T really agree with the rest of the EN, or only with what has been said in X.6? Some first-rate scholars think X.7–8 do not agree with EN I–IX (see previous lemma).[101] By contrast, Aristotle leaves the reader less in the dark about the further claim that T agrees with the truth (cf. X.8.1179a17–22), a point he bolsters with numerous arguments.

The first argument (of six) to establish T seeks to confirm that the activity of complete/perfect/final happiness is the most outstanding activity (*kratistê*, 1177a13; a19). Aristotle offers two supporting reasons. The first – intelligence in us is our most outstanding element – refers back to X.7.1177a12–13, where he asserted that the activity of our best element will be the most outstanding one. In the present passage he identifies our best element more firmly with our intelligence (*nous*, 1177a20–1) – without, however, adding any independent argument. While intelligence may be our best element, pointing to it does not support T, at least not without further argument. In other passages in which he extols intelligence as our best or most important element, he does not conceive of intelligence in purely theoretical terms, but rather stresses its practical role (IX.8.1168b28–1169a3 and a15–18). So, homing in on intelligence may equally support the thesis that some kind of practical activity should be central to happiness. But perhaps our reading of T is unduly narrow, for T need not be restricted to purely reflective activity, as *theôrein* is used throughout the EN also in practical contexts.[102] In this case, pointing to intelligence as the faculty that engenders *theôrein* would be adequate.

However, Aristotle's second point lends some support to the first, and indeed narrows down *theôrêtikê* to mean 'reflective' in a theoretical sense, excluding the practical sphere. Grammatically, the text at 1177a20–1 could mean that *intelligence* concerns the most outstanding objects of knowledge. But this would make the addition 'the objects intelligence is about' awkward (a21). So, probably he claims that the objects of the most outstanding *activity* are the most outstanding. In any case, he has

---

[101] There are two versions of this position. a) Because T does not sit well with the rest of the EN, it should not be part of it. For example, developmentalists like Jaeger 1923 see in X.7–8 remnants of a Platonising phase (cf. Nussbaum 1986, 376–7). b) One may confine T to an excursion that has no proper place in the EN (Long 2011, 108), or an unexpected reconsideration (Curzer 1990).

[102] Indeed, the popular translation for *theôrein*, 'to contemplate', captures the outward-looking aspect of *theôrein* in practical contexts, such as the following: I.7.1098b3; I.10.1100b19; IV.2.1122a35 and b17; VI.1.1139a6–8; VI.4.1140a10–12; VI.5.1140b9–11; VI.7.1141a25–6; VII.3.1146b31–5; IX.9.1169b33–4; X.9.1181b17–20. However, I translate *theôria* and cognates as 'reflection' throughout because, in the context of EN X.7–8, the word refers to reflection on systematic knowledge of first principles (see below).

explicitly discussed the objects of theoretical wisdom (*sophia*) and its practical counterpart (*phronêsis*) in Book VI. *Sophia* surpasses *phronêsis* because it deals with things of a far more divine nature than human affairs, 'such as, most obviously, the constituent parts of the universe' (VI.7.1141a34–b2). Accordingly, Aristotle defines *sophia* as a combination of systematic knowledge (*epistêmê*) and intelligence (*nous*) of the most estimable objects by nature (1141b2–3). The kind of *theôria* that stems from *sophia* would be different in kind from its practical equivalent.[103] Now, if the cognitive faculties and their objects relate to each other through 'a certain likeness or kinship' (VI.1.1139a8–11), then Aristotle can justify why we should esteem theoretical intellect more than practical intellect. The former would be more divine, partly due to its dealing with the most divine objects (which explains the epithet *theiotaton* of intelligence more generally, 1177a16).

1177a21–3 And further ... do anything else.

While the previous lemma obviously serves to extol reflective activity, the present point needs some unpacking. Why should we care whether we can engage in activity A more continuously than in activity B? Why does continuity matter?

The status of continuity in the search for happiness becomes clearer if we begin with our human limitations. According to Aristotle, 'continuous activity is impossible for everything human' (X.4.1175a4–5). The context of the quotation leaves no doubt that engaging more continuously in a good activity is better than doing so less continuously (1175a3–10, see also IX.9.1170a4–6). Consider such old-time favourite activities as eating, drinking, and sex. We can do none of them continuously, or indeed for very long, at least ordinarily. People who are into these pleasures will find ways to engage in them more frequently or for a longer time, so as to come closer to a more continuous activity. Clearly, we prefer being able to engage more continuously in activities we take to be good. However, the proviso that we care about the continuity of activities we take to be good (rather than bad) indicates that continuity is not itself a value. It does not stand on a par with the hallmarks for happiness, self-sufficiency, completeness, finality, and perfection, either in EN I or X (1176a33–b6). Continuity

---

[103] *Theôrein* (contemplating, or reflecting on) the constituent parts of the universe may be done in the course of either philosophical astronomy or more directly the science of Aristotle's *Metaphysics*, esp. E.1.

seems to increase the value of activities: it makes good ones better, and bad ones worse. Now, since Aristotle attempts to single out the supremely best activity, it should be one in which we can also engage most continuously.

We can see more clearly how continuity relates specifically to happiness through a closely related value, stability. Plato, from whom Aristotle inherits the value, attributes stability (or security, or sureness) especially to good cognitive faculties, as well as to their objects (*Philebus* 55c–59c; *Republic* 585b–d). Their stability confers stability on human life. Similarly, Aristotle thinks good people and their friendships are especially stable (VIII.8.1159b8), presumably because what makes them good, their virtues, are especially stable states (II.4.1105b3). The stability of virtue has two consequences. First, the pleasures stemming from virtuous activity will also be especially stable (see the next lemma, on 1177a23–27). Second, since happiness consists in the activity of virtue, it can account for the acknowledged stability of happiness (I.10.1100b2). The stability of happiness rests on our ability to engage in virtuous activity especially continuously: the most estimable virtues are especially stable because 'those who are blessed spend their life in them most of all, and most continuously' (1100b15–16). If 'spending one's life in virtue' means that one lives in accordance with virtue, then a virtuous person would live continuously in virtue. However, Aristotle seems to focus on more specific activities. At any rate, he does so in the present lemma, where he highlights our ability to engage most continuously in reflection – which goes beyond merely living in accordance with a certain virtue.[104]

But why are we capable of reflecting more continuously than doing anything else? Does Aristotle want to maintain the absolute claim a) of all the things human beings can do, we can 'do' reflection most continuously? Or, in light of the task set up at 1177a12–18, does he want to establish the comparative claim, b) of activities guided by intellect, we can engage in theoretical thinking most continuously? He does not *need* to establish a), because continuity is not itself a value or a guarantor of happiness. Other activities could be as continuous as reflection, but if they are less valuable, doing them more continuously would not make one happier than engaging in reflection. All he needs to establish in order to identify complete/perfect/final happiness (*teleia eudaimonia*, 1177a17)

---

[104] Aristotle's claim in I.10 may either comprise all virtue – in which case he would elevate the activity of theoretical intellect as most continuous only in X.7, or, alternatively, I.10 already zooms in on theoretical intellect – in which case X.7 reaffirms the claim made in the earlier passage, reminding the reader of the superiority of theoretical intellect over the practical virtues.

is b). One could support b) by pointing to the formal features of the relevant activities. Unlike most particular actions guided by intelligence, particular instances of reflection do not have an internal cut-off point. If we understand reflection as contemplating the constituents of the universe, say (see previous lemma), then one could in principle go on doing this forever. One cannot go on forever showing one's courage in this particular battle with the enemy.

Nevertheless, Aristotle *could* support a). Activities such as particular instances of seeing also lack an internal cut-off point. However, theoretical reflection fosters continuity more than any other activity because it is i) least tiresome and ii) least tiring. In X.4 he suggested that we tend to perceive or reflect on an object intently only as long as we find it interesting. Once our interest wanes, we find the activity tiresome and tend to stop (see 1175a3–10, with commentary for details). To i), reflection will not become tiresome because it is of the 'most outstanding objects of knowledge', i.e. the highest knowables (1177a20–1, previous lemma), and a properly trained intellect cannot become bored with the highest objects. To ii), sometimes the faculty gives out before the object. For example, our eyes can get tired before we have exhausted a particular painting. Theoretical reflection stands out because (theoretical) intelligence least of all involves the body (cf. 1175b36–1176a3, with commentary). So a) would connect with the previous point by infusing it with a further nuance: intellect is the most outstanding element (*kratistê*), because it can be active most continuously. This characteristic, moreover, points beyond the world of physical wear and tear, picking up the earlier characterisation of intelligence as our most divine element (1177a15–16).

1177a23–7 Next, we think ... for those who seek it.

The next reason in favour of reflection as complete/perfect/final happiness (*teleia eudaimonia*, 1177a17) relies on the intimate connection between pleasure and happiness, intuitively felt by everyone. Aristotle notes the connection already in Book I (I.8.1098a25), where he also indicates how his outline account of happiness – activity in accordance with virtue – explains the connection exceptionally well (1099a7–31). The happy life is pleasant because of the pleasure that virtuous activity brings.

For the present argument Aristotle invokes a more demanding criterion. The activity key to *teleia eudaimonia* will be not merely pleasant, but superlatively pleasant. He does so, because at the end of his discussion of pleasure in X.5 he has argued that the activity most characteristic of the good and happy person will be the most pleasant (1176a22–9, with commentary). By identifying theoretical reflection with the most pleasant activity, Aristotle kills several birds with one stone. He pinpoints i) the activity most characteristic of the good person, ii) the most pleasant human activity, and iii) the most pleasant way of life. He thus responds to the traditional worry, recorded in a Delian inscription (I.8.1099a27–8), that superlative pleasantness does not easily combine with the superlatives of other values key to happiness.

While his general conclusion agrees with Plato's in *Republic* IX – the philosophical life contains the most pleasures – Aristotle's different conception of pleasure requires a slightly different approach. For his present purposes, he distinguishes between theoretical wisdom (*sophia*) and the love of wisdom (*philosophia*), arguing that if the love of wisdom brings amazing pleasures, then, a fortiori, theoretical wisdom brings (even more) amazing pleasures (1177a25–7). The argument does not turn on a contrast between love and its absence (an impression one may get by looking merely at the words), but on a contrast between learner and expert (the wise person will continue to love wisdom). Every wise person started out as mere lover of wisdom. If the love bears fruit, the learner will cultivate her intellect to engage more fully with the objects of wisdom. If the mere lover of theoretical wisdom enjoys amazing pleasures through engaging with these objects, then the person who has fully attained this knowledge will have even more pleasure. An activity is most pleasant when it stems from the interaction of both an excellent state and object (1174b20–3). So, the activity of a more developed state should yield more pleasure.[105]

How could anyone argue for the superlative pleasantness of the philosophical life, surpassing even that of a dedicated pleasure-seeker? Aristotle focuses on two features of the pleasures that both philosophy and the full-blown activity of wisdom provide: purity and stability (1177a25–6). We can understand the criteria in two different ways: quantitatively or qualitatively. First, by understanding the purity mentioned here as 'purity from pain', Aristotle could argue that ordinary pleasure-seekers enjoy predominantly impure pleasures, i.e. pleasures that either rely on antecedent pain or come together with pain. Unlike philosophers, those pleasure-seekers would not tip the pleasure–pain balance of their lives towards pleasure

---

[105] On the connection between love and pleasures, as well as the significance of the Delian inscription, see Aufderheide 2016.

very much. Similarly, the lack of stability might mean that the effect of the pleasure does not last: ephemeral pleasures do not make your life (much) happier.[106] So, the pleasures of theoretical thinking would yield the most net-pleasure in the long-term.

Despite philosophy's ability to provide exceptionally durable and stable pleasures, we can still wonder whether a philosopher's life must always contain a greater amount of pleasure than that of a dedicated pleasure-seeker. We cannot answer the question on conceptual grounds. A different, and stronger, way of taking 'most pleasant' rules out that anybody but the wise person could live the most pleasant life. A pleasure-seeking tyrant misses out on pure pleasures that contrast starkly with the pleasures of the body he is accustomed to (cf. 1176b16–26, with commentary). 'Purity' recalls the argument from X.5 where Aristotle implies that the pleasures of thought are especially pure in the sense of being especially free from bodily involvement. Since pleasure belongs to the soul rather than to the body, the less the body is involved, the more the pleasure will be what it really is (see 1175b36–1176a3, with commentary). Hence, the pleasures of the theoretical intellect will be pleasures most of all – and in this sense they will be the most pleasant.

Finally, we can see how Aristotle might seek to combine both the qualitative and the quantitative consideration. Since he couples purity and stability here, he may indicate that pleasure has the two qualities for the same reason. If purity points towards freedom from bodily involvement, then we may explain the pleasures' stability in the same way. We can engage in theoretical activity most continuously because it is both least tiresome and least tiring (see previous lemma, with commentary). So, while enjoying bodily pleasures tires a person out, intellectual pleasures, Aristotle suggests, do so less. Instead of experiencing intense pleasure from some activity that comes with pain, we can engage more stably in theoretical thinking. So, at least on this score, intellectual pleasures surpass bodily pleasures in quantitative terms.

1177a27–b1 Next, the talked-of self-sufficiency ... most self-sufficient.

Self-sufficiency serves as the next reason in favour of reflection. Self-sufficiency was introduced in Book I, and recalled at X.6.1176a33–b6, to address the psychological dimension of happiness. A happy person will

---

[106] See especially *Republic* 585e3 and 586a6 for stability. While one could read Plato's argument in *Republic* 583–7 in quantitative terms, Plato seems to favour a quality-based approach (584b).

have all she needs for living well, and will feel satisfied. In line with his programme of outlining happiness in X.6–8, Aristotle seeks to identify the activity responsible for the self-sufficiency of happiness. He plays off reflection against virtuous action (*praxis*) to show that reflection is more self-sufficient, and therefore has more of a claim to being complete/perfect/final happiness (1177a17). He argues as follows: i) virtuous actions such as acts of justice, moderation, or courage presuppose other people because of the logic of the actions; ii) reflection does not presuppose others; therefore iii) the theoretically wise person is more self-sufficient than the (merely) practically wise person.

The argument seems weak, even if we do not cavil at the first premise. (The treatment of moderation at III.10–12 hardly prepares for the alleged other-directedness of this virtue.) The strength of Aristotle's reasoning obviously depends on the notion of self-sufficiency at play. In particular, the move from i) and ii) to iii) depends on a narrow understanding of self-sufficiency. We find a much broader notion of self-sufficiency when he first introduces the notion in Book I as key value to living well. He relies on self-sufficiency to identify the highest good with happiness. a) The highest good is self-sufficient, which means b) it 'on its own renders the life choice-worthy and lacking in nothing'. But c) 'we believe happiness is like this', i.e. happiness satisfies b) (I.7.1097b14–16). Prompted by b), Aristotle then expands on 'self-sufficient', explaining that he restricts 'self-sufficient' not merely to one person who lives in isolation, but includes also parents, children, wife, friends, and fellow citizens (1097b8–11). Whatever exactly the relation, somehow my attaining the highest good seems to render also the lives of other people connected to me self-sufficient. In a way, then, attaining my good comprises also attaining their good. The present passage, by contrast, seems to presuppose a much narrower conception of self-sufficiency. Here, a person counts as more self-sufficient if he can perform the activity that renders his life happy on his own. Aristotle seems to shift the meaning of 'self-sufficient' between 'that which on its own makes a man happy' (I.7) and 'that which makes a man happy on his own' (X.7).[107] Unless we can find a reason for adopting the narrower conception

---

[107] Kenny 1992, 36. Depending on how we spell out the shift, it may have far-reaching implications. E. Brown 2014 argues that the Book X understanding of self-sufficiency privileges the theoretical life, whereas the Book I account favours a more political (i.e. practical) approach to happiness. Curzer 1990, 422–4 contends that the criteria of self-sufficiency in I.7 and X.7 is so different that we cannot consider X.6–8 to be continuous with the rest of the EN (cf. commentary on 1176a30–3). Lear 2004, 47–71 discusses how the interpretation of self-sufficiency bears on the question of inclusivism vs monism (cf. Introduction §1.3).

of self-sufficiency, the i–ii–iii argument presents no cogent reason for favouring reflection over virtuous action.

One significant difference between the two contexts consists in the level of determinateness of what makes a life self-sufficient. Unlike the i–ii–iii argument, the a–b–c argument does not presuppose a specific conception of happiness. Even when Aristotle subsequently sets out to say more about happiness (1097b22–1098a20), he remains at the level of a very general outline. Happiness as the activity in accordance with virtue can mean different things, depending on what we mean by 'virtue' and which virtues we take to be central (cf. commentary on 1176a30–3). However, at the beginning of X.7, he begins homing in on the proper virtue of intelligence because *its* activity promises complete/perfect/final happiness. That is, he narrows down the determinants of virtuous activity to identify a determinate version of happiness – the best happiness. But if the account of happiness is more determinate, then also the criteria by which we judge the candidates should be more determinate. This suggests that Aristotle need not operate with two different conceptions of self-sufficiency, but may narrow it down to mirror the project of narrowing down the virtuous activity that stands at the heart of complete/perfect/final happiness.

How could he narrow down the concept of self-sufficiency (*autarkeia*) without changing it? The concept consists of two components, 'self' (*autos*) and 'sufficing' (*arkein*). Plausibly, activity A surpasses activity B in self-sufficiency if A surpasses B in either component, or both. In Book I, Aristotle concentrates on the latter component. If the practical and theoretical activities of wisdom do not differ in extent (a certain, limited group of people), or effect (they render life choice-worthy and lacking in nothing), one would naturally turn to the other aspect of self-sufficiency — the 'self'. While A would be more self-sufficient than B if it suffices for more people or for a greater goal, the 'self'-component works the other way around. The fewer people the activity needs, the more self-sufficient it will be. Aristotle contends that virtuous action requires several people, both as co-workers and as beneficiaries (1177a28–32). Without the others sharing in the activity, it could not take place. While theoretical activity also benefits a certain group of people and can also be practised jointly, the activity does not *require* people besides the single agent. A single person on her own *can* engage in theoretical thinking, but not in virtuous action. Therefore, theoretical thinking surpasses practical agency in self-sufficiency (1177a31–b1).

The result plausibly chimes with the original motivation for introducing self-sufficiency. Being able to attain a goal completely on one's own may well be more satisfying than requiring others. More importantly, how securely one is satisfied with one's life depends also on counterfactual scenarios. The counterfactual scenarios that would undermine a wise person's self-sufficiency are much more remote than the ones that would do the same to a practically wise person. For example, the death of a close friend, or moving abroad among strangers, could halt the activity of practical virtue, but not theoretical thinking. The more a person dwells on such counterfactuals, the needier she will be (think about a romantic relationship). So, the theoretically wise person will live more self-sufficiently.

1177b1–4 Next, <reflection> seems ... besides the action.

As expected from X.6, Aristotle exploits another characteristic of happiness, closely related to the self-sufficiency from the previous lemma. Self-sufficient objects of choice are those that are choice-worthy in themselves, i.e. not because of something else (cf. 1176b4–5). But this criterion appears incapable of strengthening the case for theoretical reflection. For in X.6 he identifies things 'chosen for themselves' as the ones 'from which nothing is sought besides the activity' – only to contend that 'actions in accordance with virtue are thought to be of this sort, for doing what is fine and worthwhile is one of the things to be chosen for themselves' (1176b6–9). Throughout the EN Aristotle has persistently claimed we perform virtuous actions for their own sake, or, what comes to mean almost the same, for the sake of the fine (cf. III.7.1116a12–15; III.8.1116b31; IV.2.1123a24–6; IX.8.1168a33–4). So, why should being loved for its own sake play into the hands of reflection?

Of course, in a way both practical and theoretical activities of virtue should be choice-worthy in themselves, simply because both are activities of virtue or excellence. But now Aristotle tightens the criterion to elicit a difference. He highlights that theoretical reflection is loved *only* on its own account, unlike virtuous action. At first the argument might strike us as wrong.

a) Both reflection and virtuous action are choice-worthy in themselves. (X.6)
b) Virtuous action is loved both on its own account and for its consequences. (1177b2–4)
c) Reflection is loved only on its own account, not for its consequences. (1177b1–2)
d) Therefore, reflection is superior to virtuous action.

We could present the problem as a dilemma: b) is either true or not. If it is true, then virtuous action should surpass reflection, not vice versa. If it is not true, then there is no difference between the two activities and Aristotle cannot use the argument to support reflection's bid for complete/perfect/final happiness.

Let's assume b) is true. If that were so, should we not prefer virtuous action over reflection? Plato suggested in the *Republic* that the goods we love (*agapômen*, II.357c1) for their own sakes and for their consequences, such as seeing, having good sense (*phronein*), and justice, belong to the finest class of goods. According to Aristotle, reflection is an activity loved only on its own account (*agapasthai*, 1177b1–2, the same word as Plato's). But the goods we love *only* for their own sakes seem to be less desirable than the goods we love both for their own sakes and for the goods they tend to produce. So, why does he take it the other way around?

The conclusion d) follows from a) to c) if we presuppose an underlying principle, [S]: A is superior to B if A is chosen only on its own account and B is chosen not only on its own account. But why subscribe to S? We find a distinction of different degrees of finality in Book I, where happiness is set up as a goal that is 'choice-worthy in itself and never for the sake of anything else' (I.7.1096b33–4). Other things choice-worthy in themselves may at the same time be for the sake of yet some other goal. Since happiness is the highest goal, merely being choice-worthy in itself does not suffice. The candidate activity must not be subordinate to anything. In particular, it must not be subordinate to any rival candidates. But Aristotle suggests in Book I that everything is for the sake of the highest good, except, of course, happiness, which *is* the highest good. The argument would be especially poignant if the present passage alluded to a thought expressed at the end of EN VI, that a person guided by practical wisdom also acts for the sake of reflection (13.1145a8–11) – in which case d) would follow. (Looking ahead to the next lemma, one might suggest that practical agency secures leisure in which to reflect.)[108]

But can we assume that b) is true? As stated, b) seems wrong. Consider how virtuous action contrasts with production (*poiêsis*) in Book VI: 'the end of production is different from itself, but not that of action: for acting well itself is its end' (5.1140b6–7). So, why should Aristotle assimilate virtuous action in the present lemma to production by highlighting that action 'creates something else besides' (*peripoiein*)?

---

[108] So Lawrence 2006, 65–6.

Both practical and theoretical virtue can have good consequences incidentally. But Aristotle points to an important difference between the two. Practical virtue aims at some real change in the world that is intended to remain even after the action has stopped. In this sense, the action creates something else besides itself, a non-incidental consequence that goes beyond merely creating 'the fine' for oneself besides (IX.8.1168b27). Precisely because the consequences are so closely tied to the action, we tend to assess virtuous action as a package comprised of action and result. But the package can come apart. The good consequences of virtuous actions arise only if certain conditions beyond the agent obtain (cf. previous lemma on self-sufficiency). For example, if the other people involved in the virtuous action do not co-operate, or the action simply does not pan out for reasons beyond the agent's control, then the action will not be as good as it could be. One may even be disappointed because the action does not achieve what it aims at. Virtuous action would seem especially suitable as a candidate for perfect/complete/final happiness if we consider the best version of it, which includes external results that follow from the action. Reflection does not come as a package, and hence leaves no room for disappointment, provided that we follow Aristotle in conceiving of reflection as contemplating truths, rather than trying to attain truth (for a programmatic statement of the place and status of theoretical reflection, see *Metaphysics* I.2.982b22–983a11).

1177b4–15 Next, happiness is thought ... it to be different.

With leisure (*scholê*) Aristotle broaches a topic that has not yet sufficiently surfaced in the EN. We should understand leisure as a certain framework that allows us to do what we most want or most feel like (as opposed to what we must do). Aristotle taps into a widely recognised quality of happiness by making explicit his commitment to [HL]: happiness is to be found in leisure (1177b4). We do not seek happiness for some further purpose (like building) or because we must (like keeping a promise), but merely because we want to.[109] Any candidate activity for happiness must flourish in the framework provided by leisure. But, so the argument goes,

---

[109] See Broadie 2007c for the distinction and a thorough discussion of leisure. Rose 2016, 31 subsumes several conceptions of leisure (as a specific activity, as play, as freedom from work) under the umbrella of absence from necessity. She prefers the conception of leisure as a resource to leisure as a specific good.

practical and theoretical activity differ in this respect. Or rather, Aristotle *presupposes* that theoretical reflection flourishes in leisure and *argues* in this lemma that the activities of practical virtue do not properly belong to leisurely pursuits. Therefore, the former has a better claim to happiness than the latter.

Aristotle has implicitly invoked HL already in X.6 (1176b16–19; b27–1177a1). The intuition drives the inference from a) tyrants spend their leisure in the pursuit of frivolous pleasures to b) enjoying frivolous pleasures is happiness. One of the arguments against the inference in X.6 relies on a contrast between serious and non-serious pursuits. Pleasure and amusement appear to be suitable goals for leisure, but many favourite pleasures turn out to be less leisurely than supposed (1176b27–1177a1). Insofar as frivolous pleasures and amusements take up the role of diversions and rest, they do not properly belong to the framework of leisure. They serve, ultimately, the purpose of engaging in arduous projects another time: we *must* rest in order to be ready for more work. Since amusement plays the role of rest, rather than constituting genuine leisure, amusements cannot make a person happy, according to HL.

When Aristotle concludes in X.6 that a happy life will involve serious exertions (1177a1–2), he leaves open the relationship between leisure and those serious activities. He now revisits the distinction drawn earlier. Instead of opposing serious and non-serious, he opposes leisure and non-leisure. The argument against practical activity seems to rest on the assumption that virtuous action divides exhaustively into excellence in war and excellence in politics. (The next lemma corrects this impression, proposing to understand such actions as paradigmatic.) The first argument becomes clearer if we distinguish between the virtuous actions performed in war and war as a circumstance that requires such actions. Aristotle does not deny that a courageous soldier will fight for the sake of the fine, i.e. will perform the war-like actions for their own sake. However, no one would choose the circumstance of war that makes such actions *necessary* – if one can avoid it. Since we *must* fight in war, fighting can hardly count as a leisurely pursuit. The same point emerges from considering the goal. Since we wage war for the sake of peace (1177b5), we choose courageous actions for the sake of peace, not war. Like other practical activities, war-related actions aim necessarily also at an external result (see previous lemma), attaining which makes continued action pointless (if not impossible). So, they point beyond themselves and aim at changing the condition that makes them necessary. Therefore, they do not take place in the framework of leisure. Indeed, if we engaged in war-like activities at our leisure, i.e. when we are not compelled to, we would be 'completely murderous'.[110]

Practical agency in the political sphere does not fare better. Here Aristotle simply asserts that doing politics is unleisured.[111] He seems to allude to the popular view of politicians as 'busybodies' (cf. VI.8.1142a1–2), a view in which he sees some truth. In contrast to ordinary citizens who only know and care about their own good, politicians *are* busybodies because they have goals that affect everyone in the city-state. In the bad case, politicians create positions of honour and power for themselves; in the good case, they go beyond the ordinary and care for the good of the city-state, and so provide for every citizen's happiness. In either case, politicians aim at something beyond the activity of politics, creating lasting effects (same word, *peripoieisthai*, as in 1177b3, previous lemma). Focusing on the good case – and here comes his argument – Aristotle recalls the primary goal of politics: happiness (cf. I.2). However, happiness does not consist in being a politician: 'we clearly seek [happiness] supposing it to be different' from doing politics (1177b14–15). One could therefore take politics to be subordinate to attaining goals beyond itself – which goes hand in hand with judging a politician's success in terms of results. The subordination of politics, then, reveals why it is unleisured: once you take up political office, you *must* act (even if you do not want to), and you will be assessed by standards you did not choose. Certainly, you are not free to do what you want, when you want. Hence, the activity of a politician does not take place within the framework of leisure.

In the previous arguments for the superiority of reflection, Aristotle implies that virtuous action satisfies the value in question to some extent, but tightens the relevant criterion to drive a wedge between practical and theoretical activity. So also here. While he writes as if virtuous action, and doing politics in particular, does not belong to leisure in any way, he uses a more basic notion of 'leisure' in the *Politics* that encompasses virtuous action. In the context of discussing the political relevance of leisure, 'leisure' mainly means 'freedom from paid work', not necessarily freedom to do what you want (*Politics* VII.9.1329a1–2). Excellent practical agency takes place in the

---

[110] Price 2011, 75–6 nicely develops the last point.
[111] Note, *politeuesthai* can also mean 'to live as a free citizen', but very often means 'to take part in government' or 'to hold office'. (LSJ s.v.). Since the activity is also said to create positions of power and honours (*timas*, 1177b13–14, also translatable as 'offices'), the agent requires a higher profile than merely voting in the assembly, or judging cases in court (together with more than a hundred other judges).

framework of leisure insofar as it presupposes the presence of the necessities of life. But there is also a well-motivated, tighter use of the term that makes reflection more leisurely than virtuous action because there is no sense in which we *must* contemplate, whereas a virtuous agent or a politician *must* respond appropriately to the situations they find themselves in.

Does Aristotle's argument from leisure have broader implications? Two possibilities are especially pertinent.[112] First, since tending to bodily needs takes away leisure, the body seems to deprive us from leisure – it is a source of 'unleisure' (*ascholia*). In the *Phaedo* (66b–d) Plato suggests that all our 'unleisure', including war, stems from one source: our body. How close does Aristotle come to the position of the *Phaedo*? He has already alluded to a difference between the human and the divine. He praised intelligence as 'most divine' (1177a16). He will expand on the divinity afforded to humans by their intellect after the upshot of his six arguments (next lemma). So, does the plea for leisure carry dualistic undertones? Second, he advocates here by implication reflective activity as the best use of leisure. But a person *can* acquire theoretical wisdom even without the support of a city-state, and can engage in reflection all on her own (1177a32–4). As reflection takes only things higher-than-human as its objects, the activity seems wholly apolitical. Does Aristotle here begin the strand of thought that threads through Hellenistic thought, locating happiness in the private as opposed to the public life?

1177b16–26 If, then, of the actions ... belonging to happiness.

Having provided a barrage of six arguments for the superiority of reflection over practical activity, Aristotle condenses his reasoning in a long, single sentence, concluding that the activity of reflection will be the complete/perfect happiness of a human being when it takes a complete span of life. Thus, the project commenced at the beginning of X.7 reaches the preliminary goal, to identify our best element and its proper virtue, whose exercise furnishes complete/perfect happiness. The project, note, was adumbrated in Book I with the three kinds of life (pleasure, politics, reflection, I.5), all of which are revisited in Book X. We have seen in X.6 why the life of (frivolous) pleasure does not make for a happy life. So far X.7 has examined the activities that stand at the heart of the philosophical and the political lives (their *skopos*, cf. I.2.1094a22–6). The remainder of X.7–8

---

[112] For these and further thoughts, see Solmsen 1964.

will complete the enquiry by examining whether the philosophical life really is suitable for human nature (over the next three lemmata) and then move on to other aspects of the respective lives, such as the role of external goods and good fortune.

In the previous argument, Aristotle divided excellent practical action into actions performed in war and those performed by politicians (1177b6–7), only to show that practical agency thus understood is unleisured. He now answers two naturally arising questions. First, why does he carve up virtuous action in this peculiar way? Second, why does he not consider low-level virtuous action as a candidate for happiness, comparing *it* to reflection? For instance, wittiness and the other social virtues (IV.6–8) are virtues for leisure! The context of the competition prepares his answer: we are examining how the best practical activities compare with the best theoretical activity, because only the best activities can enter the competition for the title at stake, complete/perfect/final happiness (1177a12–13; a19–20).[113] Although the exposition of the virtues in Books II–V indicates the inferiority of the social virtues vis-à-vis courage, moderation, greatness of soul, and justice, Aristotle does not leave the inference to the reader, but states clearly that 'of the actions in accordance with virtue those in politics and war stand out in fineness and greatness' (1177b16–17). Since he ranks actions in war and politics top, he must pit reflection against *them* to warrant extolling reflection as the best activity. If he were to compare theoretical thinking only to ordinary virtuous action, nothing would follow about the relative ranking between excellence in theoretical thinking and excellence in politics (the latter of which we know to be more complete/perfect/final than individual virtue since I.2.1094b7–11).

Aristotle seems to associate great fineness in action with great benefits for a number of people. But, as argued in the previous two lemmata, the external results also cast a shadow on the status of an activity. In particular, the weightiness or seriousness (*spoudê*) of politics and war provide reasons for being comparatively unleisured (vis-à-vis wit and friendliness). a) An agent cannot perform the actions at her leisure. So many people depend on the external results at which the actions aim, and within a certain time frame, that performing the actions is required. b) Failure in politics and war (through inactivity, incompetence, or infelicity) may endanger the citizens' livelihood. In this case, leisure vanishes

---

[113] Plato advocates a similar strategy in the *Philebus* in order to find the cause of happiness. See 61d–64e.

from their lives. (We all know too well the sad pictures of systematically mismanaged countries, which are, often enough, also ravaged by war.). c) Losing a war may result in the subjection of a city-state's inhabitants to slavery – which again does away with leisure. Especially b) and c) bring out the subordination of politics and war to some higher goal, one that thrives on leisure. We busy ourselves in order to have leisure (1177b4–5). But Aristotle has already made clear in X.6 that we do not toil so that we can amuse ourselves (1176b28–35). That is why he highlights here that reflection excels in *spoudê(i)*, a word that conveys both a sense of seriousness and of worth (1177b19–20). Unlike excellence in politics and war, the seriousness of reflection does not bring with it a lack of leisure. For reflection plays the role of happiness only when we have the leisure to do so (cf. 1177b4).

The praise of reflection, however, points towards the limitations of human nature, the topic of the next three lemmata. Aristotle associates reflective activity with the criteria for happiness: finality, intrinsic pleasantness, self-sufficiency, and leisure. By adding unweariness, 'so far as possible for human beings' (1177b22), he points to a higher sphere beyond the humanly possible, namely the divine. He may here hint at differing standards for human happiness and happiness without qualification (so as to include divine happiness). This comes out in a consideration related to unweariness. Reflection may be the most continuous of human activities, but we cannot engage in it continuously. a) We are worn out at times (despite its being the least wearing activity), and b) we are mortal. The latter point raises the question of how long a human life must be to qualify as a happy life. The former prompts us to consider how much one should (try to) engage in reflection. Aristotle does not answer a) or b). However, in the apodosis of the sentence, he stipulates that the happy life be complete (1177b24–5). He has not explicitly argued for the point in the previous arguments. He seems merely to recall the point about the completeness of life from the definition of happiness in Book I (1098a15), where the temporal sense of 'complete life' seems mandated.[114] Unfortunately, the present context sheds little light on the interpretation of the requirement. Still, the stipulation about the length of life serves as a *memento mori*. But it also prepares the transition to the next line of enquiry, which explicitly challenges our understanding of human nature as merely human.

---

[114] Though see Pakaluk 2005, 82–4, for alternatives.

1177b26–31 Buts such a life ... compared with a human life.

Aristotle's argument for the superiority of reflection in X.7 has so far relied heavily on comparison. Everyone knows how great excellent action in war and politics is – but look, there's something even greater! Before examining the nature of its comparative superiority more exhaustively in X.8, Aristotle concentrates on reflection in the remainder of X.7, justifying its prime position. This lemma transitions the discussion to focusing on the life of reflection (as opposed to its central activity). Subsequently, he draws out the practical implications of taking the life of reflection to be divine (1177b31–1178a2) and undergirds it with a suitable account of human nature as something divine (1178a2–4). This explains why a divine life yields superlative happiness *for us* (1178a4–8). The focus on the divine does not come unexpected. Apart from the ossified connection in *eudaimonia* (literally 'having a good god', here rendered 'happiness') between the divine and happiness, the gods were regarded as paradigms of happiness. Consequently, a happy human being 'has' something divine and will be regarded as 'most divine' (I.12.1101b23–5).[115]

Conceiving of the life of reflection as divine may have momentous consequences. For if we claim that happiness *tout court* is divine, instead of associating the divine with perfect/complete happiness only, then the present passage would seem to indicate that reflection is the only way to attain happiness, or is at least the high road.[116] Aristotle contrasts the merely human with a larger-than-human life. The life of reflection will transcend the merely human life because the person living it lives 'insofar as there is some divine element in the person' (1177b26–8) – theoretical wisdom. The argument proceeds via analogy: (A) as the divine element stands to the concrete, embodied human being, (B) so stands the activity of the divine element to that of the rest of virtue (*allên aretên*, b28–9). Therefore, the activity of theoretical wisdom will surpass the activity of the rest of virtue in the same way that something divine surpasses something non-divine. Further, if the central activity of a life is divine, so is the life (b30–1). That is, Aristotle seems to establish that the life of reflection is divine in contrast to the life of the rest of virtue, which appears to lack divinity. So, if a happy life must be divine, it looks as if only a reflective life could be happy, not a

---

[115] Long 2011 argues that Aristotle shifts his view of the divine between the bulk of the EN and X.7–8 (first virtuous action counts as divine, then it does not), whereas Aufderheide 2015 stresses the continuity (all along only theoretical reflection counts as divine).

[116] For the contrast between happiness and perfect/complete happiness, see commentary on 1177a12–17.

life of merely practical excellence. (He will expand on this implication at the beginning of X.8.)

For the analogy to work, the relata must stand in a suitable relation to each other. One way of interpreting the argument proceeds in terms of parts and wholes, suggested especially by taking a cue from 'the rest of virtue'. We can regard all the virtues as a whole, which, when we subtract theoretical wisdom, leaves us with the rest of virtue, i.e. with the practical virtues comprised of practical wisdom and the virtues of character. (Note, the practical virtues form a natural cluster: they are unified in the sense that having one implies having all the others, VI.13.1144b30–1145a6.) Analogously, a) the compound might be the human being (understood as a compound of body and soul) minus the divine element, in which case we can represent the analogy as follows: divine part : human being minus divine part :: reflection : activity of all of virtue minus reflection (= rest of virtue). Along similar lines, b) we may take the compound to be the soul, consisting of non-rational, subrational, and rational parts. In this case, Aristotle would suggest the following: divine part : soul minus divine part :: reflection : activity of all of virtue minus reflection (= rest of virtue). Unfortunately, the reprise of the terms 'the rest of virtue' at X.8.1178a9 and 'the compound' at 1178a20 does not help decide between these two ways of understanding 'the compound' in particular.

Ostensibly, the goal of the lemma is to show *that* the life in accordance with the divine element surpasses the life in accordance with the human element. But does the passage also suggest an explanation for the superiority? In other words, does Aristotle in addition to stating 'the that' also hint at 'the why'? The answer depends on how we spell out the 'stands to' in 'A stands to B…' in the analogy. Here are a few suggestions. The relationship between the items in the analogy could be 1. teleological or more narrowly instrumental (body and practical activity subserve the divine element and its activity) or 2. conditional in the sense that the body is a condition for the divine element in a human life, just as practical wisdom and its activity are a condition for theoretical wisdom and its activity (cf. VI.13.1145a6–9). More subtly, and even more fancifully, 3. both pairs could be related by their proximity to (Aristotle's) god. The human being is further away from god than her best element, just as virtuous action is further away than reflection. If the characteristics of intelligence mentioned at the beginning of X.7 linger in the background, then 4. the relation between the items in the analogy could be one of governing or regulating (not in a practical sense, though). The divine element governs the human being in the sense that a happy human being knows about her best part, and makes provisions accordingly. Similarly, in a happy life, practical wisdom knows about reflection, and makes provisions on its behalf: it is not prescriptive in relation to it, but for it (cf. 1145a10–11).[117]

1177b31–1178a2 But, one should ... esteem by far.

Having argued that the life of reflection is divine, compared with a merely human life, Aristotle draws out the practical consequences of that view. He offers straightforward practical advice [ADV]: we should 'put off the mortal as far as possible and do everything to live a life in accordance with the most outstanding thing in us' (1177b33–4). Aristotle does not usually give direct practical advice in the EN, presumably because, as here, the practical implications tend to be unclear. Should we forget about our human cares and duties to concentrate on theoretical thinking alone? Does Aristotle, in other words, extol an unethical ideal?

To answer these questions, we must start further back. Aristotle starts by citing well-known advice found in such poets as Epicharmus (cited in *Rhetoric* II.12.6.1394b24), Pindar (*Isthmian Ode* V, 14–16), Sophocles (*Tereus* fr., 590), and Euripides (*Alcestis* 799 and *Bacchae* 396). The two adages exhort us to think human thoughts because we are human (1177b32–3). More precisely, they advise the subject of the thoughts, the thinker, not to hanker after unsuitable objects of thought, objects that go beyond the human plane. While ADV on its own might seem to focus only on the subject, the poets' advice indicates that the activities are prior to any defining capacities of the subject, and that we must therefore attend especially to the objects of thought (cf. *De Anima* II.4.415a14–22). It is through the subject's *activities*, and more specifically through the subject's thinking about divine objects, that she may cast off the mortal.

We can appreciate the difference between ADV and the poets' advice by reminding ourselves of a prosaic version of the contrast in EN VI. Aristotle sums up the difference between the theoretical and practical aspects of intelligence as understood by ordinary people: the practically wise person (*phronimos*) knows things that are good for human beings, whereas the theoretically wise person (*sophos*) knows things that are 'even superhuman (*daimonion*)— but useless because what they enquire into are not human goods' (VI.7.1141b7–8). Since we should understand the poets' 'mortal thoughts' as concerned with human affairs, they ought to

---

[117] For varieties of 4. (in a slightly different context), see especially Cooper 2004 and Meyer 2011.

include thoughts about what is good for human beings, including the highest good. Thinking about happiness should count as heeding the poets' advice. The theoretically wise person does not think about happiness when engaged in thinking. They think of higher things.

Both the poets and popular opinion seem to presuppose a strict dichotomy between human and divine. But once we acknowledge with Aristotle that human beings are capable of divine thought, and that our happiness rests on divine thinking, the dichotomy must look suspicious. For if happiness consists in reflective activity, something divine (see previous lemma), then the practically wise person should think about *that*. The poets may resist blurring the line between mortal and immortal in several ways. i) They could simply reject the Aristotelian anthropology. By denying that (a part of) human intelligence is divine, the poets could insist that human happiness has nothing divine about it. ii) They could adopt a pessimistic stance. If happiness consists in thinking divine thoughts, then happiness is for the gods, not for us. Aristotle partly agrees with the latter. Happiness is for us only insofar as we cast off the mortal: don't live in accordance with (*kata*) the poets' advice, live in accordance with (*kata*) your best element!

While we can see how practically wise thinking requires taking our divine nature into account, theoretically wise thinking does not seem to consider our mortal nature. Hence the question whether ADV advocates an unethical ideal. Does Aristotle advise us to transcend our human nature, to set practical thought aside in order to concentrate on theoretical thought only? Yes and no. The two-sided answer reflects the two sides of our nature. No, because the injunction clearly appeals to us as practical agents. *We* must do everything (*panta poiein*) to live the life of reflection. Our practical agency benefits not only theoretical intelligence (cf. previous lemma), but also the human being: it is *we* who are happy through reflection. Therefore, we do not transcend our nature, but perfect it. To actualise and perfect our nature, practical wisdom, guiding our actions, sees to it that theoretical wisdom and theoretical thinking come about (VI.13.1145a8–9). It does so in two ways (on a personal or political level). a) We are born with a divine element, but in order to render it capable of thinking divine thoughts, i.e. in order to actualise its first potentiality, we must undergo long training in philosophical thinking, a process by which we become more like god, insofar as we develop a state that enables us to do what god does. At the end of this process, intelligence will be fully our most consequential and estimable part. b) Like every other state, intelligence is most what it is when active. So, practical intelligence must see to it that we use our theoretical intelligence. When we do, we and our theoretical intelligence will be most divine. Both a) and b) as practical projects are subject to the standards of conduct. To do them well requires us to do them in accordance with ethical virtue. To avoid shirking our duties for the sake of reflecting, we need leisure – time in which we can do what we want, not what we must (see commentary on 1177b4–16). Thus – and this is the positive answer to the question above – practical intelligence needs to create conditions in which we are free to transcend our ordinary human nature, a time when we can leave our human cares behind. When we have leisure and engage in reflection, we will cognise the best objects, be most self-sufficient, enjoy the sweetest pleasures, and be active most continuously (X.7.1177a18–26). Since these attributes belong most of all to god, a person engaging in reflection will be most *like* a god when doing so (for some thoughts on god – in a different context – see *Metaphysics* 12.7 and 9). Aristotle thus answers the poets with his version of the *homoiôsis theô(i)*, assimilation to god, a thesis that Empedocles (DK 31 B 146–7; 132) and especially Plato (especially in the *Timaeus* 90b–d) before him have urged.[118]

1178a2–4 And each [sc. human being] would seem ... some other being.

At the beginning of X.7 Aristotle refers to intelligence as our best and most divine element (1177a12–17). In the course of the argument, he identifies the proper virtue of this element with our (developed) capacity for theoretical thinking. Exercising this capacity makes a human both happy and divine (cf. 1177b26–31). He therefore exhorts us to cast off the mortal as far as possible by living in accordance with this part (b33–4). Now he reconsiders the boundary between the human and divine to render the exhortation suitable to *us*. Before, theoretical intelligence was our best part; now, 'each person would seem even to be this' (1178a2–4). This does not mean that a human being consists of nothing but her theoretical intelligence. For 'the authoritative and better element' (a3) entails other elements – human beings are compounds (cf. 1177b28–9). Instead, Aristotle seems to single out one element from the compound and stress that this is what

---

[118] As Plato does not differentiate so clearly between practical and theoretical wisdom, the problem of whether becoming like a god is unethical advice does not present itself. In the *Theaetetus* 176a–b, he writes that 'a man should make all haste to escape from earth to heaven; and escape means becoming as like God as possible; and a man becomes like God when he becomes just and pure, with understanding' (tr. Levitt/Burnyeat in *Plato: Complete Works* – see Cooper and Hutchinson 1997). Sedley 1999 highlights the continuity between Plato and Aristotle on the topic of becoming (like) a god, whereas Silverman 2010 stresses the differences.

we essentially are. But what a certain form of life is essentially, e.g. what makes us human, is determined by the highest and most authoritative capacities of the soul (cf. *De Anima* II.4). Accordingly, there is a specifically human way of living, because we have intelligence. Plato's *Philebus* vividly illustrates what it would mean to choose a subhuman life. Faced with the question of whether he should choose a life containing all the pleasure he could wish for, but no intelligence and cognition, Socrates' interlocutor admits that such a life would be that of a clam or mollusc, but not that of a human being, and hence not choice-worthy for us (20e–21d). Aristotle's conception of a human life is even more demanding than Plato's. Since we are essentially our better and authoritative element – theoretical intelligence – choosing a way of life that does not reflect our theoretical nature would be strange or even absurd (*atopos*, 1178a3). Such a life would miss what is essentially human. So, Aristotle seems to suggest that in order to live an essentially human life, we must live a life of reflection.

This conception of what a human being is, and how one should live, seems hard to square with the drive of EN I–IX. For the EN seems to advertise a thoroughly practical approach to life, one in which virtuous actions take pride of place. One passage from Book IX in particular seems to clash with the present lemma.[119] The question of what human beings are naturally arises when discussing the nature of self-love. One can remove the opprobrium from self-love by distinguishing between two conceptions of the self (and human nature). Those who take for themselves the larger share of money, honour, or bodily pleasures bring self-love into disrepute. But, Aristotle corrects, we should not regard their behaviour as self-love proper, because they have a skewed view of the self. They indulge their appetites, passions, and the non-rational part of the soul (1168b15–23). By contrast, true self-lovers indulge their most authoritative part. They act virtuously, and for the sake of the fine, assigning to themselves the finest and best goods (b29–31). They are *true* self-lovers, because their view of the self is correct. While the human soul has both a rational and an irrational part, Aristotle firmly locates the centre of the self in the most authoritative part: 'and just as a city-state seems to be its most authoritative element most of all (*to kuriôtaton malista*), or

---

[119] A related passage, IX.4.1166a13–23, goes in a similar direction, but contains the additional twist that it advises against becoming a god – which might seem to clash with the injunction that we should cast off the mortal. But the apparent clash disappears when we consider that Aristotle only exhorts us to cast off the mortal 'as far as possible' – which seems to acknowledge our limitations. We can try to become like gods, but we cannot replace ourselves with gods.

any other composite whole, so also a human being' (IX.8.1168b31–3). However, in IX.8 the authoritative element seems to be practical intelligence, as the two supporting considerations indicate. a) Self-control and the lack of it depend on whether intelligence (*nous*, b35) has control, and b) voluntary actions are done with reason most of all (*meta logou malista*, 1169a1). Since both illustrate that 'each is this or is this most of all' (a2), the examples seem to support a thoroughly practical notion of intelligence, reason, and the self.

On closer inspection, however, the passages in Book IX do not strictly identify the essence of a human being with practical intelligence. First, they qualify the predication with 'most of all' (*malista*), which at least makes room for other things that we may also be, but not most of all (for further discussion of *malista*, see commentary on next lemma). Second, unlike X.7, IX.8 speaks of intelligence or the rational part of the soul more broadly, without differentiating between theoretical and practical wisdom. So, one way to ease the tension between the apparently clashing conceptions of human nature would be to argue that Book X provides a more specific account, but not one that contradicts Book IX. For if we are in essence theoretical intelligence, then it is also true that we are intelligence most of all. The examples of practical agency in IX.8 would then illustrate only the broader claim that we are intelligence or reason most of all, without deciding which specific aspect of intelligence is essential to us. In an attempt to specify the relationship between the theoretical and the practical aspects of reason, one could a) understand theoretical thinking as a practical project – in which case the apparent clash between the practical and the theoretical conception of human nature would disappear (see commentary on previous lemma for the practical standing of reflection). Alternatively, b) one could unify the two functions of intelligence by making practical wisdom necessary for, subservient to, or otherwise for the sake of theoretical wisdom (see commentary on 1177b26–31). Either way, Book IX's claim that practical agency illustrates that we are intelligence most of all would fit with the claim of the present lemma that we are theoretical intelligence.

1178a4–8 Again, what was said before ... be superlatively happy.

The function argument in I.7 draws on a close connection between our nature and our happiness: human happiness must revolve around an activity that expresses our nature. In the bulk of the EN, we may get the impression that this activity is thoroughly practical. But at the beginning of

X.7 Aristotle seems to take a different view. Although human intelligence (*nous*) has a practical and a theoretical side, its proper (*oikeion*) virtue is theoretical, and hence the activity central to happiness is too (1177a12–18). Therefore, our nature must transcend the merely practical. The previous lemma tentatively elevated theoretical intelligence as the defining feature of human nature – as if practical agency was in some way alien to us, or at least not expressive of the essence of what it is to be human (see commentary on previous lemma). Now Aristotle in some way takes a stance on the previous identification of a human being with theoretical intelligence. Previously he had said that 'each person would seem even to be [theoretical intelligence]' (1178a3–4); now he says that a human being is intelligence 'most of all' (*malista*, a7).

We can read the passage in two ways. The point in the previous lemma was expressed tentatively, using the optative mood in the Greek. a) Aristotle might now be going back on the previous strict identification. By inserting *malista*, he means to forestall the misconception that a human being is nothing but theoretical intellect. Instead, a human being is theoretical intelligence more than anything else (though not in bulk, 1177b34–1178a2). So, human nature might comprise other important elements, such as practical intellect, but theoretical intellect is our distinctive mark.[120] Alternatively, b), we could take Aristotle to confirm and elaborate on the identification of human nature with theoretical intelligence. To say that each human being is theoretical intelligence *malista* is to say that, strictly speaking, human beings *are* theoretical intelligence. However, the *malista* paves the way for a looser way of speaking, according to which we can also identify human beings with some other element if suitably related to the paradigmatic case. Strictly speaking, human beings are theoretical intelligence, whereas, loosely speaking, we are intelligence more broadly, or even practical wisdom.[121]

Aristotle's supporting thought – 'what was said before will fit also now' (1178a4–5) – does not favour either reading. He presumably refers to the end of the discussion of pleasure. Following an examination of the pleasure proper (*oikeion*) to human beings (which begins at X.5.1176a3–4), he concludes that 'the pleasures completing/perfecting <the activities characteristic of the blessed person> will be said to be characteristically human in the primary way (*kuriôs*); the others will be so in a secondary way (*deuterôs*) or in ways many times removed, just like the activities'

---

[120] Charles 1999, 220.
[121] Scott 1999, 231–3.

(1176a27–9). This leaves open which activities will be characteristic of the blessed person – except that they must be the activity of virtue or excellence. The present claim narrows down the X.5 position: because we are our best element most of all, life in accordance with theoretical intelligence is, without qualification, proper to human beings (cf. 1178a5–7). But depending on philosophical temperament and background assumptions about Aristotle's way of writing in the EN, we might see either reading a) or b) confirmed. Reading a) would be correct if the *malista* made room for something other than intellect that is also part of human nature. In this case, the pleasures stemming from practical agency could count as a primary human pleasure in X.5, even if there are activities more properly human because they are more central to the human good. According to reading b), activities other than theoretical thinking would not be proper for human beings – at least not without some further explanation of how they relate to theoretical thinking. In the absence of such an explanation, Aristotle would now, retrospectively, classify only the pleasures stemming from theoretical thinking as properly human – they are most pleasant for human beings (here repeated from 1177a22–7). The pleasure from practical agency would belong to the secondary pleasures in X.5.

The question of interpretation matters because it helps determine both Aristotle's view of human nature and happiness. Calling the theoretical life 'happiest' leaves room for calling the practical life 'happy'. According to reading a), a practical life may indeed be genuinely happy when centred on the excellent activity of practical wisdom, as practical intellect is part of our nature, too. Reading b) would have the happiness of the practical life qualified. Loosely speaking, we can call such a life 'happy', but, strictly speaking, it is not happy. Aristotle grapples with the happiness of the practical life over the next few lemmata.

X.8

1178a9–14 And secondarily <so> ... to be characteristically human.

The first sentence of this momentous lemma presents the reader with several challenges. Although editors and translators mark here a new chapter, the text follows immediately from the end of X.7. Indeed, the first sentence can be made intelligible only if we supply key elements from the preceding sentence. Still, in the Greek, neither the subject of the sentence nor the predicate is entirely clear. How we construe the sentence has significant consequences for our understanding of the EN, as Aristotle claims the life of the rest of virtue is secondary in some way to the life of theoretical intelligence (see previous lemma).

Let us begin with the subject. The Greek *ho* picks up 'life' (*bios*) from 1178a7, which speaks of the life in accordance with theoretical intelligence. But 'the life of' may mean several things. Some interpreters take *bios* to refer to aspects of a life lived by one person, such as our family life, public life (if we have one), or work life, etc.[122] However, most interpreters take the different ways of life to be spread over lives lived by different people.[123] The more common interpretation takes seriously Aristotle's exhortation that life needs *one* focus (*skopos*, I.2.1094a18–24) with a view to which everything else will be arranged. This focus will be the highest good, after which the life will then be called (e.g. life of pleasure, or art, or theoretical study). An eirenic approach that makes concessions to both interpretations might allow for some variation of the goal within a life, by taking 'life' to refer to a significant phase of a person's lifetime which need not necessarily encompass the person's whole existence. So, as a child, a person may lead the life of frivolous pleasure, and, as a grown-up, the life of virtue; and, retiring from active life, she may lead the life of contemplation. Aristotle may have seen the last two lives in a successive relation in the *Protrepticus* (Düring's fragment 17, though using *phronêsis* for theoretical intelligence) and in the *Politics* – if honouring the gods is a form of the theoretical life (VII.9.1329a31–4).

Next, how is *bios* qualified? What is the life of 'the rest of virtue'? In the next two sentences Aristotle justifies and explains what he asserts in the first one. In particular, he draws attention to the fact that the activities of the rest of virtue are characteristically human (*anthrôpikai*, 1178a10), and then cites examples of virtuous actions, such as doing what is just, courageous, and so on. So, 'the rest of virtue' refers to the practical virtues (as opposed to the theoretical virtues) that are activated in such actions. The life envisaged, then, is an excellent practical life, the life implicitly contrasted with the theoretical life for much of X.7.

Now we can come to the predicate and the topic of the first sentence. Aristotle writes 'And secondarily <so> is the life in accordance with the rest of virtue: for the activities in accordance with it are characteristically

---

[122] Keyt 1989. His discussion of this topic is very helpful, even if we do not follow his particular interpretation.
[123] Cooper 1999, 229–31, n. 14, trenchantly criticises Keyt's interpretation. He argues that *bios* covers the whole of a life, not aspects thereof.

human' (1178a9–10). The bracketed 'so' is not even in the Greek; the reader must supply the predicate. Since the previous sentence reads 'Hence, this life [sc. of theoretical wisdom] will also be superlatively happy' (a7–8), interpreters almost unanimously take the present lemma also to deal with happiness (interpretation A). They understand the implicit 'so' either as 'happiest' – supplying it from the previous sentence – or as 'happy', implicit in 'happiest'. The options differ because the latter seems to suggest that the practical life, being secondarily happy, is not really or fully happy, whereas the former does not – if one can make sense of 'secondarily happiest'. But there is an alternative (interpretation B). One may go back a little further to lines a5–6, where Aristotle argues that the life in accordance with theoretical intellect is proper to a human being, and take the question 'What is proper to a human being?' to guide the present lemma. If so, he would now claim that the life in accordance with the other virtue is proper to human beings in a secondary way.[124] So, the primary topic of the lemma might be either happiness or human nature, depending on how we unpack Aristotle's compressed writing.

What is Aristotle's point? Irrespective of A or B, the justification allows for two different, opposing interpretations. He justifies his claim that the excellent practical life is secondarily A) happy/happiest or B) human by highlighting and subsequently spelling out that the activities in accordance with the rest of virtue are human. The argument could go in either of two directions, depending on what work 'human' is doing. It may show the practical life to be either i) *merely* human or ii) *also* human. Both options make sense only against the background of the discussion of human nature at 1177b26–1178a8, which first contrasts the life of theoretical intelligence with a merely human life (1177b26–31), but then goes on to make out the life of theoretical intelligence as properly human (1178a4–8). So, the question is whether i) Aristotle goes back to his initial stark contrast between the human and the divine, or whether ii) he regards the chasm as bridged, having integrated the divine element properly into human nature. Reading i) emphasises the difference between the practical and the theoretical life. He might want to do so in order to extol the happiness of the theoretical life. This reading, however, raises again the question whether the theoretical life is really human and/or whether the practical life is really happy. (This reading works less well with supplying the superlative at a9.) Reading ii), by contrast, stresses the continuity between the two

---

[124] Reece, in press, argues for this reading at length.

lives. At 1178a3–4, Aristotle suggested that choosing any life but the theoretical one would be choosing the life of some other being. Now he would stress that, properly understood, the practical life can also be human. This may either be his primary goal – in which case we should understand 'secondarily human' in a9 (i.e. B) – or the humanness of the practical life is supposed to explain how the practical life can be happy or happiest – albeit in a secondary way (A).

1178a14–19 Some <of them> are ... in accordance with practical wisdom.

The previous lemma begins an argument to show that the rest of virtue (*allên aretên*) is human to support the claim that the life in accordance with that virtue is secondarily happy/happiest, or human (depending on one's interpretation; see commentary on previous lemma). As reasons for the humanness of that life, Aristotle has so far highlighted that we act in relation to other people. Now he expands on the role of affections in action, and their connection to the body, to show that the practical virtues and the life in accordance with it are human.

The argument proceeds in two steps. First, he highlights the extremely close connection between ethical virtue as a whole (note, Aristotle uses the singular) and affective states (1178a15–16). In Book II, he suggests that the virtues of character have to do with pleasure and pain, because pleasure and pain accompany everything we do (II.3.1104b8–16). More precisely, he takes ethical virtue to be concerned with hitting the mean within action *and* affection, where the affections are differentiated more finely as fear, confidence, appetite, anger, etc. (II.6.1106b14–24). Clearly, hitting the mean within action and emotion (or missing it) *is* characteristically human. The key move in the second step brings together practical wisdom and the virtues of character. Since one cannot have the one without the other, they belong together, on the human side of the divide. Practical wisdom is not only logically distinct from virtue of character, but also different in being – hence the need to *argue* that practical wisdom is also human. The need is felt in particular after elevating (undifferentiated) intelligence pretty much to the divine (X.7.1177a12–17). Since practical wisdom is a function of intelligence, and the proper virtue of intelligence turns out to rest in a divine element, it is not obvious, and requires argument, that practical wisdom is human. One could bring out this line of thought by translating 1178a16 as 'and *even practical wisdom* is yoked to the virtues of character'. By highlighting that the virtues of character (plural) and practical wisdom mutually entail each other, Aristotle can make plausible (without going into the details) that the contrast at issue is not between rational on the one side and sub- or non-rational on the other, but between the practical and the theoretical. All of that which belongs to the practical is human.

The reasons for taking wisdom and ethical virtue so closely together presumably allude to an earlier discussion. Book VI discusses the relationship between the virtues of character and wisdom, where Aristotle argues that 'virtue [sc. of character] makes the goal correct, whereas wisdom makes what leads to it correct' (VI.12.1144a7–9). Roughly, in a practically relevant situation, a person's good character is responsible for generating a wish, providing the right starting point for further deliberation: 'badness distorts and makes a person deceived about the starting points' (VI.12.1144a34–6). With the right object of wish, the person will then deliberate and reach a decision (*proairesis*), which issues in action. Good deliberation is due to practical wisdom. So, for virtuous action, a person needs both ethical virtue and practical wisdom. Since Book VI belongs to the books common to the *Eudemian* and the *Nicomachean Ethics* (EE IV–VI = EN V–VII) that may have been added only later to the EN and without Aristotle overseeing the change, it is possible that we cannot presuppose knowledge of the discussion here.[125] However, even if a protreptic context such as the present lemma need not go into much detail, the argument hardly makes sense without (something like) the preceding discussion. Thus, the present passage can be taken as a piece of evidence for the unity of the EN, i.e. the thesis that Aristotle authored the EN roughly in the form we have it.[126]

1178a19–23 And connected as ... the present project.

At the end of X.7 Aristotle established the life of reflection as supremely happy. At the beginning of X.8, he commences an argument that comes to a close in this lemma, namely that the life in accordance with the rest of virtue (i.e. all the other virtues, except the theoretical) is human. This argument bolsters his claim that the practical life has a certain quality of the best life in a secondary way, being happiest/happy, or being human (see commentary on 1178a9–14 for the options and discussion).

Before, Aristotle has attended to our actions and affections; now, he turns to the virtues. A virtue counts as human when it belongs to the

---

[125] See Introduction §4 for a brief discussion.
[126] Frede 2019 argues against the common view that EN V–VII originate in the *Eudemian Ethics*, but supports the unity view of the EN.

compound (*suntheton*, 1178a20).¹²⁷ However, a virtue does not belong to the compound merely by being instantiated in it (like theoretical intelligence). The practical virtues belong to the compound in a richer sense, due to their being closely connected to our affective states. To explain, the virtues of character are not only responsible for acting in the way we should, but also for feeling in the way we should (II.6.1106b14–24) – which shows their connection to the compound. For although affective states belong to the soul (II.5.1105b19–21), characteristic bodily phenomena accompany them, such as reddening of shame or blanching of fear (IV.8.1128b13–15). If the other affective states necessarily involve the body, then they all belong to the compound in the richer sense of 'belong'.¹²⁸ Since the virtues governing the correct affective responses are thus concerned with the compound, they belong to it in a way that theoretical wisdom does not. Because the definition of virtue of character makes reference to practical wisdom as that which determines the correct mean for affections (and actions, II.6.1106b36–1107a1), both virtue of character and practical wisdom belong to the compound. They are characteristically human virtues.

Just as Aristotle infers from the divinity of theoretical intelligence the divinity of the life in accordance with it in the parallel passage at 1177b26–31, so he infers here the humanness of the life in accordance with the virtues of the compound. Importantly, he calls not only the practical life 'human' but also the happiness characteristic of it. Note, however, that he does not contrast human happiness with divine happiness.¹²⁹ He eschews calling the theoretical life's happiness 'divine'. In fact, his point was to reveal it as the most proper happiness for a human being (1178a4–8). So, there do not seem to be two forms of happiness, one divine and one human, of which we can fully attain only one. Rather, if he intends any contrast, it is between happiness without qualification, and happiness qualified as human. But does he intend a contrast? Now, depending on how we think the argument is set up at the beginning of X.8, we may interpret the implications of the present lemma in opposite ways. Either i) because the practical life is *merely* human (our divine element plays no active role), the happiness we can achieve in it is also *merely* human, but not happiness without qualification. In this case, the life would be secondarily happy

---

[127] The term 'compound' echoes its first occurrence in X.7 where Aristotle opposes it to the divine element, although the text does not settle whether 'compound' as the concrete human being or soul includes or excludes theoretical intelligence (see 1177b26–31 with commentary).
[128] Charles 2011 argues for the stronger thesis that desire is a psychophysical process that cannot be separated into a bodily and a mental component, not even when defining desire.
[129] *Pace* Bush 2008. For further argument, see Aufderheide 2015, 52–5.

(supplying the superlative at 1178a9 does not work so well with this interpretation). Or ii) because a happy life must be proper to human beings, a happy practical life must *also* be human. Having shown the practical life to *be* human, Aristotle can call it 'happy' (see commentary on 1178a9–14 for further discussion).

The argument ends in a flash. In contrast to human virtue, life, and happiness, Aristotle claims 'the one of intelligence is separable' (1178a22) – only to set the topic aside for another occasion. Why mention it only to set it aside? Let us begin by examining *what* he says. First, grammatically 'the one' (*hē*) should pick up on happiness (*eudaimonia*) in the previous sentence – in which case the happiness belonging to intelligence (*nous*) is (claimed to be) separable, presumably from the ordinary human happiness we can attain through living a practical life. If we take happiness through theoretical wisdom to be unattainable for human beings, it would indeed be separate (not merely separable).[130] However, since much of the argument starting at 1178a9 focuses on virtue, last mentioned in the plural as 'the virtues of the compound' at 1178a20–1, we could understand 'virtue' as the referent of 'the one' (most interpreters do so). This would open the following line of thought. The Greek pointedly stresses the connectedness of practical virtue. The syllable *sun-* (roughly 'with') highlights that virtue of character is kindred with affective states (*sunô(i)keiôsthai*, 1178a15), yoked to practical wisdom (*sunezeuktai*, a16), and connected to the affective states (*sunêrtêmenai*, a19) – which makes it a virtue of the compound (*sunthetos*, twice in a20). This reading stresses the separability of theoretical intelligence from the compound: it does not belong to the compound in the same way as do the practical virtues.

Second, Aristotle operates with various separability claims elsewhere in his works: X can be separable from Y spatially, definitionally, ontologically, or taxonomically.[131] The *De Anima* almost begins with a delicate aporetic discussion of the separability of certain parts of the soul in relation to the affective states (*pathê*, I.1.403a3–27), a topic that resurfaces several times in key passages. In particular, the discussion of theoretical intelligence in III.4–5 suggests the separability of this part of the soul.[132] But instead of rushing to the *De Anima* (or the *Generation of Animals* II.3.736b15–29; 737a7–11), we should stay with the *Ethics*. The minimal point seems to be

---

[130] For a related, possibly pessimistic, view of human happiness, see 1177b31–3, where Aristotle cites the cautioning remarks of some poets.

[131] Miller 2012 helpfully distinguishes the senses and discusses separability in *De Anima*.

[132] For an accessible overview, see Cohoe 2014.

this: if the study of subject matter X is separable from that of Y, then X and Y should also be separable (at least in definition). So, by indicating that the study of the separability of intelligence *is* separable from a study of ethics, Aristotle may suggest that theoretical intelligence is separable from the subject of ethics, human action, and affection. He does not seem to *rely* on another work to make his point: gesturing towards something exciting that goes beyond the present context may just *be* the point. He seems to extol the life of reflection partly in order to exhort the audience to the study of philosophy, and partly to establish the life of reflection as the apogee of human existence, so that the audience may orient their practical lives as citizens or politicians towards it.[133] By giving the audience a short glimpse of the separability of intelligence and its virtue, and hinting at a further discussion that would be required to explain it, Aristotle may give an example of the sort of reflective activity that would occupy the life of reflection.

1178a23–b3 And it will also seem ... the more will be needed.

In EN X.7 Aristotle commends the life of reflection by comparing it favourably with another kind of life widely agreed to be great, the life led by someone who holds high office in the city, in war or peace (1177b4–26). The editors of the text may have marked the beginning of a new chapter at 1178a9 (i.e. X.8) because they thought both the comparanda and the perspective had changed. a) Aristotle no longer compares the life of reflection with the life of a statesman, but with an ordinarily decent life based on the virtues of character. b) Instead of positively highlighting why the life of reflection is so great, he now finds fault with the life of ethical virtue, to justify its comparatively lower rank as 'only' secondarily happy/happiest or secondarily human (on which, see commentary on 1178a9–14). The editorial decision raises the question: does Aristotle begin a new chapter? Does he introduce a third life as a contender for the happiest life?

First, in response to b), Aristotle prefaces his argument (which spans this lemma and the next) by highlighting that the virtue of intelligence needs fewer external resources than ethical virtue[134] – even if he then

---

[133] Hutchinson and Ransome Johnson 2014 stress the continuity between EN X.6–8 and Aristotle's lost work *Protrepticus* (Exhortation to Philosophy).

[134] I take the subject of the sentence at 1178a23–5 – 'it' – to refer to the virtue of intelligence (a22). However, some interpreters take a22 to talk about the *happiness* of intelligence, and would therefore also take our present sentence to deal with happiness. The latter reading is awkward, insofar as it makes the comparandum 'the ethical happiness' instead of the unproblematic 'the ethical virtue'.

focuses only on the shortcomings of the practical life in this lemma. The response to a) takes longer, because we can interpret the argument in two plausible ways. Aristotle concedes that the *politikos* and the philosopher do not differ much with respect to the necessities for life. However, the activities themselves differ widely (1178a25–8). Focusing on the kind of activities characteristic of each type of life, Aristotle highlights the need for the external resources required for acts of generosity, justice, courage, and moderation (this lemma), and the absence of a need for reflection (next lemma). The kinds of virtuous action at issue require money (*chrêmata*), power (*dunamis*), and opportunity (*exousia*). We might now take the resources either i) as resources just anybody could attain – in which case the *politikos* would simply be an active citizen, or ii) as resources accessible only to those with a higher public profile, in which case the *politikos* would be a (high-profile) politician. In particular, how we take *dunamis* and *exousia* makes a difference. According to i), *dunamis* would simply be the power needed to see through one's courageous actions to the end (*epitelei*, 1178a32), and *exousia* simply an opportunity to show moderation. Alternatively, according to ii), *dunamis* would be a position of political power that allows one to reach something important with one's courage. This would be the remit of the general, not a hoplite's. Similarly, *exousia* can mean 'abundant means'.[135] A rich person's moderate behaviour is eminently more remarkable than that of someone who could not behave immoderately if she wanted to, for want of means. So, interpretation i) takes Aristotle to ask what resources we need for virtuous activity to take place at all, whereas ii) has him point out that publicly notable virtuous actions (*dêlos*, 1178a33) require grand resources.

It is difficult to decide between i) and ii), and Aristotle may not differentiate between the citizen's and the statesman's lives as neatly as we may wish (see the last paragraph of this lemma). Nevertheless, here are some considerations in favour of ii) – though they are by no means conclusive. The present lemma puts a premium on externally recognisable results stemming from virtuous action: a) 'for wishes are invisible, and even those who are not just pretend to wish to do what is just' (1178a30–1), and b) 'how else will it be clear (*dêlos*) that he, or any of the other types, is the way he is?' (a33–4). While decision (*proairesis*) plays an important role in virtue, the action (*praxis*) decided on needs to 'achieve something' (*epitelei ti*, 1178a32) if one is to show one's virtue. Merely having virtue and wishing

---

[135] LSJ, s.v. III. Lear 2004, 180 proposes this interpretation.

well does not suffice. But if recognition for one's virtue is important, then two reasons may tell in favour of ii).

First, recognition comes in degrees: it matters who and how many people recognise one's virtue. Performing a virtuous action with minimal means will hardly be recognised by any others than intimates. Contenting oneself with small-scale actions seems less desirable than performing large-scale actions – which do require many resources: 'and the greater and finer they are, the more will be needed' (1178b1–3). If we had the choice between performing greater and finer actions and performing less great and less fine actions, we would want to perform the former. In this sense, virtue tends towards greatness. But as Aristotle said before, virtuous action on a political scale stands out in terms of fineness and greatness (X.7.1177a16–17). So, the fully developed practical life aims at actions on a larger scale and therefore requires a lot of resources. The large-scale virtuous actions tend to be performed by a good politician.

Second, in I.5 Aristotle introduces three well-reputed candidates for happy lives, the lives of pleasure, politics, and philosophy (i.e. the life of reflection). It would seem plausible that he returns not only to the life of pleasure in X.6 and the life of philosophy in X.7–8, but also to the life of politics (rather than the life of mere virtue).[136] Looking at I.5 also helps to explain why, and for whom, it is important to be visibly virtuous. The politician pretty much (*schedon*) aims at honour (*timê*, 1095b23). More precisely, he aims at honour-by-good-people-for-his-virtue. But the community accords the honour only to those who contribute to the common good, i.e. only to those who are politically successful (VIII.14.1163b3–8). So, a person for whom honour is important will need to act virtuously on a grand scale – which is why the exercise of the politician's virtues *does* require many resources: outstandingly fine actions will be publicly recognised and rewarded most. If *that* is what Aristotle has in mind for the best practical life, we can explain the comparative lack of self-sufficiency (1177a27–b1) and why the relevant virtuous activity is less loved for its own sake alone (1177b1–15).

But, as often, the text defies clear-cut interpretation. For Aristotle eschews calling the best practical life in X.7–8 'political'. He could have easily said at 1178a9 'and secondarily so is the life of the politician'. But

---

[136] In this case, the *Nicomachean Ethics* would exhibit a compositional feature called 'ring-composition'. Lockwood 2014 elaborates on the EN's ring-composition. Cf. Barney 2010 on the ring-composition of Plato's *Republic*.

he does not say so, presumably because he wants to kill two birds with one stone. Both the life of the good politician and that of the good citizen are lives in accordance with practical virtue. So, Aristotle can illustrate the comparative neediness of political action even with ordinary virtuous action. He can also forestall the move that perhaps the life of ordinary virtue is better than that of politics, because the former needs fewer resources and is therefore more self-sufficient. He points out that the ordinary life will still need many resources (compared with the life of the philosopher), and that it will not be as great as the politician's life. Although the life of the politician challenges the superiority of the life of reflection most strongly, Aristotle seeks to rebut it and the life of ordinary virtue in one go.

1178b3–7 But the person engaged ... living a human life.

Comparing the external resources required for theoretical and practical virtue in a two-part argument (beginning at 1178a23), Aristotle turns in this lemma to reflection, showing that *it* does not need external resources. Interestingly, he does not pit the *life* of reflection against the practical life. Instead, he focuses primarily on the person, and secondarily on the activity of reflection. He carefully qualifies the claim that the philosopher needs no external resources: he only says the person engaged in reflection does not need resources *for the activity*. The *person* clearly does need external resources. As reflection takes place in leisure, one needs the means to afford leisure, and leisure requires at least that one's basic needs be satisfied (see 1177b4–15, with commentary). Although the philosopher needs resources to create the conditions for reflection, the activity of reflection itself does not make use of the resources. Compare the life of a politically engaged, virtuous citizen. He also needs leisure as a condition to engage in his characteristic activities, both in order to develop virtue and to engage in political actions (*Politics* VII.9.1328b33–1329a2). But the virtuous actions themselves also require external resources. Indeed, the best possible practical life, the life of virtue on a grand scale, requires resources on a grand scale (see previous lemma, with commentary). By contrast, should a philosopher happen to be extremely rich, he would *nolens volens* attain a higher public profile. He would be required to undertake work for the state at his own expense (*liturgy*), which could include furnishing the navy with a ship, providing a public banquet, or taking on responsibility for a dramatic production and other festival-related duties. Aristotle may allude to this facet of Athenian life when he decries (excessive) external resources almost as an impediment to reflection.[137] (Wittgenstein gave away all his money.)

The next step in the argument feeds into determining the shape of the best life. At the end of X.7 and the beginning of X.8, Aristotle seems to distinguish neatly between the theoretical and the practical life. For the theoretical life, we should leave behind the mortal as far as possible (1177b33). The practical life, on the other hand, is associated with the mortal and human (1177b30–1; 1178a9–22). The dichotomy might suggest that what is characteristic of the practical life, virtuous action, plays no part in the theoretical life. In a way, the present lemma serves as an antidote to this suggestion, because it simply states *that* even a philosopher, insofar as he is human, will choose to act in accordance with virtue. So, the philosopher's life will also contain virtuous action. But the status of these actions is unclear. The philosopher's happiness consists either in one activity or in more than one. If theoretical reflection is the only activity that makes her life happy, we can speak of 'intellectualism'. 'Pluralism', by contrast, denotes the thesis that activities in accordance with both theoretical *and* practical virtue make her life happy.[138]

Two questions arise, if we allocate pride of place to excellent reflective activity. a) Why does the happy person choose to act virtuously at all? b) Why, if at all, will he prefer acting virtuously to reflecting on occasions where virtuous action is required? In other words, why does the happy person not dodge the demands of ethically good behaviour in order to do what makes her happy?[139] Pluralists can readily answer question a). The philosopher would choose to perform virtuous actions because they are part of her happiness.[140] In response to b), both Pluralist and Intellectualist could assign different roles to theoretical activity and virtuous action respectively. One cannot choose to forgo virtuous action when it is required

---

[137] Aristotle also notes that the upkeep of a large estate takes time and can hinder political participation (*Politics* IV.6.1293a7–9).

[138] See Irwin 2012 for the labels and discussion.

[139] The same questions could arise for the politician: just as we don't think that intellectual accomplishment automatically makes you a good person, so we don't think that being an outstanding politician makes you a good person. Although Aristotle notes in 1179a6–8 that private citizens tend to be better people than politicians, he might persuade us that *good* politicians are necessarily good people by making a case, in VI.8, for the similarity of practical wisdom required for politics and that required for one's own life.

[140] In one variant of pluralism, the practical life in focus at the beginning of X.8 is an aspect of the best, i.e. the theoretical, life (cf. the discussion of *bios* in the commentary on 1178a9–14).

on pain of losing virtue (or rather, exposing that one did not have it in the first place). While one may pass over opportunities to display virtue that we would call 'supererogatory', there are some situations in which a virtuous person cannot but act. According to the Pluralist, failing to act in these situations would destroy the philosopher's happiness, because she would thereby deprive herself of a key constituent of her happiness. By contrast, passing over opportunities to contemplate do not automatically show that one does not have theoretical wisdom, nor that one lacks the proper love of wisdom. In particular, occasions where one *must* help a friend, or do some other virtuous action, suspend the leisure in which theoretical reflection takes place (1177b22). But since happiness is thought to be found in leisure, reflection under such conditions would not contribute to one's happiness (cf. 1177b4, with commentary). The Intellectualist can make use of the point about leisure to answer a) and b). Being placed in situations that require action explains why the philosopher would act virtuously. Having acquired the virtues, the philosopher will act when she needs to. In particular, there is no reason to dodge virtuous actions in order to reflect, because reflection under these circumstances will not benefit her, insofar as the activity of happiness belongs to leisure.

The difference between the Pluralist and the Intellectualist approach consists mainly in a distinction we impose on Aristotle's text. This comes out by thinking about what the philosopher gets in lieu of reflection. According to the Pluralist, answering to the demands of ethics still contributes to the philosopher's happiness. The Intellectualist, by contrast, deems ethically good actions part of the best life – the philosopher does act in accordance with virtue – but not part of unqualified happiness. Strictly speaking, virtuous actions do not make the philosopher (completely/perfectly) happy. Whichever interpretation we adopt, the happy life will look the same. The philosopher will perform the same actions and activities, grounded in the same consideration about leisure and what one must do. Perhaps Aristotle did not elaborate on the question whether performing virtuous actions directly makes a philosopher happy or, rather, provides the conditions under which she can engage in happy-making activities because the answer makes no practical difference.[141] In any case, he does not, here, say more about the relationship between ethical and reflective activity in the philosopher's life because he does not need to. The point is merely to concede that the philosopher will also perform virtuous actions, and

---

[141] See, however, Introduction §3.2 for further discussion.

for those actions she will need external resources. The need for resources stems from her being human (*anthrôpeuesthai*, 1178b7, translated as 'living a human life') – which contrasts with her being human in the higher sense (1178a2–7), in virtue of which she can engage in theoretical activity. (The next three lemmata, 1178b7–32, do bear on the question whether theoretical activity alone might make a life happy, or whether human beings need to combine it suitably with practical agency.)

1178b7–18 And that complete/perfect happiness is ... and unworthy of gods.

While the previous argument targets a specific point of the theoretical life's superiority to the practical life, the present lemma appears to aim for a more general conclusion, namely 'that complete/perfect happiness is a kind of reflective activity' (1178b7–8). But Aristotle has already argued for that conclusion at length in X.7 (1177a18–26). So why do it again? First, he understates his ambition. Although directed at a general conclusion, the argument (spanning over this lemma and the next) provides a specific reason for identifying perfect/complete happiness with a kind of reflection. The premises of the argument illuminate *why* the conclusion obtains. Second, and more interestingly, he has already highlighted the affinity between reflection and the divine, and will stress the point even more strongly in the next two lemmata. He has also indicated the close connection between the practical virtues and living an embodied, human life (1178a9–23). But he has not yet argued, explicitly, that virtuous action does not qualify as a paradigmatically divine activity. The present lemma provides the missing argument.

The argument proceeds in two steps. The first one establishes the negative point that the gods cannot be happy in virtue of any kind of excellent practical agency (this lemma). The second step argues for the positive proposal that the gods are happy in virtue of theoretical reflection (next lemma). In the quest for the highest human good, the activity of practical wisdom presents itself as a strong candidate for the excellent rational activity that makes a human life happy. Part of its appeal stems from its unconditional nature: human beings cannot but act in relation to other human beings. And insofar as we strive to be happy, we must do so in accordance with reason, and do so excellently (I.7.1098a12–17) – irrespective of whether we take practical wisdom to be the highest human virtue or rank theoretical wisdom even higher (see commentary on previous lemma). The gods envisaged here differ significantly from human beings. They do not act virtuously. Going through all the virtues mentioned previously in association with the practical life (liberality, justice, courage, and moderation, 1178a23–b3), Aristotle derides the idea that the gods could lead *that* life. Therefore, neither virtuous action nor the activity of practical wisdom more abstractly makes a god's life happy.

Why would a god not be just, or moderate, or simply virtuous? Abstractly conceived, we can hardly deny that a god *should* be just, etc., simply because we take gods to be good. However, we might have second thoughts if we remember that virtue can make a person happy only if she acts in accordance with it (I.5.1095b31–1096a2, cf. next lemma). As a practical disposition, we cannot attribute it to anyone who never acts. By training the spotlight on the mundane details of virtuous action, Aristotle gives us good reason to deny virtuous actions to the gods. Consider justice. Surely the gods do not have contracts, return deposits, and the like (1178b10–12). He makes a similar point for generosity (though less elaborately), and presumably also for courage (b12–15; though we can only guess, because something seems to have fallen out of the text).[142] His point against moderation focuses not on action, but instead highlights a justification unsuitable for the gods. According to a common conception (a conception that may go with attributing the virtues of character to the gods in the first place), moderation consists in the absence of unruly appetites – which would apply to the gods (b16–17). However, Aristotle and his audience reject this conception of moderation in favour of the one detailed in III.10. Moderation is the mean with regard to pleasures stemming from touch and taste – which obviously does not apply to the gods. So, looking at the details of virtue-ascriptions shows that we would have to presuppose conditions or conceptions unworthy of the gods.

Even though Aristotle's tone seems almost insolent, looking down on virtuous actions, he does nothing to diminish the status of the practical virtues for a *human life*. Suppose, as the argument might suggest, the gods

---

[142] We can explain the first accusative (*dikaias*, b10–11) by supplying *aponeimai chreôn autois* ('should we attribute to them') from the previous sentence. *Dikaias* then gives a specific instance of the kind of actions (*praxeis*) we asked about. After that, the construction breaks down a little: we still need to supply a verb that requires the accusative (like 'attribute'), but the masculine *andreious* cannot refer to the feminine *praxeis*, which is the referent of *tas*. One attempt to fix it suggests the corruption crept in because Aristotle had written *tas andreiou hupomentontos* ('the actions characteristic of a courageous person, when he withstands'). Once a change had taken place to *tas andreious*, further efforts to save the text deteriorated it, and corrupted the participles (Bywater 1892, 69). Most translators appear to read *tas andreias* – without, however, attempting to explain the corruption to the *lectio difficilior*. Without such an explanation, Bywater's elegant proposal seems to be the most plausible one. I thank Sol Tor and Raphael Woolf for discussion of this point.

are beyond good and evil. They are neither *ethically* good nor bad, and nor are their activities. What follows for us? Should we strive to imitate them 'put[ting] off the mortal as far as possible' (X.7.1177b33) and leave ethical considerations behind entirely? No, because the reasons we cannot ascribe the virtues to the gods do not apply to us. We do make contracts, we do need to return deposits, we do have a currency, we do have beneficiaries, and we can behave better or worse with respect to the pleasures arising from touch and taste. Aristotle does not ridicule the practical life; he ridicules the idea that this could be the life of the gods, and virtuous action the core, or part, of their happiness. If anything, he harks back to the question arising from the previous lemma, whether virtuous action is part of human happiness. By showing that paradigmatic happiness (1178b9) does not require virtuous action, Aristotle *might* be suggesting that human happiness also does not require virtuous action, even though a happy human *life* does require it (see commentary on previous lemma).

1178b18–23 Nonetheless, everyone assumes ... characteristic of happiness.

Aristotle provides an argument in support of conclusion [C]: reflection is complete/perfect happiness (1178b7–8).[143] The previous lemma (1178b7–18) concentrates on rendering plausible the premise that the gods do not engage in ethically virtuous activities. The present lemma, much less expansively, draws together the different thoughts in support of C. We can represent the whole argument in outline as follows (the bracketed premises are not explicitly stated):

1. The gods most of all (*malista*) are blessed and happy. (1178b8–9)
2. The gods are alive and active. (b18–19)
3. The gods do not engage in ethically virtuous actions. (b10–18)
4. The gods do not engage in productive actions. (b20–21)
5. Hence, the gods engage in reflection. (b21)
[6. For all X: if X is happy, then X is happy in virtue of engaging in an activity.]
[7. Hence, the gods are happy in virtue of their reflecting.]
8. Hence, reflection makes the gods' lives happy. (b21–2)

---

[143] For the purposes of the present lemma, I simplify Aristotle's goal as C. The text in fact aims to show [C*] 'that complete/perfect happiness will be reflection of some sort'. I return to C* in the next lemma.

9. The human activity most nearly akin to divine reflection makes a human life happy. (b23)
[10. Human theoretical reflection is most nearly akin to divine reflection.]
[11. Therefore, C.]

Aristotle 'supports' premises 1 and 2 with the same word, 'assume' (*hupolambanein*, 1178b9; b18). Everybody believes the gods to be alive, and not merely alive, but also active in some way (*energein*, b19), unlike Endymion (who was a beautiful mortal who gained immortality at the cost of being eternally asleep). Although Aristotle writes only that *we* (Peripatetics) assume premise 1, he need not imply an esoteric doctrine. The gods were widely regarded as paradigms of happiness, a point that comes out through the use of *malista*. At the end of X.7 he said 'a human being is most of all intelligence' (A is F most of all, 1178a7), where we can understand the 'is' as an 'is' of identity (see commentary on 1178a4–8 for the interpretive options and discussion). By contrast, the present *malista*-claim does not concern the identity of the gods (or happiness), but qualifies the subject of the predication, i.e. the gods (A most of all is F). Since *malista* here does not have quantitative connotations ('more gods than men are happy'), we may understand *malista* as pointing to a paradigm. To say that the gods most of all are happy is to say that the gods are paradigms of happy entities.

Conceiving of the gods as paradigms of happiness prepares for premise 9. As paradigms, the gods stand at the top of a normative framework within which less-than-paradigmatic cases earn their place by standing in a certain relation to the paradigm. Aristotle's discussion of friendship presents a case in point, insofar as less-than-paradigmatic kinds of friendship earn their name by similarity to the complete or perfect case.[144] So, similarly, if the gods are paradigms of happiness, then whoever else is happy must in some sense be similar to the gods. The present argument spells out what the gods do, and therefore in what respect we must be like the gods in order to count as happy. Aristotle expands on the similarity in the next lemma.

How do we know what gods do (or would do if they existed)? Aristotle thinks we can discover the divine activity through reasoning. Having justified premise 3 in the previous lemma, he notes *en passant* that the gods also do not engage in productive activities. He can be quick about it because a) some of the questions about ethical actions will return (Will they have

---

[144] See VIII.3.1156b7–11 with 1156b12–17, VIII.4.1156b35–1157a3, and 1157a25–b5. Aristotle uses the two words, similarity and paradigm (*homiôma* and *paradeigma*) in close conjunction at VIII.10.1160b22–3.

contracts? With whom will they trade? For whom will they produce?), and b) in any case, productive activities cannot make a life choice-worthy and happy. Production is not in itself choice-worthy, but subordinate to higher goals. Happiness, by contrast, is not subordinate to anything. But why does Aristotle not consider perception as a possible occupation for the gods? Not all kinds of perception are subordinate. Perceiving something beautiful, for example, is both pleasant and an end. Would this not qualify it as a candidate for divine activity? Not on the Aristotelian assumption that happiness revolves around the activity of intellect (just as in the function argument in I.7). So, since the gods have no share in activities stemming from the practical intellect, nor in perception, the gods are left with the activity of theoretical intellect, reflection. The supporting thoughts suggest that premise 5 implies that the gods do nothing but reflect.

On its own, premise 5 tells us nothing about our happiness. However, if we add to premises 1 and 5 the explanatory claim that the gods are happy *in virtue of* engaging in reflection (premise 6), we can transfer the explanation to human happiness. Aristotle has argued at length in Book I that happiness must consist in activity (esp. I.5.1095b31–1096a2). Since the gods engage only in reflection, divine happiness must consist in that activity. Now, 'happiness' can be that which makes a person or a life happy (I.4.1095a17–25).[145] So, engaging in the activity of happiness, i.e. reflection, makes the gods and their lives happy, a point emphasised by calling reflection 'excelling in blessedness' (1178b22). The explanatory claim in premise 8, together with taking the gods to be paradigms of happiness, does tell us about our own happiness. We need to do what the gods do if we want to be as happy as the gods – to the extent humanly possible. While we, unlike the gods, do not engage exclusively in reflection, we can engage in an activity 'most nearly akin' (*suggenestatê*, b23) to the gods' activity, namely theoretical reflection (premise 9). Since the activity is such as to render a life happy, it will do so also in the human case.[146] Reflection is *eudaimonikôtatê*, which we can translate as 'most characteristic of happiness' or 'characteristic of superlative happiness'. Whichever we choose,[147] the argument explains the rationale behind the earlier injunction to leave behind the human as much as possible (X.7.1177b33–4). We assimilate to the gods by engaging in an activity so closely related to their characteristic

---

[145] For further elaboration, see Aufderheide 2015, 37–40 and Introduction §1.2.
[146] 'Human' here takes on again the wider meaning, including our divine intellect, as in 1178a8.
[147] Our decision here bears on the question of pluralism vs intellectualism. See commentary on 1178b3–7.

activity that we can call it 'divine' (1177b30–31). Thus, when we use our divine intellect, we approximate to those who are paradigmatically happy and become happy ourselves.

1178b24–32 And a sign <for this> ... reflection of some sort.

Aristotle supports the previous argument with a sign. A sign can constitute evidence for a conclusion without being part of a fully formed deductive argument.[148] To support the conclusion [C*] 'that complete/perfect happiness will be reflection of some sort' (1178b7–8), he adduces the fact that ordinary animals (i.e. neither divine nor human) do not share in happiness. However, the evidential work is done by the explanation that ordinary animals are 'completely deprived of activity of this sort' (b25). But since there are many activities of which animals are completely deprived – in particular appreciating or acting for the sake of the fine – the sign only weakly supports C*. One could run a similar 'argument' to support the conclusion that happiness is virtuous action (i.e. acting for the sake of the fine). Aristotle seeks to strengthen the sign with two supplementary considerations. First, he situates human beings between gods and ordinary animals. Second, he expands on the close connection between theoretical reflection and happiness. Unfortunately, both points allow for different interpretations. While ordinary animals do not share in happiness, it remains moot to what extent, and in virtue of what activity, human beings share in happiness.

Aristotle begins by clarifying where human beings stand in relation to happiness: somewhere between ordinary animals and gods. Part of the difficulty of locating human beings stems from an ambiguity in the text. We can render the Greek at 1178b25–7 in two ways because *hapas* (b26) can be construed in two different ways, as 'whole' or 'every':

[A] 'Now, for the gods, the whole life is blessed, whereas for human beings, life is blessed only insofar as a certain similarity with this sort of activity exists: and none of the other animals is happy since they share in no way in reflection.'

[B] 'Now, every life of the gods is blessed, whereas for human beings, life is blessed only insofar as a certain similarity with this sort of activity exists: and none of the other animals is happy since they share in no way in reflection.'

---

[148] For Aristotle's more technical explanation of 'sign', and how it relates to a deductive argument, see the difficult *Prior Analytics* II 27, and *Rhetoric* I.2.1357b1–22.

X.8

According to interpretation A, the life of the gods is completely happy, because they engage in the activity of reflection all the time (see previous lemma for the argument). By contrast, ordinary animals never engage in reflection, and hence their lives are not happy at all. Human beings are like gods insofar as we *can* reflect, but unlike gods insofar as we cannot do so incessantly (X.5.1175a4–5). So, if Aristotle focuses on the time we spend reflecting, human beings should come out between the gods and ordinary animals. This, at least, is one way of understanding the claim that happiness extends as far as reflection does (1178b28–9). Interpretation B, by contrast, is silent about the time spent reflecting, but stresses the shape or focus of the life instead. Every divine life is happy because every god engages solely in reflection. Ordinary animals do not live a life of reflection. They do not in any way engage in an activity of this kind, and are therefore not happy. Human beings, on the other hand, can engage in reflection. Not everyone is happy, but only those who engage in an activity resembling that of the gods will be happy. Thus, happiness extends as far as does reflection insofar as those who engage in it (though not all the time) lead happy lives, whereas those who do not reflect do not live happily.

Both interpretations classify those lives as happy that are centred on reflection, and so support C*. When choosing between A and B, we must bear in mind the different underlying conceptions of happiness and the practical differences implied. Interpretation A seems to presuppose an aggregative conception of happiness, according to which the happiness of a life simply aggregates the episodes of happy-making activity in which the person engages. Gods come out as 100 per cent happy, ordinary animals as 0 per cent, while individual human beings find themselves somewhere in-between, depending on the amount of reflection. To avoid the pessimistic view that human beings cannot be fully happy – a large proportion of one's life is taken up by sleep, eating, and other basic maintenance – we could set a threshold (10 per cent of the time lived?) for counting a life as happy. In any case, the aggregative conception of happiness can make ready sense of the claim that 'to those to whom reflection belongs more, being happy will also belong more … in virtue of reflection' (1178b29–31). The more you reflect, the happier you are (all other things being equal).[149]

Interpretation B does not presuppose the aggregative conception of happiness. As long as you regard reflection as the highest good and engage

---

[149] See commentary on 1178b3–7 for a discussion of how the demands of morality can make a difference. Cooper 2004, 302–8, further discusses the aggregative conception of happiness and the topic of the next paragraph.

in reflection, i.e. as long as you live a life of reflection, your life is happy, provided you have the other goods required for living a good life. Again, there might be a threshold for counting a life as a life of reflection (reflecting once a year is too little; every day might be too demanding). However, Aristotle need not imply that reflecting more frequently or for longer means that you live more of a life of reflection and are therefore happier. The comparative claim 'to those to whom reflection belongs more, being happy will also belong more' need not compare the quantity of reflection, as it does according to A. Instead, it can also compare the suitability or capability to contemplate. By 'capability' we should not refer to the shared capacity to become theoretically wise, but rather to the developed state. So, reflection belongs to an individual only insofar as she has developed her theoretical intellect. Indeed, at the highest stage of development, a human being lives the happiest life and *is* intelligence most of all (*malista*, 1178a6–8). To those who have developed their theoretical intellect more, reflection and happiness also belong more because they live more of a life of reflection.

So far, we have taken Aristotle's talk of 'reflection' at face value. But in two prominent places, he qualifies what he says in a way that allows us to regard theoretical reflection as the central case, but not as the only possible happy-making activity. In C*, he qualifies happiness as *theôria tis*, and explains that a 'life is blessed only insofar as a *homoiôma ti* with this sort of activity exists' (1178b26–7). The indefinite article *tis* (or *ti* for the neuter) can work in opposite ways. 'Y is Z *tis*' can either mean, determinately, i) Y is a certain kind of Z, or, indeterminately, ii) Y is Z of some sort. The second option would allow activities that do not strictly speaking count as reflection to play the role of reflection. Interpretations A and B as developed so far suggest the determinate way of taking the indefinite articles. Happiness is a certain kind of reflection; the activity that makes a life happy must exhibit a certain similarity (*homoiôma*) to divine reflection. The activity most nearly akin to divine reflection is the human version of it (1178b22–3). There are two main reasons in favour of the more determinate reading. 1. Aristotle introduces C* immediately after dwelling on the person who engages in theoretical reflection in the strict sense (1178b3, with b7–8), as if he was continuing to discuss the same topic. 2. He takes the activity in question to be estimable in itself (*timia*, 1178b31), a property he might dissociate from the practical virtues in I.12.[150]

---

[150] See Aufderheide 2015.

But the reasons fall short of being decisive, and there are good reasons in turn for the less determinate reading of the indefinite articles. 3. Aristotle speaks of 'this sort of activity' (b25 and b27), not of 'this activity'. Further, stressing that ordinary animals are 'completely deprived' of this sort of activity (b25) and that they 'share in no way' in reflection (b28) leaves open the possibility that one might share in different, albeit imperfect, ways in reflection. In particular, it might suggest that human beings share in some way in reflection without engaging in the very same activity that the gods engage in. 4. If a life can be happy in virtue of an activity that exhibits a 'similarity of some sort' to divine reflection, we have a way of explaining how a thoroughly practical life that contains no theoretical reflection can nevertheless be happy (1178a21–2). For we have now a further way of interpreting the claim that 'to those to whom reflection belongs more, being happy will also belong more'. The activity of reflection may belong more to a person the closer the activity in which she engages resembles divine reflection. And to the degree that it resembles the divine paradigm, to that degree we can call it 'happiness'. If we can provide reasons for taking the activity of practical wisdom to be similar to divine reflection, we thereby provide reasons for taking practical agency to be happiness – *qua* being 'reflection of some sort'.[151]

1178b33–1179a9 And happiness for a human ... virtue will be happy.

The main point of this lemma is clear: a happy life does not need many resources.[152] But which life does Aristotle, here, consider happy? Answering the question is complicated by the fact that i) he begins by speaking about the theoretical life, but ends by confirming that 'the life of the person active in accordance with [sc. practical] virtue will be happy' (1179a9). Does the main point apply to a happy practical life, or to a happy life of reflection? ii) Read as carrying on the argument from the previous lemma, the answer depends on our interpretation of the previous lemma. It may have attempted to establish either that the human version of theoretical reflection makes a life happy, or it may have indicated a way in which

---

[151] Especially Lear 2004, 193–6, supports this interpretation. But see also Broadie in Broadie and Rowe 2002, 78 and 445–6, Broadie 2016, and Charles 1999, 2014, and 2015.
[152] The translation of the first sentence favoured here takes 'happiness' from the previous sentence to be the subject understood. We may translate alternatively: 'to the extent that someone is a human being, he will also need external prosperity' (Reeve). In this case, only the second sentence makes the topic clear.

a practical life can be happy insofar as the activity of practical intelligence resembles reflection (see commentary for details). In any case, in the present lemma Aristotle transitions to testing the truth of the proposed account of happiness, a procedure readers have already encountered in Book I. There, chapter I.7 completes the (preliminary) account of happiness, and chapters I.8–11 examine how well the account chimes with the things said about happiness, both by ordinary people and the wise. Here, Aristotle turns explicitly to the wise in the next two lemmata (1179a9–a17). He then considers a further but related topic, god-given good fortune (1179a22–32).

Let us start with the uncontroversial part of the lemma. The use of 'human' vacillates between 'merely human' and 'higher-than-human' from 1177b26 onwards. The merely human life will need resources in virtue of its central activity, whereas resources enter the life of reflection not in virtue of its central activity, but insofar as the person living it will be human (1178b1–7). One could take the present lemma as yet another argument for the superiority of the theoretical life over the practical life because of the former's greater self-sufficiency.[153] But, taken differently, it serves to make a more interesting point. Aristotle expands on the need for resources and links it to the topic of self-sufficiency. In contrast to the gods, our nature is not self-sufficient for reflection. As before, at 1177a27–b1, a person does not count as self-sufficient if she is able on her own to satisfy her needs, but only if she does not need anything external. So, while the *activity* of reflection is self-sufficient in this way, the *person* reflecting is not. In order to engage in reflection well, we need to be sufficiently healthy, fed, hydrated, warm, etc. So, while we lack self-sufficiency, we can remedy the lack easily, because we do not need many resources. For, once we reach a fairly low threshold, more resources do not increase or improve the activity of reflection. So, Aristotle admits that a life of reflection needs resources, but reassures us that it does not require many and therefore does not threaten happiness.

On to the controversial part. Why does he go on to say that *action* does not depend on excess (1179b3–4)? He argues that we can perform virtuous actions without great resources – as if to right the impression given at 178b1–3, where actions are said to require many resources. There are two ways of explaining the turn of the argument. First, we might take Aristotle to develop a response to one of the main criticisms against the practical life, its heavy dependence on resources. Suppose we take him to

---

[153] Gauthier and Jolif 1958 completely reshuffle the text to make it fit this interpretation.

have suggested in 1178b24–32 that a life can be happy in virtue of activities that saliently resemble divine reflection without being instances thereof, such as virtuous action. This opens the possibility of reading the present lemma as a continuation. If the paradigmatically practical life, the life of the politician, is happy in virtue of its use of practical wisdom, then a private person can also be happy in virtue of *her* use of practical wisdom. True, prominent actions will be finer, but ordinary acts of virtue will be fine nevertheless, as pointed out here, and that at a lesser cost (and lesser need for external resources). Therefore, a practical life can be happy without needing a great many resources.

Second, instead of shifting lives half-way through a sentence (1179a1–5), we can take Aristotle to stay with the person living the life of reflection. The need for the present lemma originates in 1178b3–7, where he declares that the philosopher, 'insofar as he is a human being and lives together with many others … chooses to do what is in accordance with virtue; therefore he will need things of this sort for living a human life' (1178b5–7). He may now want to expand on the quoted passage, and clarify its implications. a) As the philosopher's life contains the activities of both theoretical and practical virtue, readers might be tempted to take both as parts of happiness.[154] To forestall this impression, Aristotle stresses at 1178b7–32 that the philosopher's life is happy in virtue of reflection, not in virtue of practical thinking. b) Nevertheless, since the philosopher *does* act in accordance with virtue, and virtue requires resources, we might rightly worry whether the need for resources that enable her to act well threatens her happiness – especially if actions require a great many resources (as claimed at 178b1–3). By showing that we can act well on a private level (which does not exclude participation in politics; it only excludes high office) rather than merely in positions of power, Aristotle can show that 'the life of the person acting in accordance with [sc. practical] virtue will be happy'. Acting in accordance with practical virtue does not require many resources, and hence will not endanger the happiness of her life.

1179a9–13 And Solon, too … do what one should.

Aristotle now turns to the wise to support his own view of happiness. He cites Solon (this lemma) and Anaxagoras (next lemma) in support of the view that a happy life requires only moderate means. However, both

---

[154] Consult the commentary on 1178b3–7 for discussion of this possibility.

also evoke subtler thoughts about happiness that help Aristotle further to explore *his* ideal of happiness, the reflective life. In particular, he may lean on Solon to structure the discussion for the remainder of X.8 (for more detail and an alternative, see especially the commentary on 1179a22–32). Solon of Athens (military leader, 593–592 BC) was a legendary statesman and poet. By the fourth century, his wisdom, deeds, and laws were almost mythical. He counts as one of the seven sages and is perhaps best remembered through the historian Herodotus (ca 480–420 BC), rather than through his own poems. Aristotle has already engaged with Solon's dictum to judge a person happy only after he or she has died in Book I (chapters 10–11), when he compared his preliminary sketch of happiness with well-reputed opinions (I.8–11). Comparing his filled-in picture of happiness with well-reputed opinions, he picks out another aspect of Solon's view in this lemma, namely the role of external resources. Aristotle wholeheartedly endorses the point, even if he distances himself from the details of Solonic happiness (at 1179a11–12).

Solon maintains that living happily does not require many external resources. Aristotle's audience will have been familiar with Solon's view through the writing of Herodotus, who imagines Solon meeting the fantastically rich King Croesus (ca. 560–546 BC, *Histories* I.29–33). Croesus acknowledges Solon's standing and wisdom, and wants to be deemed happy in return on account of his immense wealth and political power. Solon, however, refuses to count Croesus as happiest. Instead, he ranks a certain Tellus of Athens first and a pair of brothers (Cleobis and Biton) second. What have they done that is so great? Tellus lived well, was moderately rich, and died honourably in battle, that is, he had the good fortune to end his life well ('Tellus' seems to be a pun on *telos* which means 'end'). Cleobis and Biton were prized athletes, of sufficient wealth, and outstanding strength. They also died well, after an especially fine deed for their mother. Croesus, of course, does not appreciate being ranked below men of no consequence, private citizens. However, Solon declares wealth to be insufficient for happiness, since the end of a life crucially contributes to its assessment. Wealth might even be a liability, because the divine (*to theion*) may become jealous of a rich person and ruin him. Since the gods, then, take a hand in distributing happiness (also evident in Solon's account of the brothers), the rich and powerful are not happier through their money than those who have enough only for the day. And – surprise, surprise – shortly after Croesus dismisses Solon, disaster strikes: no happy life for Croesus.

Herodotus' anecdote pertains to Aristotle's project in several ways. First, the characters of Solon and Croesus embody different conceptions of happiness. Although a statesman and poet, as portrayed in Herodotus, Solon stands for the pursuit of wisdom (*Histories*, I.30),[155] while Croesus stands for political power and money. Thus, the two characters serve to recall the contrast, staged in X.7, between the two best lives, the life of theoretical wisdom vs the life of excellence in politics. Second, Solon's view helps to keep in mind the ordinary practical life in accordance with virtue, and why it may count as happy (see 1178a23–b3 with commentary). Ruling 'land and sea' (1179a4–5) may not be necessary for a happy life of action – which obviously resonates with Solon's view. In any case, Aristotle needs to support his claim that we can act well without many resources (1179a5–6). Solon provides support for this basic point. In order to do what one should (*prattein ha dei*, 1179a13), one only needs moderate means. Since *those* actions will be part of every happy life – whether philosopher or not – they do not raise the bar for external resources very high. Self-sufficiency marks a third point of contact. While the Solonic conception of self-sufficiency differs from Aristotle's, Solon nevertheless brings out nicely how self-sufficiency pertains to happiness:

> Now no one (who is but man) can have all these good things together [sc. being free from deformity, sickness, and all evil, and happy in his children and his comeliness, and ending his life well], just as no land is altogether self-sufficing in what it produces: one thing it has, another it lacks, and the best land is that which has most; so too no single person is sufficient for himself: one thing he has, another he lacks; but whoever continues in the possession of most things, and at last makes a gracious end of his life, such a man, O King [sc. Croesus], I deem worthy of this title.
>
> (Herodotus, *Histories*, I.32, tr. Godley)

Fourth, Solon draws an important lesson from our lack of self-sufficiency, combining our need for external resources with the dependence of happiness on the gods. If your happiness depends on things outside your control, such as having good health or good looks, then good fortune seems crucial to happiness (cf. EN I.8.1099a31–b8). But if good fortune is dispensed by the gods, then the gods can directly influence an individual's happiness. Aristotle takes up the suggestion towards the end of X.8 (1179a22–32), where he examines in what sense, if any, a happy life depends on divine intervention.

---

[155] In fact, Solon is travelling abroad, among other things, for the sake of *theôria*. Nightingale 2004, 63–8, examines closely what kind of *theôria* Solon engaged in, and how it relates to philosophical reflection.

In short, Aristotle leans on Solon to support the obvious point that fine actions do not require many external resources. More subtly, invoking Solon may also help structure the 'endoxic' discussion at 1178b33–1179a32. Reviewing Solon's view on happiness also raises, implicitly, important questions for Aristotle's conception(s) of happiness and suggests specific ways of answering them. However, leaning on Solon does not mean endorsing his answers. Unlike Solon, Aristotle thinks the *finest* actions will be big-scale and hence do require immense resources (1177b16–18 with commentary). Laying down your life for your city-state, and doing something extraordinary for your family, will be fine actions by anyone's reckoning, but not the fin*est* by Aristotle's.

1179a13–17 And even Anaxagoras ... with our arguments.

In addition to Solon (previous lemma), Aristotle also discusses Anaxagoras to show that their views about happiness converge on the issue of external resources. Again, the key point is that a person can be happy without a lot of money and political power. However, invoking Anaxagoras may also serve a subtler agenda, namely, illustrating the life of reflection and its independence from doing politics. Anaxagoras of Clazomenae (ca 500–428 BC) was the first philosopher to have settled in Athens (around 456). As a foreign resident (*metoikos*), Anaxagoras was barred from political participation in Athens (just like Aristotle later). He was even tried for impiety owing to his scientific study of nature (around 436). To escape his death sentence, he fled from Athens to Lampsacus and carried on with his studies as before.[156] Anaxagoras thus vividly reminds us of the central role of theoretical thinking for happiness.

Although Aristotle has chosen only to allude to Anaxagoras, his audience will have known how to complete the picture (just as with Solon in the previous lemma). We can read up on him in Aristotle's other major work on ethics, the *Eudemian Ethics*. Apparently, just like Solon, Anaxagoras was asked whom he considered happiest by someone who puts a premium on external goods, such as being of consequence (*megas*), handsome (*kalos*), or rich (*plousios*)(EE I.4.1215b6–11). The reasons for the common preference, this lemma states, lie in people's inadequate sensibility of what is truly worthwhile. Unable to pick up on 'higher' values, such as theoretical wisdom, they believe only in what they can see. As theoretical wisdom does

---

[156] Mansfeld 1979 and 1980 contain the full story of Anaxagoras' trial and subsequent life.

not seem to produce visible results, it does not count (for them, 1179a15). But he does not only share Aristotle's values: Anaxagoras' life can even serve to exemplify the life of reflection. Importantly, fleeing from Athens does not dampen his happiness – at least, not insofar as he can still pursue his theoretical studies (as he did). So, the life of Anaxagoras may vividly illustrate the view that theoretical reflection *alone* suffices for happiness.

However, Anaxagoras' social critique and diagnosis slightly overstate the point. People do not completely overlook theoretical wisdom (*sophia*): it is just that they do not find it valuable. While they do regard Anaxagoras and others like him as *sophoi* (theoretically wise), they will nevertheless refuse to count philosophers as happy. Anaxagoras and other philosophers are taken to possess a lot of useless knowledge, but not to know what is beneficial for themselves (VI.7.1141b3–8) – presumably because their activity does not produce visible results (cf. 1178a30–b3). Living well is taken to be a thoroughly practical endeavour. So, *to the many* theoretical wisdom seems neither necessary nor sufficient for happiness, and hence not worth pursuing as though it was the most important thing. Aristotle can rebut the core of the popular view in two steps. First, theoretical prowess does not entail practical feebleness, as a tale about Thales from Aristotle's *Politics* shows (the sixth-century BC philosopher was reckoned one of the seven sages). Due to his superior knowledge of astrology, he predicted a bumper olive crop, secured all the olive presses ahead of time, and rented them out at whatever price he wanted, because he had the monopoly (I.11.1259a5–11).[157] So, among the *sophoi*, at least Thales has practical wisdom, although he tends to use it in a way most people will not be able to recognise – as part of the reflective life.

Second, leading a happy life in fact requires practical wisdom, even if theoretical wisdom alone may make it happy (1178b3–7, with commentary). While the activity of reflection is self-sufficient, the *person* living the life of reflection is not (1178b33–4). Since the person will need to act in order to compensate for the lack of self-sufficiency, she will need practical wisdom at least to the extent of enabling her to reflect (VI.13.1145a6–9). In this sense, the life of reflection as lived by human beings is a practical undertaking. But Aristotle takes a further step. He assumes philosophers live together with other people, presumably again in order to compensate for the lack of individual self-sufficiency (cf. the explanation of our social

---

[157] Anaxagoras probably inherited a large sum of money which, some say, he lost through lack of practical wisdom (Plato, *Greater Hippias*, 283a), whereas others say he gave it away to his relatives (Diogenes Laertius, *Lives of Eminent Philosophers*, II.3.7).

nature in *Politics* I.2). But the philosopher will act towards the others as one should, i.e. in accordance with virtue (1178b6) – for which one needs practical wisdom. So, Aristotle agrees with popular opinion that practical wisdom is required to live the best life, and part of being practically wise is to know what is beneficial for oneself, and to be able to attain it. But he differs by siding with Anaxagoras on what is truly beneficial: theoretical reflection.

Would Anaxagoras share in Aristotle's refutation of popular opinion? In particular, does Anaxagoras share the view that theoretical wisdom alone does not suffice for living a happy life?[158] Anaxagoras is known for having his head in the clouds. He cites 'contemplating the heavens and the order of the cosmos' as reasons for why it is better to be alive rather than not (EE I.5.1216a10–16). However, he also acknowledges that theoretical reflection alone is not all there is to living happily. He thought 'a person living without pain and with a clean record in terms of justice or who partook in some form of divine reflection is as blessed as a human being can be' (I.4.1215b11–14). All of these – to return to the ostensible point of the lemma – can be attained without a lot of money and political power. Thus, living happily does not require many resources.

1179a17–22 Now, considerations of this ... to be mere words.

Before Aristotle turns to the topic of the divine influence on our lives (raised at 1179a9–13; resumed in the next lemma), he pauses over a methodological point that also serves as a stepping-stone to X.9, where he emphasises the practical relevance of his discussion (1179a35–b4). He now returns to a topic recurrent in EN X, namely the connection between conviction, words, deeds, and lives lived. The introduction to the discussion of pleasure ends on the note that ethical claims do not carry conviction if they fly in the face of those who make them (X.1.1172a33–b7, with commentaries).[159] Therefore, he exhorts us to examine whether 'what was said before' agrees with the deeds and the lives lived (1179a20–1).

---

[158] Note, both philosophers may contend that theoretical reflection alone is happiness, while denying that reflection is sufficient for leading a happy life. For instance, Aristotle may claim that one needs also ethical virtue to lead a happy life, even if virtuous action, strictly speaking, does not form part of happiness, i.e. that which makes a life happy. For further discussion, see commentary on 1178b3–7.

[159] See also X.2.1172b15–18 (with commentary) on Eudoxus, whose words seem to be more credible because they do not seem to agree with his deeds. For a more detailed discussion of both the apparent challenge Eudoxus faces, and the connection between words and deeds in the present lemma and in the ethics more generally, see Broadie 2018.

Unfortunately, it is not clear what Aristotle means, because several important phrases can be interpreted in different ways. What is he talking about? The 'considerations of this sort' (1179a18) refer to the dicta of Solon and Anaxagoras (previous two lemmata). But how do they relate to the more general point that truth in ethics must be judged against deeds and lives? Aristotle could either say a) 'looking at the lives of Anaxagoras and Solon is really helpful for studying happiness, because in general looking at lives and deeds is key' or b) 'comparing our view of happiness with what Solon and Anaxagoras *say* confirms it, but we need to do more than that: we need to consider how our view meshes with lives and deeds'. On reading a), Aristotle would justify and explain why considerations of this sort carry conviction, whereas reading b) contrasts things said with something better that carries even more conviction. Reading b) is more plausible than a) because i) Aristotle did not actually discuss the lives of Anaxagoras and Solon, but merely evoked them, and ii) he stresses the agreement between his own words (*logoi*) and the opinions (*doxai*) of the wise just before the present passage (1179a16–17). Aristotle, then, suggests moving away from comparing words to words towards comparing words with deeds and lives.

Next, which words of Aristotle's should we compare with deeds and lives? On a narrow reading, the scope would be restricted to what he says at 1178b33–1179a9, namely that a happy life does not need many external resources. More broadly, we could take him to refer to the position advanced in EN X.7–8, that the life of reflection excels over all other ways of life. More broadly still, 'what was said before' may refer to what was said in Book X up to now, because the content of EN X seems to be bookended by the same methodological consideration. Words about action do not carry conviction unless they agree with the deeds, a point made both at the end of X.1 (before discussing pleasure) and at the end of X.8 (at the end of discussing happiness). Both the narrow and the broad readings point towards the intermediate scope, for the happy life as discussed in X.7–8 incorporates what Aristotle has said about pleasure: it will be the most pleasant life. But it will also be a life of moderate resources. So, in practical terms, he advises us to examine whether the life extolled as the best bears out what was promised. Among other things, we need to ask whether the reflective life really delivers the amazing pleasures it promised (cf. 1177a22–7), and whether it is liveable with moderate resources. The latter is comparatively easy to ascertain: we can simply see how much stuff and money a person seems to require. With pleasure, our evidence would be whether the person living the best life tends to seek out pleasures extraneous to that life more than she should. This would indicate that the pleasures intrinsic to the life do not satisfy her and are therefore not the most pleasant for human beings (cf. 1178a5–6).

But these are side-points. The real question is: whose life and deeds should we compare with life advertised as the best? Since Aristotle leaves the exercise of examining the words and deeds to his audience, we do not know against which life we should test them. There are three main options. According to the first, Aristotle's life is on the line. *He* proposed reflection as the best life. So, unless *he* lives by what he preaches, we should discard his teaching as mere words (1179a22). In the good case, his life shows the ideal he advertises to occupy a genuine position. The main point is that the life advertised is liveable and therefore should have weight in practical consideration. In particular, Aristotle does not put himself on a pedestal with Solon and Anaxagoras. His argument does not go from deeds to words. He does not mean to say: 'Look how I live. Isn't that great? Live like I do, and you will be happy! Here, I'll explain to you what I mean…' This strategy fails because the mere harmony between words and deeds falls short of providing other people with reasons for living that life. Rather, he has forestalled two possible objections to his view. 1. Due to the divinity and separability of the element responsible for reflection (cf. 1177b30–1 and 1178a21–2), one might worry that the life of reflection is not liveable for human beings. 2. If Aristotle were to do other than he says, we would have little reason to think that he means what he says. Or at least he would automatically invalidate his arguments by showing, through example, that they do not deserve to be listened to. So, while his way of life does not undermine the arguments in favour of the life of reflection, the arguments are in the driving seat: the life merely has to conform, lest it undermines the arguments.[160]

Now we come to the second option. Aristotle may exhort his audience to hold up the life of reflection to their own lives. If it harmonises with what they already practise, then they should accept his conclusions, but if not, then his argument will be mere words *to them*.[161] Aristotle does not need to take his audience to be already fully committed philosophers. Rather, he asks his congregation to search their souls as to whether they are ready to live the Aristotelian ideal, that is, whether they are prepared

---

[160] The primacy of the arguments also addresses another worry, voiced by many undergraduate students who (are made to) read EN X.7–8. Aristotle only extols the life of reflection because this is what he happens to like best! But if the arguments are true, the author's motivation in putting them forth does not matter. See Broadie 2018 for further illumination.

[161] Broadie in Broadie and Rowe 2002, 446–7, develops this interpretation.

both intellectually and affectively either to live the life he preaches or at least to recognise their own tendencies towards such a life, even if their circumstances prevent them from taking it up (e.g. when required by their father to pursue a political career). While Aristotle has stressed the good upbringing of his audience (I.4.1095b4–5), can he expect everybody to agree with his fixation on reflection? Presumably yes: they need not all want to become philosophers, but most will have some interest in abstract thinking, or else they would not have found their way to the Lyceum. Aristotle need not convert unbelievers; rather, he makes explicit convictions already held by his audience and channels them towards a certain ideal.

Thirdly, and finally, he may ask his audience to validate his view of happiness by taking an informed look at human life in general. Although Aristotle regards the many as hard to convert to the proper values if they have not had the benefit of a proper education (e.g. X.9.1179b8–10), he also harbours a very optimistic view of nature, and human nature in particular. While he clearly does not regard everybody as happy, he suggests, building on Eudoxus, that 'even in inferior animals there is some natural element of goodness better than themselves which seeks their own proper good' (X.2.1173a4–5) – which implies (in the context) that human beings have such an element also. If Aristotle's words about the reflective life are true, and we have an inbuilt element steering us towards our own good, then we should be able to discern that human lives are directed towards reflection, even if this tendency is overlaid by other behaviour that is, strictly speaking, alien to us (X.8.1178a3–4). While he does not emphasise the shared human tendency towards theoretical thinking in the EN, he does so at the beginning of his *Metaphysics*, which famously starts with the lines 'all human beings desire to know' (980a1). The knowledge in question turns out to be knowledge that goes beyond the merely practical. It is knowledge that we desire for its own sake. And at the apex of such intrinsically valuable knowledge stands theoretical reflection. So, if he is right in the *Metaphysics*, we should be able to see people striving towards theoretical reflection insofar as we should be able to observe them pursuing knowledge for its own sake (even if this knowledge falls short of Aristotle's high standards for proper reflective knowledge). The observation would not only confirm the correctness of his account of happiness in general, but would also directly appeal to his audience because they, too, are human and will therefore strive towards knowledge, whether explicitly so or not. So, they should be able to pick up on their own tendency towards knowing for its own sake.

1179a22–32 And the person active ... happy most of all.

In what appears to be a coda to discussion of the life of reflection, Aristotle maintains that 'the person active in accordance with intelligence, and devoting himself to this' (1179a22–3; i.e. the theoretically wise person) is most dear to or beloved by the gods (*theophilestatos*, 1179a24 and a30). Many interpreters seek ways of defusing the passage, because they cannot attribute such a view to Aristotle. Some think it misplaced (Gauthier and Jolif), or merely an addition by a later editor (but not genuinely Aristotelian, Stewart). Others have tried to write off the passage as 'merely' dialectical, but not expressing Aristotle's considered view (Burnet, Gauthier, and Jolif).

Why should Aristotle not be saying what he appears to be saying? Two problems compromise the passage. First, it is 'un-Aristotelian' because *Aristotle's* god, as described in *Metaphysics* 12.7–9, does not think about human beings, but engages only in 'thinking of thinking' (*noêseôs noiêsis*, 12.9.1174b34–5). And even if the account of the *Metaphysics* does not outline his definitive view of the god(s), the EN has the same implication. i) The gods continuously engage in theoretical reflection (1178b25–7). ii) Reflection deals with the best and most estimable (*timiôtaton*) things in the universe (1141a34–b3), but iii) human beings do not belong to the best things (1141a20–2). So, iv) the gods have no business even to think about human beings, let alone to do something for them. Second, the passage disagrees with Aristotle's expressed view of the gods' nature. At 1178b7–18 he has made crystal clear that the gods do not act, virtuously or otherwise. The present passage claims 'the gods benefit [sc. the theoretically wise] in return (*antipoiein*, 1179a28)' – as if they were exchanging favours with humans. Could we not try to absolve Aristotle from speaking in his own voice? We could stress the distancing qualifiers ('seems', 'is likely') and the use of the non-committal optative mode. Unfortunately, the easy way out does not work. For we do need an alternative explanation for why he says the gods benefit the theoretically wise person. One initially plausible explanation – he merely expresses popular opinions, trying to convert those who believe in tales of gods that care for human beings – cannot be right. For, as has just been recalled, if you do not believe in what you preach, and fail to act accordingly, you will not convince others. Getting others to believe in your view by dissimulation because it is better for them is setting up for failure (see commentary on previous lemma). Besides, Aristotle does not at all hedge the conclusion that the wise person is most dear to the gods, but endorses it firmly. So, how can we account for the passage in general, and the two problems in particular?

There are two approaches to making sense of the passage. A) The passage alludes to the virtue of piety – virtually absent from his works as we have them – and attributes it to the theoretically wise person. B) The passage continues discussing the relationship between self-sufficiency, external resources, and happiness. The route via piety anchors the passage on Anaxagoras (1179a13–16). Can we consider Anaxagoras' life happiest, as he himself suggests? For although he led the life of reflection, he was condemned to death by the Athenians and had to flee. One could interpret his misfortune as the result of a divine grudge, especially since he was indicted for declaring the sun and the moon, traditionally thought to be deities, to be stones (Plato, *Apology* 26d–e). The divine grudge corresponds to the charge brought against Anaxagoras: impiety. On the assumption, voiced in Plato's *Euthyphro*, of equating the pious person with the person dear to the gods (9e–11b), Anaxagoras' impious behaviour ought to make him least loved by the gods – hence the charge and conviction. Against this background, we can read the passage as Aristotle's attempt to rehabilitate Anaxagoras and the life for which he stands. In the context of rejecting Plato's theory of forms, Aristotle connects piety with a special reverence for the truth (*alêtheia*, I.6.1096a16–17), where 'the truth' is the kind of result aimed at by philosophy, including the principles of eternal things (*Metaphysics* 2.1.993b19–31). Now, the person who cares most about theoretical intelligence, and exercises it, is most pious, because she cares most about the truth, for theoretical wisdom is the capacity to grasp the truth in question. But, per *Euthyphro*, the pious person is dear to the gods. So, Anaxagoras' way of life is a genuine attempt at living piously. He will be much dearer to the gods than those who never try their hand at philosophy. And he will not only be dearer to the gods, he will also be happier, given that theoretical thinking is responsible for happiness. So, Aristotle suggests, you do not have to decide between piety and happiness: in reflection, the philosopher gets both.[162]

Though similar in many respects, interpretation B steers clear of piety. Instead of anchoring the passage in Anaxagoras, we can also turn to Solon (1179a9–13, with commentary). Solon's view on external resources is informed by the common view, underlying also interpretation A, that the gods give people what they deserve. Because it requires so many external resources, a high-profile political life requires extraordinary good fortune. But, Solon teaches, the gods may grant good fortune or take it away (as in

---

[162] Broadie 2003 has made a compelling case for detecting piety in this context. Her interpretation differs in details from my sketch here. See also Broadie and Rowe 2002, 447–9, and Broadie 2018.

the case of Croesus) – which leads many to identify happiness with being dear to the gods. Even Solonian happiness, despite requiring only moderate means, depends on divine favour, given that Solon puts a premium on how one's life ends – and the gods can influence what end a life takes. Thus, on the assumption that good fortune is granted by the gods, a *happy* life would have to be a life favoured by the gods, and the person who lives it would be dear to them. Now, if securing the supply of external resources needed for happiness indicates divine favour, then the philosopher would indeed be *most* loved by the gods. For theoretical reflection as the central activity of Aristotle's ideal does not require any external resources. Engaging in *it* by itself guarantees happiness – as if it comes automatically with good fortune! Aristotle would thus draw out a further consequence of his non-standard conception of happiness. Engaging in reflection does not only make you happy (we know that already at this point), it also makes you most beloved by the gods.

To make the interpretations work, we need to address the problems mentioned above. How *can* Aristotle make the theoretically wise person dearest to the gods without contradicting himself or being un-Aristotelian (if that were possible)? First, philosophers are dear to the gods because of a shared concern for the truth. For although gods and men are not friends, owing to the wide chasm in value between them, some human beings can nevertheless be of *one mind with* the gods, and *share the same view* of the truth – however briefly (cf. 1159b31–2 and IX.8.1168b7 on the marks of friendship, which are italicised here). But the account of human beings developed in the course of the argument for reflection allows Aristotle to go further (X.7.1177b26–1178a8). In particular, the gods delight in what is most excellent and closest in kind to them, i.e. theoretical intelligence (cf. 1178b23). So, the gods do not need to think 'mortal thoughts' (cf. 1177b32–3, with commentary) when delighting in philosophers. Instead, they can continue to engage in reflection on the best things in the universe because our theoretical wisdom is divine and does belong to the estimable things worthy of divine thought. Second, the gods benefit in return those who love intelligence most of all and honour it. Their care (*epimeleia*), therefore, comprehends the person only as far as the person *is* intelligence (1178a7). So, the benefits they return for a person's caring for intelligence and truth need not involve any physical activity, as the gods will benefit the person only insofar as they benefit intelligence. That is, Aristotle does not contradict his earlier claim that the gods do not act even if he now adds that they benefit the philosopher.

But what does the divine benefit consist in? Plato proposes philosophy as 'a gift from the gods to the mortal race whose value neither has been nor ever will be surpassed' (*Timaeus*, 47b1–2, tr. Zeyl). In the *Philebus* he similarly introduces the so-called 'Promethean method' (roughly, dialectic) as a 'gift of the gods to men' which allows us 'to inquire and learn and teach one another' (16c–e). Depending on how closely Aristotle follows Plato, we have two ways of accounting for the benefit. Suppose, i), reflecting comprises quite generally abstract thinking, including enquiry. In this case it is reasonable that gods might help an investigation along by presiding over it (cf. Plato's *Philebus* 25b5–12 and 61b11–c2; *Timaeus* 27c6–d1 and 48d4–e1; *Laws* 893b1–4), or by breathing a sudden insight into the thinker that seems to come out of nowhere.[163] In an alternative, and more restricted, view of reflection, ii), finding things out does not play a role in reflection, but only contemplating the truth that comes out of such an enquiry. In this case, the gods may benefit the thinker by simply providing content worthy of reflection. Either the gods *are* the content, or else whatever is worthy of reflection is for the gods' sake, a relation that can be spelled out in different terms of approximation or imitation. Of course, the content is, in a way, there for everyone to cognise – but only those who cultivate and attend to their intelligence, and who act correctly and finely, will in fact reap the benefit of divine thought. Either way of thinking about the benefit makes clear that only those who in fact engage in reflection will be benefited – this much Aristotle clearly shares with Plato. You can receive the greatest gift only if you take care of your intellect. But if you do, you will be guaranteed the greatest gift: happiness by doing philosophy.

---

[163] Thus, Broadie 2003, 64–5.

III Becoming Good (X.9)

X.9

1179a33–b4 Well, then, if both ... in some other way.

In this lemma, Aristotle transitions from discussing happiness (X.6–8) to thinking about applying the insights gained in the course of the *Nicomachean Ethics* – the topic of X.9. He marks the end of the discussion of happiness very clearly. At the beginning of X.6, he listed the topics already discussed (the virtues, friendship, and pleasure); now he includes 'this topic' (the Greek has a plural, 'these things') in the list of things dealt with in outline (see 1176a30–3, with commentary on 'outline'). However, Aristotle quickly forestalls the impression that ticking topics off the list means we have finished. The primary purpose of the lemma is to remind us that the list and the work of which it forms a part has a specific purpose, as stated at the beginning of the EN: 'every craft and every enquiry, and likewise every action and planned undertaking (*proairesis*), is thought to aim at some good' (I.1.1094a1–2). Since the EN *is* a planned undertaking (he uses the same word, *proairesis*, here at 1179a35), we must ask what the good of this enterprise is.

Aristotle considers two possibilities. The goal of the EN (its *telos*, 1179a34, b1) may consist in a) reflecting on and understanding a topic, or b) applying such knowledge. For enquiries falling under the broad umbrella of theoretical knowledge (including metaphysics, mathematics, and theology), the distinction does not arise, because that kind of knowledge is not, in its nature, practical. We pursue such knowledge for its own sake, i.e. for the sake of a). But *for Aristotle* the EN does not belong to theoretical knowledge. True, *we* tend to study the EN much like any other Aristotelian text, as an interesting philosophical account of topic X and as a source of insight into X. But we hardly fault ourselves for neglecting to integrate the insights gained through studying the EN into our lives. *Aristotle*, by contrast, does fault us or any reader of the EN who does not show concern for implementing the lessons learned. He does so, because he conceives of the EN as an inherently practical enterprise. And in practical matters, the goal is the action, not the mere knowledge of it (I.3.1095a5–6; II.1.1103b26–30). So Aristotle exhorts us to become good and act well: 'we must try to have and use [virtue], or become good in some other way' (1179b3–4). He considers and rejects other ways of becoming good in the next two lemmata. If we follow his injunction, we shall not only complete our understanding of the EN – in the practical case, b) contributes to a) – but also complete the EN itself. The project of the EN remains incomplete (*atelês*), unless put into action.

The injunction appears unproblematic. It seems to remind us simply of the practical nature of 'ethics'. We must not forget to practise virtue – understandable perhaps, after the lofty thoughts in X.8 (which argues that happiness consists in theoretical reflection). However, the last chapter, X.9, does not seem to add much to *that* project. Aristotle does not seem to give us any advice on how we, as individuals, can establish a practice that would make us better people. Instead, the chapter seems to focus entirely on how we can turn *other* people towards practising virtue! More precisely, the bulk of X.9 deals with the education necessary for a study of the EN that reaches both goals, a) and b). But since *our* education is mostly completed – especially the early education (cf. II.3.1104b11–13) – Aristotle seems to address us as educators of others. How can we bring the two strands of thought together? It looks as if there is a tension, [T], between the way he sets up X.9 and how he executes the project. [T]: i) he exhorts *us* to practise virtue, but ii) he only discusses how we can help make *others* virtuous.

Before we can address the apparent tension in T, we need to examine ii) more closely. Why should we care about making others virtuous? The answer emerges by taking into account the political dimension of the EN. In Book I, Aristotle characterises the knowledge of the human good as 'a kind of political knowledge' (I.2.1094b11), and the project of the EN as a 'political enquiry' (I.13.1102a12). Accordingly, he addresses 'the politician' (*ho politikos*, I.13.1102a18 and a23), to ensure he knows enough about the soul to understand the definition of happiness as activity of the soul in accordance with excellent reason. The present lemma announces the end of the project of outlining the virtues and happiness. The politician has now attained a sufficient grasp of what virtue and happiness consist in. Therefore, Aristotle can address the politician's 'proper' concern, namely making the citizens good and capable of fine deeds (I.9.1099b29–32; cf. I.13.1102a7–13). So, by taking into account the framing of the EN as a political work, we can explain why Aristotle now veers into discussing how we can improve others.

Conceiving of the EN as a political work, however, does not prevent it from also addressing private individuals.[164] In particular, while attaining the human good for a city is finer and more complete than attaining it only for one person, Aristotle nevertheless acknowledges that we should also welcome the latter outcome (I.2.1094b7–11). And nothing indicates that it must be someone else's happiness that is achieved: it could also be one's own. So, Aristotle's disquisitions on happiness and the soul seem to serve politicians as well as private individuals (provided we can make sense of the 'political enquiry' in this case). The two sets of audiences suggest two ways of releasing the tension in T. A) We have learnt enough about happiness of the individual. We can make ourselves and perhaps our friends good (and happy?), provided we enjoyed a proper upbringing and have the right amount of the goods of fortune. But the EN is incomplete, insofar as it does not reach its full potential. In order to use the knowledge gained through its study more completely, we need to operate on a larger scale. Making a city good is more complete than making just one person good. So, there is no real tension in T. We can be happy while leading completely private lives. But Aristotle suggests that we can be even more virtuous, and therefore lead happier lives, if we try to improve others *en masse*.

Alternatively, B), he may suggest that his treatise up to this point does not suffice even to attain virtue in one's own case. The political context in which we may hope to lead happy lives requires us in any case not to keep our knowledge of the highest good to ourselves, but to share and actively promote it among other citizens. At the heart of the city-state (*polis*) stands the community (*koinônia*). Being a good citizen, and using one's practical wisdom well, consists in reflecting, jointly, on shared values and trying to exhort others to share those values and to make them live virtuously. So, if it is only within a *political* context that the use of practical intelligence makes a practical life happy, and this use involves making *others* better, Aristotle would have to say more about how to educate others towards virtue – which corresponds to the content of X.9. Thus, T does not contain a tension, but shows us two sides of the same coin.[165]

---

[164] *Pace* Bodéüs 1993.
[165] See Cooper 2010 for the importance of *koinônia*. He raises and discusses similar interpretive options.

While Aristotle may simply towards the end come back to the political dimension with which the EN begins, the options outlined here may also emerge more immediately from EN X. For X.7–8 seems to establish the statesman's life as the most outstanding practical life, the paradigm that other practical lives must resemble if they are to be happy (cf. X.7.1177b16–26 and 1178a23–b3, with commentaries). So, interpretation A) would have X.9 complement the two previous chapters by spelling out in more detail what the best practical life involves, whereas interpretation B) focuses more on how the private individual can imitate the politician. By becoming 'more political', and cultivating virtue with a view to the good of the community, even a private individual would be able to lead a happy life.

1179b4–20 Well now, if words ... thought to become decent.

In the previous lemma, Aristotle raised the question how we become good, the dominating topic of X.9. In this lemma, he takes up the suggestion from the previous lemma that we might become good through some other way than having and using virtue. He considers whether words (alone) can make us virtuous. In illuminating what turns out to be a blind alley, Aristotle sheds further light on the status of his own treatise. In the previous lemma, he posited becoming good as the express goal of the EN. However, a) reflecting on and understanding a topic do not suffice for acquiring virtue – for if knowledge were sufficient to make us, the readers, good, the EN would have achieved its aim. All we would need to do to make others good would be to spread the word. However, since the EN has not yet reached its goal, we must also b) apply the knowledge gained, which involves turning others towards virtue.

Long before Aristotle, however, others had expressed their pessimism about the possibility of improving other people. In particular, Theognis, an elegiac poet probably of the late sixth century BC, found the power of words insufficient to make people good. Theognis, whose verses are appropriated here, fuels his pessimism with the observation that *doctors* would earn a handsome fee if they could cure baseness and muddled wits: there is no method for turning around a bad or a stupid person (432–4). Aristotle's version of the verse, implying that *words* would earn a handsome fee, reflects Theognis' next lines: 'and if good sense could be made and placed in a man, there would never be a base son of a noble father, since he would heed words (*muthoisi*) of wisdom. But you will never make the base man noble through teaching (*didaskôn*)' (435–8, tr. Gerber 1999). So, Aristotle does not buy into Theognis' wholesale pessimism about education, but limits it to the power of words. His outlook differs from Theognis' insofar as the philosopher takes into consideration the conditions under which teaching does and does not work. Words alone do not suffice to make people good, but if the audience satisfies certain conditions – being free and well-born, loving the fine – words may have some force yet (1179b7–9).

However, Aristotle does not now pursue this ray of light cutting through the gloom of Theognis' thought. He saves consideration of how to attain the conditions under which words can make people better for the next few lemmata. For now, he latches on to Theognis' pessimism and dwells on the bad case. Why do words not work on the many? Appropriately, he takes a good look at the psychological conditions. First, the many live by passion (1179b13). The examples of what makes them act – fear, punishment, basic pleasure and pain – suggest the identification of living by passion (*pathos*) with the pursuit of base pleasures and the avoidance of pain. Like the paradigm of this kind of life, the tyrant (discussed in X.6), they have not tasted what is truly pleasant and therefore remain on one level with children in their choice of pursuits (1176b16–27, with commentary). Second, the many do not have a sense of shame (1179b11). Although an emotion (*pathos*, IV.9.1128b11), shame commands a special role in education because it requires that some grasp the fine. In order to experience shame, we need to acknowledge that we have fallen short of what was expected of us. And since this expectation is often articulated in words – either before or after – shame seems to be susceptible to words in the way many other emotions are not. For instance, using words only, one cannot instil a bodily pleasure or pain. But one can make a person feel ashamed. So, Aristotle diagnoses, a learner needs a sense of shame insofar as it helps her to outgrow the primacy of passion, i.e. bodily pleasure and pain. It is an important trait of character for the young who want to become good (IV.9.1128b15–16), because it helps to put their grasp of the fine into action.[166]

What does Aristotle recommend we do with people who live in accordance with (low) passion? He is under no illusion that *logos* fails as a method of turning them around. *Logos*, here translated as 'talk', is the singular of *logoi*, translated as 'words'. Using the singular here helps accentuate the opposition that underlies the discussion: passion vs reason (another viable translation of *logos*). We cannot get them to live in accordance with *logos* (reason) because they do not listen to *logoi* (words). And they do not listen

---

[166] See further Burnyeat 1980, who calls shame a 'semivirtue of the learner', 78.

to *logos* because their character is oriented towards the baser pleasures, a fault that can be remedied at an earlier stage of development, for instance through cultivating shame, but can hardly be altered once the orientation has become engrained in a person's character (1179b16–18). Thus, Aristotle seems content to write off the many – at least the many who did not grow up with a sense of shame. The important point, and the practical message derived from the engagement with Theognis' pessimism, is to attend to the conditions that must be in place for people to benefit from words of wisdom.

1179b20–31 And people become good ... by what is disgraceful.

By appropriating Theognis' pessimism in the previous lemma, Aristotle supported his claim that we do not become good through words alone (1179a35–b2). Having an eye on the goal of the EN – becoming good – he now considers three well-known alternatives. We become good by nature (*phusis*), habit (*ethos*), or teaching (*didachê*, 1179b20–1). We can avoid Theognis' pessimism about becoming good only if we attend properly to the preconditions under which successful teaching takes place. This lemma stresses the role of habituation in readying the learner.

The locus classicus for discussing the problem of becoming good remains Plato's *Meno*. The dialogue begins with Meno asking, 'Tell me, Socrates, can virtue be taught (*didakton*)? Or can it not be taught but be acquired through practice (*askêton*)? Or if neither acquired through practice, nor learning (*mathêton*), whether it comes to human beings by nature (*phusei*) or in some other way?' (70a). Aristotle obviously alludes to the *Meno* – the *Meno* also cites the Theognis passage to which 1179b6 refers (though more fully, 95c–96a). However, Aristotle uses the allusion only as a springboard for recalling his own discussion, both in Book I and II of the EN. In Book I, he asks whether happiness 'is acquired through learning (*mathêton*) or through habituation (*ethiston*), or in some other way through practice (*askêton*), or whether it comes through some kind of divine dispensation, or even through chance' (I.9.1099b9–11). He rejects chance as a cause and foreshadows the connection between happiness and the divine (1099b17–18) explored further in X.7–8. In Book I, Aristotle makes happiness the prize of virtue – without, however, giving a straight answer to Meno's question as to how we acquire virtue (he mentions a certain kind of learning and care, 1099b19–20). Presumably, Aristotle could not give a straight answer, because he had not yet introduced the distinction between intellectual and character virtues (I.13) that structures the EN. Books II–V focus on the character aspect of virtue, turning to the intellectual aspect only in Book VI. Naturally, the different aspects of virtue require different methods of acquisition. We acquire and increase intellectual virtues mostly through teaching (*didaskalia*), whereas character virtue comes through habituation (*ethos*, II.1.1103a14–18). Having ruled out the natural element as practically irrelevant – it is not up to us (1179b21–2) – Aristotle now turns to reconsidering the earlier picture of the acquisition of virtue by examining the different roles played by habituation and learning.

Despite the similarities between the Book II account of the acquisition of virtue and the present lemma, both in the word 'habituation' and in the recognition that words alone will not suffice to make anyone good (cf. II.4.1105b11–18), we should pause over some important differences. The most obvious difference between the account of acquiring virtue in Book II.1–4 and the present discussion lies in the role of reason. Book II notes that human beings in general have a nature that can be perfected/completed by habit (1103a24–6). The earlier account of habitation likens the acquisition of virtue to that of craft (1103a31–b2), and emphasises the practical element. It is through doing the just or moderate things that we become just or moderate – just as we become builders through actual building. Because of the analogy to craft, i.e. a kind of knowledge, the 'doing' in question cannot be devoid of intelligence ('mindless following'). While we may wonder how rich, intellectually, habituation will have to be in order to succeed, Aristotle suggests habituation suffices for the acquisition of character virtue. In particular, he seems to curtail the remit of learning (*didaskalia*) to the acquisition of intellectual virtue (II.1.1103a14–18). In light of the interceding discussion of virtue, he now corrects the misleading impression that habituation alone could instil virtue. At the end of Book VI (which treats of good states of the rational part of the soul), he contends that the practical virtues of character and intellect mutually depend on each other. One cannot fully acquire the one without the other (VI.13.1144b26–32) because both elements, intellect and character, are required in virtuous action. Therefore, the division between the virtues of intellect and character and their different methods of acquisition cannot represent two sharply distinguished, subsequent stages of development.[167] If it takes time and experience to acquire practical wisdom

---

[167] More precisely, Aristotle writes at the beginning of II.1 that intellectual virtue for the most part (*epi to pleon*, 1103a15) stems from teaching. As there are several intellectual virtues, he might mean either that i) most of them are acquired through teaching, or that ii) all of them are for the most part acquired through teaching. Reading i) would leave space for excluding the development of practical reason from the remit of teaching. I thank Margaret Hampson for alerting me to this possibility.

(II.1.1103a16–17), then the same applies to the virtues of character. So, in order to acquire virtue *tout court*, we need both habituation *and* teaching. In the Book X discussion, Aristotle seems especially concerned with the intellectual element, the element susceptible to teaching. He stresses that it can blossom only if the soul is prepared by habituation.

Putting the Book II discussion of virtue into perspective, Aristotle now presupposes a more nuanced view of the acquisition of virtue. He proposes a two-stage model, with three aspects of education. Phase one concerns habituating the person's emotions. The learner must move away from being swayed merely by baser pleasures and pain towards the finer pleasures and pains, a process that succeeds only if 'the natural element' (1179b21–2) supports this tendency.[168] Habitually enjoying the fine goes hand in hand with the learner's becoming a lover of the fine. The state acquired in this process will also be responsible for 'yearning for the fine and being disgusted by the disgraceful' (1179b30–1). Phase one also addresses a further desideratum. Virtue crucially takes into consideration the motive of an action: a virtuous action must be decided on for its own sake (II.4.1105a31–2). Beginning with the emotional education targets the motive right away. Learning to love the fine, the learner will do the actions for the sake of the fine. Without attending to motive and emotions, it is unclear how the next phase could possibly succeed in making people virtuous.

Phase two concerns the acquisition of virtue proper, and comprises two aspects. a) The learner must come to do habitually what the just, moderate, courageous, etc., person would do in the situation. The emphasis is on action. b) The learner must come to assess the situation correctly, become excellent at deliberating, and generally master the intellectual aspect of virtue. The emphasis is on intellect. Although Aristotle proposes phase one to start before phase two, it need not finish before it. In fact, the agricultural metaphor suggests as much. While the soil needs attention beforehand if it is to nourish the seed, it also requires tending while it nourishes the seed.[169] However, education towards virtue seems even more 'natural' than growing crops. For if *we* have to prepare the soil to grow good crops, *we* also need to tend the soil, making sure the crop does not use up all

---

[168] Aristotle might here refer to the 'natural virtue' that we can attribute to children and even animals. Adding intelligence to the natural virtues is the most important step in turning them into full-scale virtues (VI.13.1144b1–16). He might suggest that phase one covers the same ground as natural virtue. Some are simply ready to receive virtue (by nature), whereas others need habituation to get to that point.

[169] Aristotle recycles an image used by Antiphon the Sophist. In B60 Antiphon likens implanting education in the young to planting seeds in the soil.

the nutrients, that there is enough water, etc. By contrast, our emotional development does not need outside help. As the learners gain experience through acting for the sake of the fine, their actions will continue to habituate their emotional responses. Just as teenage love matures into adult love, teenagers' love of the fine grows through experience and reflection. The three aspects of virtue, emotion, action, and intellect mutually further each other's development as the person becomes more experienced.[170]

1179b31–1180a1 It is difficult to meet ... they have become habit.

How does one become good? Aristotle asks this question because educating others towards virtue seems to be characteristic of a good person – the sort of person his audience want to become, partly through studying the EN (cf. 1179a33–b4 with commentary). In the previous lemmata he has highlighted three factors that contribute to becoming a good person: nature, habituation, and learning. He also noted two conditions that must obtain before the acquisition of virtue proper can begin. The person to be educated must have the right nature, and she must have begun the habituation of her emotions. Our nature, Aristotle points out, is not up to us. Because we are human, our function (*ergon*) consists in leading some kind of practical life of reason (I.7.1098a3–4). We must simply trust that we have the capacity to leave living by passion behind and turn towards living by reason. Part of the process consists in developing the capacity to love and enjoy things for their own sake, in particular the fine (cf. III.10.1118a16–26). But developing the capacity to appreciate the fine for its own sake *is* up to us. It is with habituating our emotional responses to the fine that education towards virtue must begin (1179b30–1).

The main obstacle to educating the young is their living by passion (I.3.1095a2–6), because it constrains the educative methods. As they do not listen to reason, two options seem initially promising. We may be tempted i) to 'correct' the young with pain when they fall short of our expectations (cf. 1180a8–9), or ii) to entice them to do what we want them to do by the promise of some treat. Although both ways, or a combination, get the learners to do what is just, what is moderate, and so on, neither

---

[170] Burnyeat 1980 puts prime emphasis on phase one, because, he argues, we come to build the virtuous state through taking pleasure in the fine. By contrast, Broadie 1991 seems to fold phase one into phase two. According to her, we can only enjoy the fine once we have the right disposition – which we gain from habituating ourselves to doing what is fine. Jimenez 2016 tries to adjudicate between the two views.

option is a recipe for success. They fall short of fostering virtue because they neglect the role of the motive (see commentary on previous lemma). Both i) and ii) simply work with the motive of getting pleasure and avoiding pain. So, they tend to instil a practical efficacy in avoiding punishment or getting the promised treats. But we would need something like magic to get from there to virtue. For a virtuous person characteristically performs a virtuous action for its own sake, or (in other words) for the sake of the fine. The educator's task, then, consists in changing the learner's core motivation, away from bodily pleasure, towards the fine.

Noting the difficulty of going through the educational programme required for acquiring virtue, Aristotle suggests at once a surprising remedy: the right laws! He argues as follows:

1) Living moderately and with self-restraint is either a necessary stage or the goal of education. (1179b32–3)
2) Living moderately and with self-restraint is not pleasant to the young. (b32–3)
3) Practices prescribed by the law will not be painful to the young once they have become habitual (*sunêthê*), i.e. once the young have become used to them. (1179b32–1180a1)
4) Therefore, the upbringing and practices should be prescribed by the laws. (1179b34–5)

The argument for the conclusion, 4, pivots on premises 2 and 3. Since the young attach themselves firmly to pleasure and pain, a painful educative programme will hardly meet with success. But 2 indicates that the way towards virtue involves phases that would normally be perceived as painful. So, Aristotle suggests in 3 a way of eliminating the pain, thus clearing the path towards virtue for those who shun pain. To reach 4, he must claim that the laws take away the pain, or at least that they contribute significantly to alleviating the pain and so make the painful path to virtue viable. The laws should therefore guide the education towards virtue.

Unfortunately, the argument seems to fall short of establishing the conclusion, for three reasons. First, one might cavil at the lack of a further premise, 3*: nothing else eases the pain of living moderately and with self-restraint. For 4 only follows if the laws are the only way of achieving that goal. Second, and much more seriously, premise 3 does not seem suited to reaching 4. Why would it make a difference to the young whether *the law* prescribes how they are to be brought up? If the laws do make a difference, they do not seem to do so *qua* law. In the *Rhetoric* Aristotle notes that 'there are many actions not naturally pleasant which men perform with pleasure, once they have become used (*sunethisthôsin*) to them' (I.10.1369b15–19). So, without further explanation, we must assume that the work of easing the pain seems to be done by getting used to the things prescribed, not by getting used to the-things-prescribed-by-law, or by the law itself.

Third, it is difficult to see how it could make a difference to a youth whether a) his parents prescribe, say, one hour of music practice a day, or b) the law prescribes the same practice. Because b) will be passed on to the child through the parents, the ultimate source of the prescription hardly makes a difference to the child – unless c) the young have a special reason not to listen to their parents or d) they have a special reverence for the law. Now, a special reverence for the law seems hard to square with the tacit assumption that generated the problem of education in the first place, namely that the young live by passion. Moreover, if revering the law involves following the law for its own sake we would only shift the problem, but not solve it. For in this case, the problem would be to get the children who live by pleasure and pain to acknowledge the status of the law, and to revere it as something worthwhile in its own right. But if a parent can do that, why can they not instil a reverence for the fine more generally?

Despite the apparent weakness in Aristotle's argument, we should not dismiss it prematurely. If we take the argument to lead on to a discussion of law in an educational context, the 'argument' becomes much more suggestive and interesting. It raises questions that need to be addressed in evaluating the law's contribution to education. To the first problem, the *Rhetoric*'s emphasis on getting used to things might suggest a special role that the law could play. If the goal is to live moderately and with self-restraint without being averse to it, and time takes away the aversion, then the law's role might be to guide the young over the rough patch where living in this way *is* painful. Since the law does not appeal much to young people's baser motivations, it would thus clear the path for the young to enjoy living moderately and with self-restraint, not for external rewards or punishments, but for its own sake.[171] Further, addressing the second problem, it might be important that it is the laws rather than the parents that compel the young to stick with living moderately and self-restrainedly when they experience this way of life as painful. Indeed, at 1180a18–24 Aristotle returns to c) and d). He notes in particular c) as a problem and discusses how laws could avoid the potential conflict between children

---

[171] In working out this option in detail, one has to examine to what extent the *Rhetoric*'s claim replaces the magic mentioned in paragraph 2, and whether the claim that 'the law has no power to secure obedience except habit' (*Politics* II.8.1169a20–1) undermines any such attempts.

and parents (only to admit that we might need to do without 'official' laws after all). So, even if the present lemma does not present a cogent argument for the primacy of laws in education, the lemma successfully shifts our attention to the role of the laws. How do the laws make it more likely to meet with the right sort of education? Aristotle raises, but does not address, that question in this lemma. He expands on, and continues to justify, their place in education in the next few lemmata.

1180a1–5 And presumably it is not ... more than the fine.

Aristotle now puts forward a further reason for the importance of laws in the project of becoming good. The basic unit of life in fourth-century Athens was the household, which comprised the core family, but also grandparents, servants, lodgers, and so on. The ruler (*kurios*) of the household was the oldest (capable) male. He took all the important decisions, both for the household, but also for individuals living in the household. Everyone in the household was under his command. This applied in particular to children and youths. Education was seen as a private affair, overseen by the *kurios*. When coming of age (i.e. after having turned 18), young men would be entered into the registry of the deme (roughly, 'tribe'), the next most important political division after the city-state (*polis*). Being enrolled in a deme meant that the young men were full citizens. Their first duty was to leave home for two years' military service. After that, their main duties consisted in paying taxes (if they had sufficient property), and being on call for military action (between the ages of 20 and 58). But they also enjoyed certain rights. In particular, as citizens, they were allowed to attend the assembly, thus participating in governance. They were also allowed to marry other citizens and start a legitimate family on their own. Since the reaching of manhood marks the completion of their upbringing, we might expect that their education towards virtue also ends here. But we would be wrong: the young men have not yet acquired virtue. But in lieu of an authoritative figure, like the ruler of the household, or the guardian that oversees their military service, who can tell the young men what to do? Aristotle answers: the laws.[172]

But why *should* the parental education and the military service not suffice to make the young men good? The answer lies in the different

---

[172] See Aristotle's *Constitution of Athens*, chapter 42, for most of the details in this paragraph. Hansen 1991, 86–124, provides a well-rounded and accessible discussion.

way of life the young will lead. The process of habituation does not stop when the young become citizens: for a large area of responsibilities, it is only just beginning. To mention two examples. i) Courage develops through doing courageous actions, and courage is shown on the battlefield (III.6.1115a29–35). So, in order to become courageous, one must gain experience and fight in war – which only grown-up men are allowed to do. ii) Only as citizens, standing on their own two feet, can the young properly deliberate about both the good of the city-state and their own good. For we deliberate only about what is practicable and up to us (III.3.1112a30–1). Belonging to a household as a subordinate member severely limits the range of deliberation, because most of the important decisions are made by the ruler. The lack of practice extends into the public sphere. After being admitted to the assembly, it requires careful study and experience to contribute meaningfully to the process of deliberation about the good of the city-state. (Magistracies tended to have an age restriction, to ensure the relevant experience.) In short, the whole process of acquiring virtue requires experience, experience that the young men can gain only through engaging in real-life activities, such as participating in an assembly meeting or a war. Since many of the actions citizens will have to perform are prescribed by the law, then the laws will, in a way, continue to habituate the men in the practices that befit them (provided the laws are good). So, since the young cannot learn everything they need to learn for living well while still exclusively under their parents' care, the education continues after that – indeed, through the whole of one's life. And instead of the parents, the laws take on the guidance.

So far Aristotle seems to have spoken about the privileged few who have a genuine chance to live well. But at 1180a4–5 he brings in the many, highlighting the coercive power of the law. What does that have to do with the point at issue? Surely, he does not flag the inefficiency of education by highlighting that the many remain hankering after pleasure, unable to obey words, rather than brute force. Rather, he mentions the many and their shortcomings to explain why *laws* rather than another expedient, such as friendly advice or positive incentives, should guide the character development of adults. In a realistically conceived city-state, not everyone will have a good character (cf. *Politics* III.4.1277a4–5). Indeed, as Aristotle's use of 'the many' suggests, most people will not have a good character. In order to guide *their* behaviour, exhortations will not do, 'for the many obey compulsion more than talk, and <they obey> penalties more than the fine' (1180a4–5). The law, however, has the power to coerce even those unwilling to behave in accordance with the laws.

While he does not expect the character of the many to change through lawful coercion, he does expect the same laws to afford guidance to the well-brought-up. At this stage, the good or soon-to-be-good people have formed a lasting commitment to the law. For a) they are committed to reason (*logos* – in contrast to *pathos*, passion), and b) the law is 'a form of words (*logos*) that stems from practical wisdom of some kind and from intelligence' (1180a21–2). As they adhere to 'the word' (*logos* at 1180a5, also rendered 'talk' in the translation), decent people will not usually transgress the law. So, rather than having in place two systems for guiding behaviour, we need only one sufficiently versatile system that works differently for different groups of citizens. We need a system that appeals to the reason of decent people, while at the same time exerting coercive force on those incapable of listening to reason. This system is, of course, the law. The law applies to all citizens equally, but it guides them in importantly different ways.

1180a5–14 That is why some think ... to their beloved pleasures.

Aristotle continues the thread begun in the previous lemma. If laws govern both education and conduct later in life, we have an expedient that caters to the relevant groups of moral development. Now he sketches how the laws do the job with respect to three different groups: the good, the bad, and the incurable (interestingly, he leaves out the middling sort). Washing his hands of the incurables, he highlights the fact that good and bad people are differently motivated. Only those properly habituated emotionally and practically will be able to listen to reason, whereas those not so habituated will be checked by (the prospect of) brute pain (cf. previous lemma). The emotional education orients the learner towards the fine, and living with a view to the fine already presupposes trying to live in accordance with reason. For Aristotle, virtuous agents perform their characteristic actions both in accordance with correct reason (II.2.1103b31–2) and for the sake of the fine (Books III–IV, *passim*). As their actions show, the good rightly regard reason as their authoritative element (IX.8.1169a2–3). Living in accordance with reason sharply contrasts with living in accordance with passion (*kata pathos*, I.3.1095a7–8). Those guided by appetite or passion more generally will of course be able to hear the words, but they will not habitually listen – unless the words appeal to (their expected) pleasure and pain. So, the good and the bad are differently motivated, because different elements of the soul are authoritative. The bad will not listen to exhortations, while the good will feel alienated by threats. The lawgiver must take this difference into account when making the laws. The laws must appeal both to reason (for the good) and to appetite (for the bad).

Why the need to spell out at such length a point already contained in the previous lemma? Aristotle, note, does not put forward the proposal in his own name, but refers, indeterminately, to 'some' (1180a6). An educated guess leads us to the works of Plato, who not only says what the 'some' say, but also presents the following kind of problem to which the position answers. Everyone knows how annoying it is to be told 'you must do chore C, or else…!' when you had already resolved to do C. Children and other learners react especially acerbically to such exhortatory threats. But if the laws guide everyone's conduct, and if we need to compel the many to behave decently (previous lemma) – would those laws not undermine the education of those who are brought up well? Plato observes in the *Laws* that those who have undergone some training towards virtue and are anxious to become good will be put off if the further guidance comes only in the form of savage and hostile threats that address only brutes or slavish people but not the well-born and well-educated. To cater to both kinds of people, the well-educated and the many, Plato suggests prefacing the 'business part' of a law with a proem, explaining why it is right and good to follow such-and-such a practice, words that appeal to reason (718a–723e). So, by making the law a complex that can appeal to both reason and appetite, Plato has at least found a solution to the problem posed by the different natures of those to whom the law applies.[173]

Aristotle does not go into any detail about the provisions for the good. Instead, as before, he focuses on the bad. He distinguishes between two kinds of bad people, the corrigible and incorrigible. The bad are led by pleasure and pain. So, getting them to behave in certain ways requires steering them by pleasure and pain, if it is to work at all (1180a11–12; cf. X.1.1172a19–21 on the young). The reference to yoked animals suggests that Aristotle does not expect the bad to learn in any meaningful sense. Oxen will do as they should under the command of a skilful driver, but once the driver disappears, the oxen will do as they like. Nevertheless, one might understand 'chastisement and punishment' (1180a9) as a special case of a medical cure (*iatreia*), licensed by the contrast with the incurable ones (*aniatous*).[174] Since 'it is in the nature of medical treatments to come

---

[173] Unsurprisingly, scholars do not agree on the exact nature and function of the preludes to the laws. Annas 2010 provides an accessible entry to the topic.

[174] For an example of offence and punishment appealing to the slavish nature of the offender, see *Politics* VII.15.1336b4–12.

about through opposites' (II.3.1104b17–18), pain as corrective punishment is more likely to succeed in delivering the message if it squarely opposes the seductive pleasure. If even that expedient fails, it is suggested, one should expel (*exhorizein*, 1180a10) the incurables, as there seems to be little else short of capital punishment that one could do to neutralise them (Athenians in Aristotle's time did not imprison wrong-doers as punishment). Although this suggestion does not seem to stem from the *Laws*, Plato may nevertheless sponsor this point also. Responding to Socrates' challenge that virtue cannot be taught, Protagoras in the eponymous dialogue argues that fathers do their utmost to instil virtue in their sons because we exile those who do not respond to punishment and instruction to make them better (325a–c). So, this lemma's recommendation as to how to deal with the bad – use force and, failing that, expel – is not outlandish, but fairly accepted. (Note, Aristotle may prefer to speak of 'some' rather than Plato, because Plato need not share the view of any of his characters, be they Protagoras or an unnamed Athenian.)

1180a14–24 Well, as has been said ... prescribing what is decent.

In this long and difficult sentence (in the Greek it is one sentence), Aristotle pulls together the threads pursued so far in X.9. a) Since the EN is a practical endeavour, we must examine, practically, how to acquire virtue. b) Discourse does not suffice: the learners must undergo both emotional and practical training before they fully benefit from teaching. c) The acquisition of virtue extends into the adulthood – which is why d) laws, not parents, should govern the whole of education, provided that e) the content of the laws also appeals to reason. Aristotle now adds two further considerations in favour of the laws' educational role: f) the laws have the required power to compel; and, almost as an afterthought, g) the laws help prevent an intergenerational conflict. As before, points f) and g) owe much to Plato.

Becoming and remaining a good person, i.e. being properly educated and living decently as an adult, depends on 'some sort of intelligent system of right order' (alternatively, 'intelligence of some kind and right order', 1180a18) that exerts the right influence. Aristotle gives this role to the law after having rejected the only alternative, a father's prescriptions. The father is responsible for the existence of his children, their nurture, and their education (VIII.11.1161a15–17). Why, then, would a father not be able to educate his children to virtue even if he is responsible for so doing? Because his prescriptions do not come by default with the right sort of force or compulsion. This claim raises the important question of in what way a father's prescriptions differ from the law. The difference cannot consist in the law's having 'more muscle'. For Aristotle has argued that the good must *not* be compelled by brute force to live decently. Therefore, the force or compulsion in question must stem from some element other than brute force. Nor can the difference rest on a position of power that imbues the prescriptions with the relevant force, as the example of the king might suggest (1180a20–1), for 'by nature a father is such as to rule over his sons', just as a king rules over his subordinates (VIII.11.1161a18–20). So, how can we make sense of the claim that fathers are *by nature* such as to rule their sons, and indeed are responsible for their education, while they do not have the power to make their sons live in accordance with reason? Aristotle, not acknowledging the tension, merely suggests the laws should govern the education. So, what do the laws have that a father does not have?

We can discern two relevant features of the law, features that personal prescriptions tend to lack. First, Aristotle locates the difference in the law's 'being a form of words (*logos*) that stems from practical wisdom (*phronêsis*) of some kind and from intelligence (*nous*)' (1180a21–2). We can explain the connection between having the power to compel and stemming from reason by reference to a passage from Plato's *Laws* (713d–714b) that also associates law with reason (*nous*). As a principle of ruling, the better should rule over the inferior, and if possible the rulers should be superior in kind (a shepherd rules the sheep, a cowherd the cows). According to an old tale, human beings were once ruled by benevolent daemons – to the benefit of all. In the absence of daemons taking an interest in us, 'we should run our public and our private life, our homes and our cities, in obedience to what little spark of immortality lies in us, and dignify these edicts of reason with the name of "law"' (714a, tr. Saunders). For Plato, authority goes hand in hand with being better in kind. An ordinary human being can hardly command this kind of authority – Aristotle notes the king, an ideal ruler, as a limiting case at 1180a20–1 – and certainly fathers are not better in kind than their children. So, being ruled by law instead of a person resembles being ruled by intelligence, something better in kind than a mere person.[175] The precepts of the better element, accordingly, have a special authority over us.

---

[175] For the two competing views of human nature as merely human (i.e. purely practical), and higher-than-human (i.e. engaging in theoretical reflection), see X.7.1177b26–1178a8.

The second point, addressing g), rests on the difference between personal and impersonal rule. Again, Plato's *Laws* help, because immediately after the passage quoted, Plato goes on to illustrate the benefits of being governed by law. Highlighting the dangers of human corruption, he worries especially about the rulers' growing appetites that will lead to the ruin of the ruled (714d–715d). Again, although Aristotle keeps silent, we can attribute a similar thought to him, since he says as much in a strikingly similar passage of the *Politics*. 'Anyone', he warns us, 'who instructs law to rule would seem to be asking god and intelligence (*nous*) alone to rule, whereas someone who asks a human being asks a wild beast as well. For appetite is like a wild beast, and passion perverts rulers even when they are the best men. That is precisely why law is intelligence without desire' (III.16.1287a28–32, tr. Reeve, slightly modified). Both philosophers extol one aspect of the impersonality of the law: a person has desires that may interfere with ruling, whereas law as something impersonal does not (cf. EN V.6.1134a35–b1). So, being ruled by law rather than by a person makes us subject to something both higher than ourselves and something impersonal, not pursuing its own agenda.

The impersonality of the law helps prevent the looming conflict between parents and children. When educating their children, many parents pursue their own appetitive goals. We are too familiar with over-ambitious parents who demand too much of their children, at the wrong time, and without proper guidance. Equally familiar are parents who do not attend to their children's upbringing properly because of ill-health, or the need to make ends meet, or because the parents are too engrossed in pursuing their own careers (Plato's *Protagoras* mentions the great mid fifth-century politician Pericles as a case in point, 319e–320a). The law, by contrast, never falters. However, the impersonal character of the law aids education not so much because it will refrain from pursuing its own goals at the children's peril, but rather because of the children's attitude towards it. First, the law is not a proper object of anger, because anger is directed at individual people (*Rhetoric* II.2.1378a32–4). Second, extrapolating from her own experience, the child will assume the father asks her to do onerous things for his own benefit. But the child cannot accuse the laws of the same affront. Third, while children get angry at their parents for curbing their impulses (1180a22–4), they will not buck the law, because they perceive the law as 'higher' than their parents. This attitude does not require a special reverence for the law as such – remember, Aristotle's children tend to be motivated by pleasure and pain (I.3.1095a2–11, cf. VIII.3.1156a31–4 and X.1.1172a19–21). The asymmetry in the children's assessment of the father's prescriptions and the law stems, rather, from the laws' impersonality. Children take offence especially when parents forbid them to do X, while other children are visibly allowed to do so. But if doing X is forbidden to all children by law, then children should not feel offended *personally*. That is, the law removes the opprobrium of arbitrariness that children may, often rightly, discern in their parents' educational regime. This helps to assuage the lingering doubt that parents tell them to do X only out of self-interested motives – which would rightly alienate the children.

1180a24–32 But only in the city-state ... of deciding on it.

Having argued for the importance of law in the upbringing and education of the young, Aristotle now turns to the proposal's practical and political implications. He bemoans the fact that almost all lawgivers neglect to make educational laws. The lawgivers (*nomothetai*) were a body of the city-state (*polis*) that dealt with introducing new laws or additions or changes to existing laws. The Athenian lawgivers were not necessarily legal experts, but were drawn also from the ordinary citizenry. In any case, the role of lawgiver entailed working in the interest of the city-state.[176] Judging by their inaction, the lawgivers either did not understand the importance of law to education, or they did not see education as a public good.[177] But instead of dwelling on the reasons for the neglect, Aristotle proposes private education as second best. Over the next lemmata, until 1180b28, he explains how to combine the benefits of law-based education with private education.

Aristotle begins by taking stock. The vast majority of city-states do not govern education by law. He singles out for praise those few cities that do offer a public education. The Lacedaemonian (or Spartan) system of education was not only public, but communal. It supervised the common upbringing of free-born males aged 7 to 29, exempting only the direct heirs to the king, and extended into adult life in the form of common messes. But who are the others? While Plato proposes a communal education both in the *Republic* and in the *Laws*, the 'few others' (1180a25) presumably also refers to actual city-states. With an educated guess we might identify Crete and Carthage, whose constitutions Aristotle classes together with that of the Spartans in his critique of constitutions in the *Politics* (II.9–11).

---

[176] Hansen 1991, 161–77 provides an excellent overview of the role of the lawgivers in Athens.
[177] Ober 2001 suggests that a public education of the kind Aristotle envisages jars with the democratic values prevalent in Athens at that time.

(He mildly praises the group – they are better than all the other extant constitutions – without, however, dwelling on the aspect of education.) However that may be, the only city-state named here that pursues education within the correct framework – as a communal undertaking, aimed at the common good – is that of the Lacedaemonians. Everyone else has either to change educational regime, or else make do with private education as second best.

The status of private vis-à-vis public education is difficult to pin down, because the nature of Aristotle's proposal is so elusive. This lemma connects public with communal education, which, in turn, results in shared values. Moreover, he writes as if the form of the education (public or private) determines the content of what the young learn. On the basis of these two points and the examples of the Lacedaemonians and the cyclopes, we can pinpoint an assumption that we can express as a biconditional: (A) the young attain shared values and virtues if and only if they are educated by the city-state. We have some evidence in the case of the Spartans for the one direction. All prospective male citizens receive the same education because the state educates everyone in the same way. They end up with a very tightly knit community of shared values and virtues. On the other side, Aristotle suggests that the absence of a city-state education leaves the young with whatever values their parents happened to endorse. The cyclopes vividly illustrate the point that the absence of a centrally organised education goes hand in hand with the absence of shared or common values, for the cyclopes live without common assembly or common law (Homer, *Odyssey* IX.112). They live without any conception of the common good and do not take each other's good into consideration. Although they live next to each other on the same island, they do not live together in any sort of community. Each lives in his own cave, 'wielding law over children and spouse' (114–15). So, in the absence of any kind of community, the 'laws' laid down for spouse and children, and instilled in the offspring through education, are idiosyncratic. Aristotle puts the same contrast, though less dramatically, in a *Politics* passage, which winds up praising the Spartans for rightly regarding education as a public good: 'since the whole city-state has one single end, however, it is evident that education too must be one and the same for all, and that its supervision (*epimeleia*) must be communal, not private as it is at present, when each individual supervises his own children privately and gives them whatever private instruction he thinks best' (VIII.1.1337a21–6, tr. Reeve). So, both sets of examples together provide some support for (A).

If (A) were true, then private education would be confined to instilling in the young virtue as privately conceived. But private education *need not* instil 'private' values, because parents need not educate their children in accordance with their own 'private law', like the cyclopes, but might do so in accordance with the values of the community (*koinônia*) to which they belong (family, clan, deme, city-state). Because the education takes place in a city-state, any individual stepping in to educate to virtue those over whom he has authority may not only look to the good of the family, but also to the good of the city-state. Aristotle seems to indicate this possibility by likening the pre-city-state way of life to that of the cyclopes. When families live scattered, the oldest capable male sets down the code of conduct for the household – without a view to the good of a group larger than the family (*Politics* I.2.1252b20–4). By implication, when households belong to a city-state, the rulers of the household must act in line with the view of the city-state's ruler(s). When both shared discourse about what is good for the city (discussed, e.g., in assembly meetings) and some more general grasp of what is good for human beings inform private education, the values instilled through private education should converge, or at least not widely diverge, as they might in the case of the cyclopes. So, even if a system of private education cannot quite produce the highly unified citizenry that results from Sparta's compulsory and common military training, private education can nevertheless produce citizens who share the same goals and ideals. So, even though (A) seems plausible initially, private education can also lead to common values and shared virtues.

It is not clear whether Aristotle conceives of private education as completely private and idiosyncratic, or as public in spirit. Does he endorse or reject (A)? Although the following lemmata do not decide it one way or the other, they probably indicate that he rejects (A), and that even private education takes shared values into account. One shared value about which Aristotle says surprisingly little is correctness or truth. In this lemma he praises Sparta only for the arrangement of the education, not its content. Sparta has cleared only one bar for a good education. In the *Politics*, by contrast, he criticises Sparta heavily for failing on the second, the correctness of the education.[178] This affords a new aspect on private education as second-best. Since it need not pass on the value of the city-state to the children, private education can produce virtuous people even in a badly

---

[178] Due to their war-oriented constitution, the Spartans reverse the value of virtue and other goods: they take virtue to be instrumental in attaining other goods (*Politics* II.2.1271a41–b10). This misconception especially undermines a correct education (VII.2.1324b5–11 and VII.14.1333b5–11; cf. VII.14.1334a2–b5). Hitz 2012 helpfully discusses the differences between Spartan and Aristotelian education.

governed and badly organised city-state. In a misgoverned city-state, private education would therefore be better for the young insofar as they will not be turned into people that match the bad city-state. So, the desirability of private and public education depends on the circumstances. In a well-governed city-state, educating the young in a communal spirit seems desirable, whereas in a badly governed city-state a purely private education both in administration and spirit would seem preferable. Aristotle may leave it genuinely open whether he advocates private education in a public spirit or not.[179]

> *1180a32–b7 But from what has been said ... to love and obey him.*

Having noted the absence of a communal education programme in most city-states, Aristotle recommends private education as a second-best in the previous lemma. He now expands on the second-best option. Since good education rests on laws, he suggests that even private education should be law-based. He proposes [P]: The educator, i.e. the father, should become proficient in making law (1180a32–4). P immediately raises two questions. First, what does it mean to become proficient in making law, and, second, what does 'law' mean here?

Two reasons support P: one dealing with the laws in question, the other with the father's role in connection with these laws. The first reason, [R1], states that 'communal types of supervision depend on laws, and decent ones on good laws' (1180a34–5). If we take education to be a communal type of supervision, then it requires good laws. Aristotle's use of the word 'law' differs from the way in which his Athenian contemporaries tend to use it. In the latter sense, a law must be an entirely general written statute passed by the lawgivers (*nomothetai*). In the former sense, the educational 'laws' in question can be written or unwritten, general or individual. 'Law' in this sense even pertains to the prescriptions of an instructor in music or gymnastics. While the examples illustrate R1 in the sense that good practice of music and gymnastics requires good prescriptions, we may wonder why Aristotle insists on the term 'law'. What does he gain by stretching the concept beyond its common usage? i) 'Law' keeps the connection to the communal supervision, because they both aim at the benefit of the community. The examples of music and gymnastics belong to a common

---

[179] Scholars have tried to pin Aristotle down. Schütrumpf 1991, 81–93 takes him to propose a purely private education as second best, whereas Bodéüs 1993, 66 and 124 takes private education to be public in spirit.

concern, insofar as both belong to a good education: the next generation needs to be both healthy and cultured if they are to perform their duties as citizens well.[180] ii) The examples also illustrate the generality of the law. Both music and gymnastics are governed by norms. The instructor does not arbitrarily set the norms to which his pupils must conform. Rather, taking the goal for granted – health and a proper appreciation of music — the instructor's role is to enable the pupil to attain the goal. He does so primarily by issuing, and overseeing adherence to, general prescriptions, aimed at a general norm (for discussion of one-size-fits-all prescriptions, see next lemma, with commentary). If, as Aristotle suggests, we call these prescriptions 'laws', then the instructor needs to be proficient at making laws in order to make his pupils meet the norm.

The reasoning transfers to the fathers as private educators. By using 'law' in the wider sense, Aristotle establishes that some parts of a good *private* education are governed by laws.[181] From here, it is only a small step to conceding that the whole of the private education must be governed by laws. This has two implications. a) Fathers must become proficient in making laws (= P). That is, fathers must devise and issue prescriptions governing the education of their children. b) The father does not operate with an idiosyncratic notion of goodness according to which he seeks to educate his children. Rather, the prescriptions must aim at meeting some general norms. The generality of the norms pertains to the question of the spirit of the education (raised in the commentary on the previous lemma). Is the spirit private or public? In public-spirited private education, the educator would devise the prescriptions with a view to the norms and customs prevalent in the city. The absence of public spirit in private education would have the educator aim at even more general norms, such as the norms of human nature. A private education oriented towards human goodness would pay heed to the city-state only incidentally, if the city happened to have the values right (more on the universality of the standards in 1180b13–23).

Without settling the question, Aristotle gives a further reason, ultimately for P, namely [R2]: 'just as the legal provisions and customs in a city-state have force, so too do the words and habits of a father in a household'

---

[180] In this sense, Aristotle uses 'law' and related terms in *Politics* VII.16–17 and VIII to prescribe everything from how to beget strong children to which sort of poems they should listen to. Plato had done so before him in *Republic* V.449–471 and *Laws* VII.

[181] The close connection between law and education had been established by political thinkers before Plato and Aristotle (see Too 2001). The new point is to extend 'law' to private education.

(1180b3–4). R2 sits less easily with the main thrust of the previous lemmata. Does R2 not directly conflict with the earlier thesis in support of a law-based education, that a father's prescriptions do not have the right force (1180a18–22)? To make matters worse, Aristotle now contends that a father's words have even more force in the family than do the laws in the city (1180b5). We can relieve the tension by taking into account the differences between the conception of a father in the earlier and the present passage. Having widened the notion of 'law', we can now see the father as occupying the same position as the law-makers in the city. It is his responsibility to ensure that some general norm be met by his charges. This role rules out idiosyncratic or arbitrary prescriptions, which are apt to alienate the children and undermine the father's authority (see commentary on 1180a14–24). On condition that the father exercises his proficiency in making laws, the laws will be especially forceful. But while the laws set down by the father are impersonal, *he* is not. If, as expected, the prescriptions benefit the children, they can be grateful *to him*. Citizens cannot be grateful to the office of the lawgivers in the same way (note, the lawgivers were drawn by lot and changed from occasion to occasion). Similarly, the children 'are naturally predisposed to love and obey [their father]' (1180b6–7), a predisposition that goes deeper than the ties we may have with the city. The latter have to be acquired; the former are part of being human. So, the father as lawgiver (in the wider sense of 'law') should prove especially effective.[182]

1180b7–13 And further, individualised regimes … suitable for him.

Previously, Aristotle has praised communal education (1180a24–32). In default of communal education, he suggested private education as a second-best. Having 'upgraded' private education to a law-based education, he started in the previous lemma to address the problems inherent in private education (cf. 1180a14–24). Now he questions the status of private education as *merely* second-best. Unlike communal education, private education can cater to the individual. This way, he suggests, education may produce better results.

---

[182] On a more speculative note, what about the father's habits at 1180b5? Hampson 2019 suggests that children will unreflectively imitate their father. So, if the father is proficient in making law and shows good conduct himself, the children will be predisposed to listen, because they have already practised the relevant types of action when imitating their father.

He advertises greater accuracy as the main benefit of private over communal education (1180b11–12). Elsewhere, Aristotle uses 'accuracy' (*akribeia*) to highlight various good qualities of broadly scientific thinking (cf. *Posterior Analytics* I.27). Here, by contrast, he suggests merely that prescription P1 is more accurate than P2 if a) P1, but not P2, correctly applies to the situation, and b) P1 yields better results than P2. The two examples illustrate the points. As for a): 'Fevers are cured by rest and fasting' is a general statement, from which we can derive the general prescription: [P3] 'Anyone suffering from a fever should rest and fast.' P3 lacks accuracy, insofar as it incorrectly prescribes fasting for pregnant women and those suffering from diabetes to cure their fever. Adding the relevant exceptions will make P3 less general, but more precise (in the sense used here). As for b): if we stipulate knocking out the opponent as the goal of boxing, we can again derive a general prescription: [P4] 'To win a boxing fight, knock out your opponent.' If a boxing trainer only offered P4, together with the other general rules of boxing, he would not be a good trainer. He would improve slightly by offering further general advice, such as 'keep your defence up' and 'mind your footwork'. But a good trainer will prescribe a more personalised fighting style. For example [P5] 'Keep the opponent at a distance, tire him out, and then aim for the chin.' P5 may work only for boxers with a long reach and is not profitably followed by shorter boxers. So, while P4 is more general than P5, P5 is more precise if prescribed for a boxer who would profit from following it. Returning to education, Aristotle suggests that communal education issues less precise prescriptions than private education. The 'laws' of education will hardly specify all the relevant exceptions in circumstances that render the prescriptions less efficient than they should be. Private education, by contrast, can customise the educational prescriptions to fit the specific learner.[183]

The preceding lemmata have hailed law as a great boon to private education. Does Aristotle now undermine his support of law-based education by suggesting that we need a more particularised approach? No, for two reasons. First, he does not say anything to undermine the need for perfectly general prescriptions that could be called 'law' (on which see previous lemma, with commentary). He does not seek to replace laws

---

[183] At V.10.1137b13–34 Aristotle notes that laws (in the strict sense of the word) cannot deal with all the specific circumstances that may arise and therefore need to be supplemented by a mechanism that can deal with those situations. (More specifically, he suggests that decrees, *psêphismata*, would do the job.)

with more accurate prescriptions. Instead, he proposes that educating the young in the best way requires that we supplement the 'laws' with more accurate prescriptions, suitably qualified or particularised. Second, and relatedly, the law-based approach was introduced to remedy the defects of a certain type of private education, the idiosyncratic education which the cyclopes stand for (1180a24–32, with commentary). But Aristotle does not suggest we go back to *that*, but assumes instead that the general framework of education remains set by 'laws'. Private education should be individualised, but not individualistic. The chosen examples support this point. The norms of success in boxing or medicine are not private. While I can define my own idiosyncratic account of what health or winning at boxing consist in, and while I can follow my prescriptions deriving from my accounts, my success will be measured by how things are, not by how I think they are. I do not win or am healthy merely because I think so. So, just as in medicine and boxing, the particularised prescriptions are devised to help follow general norms. For the best education, the laws need to be supplemented.

In spelling out what the best possible (private) education consists in, Aristotle has subtly distinguished between three kinds of knowledge (broadly speaking) needed to make the right prescriptions. First, because the educator's prescriptions aim at conforming with general norms, he must have knowledge of these norms. Second, the educator must know how best to frame the prescriptions for maximum accuracy. This knowledge comprises, or should be informed by, knowledge of educational methods. Third, in order to individualise the prescriptions, educators must know both the general and peculiar strengths and weaknesses of the learners. Thus, they also need intimate knowledge of their charges. While a father should know his children well enough, the first two would presumably be acquired by becoming 'proficient in law' (1180a33–4). In the following two lemmata, Aristotle considers more closely the kind of knowledge required for making people good.

1180b13–23 But a doctor ... branches of knowledge are about that.

This lemma further elaborates on the kind of knowledge required to improve other people. Aristotle seeks to correct the impression the previous lemma may have created, that private education, and individualised supervision more generally, is idiosyncratic. But individualised supervision is not idiosyncratic, because it should be governed by knowledge of what is common. While he acknowledges that one *can* take care of a person properly without general knowledge, Aristotle would not call such a person 'expert'. To become an expert, one needs knowledge of what is general and applies to all cases.[184]

One could construe the thought here as an inductive argument. If my child lacked health, I would go to a doctor, i.e. an expert. If I wanted my child to become fit, I would sign him up for athletics, to be trained by experts. And so on. However, while parents tend to rely on expert tuition in many areas, in the case of education towards virtue, many would hesitate to hand over their children to experts (in a boarding-school, say). Apart from the importance of a close relationship between children and parents, parents might justify their sentiment by claiming that they know their children best. They know how their child reacts to affection, incentives, threats, rewards, and punishments. Experts have less intimate knowledge and can, therefore, educate children less effectively. Or so the parents' argument goes.

Both the induction argument for expertise and the parents' counter-argument do not distinguish the kinds of knowledge required for the best care. The parents stress their particular knowledge of their child and the knowledge of the particular method that works for her. The induction argument, by contrast, points towards knowledge of the general norms with a view to which we undertake the supervision in the first place (health, physical fitness), and general knowledge of the methods required to attain the goal. Ideally, the supervision would be informed by both: general expertise and knowledge of the particular. To this effect, Aristotle suggested the private educator become 'proficient in making law' (1180a33, cf. next lemma). The previous lemma argued that this requires knowledge of the general norms that govern good education, especially knowledge of the goal. But as a parent I am only concerned with bringing up my own

---

[184] I take *kath' hen* in 1180b14–15 to be synonymous with *kath' hekaston* in b8, translating both as 'individualised'. Many translators render *kath' hen* as 'for each individual'. Hasper and Yurdin 2014 dispute this rendering and instead translate '(i) But the best care can be given in virtue of one thing (*kath' hen*) and (ii) by a medical expert and a trainer and everyone else who knows of the universal that it [applies] to all people or to such people – for (iii) the branches of science are said to be, and indeed are, of what is common.' If this reading is correct, then Aristotle would seem to focus exclusively on universal knowledge, pinpointing what about it enables giving the best supervision, whereas the more common reading brings in the reference to the individual because it helps to continue the thought from before (which is about individuals). On this reading, Aristotle does not spell out just what it is about knowledge that makes the experts especially apt to administer the best care. The difference, I take it, is a difference of emphasis, not of substance.

children. Why would it not be enough if I can bring up my own children well? Why do I need to know 'what applies to all or to people of such a kind' (1180a14–15)?

The answers become clearer by considering the relevant kinds of knowledge more thoroughly. Expertise in medicine involves both a firm understanding of health in general, and knowing general ways in which to instil or preserve health. In branches of practical knowledge, the former is crucial for the latter, as knowledge of the general comprises knowledge of the causes (*Metaphysics* 1.1.981a1–b6). Being able to explain *why* a person is ill enables the doctor to prescribe a suitable cure that addresses the cause of the illness. Aristotle admits that experience can teach us that this remedy helps that ailment, sometimes very effectively (cf. *Metaphysics* 1.1.981a28–30). But the more thorough the understanding of the goal, the more effective the means to attain it in the face of difficulties and variation. Only if I have expert knowledge of the goal, and thus of the causes, can I think properly about contributing factors, defeaters, enablers, and so on. Moreover, knowing the cause enables me to analyse mistakes, to think about improvements, and to improvise intelligently when tried methods seem not to work. Experience, by contrast, is confined to a more narrow set of conditions that must resemble past occurrences closely. To give an example, let us say chicken soup helps with a cold. You might know this from experience. But the knowledgeable person will also know the cause: light meats are healthy. The knowledgeable person will be able to substitute the chicken with some other light meat, whereas the merely experienced person will hit or miss with her substitution.[185] Therefore, individualised supervision should be guided by general knowledge. An expert will usually produce good results thanks to her knowledge.

So far we have one answer to the parents' question. Experts tend to produce better results. They do so because their expertise comprises knowledge of the causes – which, in turn, helps analyse the present condition of the 'patient' and to deliberate how best to reach the goal. But conceiving of expert knowledge as comprising knowledge of the causes also provides material for a second answer. General knowledge most of all enables a person to teach, whereas experience does not (*Metaphysics* 1.1.981b7–12). While a doctor does not need to teach in order to heal the

---

[185] Cf. VI.8.1141b16–21, where Aristotle also notes that knowledge can be too general to be practically helpful. If A knows that light meats are healthy, but not the less general claim that chicken, veal, etc. are light meats, while B knows from experience that chicken is healthy, then B will probably attain better results.

patient, educating one's children towards virtue *does* have an element of teaching or instruction. For becoming virtuous comprises two overlapping phases, with three aspects: i) habituating the emotional responses, ii–a) habituating the actions, and ii–b) mastering the intellectual aspect of acting well (1179b20–31, with commentary). Since the latter requires teaching (II.1.1103a15–16), the educator must have expert knowledge. So, without general knowledge, I might be able to bring up my children well if I am lucky, but the education would be less robust in times of adversity, and it would not pass the theoretical underpinning that helps the attainment of the full mastery of virtue. General knowledge would remedy these defects.

1180b23–8 Maybe, then, someone ... supervision and practical wisdom.

The previous lemma adduced the fields of medicine and gymnastics in order to highlight the role for expertise. An expert will be able reliably to improve those of whom she takes care. In this lemma Aristotle draws the same conclusion for education. If an expert in health makes people healthy and an expert in gymnastics makes people fit, then an expert in education makes people virtuous. The point applies regardless of numbers and the character of the education, whether it be private or shared in some way. Going back to the discussion of the law-based education (cf. commentary on 1180a14–24), Aristotle now sums up his points in the claim that we become good through laws (1180b25). If so, expertise in law-giving would be necessary and possibly sufficient for expertise in educating the young towards virtue.

The lemma raises two questions. First, who is the addressee? Second, what does proficiency in law amount to? Had this lemma followed the argument for a law-based education running from 1179b31 to 1180a24, any reader would take Aristotle to speak about laws in the prevalent sense. He mentions the lawgivers as an institution of the city-state (1180a6), who should make the provisions to turn people towards virtue. The laws they make are expected to govern the whole of life (1180a4). However, Aristotle veers away from state-run education towards private education, because only the Spartans and a few other city-states provide communal education. So, if this lemma strictly follows the line of thought beginning at 1180a24, then the person 'who wishes to improve people' (1180b23–4) ought to be the private educator. Accordingly, the laws through which we become good would not be laws governing conduct in the city-state, but rather the precepts laid down by the private educator (cf. 1180a32–b7 with commentary). The two questions would not ordinarily arise – of course Aristotle continues with private education! – were it not for the next lemma, in which he plainly assumes proficiency in law-giving to be part of political expertise more generally (1180b30–1). So, how can we square the political aspect of expertise in giving law with its role in private education?

How could proficiency in law-giving in the proper sense possibly further the goals of private education? We can give two different kinds of answer. Interpretation A insists on the results achieved so far. Like an expert in music or a gymnastics teacher, the expert educator must lay down precepts with a view to general norms. However, the responsibility of the educator greatly exceeds that of the specialist teachers (according to Aristotle's *Politics*, music and gymnastics form part of the education towards virtue).[186] Therefore, the educator's expertise needs very firm grounding. In order to establish a coherent regime based on good laws (cf. 1180a34–5), to devise sanctions for non-compliance, etc., the private educator needs an expertise that resembles proper law-making so closely that it can be called 'proficiency in making law'. This expertise can best be attained by studying the paradigm case of 'proper' law-giving thoroughly. That is, the study of law-giving would be instrumental in acquiring the relevant expertise for good education.

Stressing the communal nature of virtue, interpretation B makes the study of 'proper' law-giving constitutive of the educator's becoming proficient in law-giving. There are two ways in which we can spell out this suggestion. i) One might highlight the connection between being good and being obedient to the law. A true politician, Aristotle contends, 'wants to make the citizens good and (or i.e.?) obedient to the law', as they do in Crete and Sparta (I.13.1102a7–12). We can spell out the connection between obedience to the law and goodness through the virtue of justice. Being unlawful is being unjust, whereas being lawful is being just (V.1.1129b11). Of course, this does not exhaust the notion of justice, but integrating into the community to which one belongs and submitting to its rules and customs are part of being just. While knowing the laws is crucial to making the young obedient to the laws, expertise in law-making goes further. It requires a level of understanding that enables the educator to explain and give reasons for the laws. As the young become more accustomed to being guided by their reason, they need to understand that being guided by law is being guided by reason (1180a21–2). Thus, expertise in making law comprises not only the *that* but also the *why* of the laws. The latter helps with the teaching aspect of educating the young when

---

[186] See especially *Politics* VII.15; 17; VII.1–7.

they shift their perspective from being driven by passion to being guided by reason.

ii) Thinking more about the why of the laws brings out the orientation towards the community. Expanding on the connection between justice and lawfulness, Aristotle explains that 'in one sense we call <those actions> just that tend to produce and preserve happiness and its parts for the community of citizens' (V.1.1129b17–19). The laws, Aristotle suggests, are set up with a view to achieving the highest good, happiness (I.2.1094b4–7). And since the law requires us to perform virtuous actions, such as fighting in a war, abstaining from adultery, or libel (V.1.1129b19–25), these actions will preserve or contribute to the good of the city-state. Virtuous actions, in short, are not a private affair, but concern the city as well. But there is a difference between doing what is required and acting virtuously. One may either act out of fear of punishment or for the sake of the fine (cf. 1180a5). Acting virtuously (as opposed to merely doing what is virtuous) requires both knowledge and the right motive (II.4.1105a30–2). Both conditions together suggest that in order to act virtuously one must understand the place and role of virtue in the community, and see it as a shared activity. So, while private education towards virtue aims at the goal of living well, it is at the same time a political act, because virtue is at home in the city-state. This may explain why Aristotle calls someone who makes people better, or enables them to act virtuously, a 'politician' (I.9.1099b29–32; cf. I.13.1102a7–13). This 'politician' will again need a solid grasp of politics, especially its architectonic (and more authoritative) branch, law-giving (VI.8.1141b24–6).[187]

Which interpretation we adopt has far-reaching consequences for our reading of the EN. Since either version of interpretation B makes the study of law-making and politics more generally constitutive of acquiring virtue, the EN on its own would be an *incomplete* course in ethics! Unless we go on to study the *Politics*, we cannot even attain virtue for ourselves because we need the knowledge expressed in the *Politics*, or something like it, to be just and to live well. It is knowledge that we ourselves need in order to attain happiness, because, as Aristotle puts it, 'one's own well-being is inseparable from the management of a household, and is dependent on a political system' (VI.8.1142a9–10). But we also need this knowledge to instruct our children towards virtue. According to interpretation A, by contrast, the EN need not be incomplete, but would benefit from a

---

[187] Cooper 2010 proposes a similar interpretation in great detail (though without the focus on justice). He stresses in particular the consequence noted in the next paragraph.

complementary study of the *Politics*. That is, it allows that individuals *can* become good even without good laws and without the study of good laws. (See 1179a33–b4, with commentary, for further discussion.)

1180b28–1181a9 So should we examine … those dearest to them.

Aristotle begins X.9 with a plea for practising the virtues – or else the project of the EN would remain incomplete. Highlighting the conditions under which instructions such as the EN can bear fruit, he stresses the need for proper education. Bringing the programme of the EN to completion therefore requires thinking about educating others (see 1179a33–b4, with commentary). So far, Aristotle has argued at length for the claim that educating others well requires some expertise in law-giving. The present lemma therefore asks, appositely, how we acquire that expertise. Answering the question occupies the discussion until the end of the EN.

How do I acquire knowledge of law-giving? We can approach the question by extrapolating from the account of habituation in II.1 and II.4. A person becomes proficient in a branch of productive knowledge through the process of habituation. Although the learner's doing the activities related to the relevant branch of knowledge leads to acquiring the knowledge, doing them well and with a view to knowledge-acquisition tends to require the guidance of a teacher (II.1.1103b6–13). Aristotle extends this model of learning beyond productive knowledge. He modifies it to accommodate another kind of practical knowledge, virtue. While he does not emphasise the role of the teacher in Book II, he clearly recognises its importance in Book X. Without expert guidance hardly anyone would become virtuous because performing the right actions in the right way involves the use of reason, which the learner still needs to develop (cf. commentary on 1179b20–31). All kinds of practical knowledge have an important intellectual element. The acquisition of virtue relies in part on good teaching because the intellectual element of virtue, practical wisdom, is acquired mostly through teaching (cf. II.1.1103a14–16). Law-giving also falls under practical knowledge, and also counts among the more intellectual pursuits. It will therefore be largely acquired through teaching (but the learner must also exercise and practise the knowledge to become proficient).

As the teacher plays a prominent role in a person's becoming proficient in law-giving, Aristotle now examines who would count as a suitable teacher – for a suitable teacher at the very least *can* teach the relevant knowledge K, be it productive or practical. We can formulate the assumption that informs the present lemma in the form of the biconditional, explicating who can teach [CT]: a person can teach K if and only if she has expertise in K and practises K. However, Aristotle considers whether law-giving and political expertise more generally might not present a special case to which CT does not apply. On the one hand, the sophists appear to present a counter-example to the left-to-right direction. They teach political knowledge, but they do not actively exercise their political knowledge (1180b35–1181a1). Active politicians, on the other hand, cast doubt on the right-to-left direction of CT. They appear to be experts who do not, and in fact cannot, teach political knowledge (1181a1–7).

Instead of rejecting CT, Aristotle explains away the counter-examples. First, he reports only that the sophists *profess* (*epangellontai*, 1180b35) to teach knowledge of politics – which leaves open whether they achieve their goal. He alludes here to the memorable discussion in Plato's *Protagoras* that examines in detail whether Protagoras can (and does) teach 'the art of citizenship' (319a).[188] One argument for denying Protagoras the status of a teacher relies on his lack of knowledge of the subject matter: he has difficulty spelling out the nature of the excellence that he professes to instil in his pupils. Aristotle, similarly, undermines the alleged expertise of the sophists in the next lemma. He alleges, in Socratic fashion, that the sophists do not even know what political knowledge is – and hence cannot teach it. If so, they do not threaten CT.

Second, Aristotle contends that actual politicians, past and present, lack understanding, but operate from experience instead (*empeiria*, 1181a2). But experience falls short of the kind of general knowledge required for expertise (cf. 1180b13–23, with commentary). He musters two reasons in support of his contention. i) Practising politicians show no signs of theoretical understanding required for expertise, since they do not discuss the nature of political knowledge (1181a3–4). ii) Politicians do not actually teach anyone, not even their sons (a5–6). Although both reasons are defeasible — the politicians may not have the time to do either of these because they are busy doing their jobs – especially ii) undermines the example

---

[188] Protagoras of Abdera (ca 485–415 BC) was one of the earliest and most successful 'sophists'. In fact, he defies the charge of political inactivity because he probably drew up the laws for the Greek colony at Thurii in southern Italy (Diogenes Laertius, IX.50). Similarly, the Athenian Isocrates, whom Aristotle counts among the sophists (see next lemma), tried to influence current political affairs in the Greek world.

Sophists were a disparate group of usually itinerant providers of higher education who charged (sometimes high) fees for their services. Plato's dialogue *Sophist* shows among many other things the difficulty in giving a suitable definition of the Sophist's nature. Plato stresses the shortcomings of sophists in many dialogues; the *Protagoras* and the *Gorgias* are especially memorable.

of the politicians as a threat to CT. His reasoning gains force if we fill in the backstory from Plato's *Protagoras*, to which Aristotle alludes. In the *Protagoras*, Socrates points to Pericles, the most eminent politician of the fifth century (ca 495–429 BC), who did not succeed in bringing up his sons well (*Protagoras* 320a–b). But since anyone would want to make his own children good, Socrates concludes that Pericles simply lacked the expertise to do so.[189] Aristotle follows Socrates by suggesting that a) a politician would want to turn his sons into politicians, because there is nothing better to leave for the cities (1181a7). But b), no politician turns his sons into politicians. Therefore, c) practising politicians lack the expertise required to teach others political knowledge.

In the remaining lemmata of the EN, Aristotle further explores how we might become proficient in law-giving. He wrestles with the following problem: we seem to need teachers in order to become proficient in law-giving, but there do not seem to be any group of people that can teach this knowledge, given CT. Nevertheless, he considers what, if anything, we can learn from the sophists and active politicians.

1181a9–23 Still, experience does ... the case of painting.

In the previous lemma Aristotle considered how we might acquire the expertise in law-giving required for educating the young to virtue. He ruled out two sets of possible teachers because they do not seem to satisfy the basic conditions for qualifying as a teacher: a person can teach practical knowledge K if and only if she has expertise in K and practises K (this is CT from the previous lemma). Both the sophists and active politicians turn out to be unsuitable teachers. If we acquire practical knowledge especially through teaching, how *could* we acquire political knowledge in the absence of suitable teachers? In this lemma, Aristotle examines whether we can learn more from the sophists or from active politicians. He focuses especially on the role of experience, a quality of a good teacher of practical knowledge that has not yet been sufficiently stressed (though CT implies it, as practising K entails experience), for the acquisition of any kind of practical knowledge requires some practical doing – a process called habituation in EN II.1 and II.4 – through which the learner acquires some experience. To become proficient in any kind of practical knowledge, the learner must gain experience through long-time practice, reflection on

---

[189] Similarly *Meno* 93b–94d.

what works and what does not, and feedback from peers and others. So, an expert will not only have general knowledge that allows him to teach others (see 1180b13–23, with commentary), but also experience gained through reflective practice.

Against the sophists as teachers of political expertise, Aristotle has cited in the previous lemma their lack of experience. They do not practise the knowledge they profess to teach. But if expertise in branches of practical knowledge requires experience, how can the sophists be experts? Well, they are not, he argues, because they do not even have the general knowledge on the basis of which genuine experts teach. The sophists do not know the subject they profess to teach. He no doubt expects the reader to be familiar with Plato's dialogue *Protagoras*, which undermines the teaching credentials of the eponymous character (who is a sophist) in a similar way. But Aristotle also supports the point with his own arguments.

First, sophists wrongly class political knowledge either together with rhetoric or even below it in the hierarchy of the branches of knowledge.[190] The classification betrays a misunderstanding of politics. For political knowledge oversees and regulates all other practical knowledge, and therefore ranks as the highest and most architectonic practical knowledge. Rhetoric therefore ranks lower (explicitly stated at I.2.1094b3).[191] Second, turning now from the discipline to the content, Aristotle musters a further sign that betrays the sophists' incompetence. At 1181a15–17 he cites, almost verbatim, a snippet from Isocrates' *Antidosis* which cleverly argues that making good speeches is difficult because one must avoid saying what one's predecessors have said, while making laws is easy because one only needs 'to collect those [sc. laws] which are reputable in other states, which anyone who wishes can easily do' (83.3–5). Unlike rhetoric, law-giving as part of political expertise does not even appear to be worthy of teaching! But this approach to choosing the right laws only highlights the misunderstanding of what law-giving involves: it completely underestimates the importance of experience. For in order to choose the best laws, we need to be able to identify the best ones. But i) even discerning correctly requires experience, as the example of music indicates. In the educational programme of the 'city of our prayers', Aristotle suggests children learn to play musical instruments in order to judge and appreciate music correctly (*Politics* VIII.6.1340b35–9). In music, you do not have

---

[190] Cf. Plato's *Gorgias* 466a–c, where Polus attributes the greatest power in the city to orators. The more proximate target seems to be the influential rhetorician and teacher Isocrates (436–338 BC).
[191] Cf. Plato, *Statesman* 304d–e.

to be a professional to judge the music correctly, but you need to have practised playing at some point in your life.[192] Plausibly, the point transmits to many other branches of practical knowledge, and applies in particular to discerning the qualities of good laws. ii) Discerning which laws are best requires comprehension (on which, EN VI.10). Comprehension enables its possessor to understand the wisdom in someone else's proposals – and good laws do stem from practical wisdom (VI.8). But just as acquiring practical wisdom requires experience, so acquiring comprehension will too (VI.11.1143b4–14). So, the sophists (with whom Aristotle classes Isocrates) wrongly suppose that correctly picking the right laws is easy because they do not understand the role of experience in making good choices.

Being able to teach others in the branches of political knowledge requires experience of the right kind – which only an experienced teacher can engender in a learner. For only an experienced person can see why a particular law worked well in this or that situation, and can understand why a different and apparently better law would not have worked. These practical insights are crucial for successful, practice-oriented learning. Although even the inexperienced can appreciate when a city-state is well-governed, they can do so only by 'looking' at the state, as the analogy to painting shows (1281a22–3). But, crucially, the inexperienced lack the ability to extrapolate from a collection of actual laws and judge whether any of them would suit this or that context. For doing *that* would take experience, not least because it requires a correct appreciation of the current situation to which the laws are supposed to apply. And the correct perception of particulars is the domain of comprehension and practical wisdom, both of which only develop with experience (VI.11.1143a32–b14; cf. VI.8.1142a11–19). Thus, if we had to choose between two suboptimal sources of political knowledge, an experienced politician and a sophist, we should try to learn from the politician, because experience clearly counts for more in the field of political knowledge than whatever the sophists have. With experience, an active politician shares at least one characteristic with an expert in the field of politics. Sophists, by contrast, turning out to be both ignorant and inexperienced, share none.

---

[192] Relatedly, Aristotle distinguishes between professional and general education in some branches of practical knowledge in *Politics* III.11.1281b40. The latter tends to suffice to render competent judgement. In productive knowledge, the user of the product can also judge whether it is well-made or not – as in the example of painting adduced in the present lemma.

1181a23–b12 But the laws are ... comprehend these things better.

We need to become proficient in law-making in order to make other people good, whether we are private or public educators (cf. 1180b23–5). Unfortunately, two potential groups of teachers, sophists and active politicians, turn out to be insufficiently qualified, because they lack either the theoretical understanding or that and the practical knowledge – both of which a good teacher must command (1180b28–1181a9 and 1181a9–23, with commentaries). Aristotle's negative assessment of current conditions raises the acute question: how *do* we acquire expertise, if not from an expert? Now he proposes and examines an answer raised in the previous lemma. By studying an expert's work (*ergon*), one can 'comprehend through which means or how they are attained' (1181a20–1). The same problem mentioned there also impedes the proposal in this lemma. It takes experience to gain from such a study, but the learners envisaged here do not seem to possess the relevant level of experience.

Why does Aristotle try the same answer again? First, because he now identifies the laws as a politician's work. In the absence of written treatises on the art of politics (1181a3–5), we must examine the laws, because they too encapsulate their authors' wisdom (if made well). Second, he dismissed the sophists' proposal simply to select the good laws partly because we need experience to judge whether a law suits the present situation (see commentary on previous lemma). But now he considers a rejoinder (indicated in Greek at 1181b3 by *kaitoi*, 'surely'), driven by the example of medicine. For in the medical case, it seems as if written texts *can* make us experts after all. In the absence of formal qualifications, pretty much everybody could practise medicine. Medical aid was sought, among others, from so-called root-cutters and drug-sellers, as well as those who sold 'magic' in the form of amulets, incantations, or charms. But some practitioners also pursued medicine in a more scientific way.[193] Part of the scientific approach to medicine is to think systematically about the causes of disease in order best to restore or preserve health. An expert in this approach to medicine would therefore also be able to teach medical knowledge to others. Some experts, indeed, have produced books or lecture notes (*sungrammata*, 1181b2–3), presumably for the purpose of teaching. As teachers of medicine, the physicians do not only write or talk abstractly about cures and treatments, they also distinguish between

---

[193] The Hippocratic treatise *On Ancient Medicine* tries to establish medicine as a form of knowledge (*technē*).

different conditions in order to differentiate between different types of patient (1181b3–5).[194] Given the detail about each type, and the experience that went into differentiating these types, why would we not be able to learn from those texts? For if we follow the instructions, would we not become doctors? No. Aristotle's reserved answer takes into account the eventual application of the example. If there were no true experts to consult (as in the case of politics), and all the teaching had to come from the texts alone, then, Aristotle suggests, the 'learning' will be unsuccessful. For applying even explicitly practical advice requires experience (1181b5–6). To begin with, we would need to be able to diagnose the condition of the patient, and be able to rule out that another illness masks or alters the symptoms — both of which requires experience.[195] Further, choosing the correct treatment for this type and administering it properly to this patient will also require experience. So, the example of medical knowledge does not, after all, show a way for acquiring political knowledge, because we cannot presuppose the required level of experience.

Nevertheless, by analogy with the medical case, written texts may play an important role in acquiring political expertise. But Aristotle seems to assign to the learners in the political case more chances of success. In particular, 'collections of laws and constitutions would be especially useful to those who are capable of reflecting on and discerning what goes well or the opposite and which kinds of things harmonise with each other' (1181b7–9). The salient difference to the medical case is the capacity to reflect on and discern the good and bad contained in the collection of laws and constitutions. However, the capacity to discern the relevant works correctly seems either to consist in experience, or at least to presuppose it, as is clear from a passage to which the present lemma alludes: 'those experienced in each case discern the relevant works correctly, and they comprehend through which means or how they are attained', while those without experience cannot discern correctly (1180a19–22). One could formulate the problem that stands in the way of acquiring political expertise as a dilemma, [D]: either a) the learners in the case of politics have sufficient experience to make use of written texts (by being able to judge well about the content of

---

[194] The subject of *peirôntai* (try) cannot be the texts, but must be their authors (*iatrikoi*, doctors, from the previous sentence). When they distinguish types, Aristotle may allude to the four-humours doctrine – the humours being blood, phlegm, yellow bile, and black bile – prevalent in Hippocratic medicine. On this basis, one may distinguish between types by reference to the preponderance of one of the humours, such as the sanguine or the melancholic type.
[195] This is despite the very practical advice given in the Hippocratic *Prognostics*.

collections of laws and constitutions), or b) they do not. If a), they do not need the texts to become proficient (though the texts may improve their practice). If b), the texts do not help them to become proficient. So, taken at face value, both the medical and the political case seem to be parallel. Normally, expert teachers help to overcome D. Through their experience, they can show learners how to apply the knowledge to particular cases. This is why knowledge from medical text-books is – now and then – supplemented by a practice-oriented 'apprenticeship' with experts who practise the knowledge they teach. Unfortunately, this solution is not available to students of politics because there seem to be no experts: neither sophists nor active politicians fit the bill (1181a12–19 and a3–9). Without teachers and without experience in the subject matter of politics, students seem unable to learn from a text-book only.

Aristotle does not seem to proffer an explicit solution to the dilemma. Two interpretations suggest themselves. Either i) there is no straightforward answer, or ii) the dilemma admits of a simple solution from resources available to the EN's reader. What is at issue? Nothing less than the success of the EN! The course in ethics would remain incomplete if we did not put it into action (1179a33–b4). But in order to become good ourselves, we may need to make others good, a task that requires some kind of political expertise (1180b23–5). Now, ii) suggests that we can acquire the relevant expertise, whereas i) casts doubts on our prospects. According to interpretation i), Aristotle's main points from 1181a24 to the end would be first to criticise the present state of political expertise by discrediting everyone who now professes to teach political knowledge, and then to propose an ideal towards which anyone who is serious about becoming a good person should strive: the ideal lawgiver who has both a grasp of political and ethical theory *and* practical experience of politics. Aristotle accepts that people do not yet have the right combination of experience and theory. So, his positive contribution consists in making a plea for the study of political theory – of the kind contained in the *Politics*. While this study by itself does not suffice to instil expertise in law-giving, it is an essential step that should no longer be neglected.

There are different ways of spelling out interpretation i). Perhaps the most promising version runs as follows. One can reject the thought that went into formulating the dilemma: Aristotle *can* presuppose that his readers have the capacity for reflecting on, and discerning, the good and bad in the collected constitutions – *without* requiring them to have experience in politics. How can we do justice to the similarity between musical and political expertise highlighted at 1181a17–19, while at the same time driving a wedge between the two domains? The trick is to claim that the reader of the EN is already capable of reflection and discernment (in part through having studied the EN). In particular, the would-be (private) legislator has already made some progress in acquiring the virtues and developing practical wisdom. But political knowledge and practical wisdom are the same state, although they differ in definition (cf. VI.8.1141b23–4). So, while a good person already has the basic state (*hexis*) that enables her to learn politics from a text-book, she nevertheless will need to study the book in order to become expert at political knowledge. (Note that this solution works only on the assumption that the would-be educator is good and practically wise to a sufficient degree, an assumption that may or may not chime with the beginning of X.9; cf. 1179a33–b4, with commentary).

1181b12–24 Since, then, the topic ... from the beginning.

The final lemma falls into two parts. The second part lays out a programme of study, the need for which is justified in the first part, as follows. In X.9 Aristotle pressed the importance of being proficient in law-giving (*nomothetikos*) for educating others to virtue because of the role that laws themselves should play in education (cf. 1179b31–1180a24). Educating others to virtue belongs to the task of putting one's own virtue into action. But since action is the express goal of the EN, the enquiry into human nature and virtue would be incomplete without some guidance on how to become proficient in law-giving. Aristotle proposes to examine law-making (*nomothesia*) as well as the theory of a political system[196] more generally in order to bring the philosophical study of human affairs to completion (1181b13–15).[197]

Astonishingly, he maintains that the topic of law-making has been left unexamined by those before (*tôn proterôn*) – which seems both to disregard Plato's *Laws* (to which he alludes in 1180a5–19) and jars with the proposal to go through the views of his predecessors. We can make sense of this claim if we take Aristotle to count himself among the Platonists: before *us* no one studied those topics (this solution was especially favoured when scholars were keen on identifying older, Platonist layers of

---

[196] Many translate *holôs dê peri politeias* as 'political systems in general' (Irwin; Crisp) or 'constitutions in general' (Rowe; similarly Reeve). However, *politeias* is most likely genitive singular, not accusative plural. We should translate the singular accordingly as 'of government' or 'of the form of government' or 'of a political system'.

[197] We may query whether Aristotle takes his treatises indeed to complete the study of human nature, or whether he merely proposes, more humbly, that studying his works is the best one can do at present. The force of 'as far as possible' (*eis dunamin*, 1181a14–15) is crucial here, especially in connection with the interpretive options outlined at the end of the previous lemma.

text in the Aristotelian Corpus). Less significantly, *hoi proteroi* can simply mean 'the ancients' – to which Plato would not belong. In either case, Aristotle would set his own work apart from non-philosophical thinkers. Alternatively, he might think that nobody before him has conducted the enquiry in the way that would make the audience (more) proficient in law-giving. Indeed, Aristotle *can* use 'philosophy' and cognates to indicate *mere study* that lacks practical application.[198] In particular, he might discount Plato's works because they are neither sufficiently praxis-oriented nor empirically informed: they do not discuss actual constitutions that people in fact encounter (see below). So, the topic is left unexamined in the proper, praxis-oriented way.

How does the programme work for those who have neither teacher nor the relevant experience in politics? (For the formulation of the problem, see previous lemma.) Aristotle proposes the following (1181b15–22):

[1] if there is anything on some part of the topic that has been said correctly by our predecessors, we should attempt to go through it,

[2] [a] on the basis of the collected constitutions, [b] <attempt> to reflect on what sorts of things preserve or destroy cities and what sorts of things preserve and destroy each constitution, and [c] through which causes some cities are governed [b20] well and others the opposite.

[3] For having reflected on these matters, we will probably be in a better position to see comprehensively even [a] which constitution is best, [b] and how each is ordered, and [c] which laws and customs it will have.

The gist of the programme is clear. We should begin by examining what other thinkers (including Plato) have said on the topic – a method ubiquitous in Aristotle's writings. Since he has remarked on the lack of theoretical studies by actual politicians (1181a3–4), he will have to contend with other philosophers.[199] However, Aristotle goes beyond a merely theoretical study of statesmanship and related topics. He suggests in 2a a study of actual constitutions. Presumably he refers to the collection of 158 constitutions that has been completed in his school, the Lyceum (only the Athenian constitution has been preserved more or less complete). We should take the constitutions as case-studies (2b), serving to uncover

---

[198] In this vein, he criticises the many who do not want to go through the labour of habituation, but rather think they can become good by philosophising (i.e. only talking, II.4.1105b12–18).

[199] For similar programme description at the beginnings of major works, see *Physics* I.2ff; *De Anima* I.2; *Metaphysics* I.3ff.; *Generation and Corruption* I.1–2.

the causes of good and bad government (2c). This approach importantly seems required in order to expand into the realm of the political, whatever comprehension and good judgement a person may have. This may be a way of becoming a good lawgiver (1181a15–23, with commentary) without experienced teachers and without the student's having the relevant experience in politics already. For even the inexperienced can judge whether a product came out well or not. We do not need to be experts to judge whether a city-state is doing well or not. But we do need to be experts, or to have the help of experts, to understand why. A theoretical study of what contributes to preserving or destroying a city-state, together with the empirical knowledge of its conditions, puts us in a much better position to assess and choose good laws and constitutions (3).

The exact goal formulated in 3 is less clear and can be taken in either of two ways. We might be in a better position either A) to see *the* best constitution, or else B) to judge which constitution for various general forms of government is best, i.e. to judge the best of its kind. Interpretation A does not sit well with 3b if 3b means 3b–1 'how each of the constitutions [sc. from the collection] is ordered…' (2 made us study those points already), or 3b–2 'how each best constitution is ordered', because there seems to be no plurality of best constitutions 3b could refer to. One could make sense of it by understanding 3b–3 'how each is ordered [with a view to the best one]'. Interpretation B, by contrast, can make room for the implied plurality in 3b and 3c. For 2 helps us to comprehend the positive and negative features of actual constitutions well. This puts us in a position to classify constitutions according to type and subtype. Based on our study of the collected constitutions, we are then able to pair a certain order and certain customs with a certain type of constitution to bring out the best of it.

Apart from the immediate context, two further considerations may inform our choice between A and B. First, both interpretations can muster support from the *Politics*, the work to which Aristotle apparently alludes. The introduction to Book II resembles the programme outlined in our passage:

> Since we propose to study which political community is best of all for people who are able to live as ideally as possible, we must investigate other constitutions too, both some of those used in city-states that are said to be well governed, and any others described by anyone that are held to be good, in order to see what is correct or useful in them, but also to avoid giving the impression that our search for something different from them results from a desire to be clever. Let it be held, instead, that we have undertaken this enquiry because the currently available constitutions are not in good condition.
>
> (*Politics* II.1.1260b27–36, tr. Reeve)

Since the *Politics* passage clearly points towards *the* best constitution, and suggests we attain it through a programme similar to [1] to [3], we may be drawn towards interpretation A. However, in the *Politics* Aristotle writes as if *the* best constitution does not exist, whereas the last words of X.9 sound as if we could select it from among the constitutions canvassed. In any case, *Politics* V–VI does not merely seem subordinate to devising the best constitution. That part of the *Politics* seems primarily interested in constructing the best versions of suboptimal constitutions – which chimes better with B. This approach to supporting A or B is complicated through the difficult relationship between the EN and the *Politics* as we know it. Some scholars map the programme neatly onto the *Politics* as we have it ([1] corresponds to *Politics* II; [2] to III.6–VI; [3] to VII.13–VIII), whereas others stress the differences (the presence of *Politics* I; the impulse to preserve the constitution rather than producing virtuous citizens).

Finally, are there philosophical reasons for preferring the one over the other? This depends on the role of the study of law-giving. If the study is instrumental in acquiring expertise in law-giving and hence passing on virtue, then interpretation A may suffice, for the father's role in the household resembles that of a king (cf. 1161a18–19). So the 'constitution' at home will remain the same, and we do not need to think about how to adapt our rule to suboptimal conditions. If, however, the study of law-giving and constitutions is constitutive of exercising virtue (and hence to passing it on) because virtue is in an important sense political, then being able to bring out the best in each form of government seems crucial to becoming a good and virtuous citizen. (For the constitutive vs instrumental study of law, see commentary on 1180b23–8.)

Epilogue

Book X of the *Nicomachean Ethics* presents a high point, if not *the* high point, of the whole treatise. Similar to some of Plato's dialogues, it does not end with a congratulatory 'mission accomplished', but instead indicates further work that lies ahead if we are both to become fully knowledgeable about human affairs and to embody this knowledge in our actions.

Anyone who has dipped into the commentary will know that there are many points of detail that cannot be resolved easily – and it is anyone's guess whether his students questioned Aristotle about those or similar points of interpretation. Some points do not make a practical difference and fall therefore outside the scope of ethics (as conceived by Aristotle). For example, whether pleasure *is* an activity or whether it is merely *like* an activity, or whether pleasure is *the* perfection of an activity, or *a* perfection. Nevertheless, these questions are important *to us* who have elevated (or denigrated?) ethics to the status of an academic discipline that can be studied simply for the sake of knowledge. Other moot points do carry practical relevance, and would need to be addressed by those who wish to achieve the self-stated goal of the EN, namely to act out the knowledge gained through its study. To name two examples for this sort of question: can one possibly be happy without studying law-giving and political systems more generally? And can one live happily without engaging in, or living otherwise for the sake of, reflection? The commentary does not distinguish between the status of these different kinds of query, but instead tries to motivate the questions, and suggest possible solutions. It will have achieved its primary goal when it aids the reader in thinking philosophically about the issues as they arise from the text. Although the commentary indicates at important points where one interpretive decision affects another one, it does not usually try to harness these options into 'lines' of interpretation. The reader is invited to work out her own 'line' on the topic that interests her, whether for practical or theoretical purposes.

While the primary benefit for the reader of the commentary probably lies in helping her to understand a particular passage or arrive at a certain view, I hope it also benefits the reader in another, albeit less straightforward, way. The commentary proposes, through example, a certain way of engaging with the text, a way that I take to be especially conducive to engaging with Aristotle philosophically. First, it takes Aristotle seriously as a philosopher (as opposed to an object of antiquarian interest). This means that we can bring our analytical tools to the text, trying to pin down what he says, why he says it, and whether it is plausible. But he is not a contemporary philosopher, nor did he write in a historical vacuum. So, second, where suitable, the commentary tries to illustrate how we can bring to life Aristotle *as a philosopher* by imagining him in implicit dialogue with Plato and other intellectuals. Bringing the other thinkers to the fore when thinking about the arguments helps not only to set Aristotle's position and arguments in EN X into perspective, but also shows how he does philosophy. Finally, and most importantly, the commentary tries to demonstrate the benefit of open-minded discussion. Instead of bringing a view to the text (which the text must then bear out), I have tried to explore options suggested by the text, often without settling for one option in particular. While this can seem like unfinished business, I take it to be in the spirit of Aristotle's own philosophising not to present simple points to take away, but instead to engage the audience actively in the activity of thinking that might lead to those points.[1] It is only by thinking through several options that one can understand the strength of the position one eventually adopts. Because embracing this attitude wholeheartedly is difficult – especially for those who work professionally on Aristotle – the commentary may not always have succeeded in living up to its aspiration. But hopefully the approach as a whole inspires the reader, veteran or novice, to follow suit.

---

[1] Many contributions in Wians and Polansky 2017 stress the pedagogic intent of Aristotle's more scientific writing.

List of References

Ackrill, J. L. 1997. Aristotle on eudaimonia. In his *Essays on Plato and Aristotle*. Oxford University Press, pp. 179–200.
Annas, J. 2010. Virtue and law in Plato. In *Plato's 'Laws': A Critical Guide*. Ed. C. Bobonich. Cambridge Critical Guides. Cambridge University Press, pp. 71–91.
Aufderheide, J. 2013. Processes as pleasures in EN vii 11–14 – A new approach. *Ancient Philosophy* 33 (1): 135–57.
  2015. The content of happiness: A new case for *theôria*. In Aufderheide and Bader 2015, pp. 36–59.
  2016. Aristotle against Delos: Pleasure in *Nicomachean Ethics* X. *Phronesis* 61 (3): 284–306.
  2017. Is Aristotle a virtue ethicist? In *Rereading Ancient Philosophy: Old Chestnuts and Sacred Cows*. Ed. V. Harte and R. Woolf. Cambridge University Press, pp. 199–220.
Aufderheide, J. and R. M. Bader (eds.). 2015. *The Highest Good in Aristotle and Kant*. 2015. Oxford University Press, pp. 36–59.
Bader, R. M. 2015. Kant's theory of the highest good. In Aufderheide and Bader 2015, pp. 183–213.
Baker, S. H. 2015. The concept of ergon: Towards an achievement interpretation of Aristotle's 'function argument'. *Oxford Studies in Ancient Philosophy* 48 (1): 227–66.
Barnes, J. (ed.). 1991. *Aristotle: Complete Works*. Princeton University Press.
Barney, R. 2008. Aristotle's argument for a human function. *Oxford Studies in Ancient Philosophy* 34 (1): 293–322.
  2010. Platonic ring-composition and *Republic* 10. In *Plato's 'Republic': A Critical Guide*. Ed. M. L. McPherran. Cambridge University Press, pp. 32–51.
  2015. The inner voice: Kant on conditionality and god as a cause. In Aufderheide and Bader 2015, pp. 158–82.
Bodéüs, R. 1993. *The Political Dimensions of Aristotle's Ethics*. Tr. J. Garrett. Albany: State University of New York Press.
Bonitz, H. 1870. *Index Aristotelicus*. Berlin: Reimer.
Bostock, D. 1988. Pleasure and activity in Aristotle's *Ethics*. *Phronesis* 33 (3): 251–72.

2000. *Aristotle's Ethics*. Oxford University Press.
Broadie, S. 1991. *Ethics with Aristotle*. Oxford University Press.
  2003. Aristotelian piety. *Phronesis* 48 (1): 54–70.
  2007a. The good of practical beings: Aristotelian perspectives. In her *Aristotle and Beyond: Essays on Metaphysics and Ethics*. Cambridge University Press, pp. 166–83.
  2007b. On the idea of the summum bonum. In her *Aristotle and Beyond: Essays on Metaphysics and Ethics*. Cambridge University Press, pp. 135–52.
  2007c. Taking stock of leisure. In her *Aristotle and Beyond: Essays on Metaphysics and Ethics*. Cambridge University Press, pp. 184–98.
  2007d. What should we mean by 'the highest good'? In her *Aristotle and Beyond: Essays on Metaphysics and Ethics*. Cambridge University Press, pp. 153–65.
  2016. Practical truth in Aristotle. *American Catholic Philosophical Quarterly* 90 (2): 281–98.
  2018. Words, deeds, and lovers of truth in Aristotle. In *Authors and Authorities in Ancient Philosophy*. Ed. J. Bryan, R. Wardy, and J. Warren. Cambridge University Press, pp.102–19.
Broadie, S. and C. J. Rowe. 2002. *Aristotle: Nicomachean Ethics*. Oxford, New York: Oxford University Press.
Brown, E. 2014. Aristotle on the choices of lives: Two conceptions of self-sufficiency. In *Theoria: Studies on the Status and Meaning of Contemplation in Aristotle's Ethics*. Ed. P. Destrée and M. A. Zingano. Louvain: Peeters, pp. 113–33.
Brown, L. 2013. Why is Aristotle's virtue of character a mean? In *The Cambridge Companion to Aristotle's Nicomachean Ethics*. Ed. R. M. Polansky. Cambridge University Press, pp. 64–80.
Burnyeat, M. F. 1980. Aristotle on learning to be good. In *Essays on Aristotle's Ethics*. Ed. A. O. Rorty. Berkeley: University of California Press, pp. 69–92.
Bush, S. S. 2008. Divine and human happiness in *Nicomachean Ethics*. *Philosophical Review* 117 (1): 49–75.
Bywater, I. 1892. *Contributions to the Textual Criticism of Aristotle's Nicomachean Ethics*. Oxford: Clarendon.
  1894. *Aristotelis Ethica Nicomachea*. Oxford University Press.
Carone, G. R. 2005. *Plato's Cosmology and Its Ethical Dimensions*. Cambridge University Press.
Charles, D. 1999. Aristotle on well-being and intellectual contemplation. *Aristotelian Society Supplementary Volume* 73 (1): 205–23.
  2011. Desire in action: Aristotle's move. In *Moral Psychology and Human Action in Aristotle*. Ed. M. Pakaluk and G. Pearson. Oxford University Press, pp. 74–94.
  2014. Eudaimonia, theôria, and the choiceworthiness of practical wisdom. In *Theoria: Studies on the Status and Meaning of Contemplation in Aristotle's Ethics*. Ed. P. Destrée and M. A. Zingano. Louvain: Peeters, pp. 89–109.
  2015. Aristotle on the highest good: A new approach. In Aufderheide and Bader 2015, pp. 60–82.

Cheng, W. In press. Aristotle and Eudoxus on the argument from contraries. *Archiv für Geschichte der Philosophie.*
Cohoe, C. M. 2014. Nous in Aristotle's *De Anima*. *Philosophy Compass* 9 (9): 594–604.
Coope, U. 2005. *Time for Aristotle: Physics IV.10–14.* Oxford, New York: Oxford University Press.
Cooper, J. M. 1975. *Reason and Human Good in Aristotle.* Cambridge, Mass.: Harvard University Press.
  1999. Contemplation and happiness: A reconsideration. In his *Reason and Emotion: Essays on Ancient Moral Psychology and Ethical Theory.* Princeton University Press, pp. 212–36.
  2004. Plato and Aristotle on 'finality' and '(self-)sufficiency'. In his *Knowledge, Nature, and the Good: Essays on Ancient Philosophy.* Princeton University Press, pp. 270–308.
  2009. *Nicomachean Ethics* VII. 1–2: Introduction, method, puzzles. In *Aristotle's Nicomachean Ethics, Book VII: Symposium Aristotelicum.* Ed. C. Natali. Oxford University Press, pp. 9–39.
  2010. Political community and the highest good. In *Being, Nature, and Life in Aristotle: Essays in Honor of Allan Gotthelf.* Ed. J. G. Lennox and R. Bolton. Cambridge University Press.
Cooper, J. M. and D. S. Hutchinson (eds.). 1997. *Plato Complete works.* Indianapolis, Ind.: Hackett Publishing.
Curzer, H. J. 1990. Criteria for happiness in *Nicomachean Ethics* I 7 and X 6–8. *The Classical Quarterly* 40 (2): 421–32.
Delcomminette, S. 2006. *Le Philèbe de Platon: Introduction à l'agathologie platonicienne.* Leiden, Boston: Brill.
Denniston, J. D. 1934. *The Greek Particles.* 2nd edn. Oxford: Clarendon Press, 1950.
Dirlmeier, F. 1983. *Nikomachische Ethik.* Berlin: Akademie Verlag.
Dow, J. 2011. Aristotle's theory of the emotions. In *Moral Psychology and Human Action in Aristotle.* Ed. M. Pakaluk and G. Pearson. Oxford University Press, pp. 47–74.
Düring, I. 1961. *Aristotle's Protrepticus: An Attempt at Reconstruction* (12). Gothenburg: Acta Universitatis Gothoburgensis.
Engstrom, S. 2015. The complete object of practical knowledge. In Aufderheide and Bader 2015, pp. 129–57.
Evans, M. 2007. Plato's rejection of thoughtless and pleasureless lives. *Phronesis* 52 (4): 337–63.
  2008. Plato's anti-hedonism. *Proceedings of the Boston Area Colloquium in Ancient Philosophy* 23: 121–45.
Frede, D. 1993. *Plato's Philebus, Translated with Introduction and Notes.* Indianapolis, Ind.: Hackett.
  2012. The *endoxon* mystique: What *endoxa* are and what they are not. *Oxford Studies in Ancient Philosophy* 43 (2): 185–214.
  2019. On the so-called common books of the *Eudemian* and the *Nicomachean Ethics. Phronesis* 64 (1): 84–116.

2020. *Aristoteles Werke: Band 6 Nikomachische Ethik*. Berlin, Boston: De Gruyter.

Gauthier, R. A. and J. Y. Jolif. 1958. *Aristote: L'Ethique à Nicomaque*. 2nd edn. Louvain: Publications Universitaires, 1970.

Gerber, D. E. (tr.). 1999. *Greek Elegiac Poetry: From the Seventh to the Fifth Centuries BC*. Cambridge, Mass.: Harvard University Press.

Godley, A. D. (tr.). 1920. *Herodotus: The Persian Wars*. Vol. I. Cambridge, Mass.: Harvard University Press, 1975.

Gonzalez, F. J. 1991. Aristotle on pleasure and perfection. *Phronesis* 36 (2): 141–59.

Gosling, J. C. B. 1973. More Aristotelian pleasures. *Proceedings of the Aristotelian Society* 74: 15–34.

Gosling, J. C. B. and C. C. W. Taylor. 1982. *The Greeks on Pleasure*. Oxford University Press.

Hadreas, P. 1997. Aristotle's simile of pleasure at NE 1174b33. *Ancient Philosophy* 17 (2): 371–4.

2004. The functions of pleasure in *Nicomachean Ethics* x 4–5. *Ancient Philosophy* 24 (1): 155–67.

Hampson, M. R. 2019. Imitating virtue. *Phronesis* 64 (3): 292–320.

Hansen, M. H. 1991. *The Athenian Democracy in the Age of Demosthenes: Structure, Principles, and Ideology*. Norman, Okla.: University of Oklahoma Press, 1999.

Hardie, W. F. R. 1965. The final good in Aristotle's ethics. *Philosophy* 40 (154): 277–95.

Harris, W. V. 1989. *Ancient Literacy*. Cambridge, Mass.: Harvard University Press.

Harte, V. 2014. The *Nicomachen Ethics* on pleasure. In *The Cambridge Companion to Aristotle's Nicomachean Ethics*. Ed. R. M. Polansky. Cambridge University Press, pp. 288–319.

Hasper, P. S. and J. Yurdin. 2014. Between perception and scientific knowledge: Aristotle's account of experience. *Oxford Studies in Ancient Philosophy* 47: 119–50.

Hatzimichali, M. 2016. Andronicus of Rhodes and the construction of the Aristotelian corpus. In *Brill's Companion to the Reception of Aristotle in Antiquity*. Ed. A. Falcon. Leiden, Boston: Brill, pp. 81–100.

Heinaman, R. 2011. Pleasure as an activity in the *Nicomachean Ethics*. In *Moral Psychology and Human Action in Aristotle*. Ed. M. Pakaluk and G. Pearson. Oxford University Press, pp. 7–46.

Henry, D. and K. M. Nielsen (eds.). 2015. *Bridging the Gap between Aristotle's Science and Ethics*. Cambridge University Press.

Heylbut, G. (ed.). 1889. *Heliodori in Ethica Nicomachea Paraphrasis*. Vol. XIX.2 of *Commentaria in Aristotelem Graeca*. Berlin: Reimer.

Hitz, Z. 2012. Aristotle on law and moral education. *Oxford Studies in Ancient Philosophy* 42 (1): 263–306.

Hornblower, S., A. Spawforth, and E. Eidinow (eds.). 2012. *The Oxford Classical Dictionary*. 4th edn. Oxford University Press.

Hursthouse, R. 2006. The central doctrine of the mean. In *The Blackwell Guide to Aristotle's Nicomachean Ethics*. Ed. R. Kraut. Oxford: Blackwell Publishing, pp. 96–115.

Hutchinson, D. S. and M. Ransome Johnson. 2014. Protreptic aspects of Aristotle's *Nicomachean Ethics*. In *The Cambridge Companion to Aristotle's Nicomachean Ethics*. Ed. R. M. Polansky. Cambridge University Press, pp. 383–409.
Irwin, T. H. 1985. *Nicomachean Ethics*. 1st edn. Indianapolis, Ind.: Hackett Publishing, [2nd rev. edn. 1999].
  2012. Conceptions of happiness in the *Nicomachean Ethics*. In *The Oxford Handbook of Aristotle*. Ed. C. Shields. Oxford University Press, pp. 495–528.
Jaeger, W. 1923. *Aristoteles: Grundlegung einer Geschichte seiner Entwicklung*. Berlin: Weidmann.
Jimenez, M. 2016. Aristotle on becoming virtuous by doing virtuous actions. *Phronesis* 61 (1): 3–32.
Kenny, A. 1978. *The Aristotelian Ethics: A Study of the Relationship between the Eudemian and Nicomachean Ethics of Aristotle*. Oxford: Clarendon Press.
  1992. *Aristotle on the Perfect Life*. Oxford: Clarendon Press.
Keyt, D. 1989. The meaning of ΒΙΟΣ in Aristotle's *Ethics* and *Politics*. *Ancient Philosophy* 9 (1): 15–21.
Kirwan, C. 1993. *Metaphysics: Books Gamma, Delta, and Epsilon*. Oxford, New York: Oxford University Press.
Kraut, R. 1979. Two conceptions of happiness. *The Philosophical Review* 88 (2): 167–97.
  2006. How to justify ethical propositions: Aristotle's method. In *The Blackwell Guide to Aristotle's Nicomachean Ethics*. Ed. R. Kraut. Oxford: Blackwell Publishing, pp. 76–95.
Kullmann, W. 1995. Theoretische und politische Lebensform. In *Aristoteles: Nikomachische Ethik*. Ed. O. Höffe. Berlin: Akademie Verlag, pp. 253–76.
Lawrence, G. 1997. Nonaggregatability, inclusiveness, and the theory of focal value: *Nicomachean Ethics* 1.7. 1097b16–20. *Phronesis* 42 (1): 32–76.
  2001. The function of the function argument. *Ancient Philosophy* 21 (2): 445–75.
  2006. Human good and human function. In *The Blackwell Guide to Aristotle's Nicomachean Ethics*. Ed. R. Kraut. Oxford: Blackwell Publishing, pp. 37–75.
Lear, G. R. 2004. *Happy Lives and the Highest Good: An Essay on Aristotle's Nicomachean Ethics*. Princeton University Press.
Liddell, H. G., R. Scott, H. S. Jones, and R. McKenzie. 1996. 9th edn. *A Greek–English Lexicon, with Revised Supplement*. Oxford: Clarendon Press.
Lockwood, T. 2014. Competing ways of life and ring composition. In *The Cambridge Companion to Aristotle's Nicomachean Ethics*. Ed. R. M. Polansky. Cambridge University Press, pp. 350–69.
Long, A. A. 2011. Aristotle on *eudaimonia, nous*, and divinity. In *Aristotle's Nicomachean Ethics: A Critical Guide*. Ed. J. Miller. Cambridge University Press, pp. 92–113.
Lorenz, H. 2009. NE VII.4: Plain and unqualified *akrasia*. In *Aristotle's Nicomachean Ethics, Book VII : Symposium Aristotelicum*. Ed. C. Natali. Oxford University Press, pp. 72–101.
Mackie, J. L. 1977. *Ethics: Inventing Right and Wrong*. London, New York: Penguin, 1990.

Mansfeld, J. 1979. The chronology of Anaxagoras' Athenian period and the date of his trial. *Mnemosyne* 32 (1): 39–69.
  1980. The chronology of Anaxagoras' Athenian period and the date of his trial. *Mnemosyne* 33 (1): 17–95.
Meyer, S. S. 2011. Living for the sake of an ultimate end. In *Aristotle's Nicomachean Ethics: A Critical Guide*. Ed. J. Miller. Cambridge, New York: Cambridge University Press, pp. 47–65.
Miller, F. D. 2012. Aristotle on the separability of mind. In *The Oxford Handbook of Aristotle*. Ed. C. Shields. Oxford University Press, pp. 306–27.
Natali, C. 2005. *Analysis and Commentary of Nicomachean Ethics Book X*. Project Archelogos. Edinburgh: Project Archelogos. http://archelogos.com/xml/toc/toc-enx.htm
  2013. *Aristotle: His Life and School*. Ed. D. S. Hutchinson. Princeton University Press.
  2017. Varieties of pleasure in Plato and Aristotle. *Oxford Studies in Ancient Philosophy* 52 (1): 177–208.
Netz, R. 2001. On the Aristotelian paragraph. *Proceedings of the Cambridge Philological Society* 47: 211–32.
Nightingale, A. W. 2004. *Spectacles of Truth in Classical Greek Philosophy: Theoria in Its Cultural Context*. Cambridge University Press.
Nussbaum, M. C. 1986. *The Fragility of Goodness: Luck and Ethics in Greek Tragedy and Philosophy*. 2nd rev. edn. Cambridge University Press, 2001.
Ober, J. 2001. The debate over civic eduation in classical Athens. In *Education in Greek and Roman Antiquity*. Ed. Y. L. Too. Leiden: Brill, pp. 176–207.
Owen, G. E. L. 1986. Aristotelian pleasures. In *Logic, Science and Dialectic: Collected Papers in Greek Philosophy*. Ed. M. Nussbaum. London: Duckworth, pp. 334–46.
Pakaluk, M. 2005. *Aristotle's Nicomachean Ethics: An Introduction*. Cambridge University Press.
Pearson, G. 2012. *Aristotle on Desire*. Cambridge University Press.
Penelhum, T. 1964. Pleasure and falsity. *American Philosophical Quarterly* 1 (2): 81–91.
Polansky, R. M. 2017. Aristotle's *Nicomachean Ethics* is a work of practical science. In Wians and Polansky 2017, pp. 277–314.
Price, A. 2011. *Virtue and Reason in Plato and Aristotle*. Oxford University Press.
  2017. Varieties of pleasure in Plato and Aristotle. *Oxford Studies in Ancient Philosophy* 52 (1): 177–208.
Primavesi, O. 2007. Ein Blick in den Stollen von Skepsis: Vier Kapitel zur frühen Überlieferung des Corpus Aristotelicum. *Philologus* 151 (1): 51–77.
Reece, B. C. In press. Are there really two kinds of happiness in Aristotle's *Nicomachean Ethics? Classical Philology*.
Reeve, C. D. C. 1998. *Aristotle: Politics*. Indianapolis, Ind.: Hackett Publishing.
Robb, K. 1994. *Literacy and Paideia in Ancient Greece*. New York: Oxford University Press.
Rose, J. L. 2016. *Free Time*. Princeton University Press.

Ross, D. (tr.). 1954. *The Nicomachean Ethics of Aristotle.* Vol. 546 of The World's Classics. London: Oxford University Press.
Schütrumpf, E. 1991. *Aristoteles: Politik Buch 1.* Vol. I. Berlin: Akademie Verlag.
Scott, D. 1999. Aristotle on well-being and intellectual contemplation. *Aristotelian Society Supplementary Volume* 73 (1): 223–42.
Sedley, D. N. 1999. The ideal of godlikeness. In *Plato 2: Ethics, Politics, Religion and the Soul.* Ed. G. Fine. Oxford Readings in Philosophy. Oxford University Press, pp. 309–28.
Shields, C. 2011. Perfecting pleasures: The metaphysics of pleasure in *Nicomachean Ethics* X. In *Aristotle's Nicomachean Ethics: A Critical Guide.* Ed. J. Miller. Cambridge University Press, pp. 191–210.
Silverman, A. 2010. Contemplating divine mind. In *Ancient Models of Mind: Studies in Human and Divine Rationality.* Ed. A. Nightingale and D. Sedley. Cambridge University Press, pp. 75–96.
Solmsen, F. 1964. Leisure and play in Aristotle's ideal state. *Rheinisches Museum für Philologie* 107 (3): 193–220.
Stewart, J. A. 1892. *Notes on the Nicomachean Ethics of Aristotle.* 2 vols. Oxford: Clarendon Press.
Strohl, M. 2011. Pleasure as perfection: *Nicomachean Ethics* 10.4–5. *Oxford Studies in Ancient Philosophy* 41 (2): 257–87.
Susemihl, F. 1880. *Aristotelis Ethica Nicomachea.* Leipzig: Teubner.
Taylor, C. C. W. 2008a. Plato and Aristotle on the criterion of real pleasures. In his *Pleasure, Mind, and Soul: Selected Papers in Ancient Philosophy.* Oxford University Press, pp. 91–106.
  2008b. Pleasure: Aristotle's response to Plato. In his *Pleasure, Mind, and Soul: Selected Papers in Ancient Philosophy.* Oxford University Press, pp. 240–64.
Too, Y. L. 2001. Legal instructions in classical Athens. In *Education in Greek and Roman Antiquity.* Ed. Y. L. Too. Leiden: Brill.
van Riel, G. 2000. *Pleasure and the Good Life: Plato, Aristotle, and the Neoplatonists.* Leiden, Boston: Brill.
Walker, M. D. 2018. *Aristotle on the Uses of Contemplation.* Cambridge University Press.
Warren, J. 2009. Aristotle on Speusippus on Eudoxus on pleasure. *Oxford Studies in Ancient Philosophy* 36 (1): 249–81.
  2015. The bloom of youth. *Apeiron* 48 (3): 327–45.
Wians, W. R. and R. M. Polansky (eds.). 2017. *Reading Aristotle: Argument and Exposition.* Vol. 146 of Philosophia Antiqua. Leiden: Brill.

Index

activity
   activation of capacity 131–2
   best 167–9, 182
   chosen for itself 67–8, 113–14,
      152–3, 176–8, 209
   complete 108
   continuity of 122–4, 159, 169–71,
      173, 183, 211
   incomplete 108
   individuation of 94, 132–5, 137–8
audience, Aristotle's 2, 6–7, 27–8,
   60–1, 97, 199, 222–3, 229–30
akribeia see precision
Alexander of Aphrodisias 62
amusement (*paidia*) 158–9, 179
Anacharsis 158–9
Anaxagoras 218–20, 225–6
animals 13–14, 55, 62–6, 71–3, 114,
   128, 142–4, 210–11
authority
   authoritative element determines whole 189–90
   of a father 239, 244–6, 250–1
   of judgement 156–7
   of the law 244–6, 251

bios see life
bloom (*hôra*) 119–20

book
   ancient division xi
   'common books' 30–1, 53–4

Callicles 17, 90–3
character 18–19, 56, 92–4, 124–6,
   232–2; *see also* virtue of character
childhood 96
choice *see also* activity, chosen for
   itself, *kalon, to*
   de dicto vs *de re* 126–7
   motive 235
   'package' view of choice 92,
      126–7, 178
community, political (*koinônia*)
   230, 247–8
completeness *see teleios*
contemplation *see theôria*

desire 14, 17, 20, 124–7, 138–9, 223, 245
divine
   activity 183–4, 205–10, 212
   benefit 224–7
   element 165–7, 169, 171, 184–5, 187
   human beings as 188–90
   influence on happiness 7,
      216–17, 224–7, 233

development, ethical 158–9; *see also* virtue, acquisition of
doctor 115–16, 231, 254, 264–6

education 55–6, 229, 236–7; *see also* teaching
    general vs particular knowledge required 254–6
    private 246–53
    public 246–8, 252
Empedocles 188
energeia see activity
endoxa see method
enquiry, the goal of 27–8, 228–9; *see also* audience, Aristotle's
ergon 13–17, 101, 128–9, 142–4, 147–8, 166, 264
    argument 13–15, 148, 164
    human 13–15, 142–4, 148, 191–2
eudaimonia see happiness
Eudoxus
    his argument from addition 68–71
    his argument from opposites 65–8, 73–5
    his argument from universal pursuit 61–4, 71–3, 142
    his character 64–5
exactness *see* precision
excellence *see* virtue
experience 234–6, 240, 255, 260–7, 269
expert 254–6, 261–2, 264

father 243–4, 250–1, 253
finality *see teleios*
fine *see kalon*
flatterer 95–6
friend 95–6, 120
function *see ergon*

genesis see pleasure, not a process of coming to be
god(s) 205–9, 216, 224–7 *see also* divine
good, the highest 4–7, 10–12, 16, 24–6, 27–8, 68–71, 150, 152–3, 158, 174–5, 193, 258; *see also* happiness
goods
    as qualities 75–6
    as something limited/determinate 77–80
    common 247, 258
    conditional 69–70, 93
    good for 17, 62–3, 72–3, 91–3
    intrinsic / in themselves 11, 24–6, 68–70, 80–3, 152–3, 223

habituation 233–8, 240, 259
happiness 24–7
    activity of happiness 152–3, 164, 182, 209
    acquisition of 233
    aggregative conception of 211–12
    as translating *eudaimonia* 7–8
    as what makes life happy 10, 70–1, 153, 209
    complete/perfect/final (*teleia*) 148, 164–7, 181–3, 207–9
    criteria for 10–11; *see also* self-sufficiency, *teleios*
    divine 7, 184–5, 197, 207–12
    found in leisure *see* leisure
    extension of 210–13
    in virtue of resemblance 212–13, 215, 231
    level of determinateness of 175
    outline of 7–17, 150–2
    pleasures of 171–3
    stability of 170
    superlative 191–2, 209

health 80, 90–2, 94, 115–16, 145, 250, 253–5
hedonism *see also* Eudoxus
 culture hedonism 154–5
 normative 57, 62–4, 65–8
 psychological 62–4, 65–6
 'sober' hedonism 64–5
 sybaritic hedonism 155–9
Heraclitus 142
Herodotus 216
Homer 247
honour 9–10, 68, 152, 180, 200–1
household 239–40, 248, 258, 270
human beings as compound 184–5, 188, 198
human nature 14, 22, 55, 58, 65, 97, 142–4, 147–8, 166–7, 183–92, 194, 214, 234, 236, 250
human needs 181, 199–200, 202, 214; *see also* self-sufficiency
human soul 14, 18–19, 161–2, 166, 185, 189–90, 197–8

illness 90–3, 145, 255
immortality 186–8, 244
inclusivism 11–12, 16, 24–7, 69, 203–4
intellectualism *see* monism
intelligence *see nous*
Isocrates 262

kalon, to (the fine) *see also teleios*
 chosen for its own sake 68, 113–14, 127, 153–4, 176, 178–9, 189, 210, 236–7, 258
 love for 232, 235–6
 orientation towards 236–7, 240–1
Kant 56, 93
kinêsis see Movement *and* Pleasure not a movement

law 237–46, 249–51, 257
law-giving 249–51, 254, 256–9
 how to become expert at 259–70
learning 125–6, 144, 172, 232–6, 240–2, 259, 261–7
leisure 155–6, 163, 178–83, 188, 202, 204
life
 of frivolous pleasure 9–10, 152, 155, 161–4, 193, 201
 of practical virtue 9–10, 161, 184–6, 192–202, 207, 213–14
 of reflection 184–8, 193, 201, 216, 218–20, 221
 political 9–10, 152, 201–2
 translating *zôê* or *bios* 163, 193
limit 77–9
liturgy 203
locomotion 106–7
logos (word, talk, reason) 232–3, 241, 244
love 124–6, 172, 176–7, 189, 224–6, 235–6, 251

malista (most of all) 189–92, 207–8
many, the 58–60, 218–20, 223, 232–3, 240–2
measure, the good man as 144–9, 156–7, 160
medicine 242–3, 255, 264–6
method
 Aristotle's method 2, 8–9, 60–1, 74–5, 89–90, 100, 150, 214, 268–9
 genus et differentiae 100–2
 match between word and deed 58–60, 64–5, 220–3
 pragmatic considerations 57–9

monism 11–12, 16–18, 24–7, 70–1, 203–4
mortality 183, 186–8, 203, 207
movement
　completion of 103–4, 107–8
　definition of 108
　difference in form 106–7
　divisible into subprocesses 105–6, 131–2
　taking time 109–10

nature 63, 85–6, 146–7, 233, 244
　see also human nature
neutralism 76
nous (intelligence) 156, 165–9, 186–2, 198–9, 224–7, 243–5
now, the 109–10
nutrition 89, 146

outline (*tupos*) 24, 27, 150–2, 175, 228

pain 66–7, 73–5, 88–9, 237–8
perception
　as end in itself 113–14, 209
　norms of 118, 145
perfection *see teleios and* Pleasure and completion/perfection
Pericles 245, 261
philosopher 199, 200, 202–4, 215, 218–20, 225–6, 272
philosophy 2, 172–3, 199, 225, 227, 268, 272; see also *theôria*
phronêsis 18–21, 153–4, 167–9, 185–7, 190, 195–8, 205, 213–15, 219–20, 230, 234–5, 263
piety 225
Plato
　extent of background knowledge required 2–3

　on the role of the highest good 11, 69–71
　Apology 225
　Euthydemus 93
　Euthyphro 225
　Gorgias 90
　Meno 233
　Laws 227, 242–5
　Phaedo 181
　Philebus 69–71, 77–9, 81–3, 86–9, 99, 134, 140–1, 170, 189, 227
　Protagoras 243, 245, 260–1
　Republic 87, 97, 140–1, 157, 170, 177
　Timaeus 188, 227
pleasure
　alien (*allotrios*) 135–8
　and virtue 98, 235
　and completion/perfection 22–3, 113–20, 128–30
　and fit 120–4
　as superadded end 118–20
　bad pleasures 89–94
　bodily pleasure 88–9, 155–7, 162–3, 232
　conditions of 113–22
　continuity of 122–4
　desire for 124–6, 138
　dim when too familiar 122–4
　enjoyment 91–3, 121, 124–6, 136, 139
　functional definition of 101–2
　human 142–9
　kinds of 93–6, 127–38
　likened to seeing 102–3
　metaphysics of 75–6, 80–3, 102–3
　not a movement 83–4, 103–12, 131–2

pleasure (cont.)
  not a process of coming to be 84–9, 111–12
  object of 139–40
  proper (*oikeion*) 130–8, 142–4, 191–2
  proximity to activity 126–7, 139
  pure 79, 89, 140–1, 148–9
  response-(in)dependence of 146–7
  source of 91–4, 98
  subject of 84–8
  translation 23–4
  uniformity of 131–3
  value of 57–8, 68–71, 75–6, 89–100, 136–40, 142
pluralism *see* inclusivism
politician 6–7, 200–1, 229–31, 257–8, 260–1
politics
  goal of 180, 229, 257–8
  political life 199–202; *see also* life of practical virtue
  political science 229, 264
practical wisdom *see phronêsis*
praxis see virtuous action
precision
  of activities 136
  of exposition 150
  of prescriptions 252
purity 79, 140–1, 148–9, 172–3

reason
  as human characteristic 14, 15–16; *see also* human nature
  as authoritative element 165–8, 184–5, 187–92, 241, 244
  practical vs theoretical 19–21, 166, 168–9; *see also theôria* and *phronêsis*

reflection (theoretical) *see theôria*
resources 200, 202–4, 213–20, 225–6
response–dependence 146–7

Sardanapallus 155
self-sufficiency 11, 153, 173–6, 214, 217
seriousness 159–62, 179, 182–3
sign 210
slave 162–3
Solon 216–18
sophia 20–1, 167–9, 172, 219; *see also theôria*
sophist s 260–3
Speusippus 75
statesman *see* politician
spoudaios see measure, good man as

taste 90–1, 145
teaching 231–2, 234–5, 255–6, 259–61, 263
teleios 10–11, 28–9, 81, 113–14, 129, 152–3
Theognis 231–2
theoretical wisdom *see sophia*
theôria 168–9, 170–1, 183, 202, 212–13
time 110, 211–12
Thales 219
tyrant 154–7, 163

virtue
  as measure 91
  acquisition of 231–41, 254–6; *see also* habituation
  characteristically human 195–9
  of character 18–19, 56, 195, 206–7, 233–5

of intellect 19–21
political dimension of 258, 270
proper virtue of intelligence 166
rest of 184–5, 193, 196–7
stability of 170
virtuous action *see also kalon, to*
lack of leisure 179–81, 204
resources required for 200–2
self-sufficiency of 174–6
the internal and external goal(s) of 153–4, 176–8, 179–80, 219, 258

war 179–80, 182–3, 240
wealth 91–3, 200, 216, 218–19
wise, the 219
work *see ergon*

young, the 55, 236–40, 242, 251

zôê see life